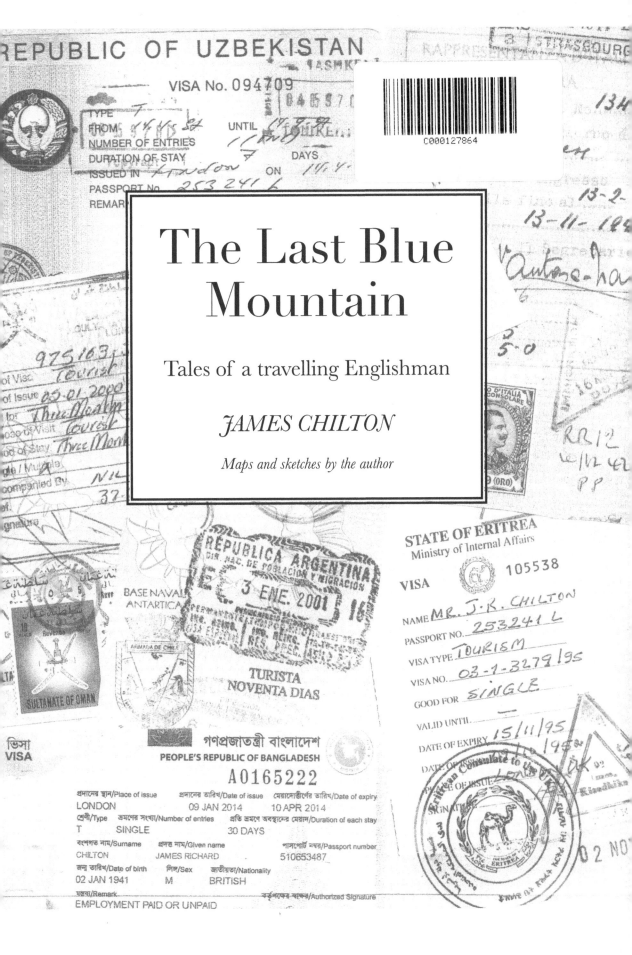

The Last Blue Mountain

Tales of a travelling Englishman

JAMES CHILTON

Maps and sketches by the author

Published by Clink Street Publishing 2015

Copyright © James Chilton 2015

Second edition.

ISBN: 978-1-909477-51-3
Ebook: 978-1-909477-52-0

London | New York

For Sarah —

— take the road less travelled —

with best wishes —

James.

June 2015.

We are the Pilgrims master; we shall go
Always a little further; it may be
Beyond the last blue mountain barred with snow,
Across that angry or that glimmering sea.

James Elroy Flecker. The Golden Journey to Samarkand

For Maggie.
Impatiently waiting

Table of Contents

Introduction

'Travel is the most private of pleasures. There is no greater bore than the travel bore. We do not in the least want to hear what he has seen in Hong Kong' – Vita Sackville West

When the Sunderland flying boat of Imperial Airways took off from the Irrawaddy River bound for the Hooghly River in north east India, on the morning of 8th March 1942, on board were my mother, my sister, an English nanny and myself. This would be the last flight from Rangoon for three years. The 214th Infantry Regiment of the 33rd Division of the 15th Army of the Imperial Japanese Forces entered Rangoon the next day and Colonel Takanobu Sakuma, the commander of Rangoon District, settled himself into my parents' old home – it had a nice position beside Inya Lake. Since I was only one year old at the time, I did not realise that I might never see my father again, nor that this long journey was the first of so many to come.

From India, we travelled to Quetta in Pakistan and when my father arrived six months later, tragically thin, we moved to Ootacamund in southern India. Two years later, we were all on a troop ship that zig-zagged around the eastern Atlantic to avoid U Boats. My grandfather, an admiral in naval intelligence, knew the rough positions of the U Boats and the exact position of his whole family. Arriving in Liverpool we boarded the train for London and my sister and I carefully unpacked our little suitcases and put out our pyjamas; we had never been on a train journey of less than two days. My father always maintained that any wanderlust I might have acquired had come from 20,000 miles of travel before I was three.

I write spontaneously and in what some of my friends might describe as unusual places: a village house in Upper Burma, a guest house beside a Siberian volcano, a tent in a Himalayan winter or a hammock under an Amazonian kapok tree. These places are not very unusual of course, simply a little off the track heavily beaten by the groups of organised tourists. Friends tend to go to the Mediterranean, spend two days in the Uffizi and will scramble for days over the ruins of Carthage. These may be interesting and occasionally fun, but they are not for Travellers; at least, not this one. As a boy, I was fascinated by the story of Colonel Fawcett who entered Brazil's Matto Grosso never to be seen again. Under the bedclothes of the senior dorm at Abberley Hall, my torch shone upon the pages of such excitements as The Lost City and Peter Fleming's *Brazilian Adventure*. Later, with a little more worldliness, the realities of a lingering death from a curare-smeared spear did not seem so attractive and my adventurer loyalties switched to Frank Kingdon Ward. Part of me, the romantic and possibly morbid part, follows this energetic plant hunter as he hacks his way through the forests of Northern Burma or struggles through the steep valleys to discover the uncharted course of the Tsangpo River, collecting the original material for my garden as he goes. How dreadful it would be to expire in the humdrum hinterland of John Lewis, falling between haberdashery and hardware.

On the whole, cities do not hold many attractions for me; there are no horizons, little honesty, they tend to be electronic and their inhabitants are concerned only for themselves. They hold many testaments to man's creative genius but in spite of attending many courses on all forms of art, I prefer the spaces in between the art. Paul Theroux puts it this way:

'.... *people who are glamorised by big cities and think of themselves as urbane are at heart country mice – simple, fearful, over domesticated provincials dazzled by city lights.*'

This meander is simply to explain that I am not a pioneering adventurer who drags tyres around muddy fields to limber up for rigours to come; not an expert in anything nor even passionate about particular places. I just like to observe the silent beauty of the wild, disturbed only by birds and beasts, and enjoy the quirks of human nature wherever they are found – preferably indigenous although fellow travellers can be interesting too. A wet tent is bearable for a short time, but the more so if you know it will be followed by a deep and hot bath, a whisky sour, soft pillows and crisp linen.

My wife Maggie is not an enthusiastic traveller. This is disappointing as one of the pleasures of travel is to share the good and the bad moments and reminisce about the day in a post-mortem of praise, criticism and discussion. After we had travelled the Silk Road from Tashkent to Beijing, she said she would never travel with me again. It was, of course, hot and dusty and the edge of the Taklimakan Desert is depressingly boring but the bit she loved best was getting stuck in an unseasonable June blizzard that blanketed the Tien Shan Mountains and being holed up for a day and a night in a yak herder's tent. (I am glad to say that we have travelled again together many times since.) As I do not always have her witty and comforting companionship, I sometimes go alone or with a group. Both of these have their merits and disadvantages but unless the group is certain to be congenial, the lone traveller option is usually the best.

The travel pieces you may be about to sample do not record every journey. The Silk Road, for example, is not here, nor are nor are Alaska, Bali, Bangladesh, Bolivia, Costa Rica and Lapland amongst others and most of Europe. The pieces here are not chosen because I enjoyed the places most; it is simply that they are the only places I wrote about at the time.

These are not a travelogues – heaven forbid! – but it seems a pity to waste some of the moments on the way that have entertained or excited. If any of these pieces tickle your spirit, get out there fast, for the byways are being trampled into a tourist track every day.

A fellow Wykehamist, Ian Graham, an expert in Mayan iconography and a real life Indiana Jones in the '40s, described himself as '*A bushwacker outfitted with a camera, a pencil, some grains of common sense and an instinct for self-preservation*'. That would be a headstone I think I might like.

Chipping Norton
June 2014

Washington for the Weekend

January 1994

'To awake quite alone in a strange town is one of the pleasantest sensations in the world'
– Freya Stark

The Potomac was frozen, there was snow in the street, ice on the sidewalks, the first five cab drivers were Afghan ex-mujahidin and the waiters seemed to be all Puerto Rican. I hailed a stubbled freedom fighter and there, between Constitution and Pennsylvania, stood the White House. So this was Washington after all. A blizzard littered the highways with skewed cars as the townies slithered to their country homes but it swept on to Virginia and left behind a bright, clear weekend.

I was fortunate; winter weekends are not known for balmy weather but take off for a city trans-Atlantic and you are assured of bargains galore. The cheapest fares of the year, hotel staff anxious to please, short queues at the high spots; a city at your feet, empty of tourists and commuters but full of the bonhomie of local traders who have not yet honed their sales pitch on the whetstone of the holiday trade. Never mind a few murky days, escape to the galleries, the tea shops and theatres and a king sized bed bought for the price of a summer pillow.

Washington is on the boundary of the Confederate and Northern states and although firmly Yankee, there seemed to be an even distribution of generals cast in the bronze of posterity; with school-boy familiarity one came upon Grant, Sherman, Jackson and Lee. It is a city of monuments and memorials, huge and arrogant in the past, humbler in the present. The massive bronze (the largest ever cast) of raising the stars and stripes at Iwo Jima is unashamedly vainglorious, the Vietnam Veterans' Memorial stark in its simplicity.

If you removed the few blocks of Georgetown and Alexandria there would be little left to charm but plenty to be in awe of. The buildings of the Smithsonian on

Arlington Cemetery, Washington

Independence Avenue lie on one side of the great green expanse in front of Capitol Hill while opposite, along Madison Drive, are the great national museums. At the Library of Congress is one of the world's greatest repositories of knowledge with a scale to dominate and impress. The Castle, the original headquarters of the Smithsonian Institution, seems curiously out of place with its turreted and eccentric skyline – an American pastiche whose architecture reflects the Liverpudlian origins of its benefactor, Henry Smithson. In the crisp air, the subway steamed through the pavement grilles and the mere scattering of people gave an eerie feeling. I felt the humility of a mouse on a harvested prairie but with Doctor Strangelove at my elbow. Suddenly the melancholy but fruity notes of a tenor sax cut into self-indulgence. Here on a deserted sidewalk, black, aged, grey haired, stubbled, darned and stooped was unwelcome reality. Like a junior rope rigger caught in the footlights of the Metropolitan, the uncomfortable truth of what lies behind the grand façade stubbed my sprightly toe. I put a dollar in the musician's hat and for a while winced each time his faulty A flat tarnished the blues.

The cordoned queues at the FBI building indicated the popularity of its tours but on an off-season Monday we were only eight and not a G man in sight. We wandered down endless corridors, occasionally peering through plate glass into laboratories that examined bullets, matched DNA and identified the pin head flakes of paint of a getaway car. The inactivity was disturbing but perhaps crime too was out of season. The shooting demonstration in the basement range gave a tweak of excitement and here a genuine agent with a Beretta revolver and a Koch submachine gun convincingly pumped 40 lead slugs through the heart of a paper cut out. The agents are tested four times a year; 'Hostage and Rescue' require 95% accuracy but for others 75% is sufficient. As I left I pondered on the fact that in a shootout the good guy has a one in four chance of being shot.

South of the Potomac in Virginia on gently sloping ground amid maple, oak, ash and linden America buries it military heroes and political heavyweights in Arlington National Cemetery. It is tranquil, serene and compassionate and the rise and fall of the ground prevents too many of the two hundred thousand head-stones being seen at once; the graves of John Kennedy and Robert Kennedy are poignant in their simplicity. The leafless trees are elegant but sombre.

'Bare ruined choirs, where late the sweet bird sang.'

I hurried up the hill towards Robert E. Lee's old house to watch the changing of the guard by the tombs of the unknown soldiers from World Wars I and II, Korea and Vietnam. Europeans, whose military pageantry tends to be colourful, musical and large scale, find this is a tame affair. A single soldier from the Old Guard – America's oldest infantry unit, head cropped as close as a coconut, is replaced for another via a staff sergeant who inspects the rifle of each in an elabo-rate ritual of much slapping of butts and rattling of bolts; whether to ensure that the rifle is loaded or unloaded I was not sure.

On a Sunday morning the old tobacco port of Georgetown had a middle class, middle browed but moneyed feel with BMWs, Saabs and Volvos, designer track-suits for dog walkers, and dressing gowned figures taking the first strenuous exer-cise of the day as they pick up 2½lbs (1 kilo) of Sunday papers. A corner shop beckoned with the smell of fresh brewed coffee and toast (rye, wholewheat, sour dough, black, brown, thick or thin), eggs (up, down, scrambled, trampled, wink-ing, blinking) and most enticing of all, bacon fried to a crisp. I expected Woody Allen to open a door rubbing his eyes or Meryl Streep to flash a crooked smile. This was a setting for romantic comedy, secure, comforting and fun. Saunter past an agreeable palette of ranch red ochre, prairie green, mustard and cornflower and you might bump into Norman Rockwell painting on a street corner or Mable

Lucie Attwell spreading a gingham table cloth, but come Monday morning, although the set remains, the dream vanishes in a flurry of overcoated executives, career wives and traffic jams.

Add a fourth day and you could take in Baltimore (an ancient port and wonderful aquarium) and Annapolis (an 18th century architectural gem) and with a fifth day, Williamsburg (living history) and Yorktown (where Admiral Cornwallis surrendered). But stretch a weekend this far and the thrill of a few stolen days will snap. I hurried home to humdrum and to reach for the atlas – winter had another six weeks to go.

Egypt for the Weekend

January 1995

'But why, oh why do the wrong people travel when the right people stay at home?'
– Noel Coward

Never ask an Egyptian taxi to hurry – at least not in Cairo. Speed is their creed, daring their hero. If you escape being maimed by a taxi, you will probably die of fright inside one. Cairo has the worst drivers on earth and its taxi drivers come from hell.

This is a monster of a city. Clogged, chaotic, cacophonous; it heaves and writhes giving birth to new cement-grey suburban blocks each week which in turn strain services already convulsed. Dominated and divided by the Nile, the river carries surprisingly little traffic. Bright feluccas, sullen in the lack of wind, floating restaurants and flocks of seagulls feeding on the detritus of fifteen million inhabitants are about all that moves. But step onto the Corniche el Nil and press further into the tangle of back streets and there nothing is still or silent. Rusty buses, mangy donkeys, shiny Mercedes and 10,000 black and white taxis jostle with people, people, and people. Women in berber black galabiyas, academics in grey, clerics in white, sharp suited businessmen, tradesmen in sweaters so hideous they would never make the final reduction rail of a north country market, rags and this year's best seller, dayglo pink trimmed with nylon lace. Architecturally barren (although the newer mosques in white limestone and marble have a refreshing delicacy), the charm comes from the people who seem universally glad to see one. Information will be smilingly volunteered and although there may often be a commercial motive for bonhomie, once it is clear that you already have ten packs of postcards, enough rugs for a warehouse and papyrus pictures by the gross, it is likely you will be genuinely wished a happy stay.

Commerce is the single ingredient that binds the vastly varied colours, religions and incomes of Egypt. Passengers pass through duty free shops to <u>enter</u> the country (the attractions include immersion heaters, refrigerators and central heating components) and in the last week of the year, Mohammed slips temporarily into the shadows to make way for the more profitable Father Christmas. A Muslim, desert, third-world country is strange enough to a visitor from frozen Oxfordshire; add 'Merry Christmas' 14 feet (4m) high across the façade of the Nile Hilton and the effect is surreal.

The pyramids are on the edge of the city and from our hotel balcony their peaks cut through the urban horizon of the industrial suburb of Giza. I felt betrayed that this preview had stolen their mystery. These sacred wardens of the greatest Pharaohs seemed reduced to sandcastles. Nevertheless, go west towards a setting sun, turn your back to the grime and the tourist tack, hire a horse or a camel and approach them over a dune and the mystery is restored.

Luxor had been our particular goal but Saudis, Japanese and others with more time to plan had filled all the planes, so Alexandria was second best. Advised to reserve train seats I selected a taxi driver from a clammering throng for his ability to understand the word 'railway station'. Unfortunately, I had assumed that this multilingual capability would mean that he could read as well. I was mistaken; his eagerness to help simply added to the confusion. The railway tickets were about the size of a postcard, nicely designed in several pastel colours. The essential information was naturally in Arabic and to check departure time, carriage and seat number, no smoking etc. the comic gestures on both sides of the plate glass window emphasised the patience of an Egyptian and the thespian ambitions of an Englishman.

The 0805 Turborini sped due north along rails arrow straight and across land pancake flat, parallel to a dual carriageway and beside fields of alfalfa, carrots and cabbages. There were bullocks, egrets, donkeys working irrigation wheels and huddles of breeze block farms each with flat roofs piled high with dried maize, papyrus, hay and sugar cane. Magpies fidgeted about the landscape and an unstable confetti of gulls whitened the furrowed ground. On board, the service of coffee was a local art form. Nescafé, powdered milk and sugar in equal proportions are whisked with a drop of water in a glass until creamy; filled to the brim with boiling water, this is then handed to the passenger who is left to juggle the scalding glass from hand to hand. In the town, the ritual is quite different; finely powdered coffee, cardamom, sugar and water are prepared to a consistency only slightly more viscous than treacle and then poured shoulder high into a thimble. Two of these sipped slowly produce a sleep-defeating buzz and a spring-in-the-step nirvana that brings energy for three more mosques and a carpet factory.

Sultan Hassan Mosque
. Cairo

Alexandria had nothing to offer of its romantic past. Even the Hotel Cecil and Café Pastrudis were uncompromisingly furnished with plastic pastiche. Lawrence Durrell placed Justine here, of course.

'A city shared by five races, five languages and a dozen creeds. Five fleets turning through their greasy reflections behind the harbour bar.'

Now, one race, one language, one creed and a monoglot metropolis. But to the west there is one of the most eccentric restaurants of the Mediterranean. Fight your way through the grime and clatter of marine workshops, chandlery, anchor chains, vast bales of cotton and belching diesel lorries and there suddenly appears a castle. Bannered, battlemented with plaster knights, concrete cannons and a menagerie of stuffed monkeys, owls, flamingos and turtles, it is modestly called 'Seagull'. Inside, many rooms cater for 1,000 customers amongst an extraordinary array of *objects d'art*, *brocante*, trivia, ephemera and the flotsam and jetsam gathered from the past elegance of a city now lost to the stuccoed drabness of countless identical high-rise blocks, rented to Cairenes seeking summer breezes. It is amusing, decorative and original but for a moment I found it disturbing. I heard the mocking voices of Justine, Clea, Olivia et al, and saw a figure in spats and patent leather wince at his domesticity displayed as a carnival and his personal possessions stripped of intimacy. There were whispers from an elaborate Victorian armoire, a hiss of 'shame' from a sepia portrait. Fortunately this nostalgic discomfort was given a sharp shove by the arrival of numerous salads – baby spiced aubergine, tahina, glutinous rice, chilli-hot okra and cucumber-cool yoghurt and then there was confusion as we were given a piece of paper with an Arabic numeral while an arm beckoned us to follow. Leaving the paper on the table, it was given back; we smiled, nodded and replaced it. After two more attempts, it was picked up by a patient waiter who led us from the dining room. Suddenly a saviour with soft and perfect English came to rescue us.

"There is no menu, just fish – whatever has been caught in the last few hours. Please give your table number."

We chose from heads of sea bass, mullet and sardines that poked up through crushed ice like a Stargazy Pie; there were also octopus, calamari and shrimps.

"Perhaps grilled on charcoal with garlic and a few spices?"

Washed down with Stella beer, juices scooped up with warm pitta bread, that was reality. We left past parrots and pelicans, Nubians, Saracens and Mamelukes. At the road, a backward glance seemed to catch a slight figure in starched collar sipping from one of those thimbles of coffee and then a sixteen wheeler loaded with pig iron thundered by and a taxi had us in its sights.

Weekend in Palm Beach

February 1995

'I did not understand the term 'terminal illness' until I saw Heathrow for myself'
– Dennis Potter

For a town as photogenic as Palm Beach – an oasis of respectability 100 miles (160kms) north of Miami – it is surprisingly difficult to find a picture postcard. With azure sea, palm trees, pelicans, elegant architecture and inhabitants, hedges trimmed to set square perfection and streets so spick and span one doubts if anybody has dropped a raspberry ripple or tossed an empty Budweiser in fifty years, a carousel of gorgeous views might be expected on every corner. But Palm Beach is as close to reality as Kubla Khan. Its main shopping street, Worth Avenue, is aptly named – unless you know how much you are worth there is nothing you are likely to be able to afford.

However, there is an exception in The Church Mouse, the charity shop run by the Episcopalian Church of Bethesda-by-the-Sea. Here Palm Beach bric-a-brac and cast-offs start at a price that most of us would consider appropriate for an heirloom and car spaces beside the shop are 'Reserved for Donors'; I thought I had uncovered an illicit trade in spare parts for the aging population. Inside Betsy Mitzer, groomed and cool in crisp linen, explained, "We really prefer a good name on our clothes and anything for the home needs to be perfect. Items are often brought in by maids – they have little use for a designer cocktail dress."

The Church of Bethesda-by-the-Sea is solid, anglo-saxon and turreted. It could well have been brought stone by hand-crafted stone from a shire county and bears an uncanny resemblance to St. Mary's at Frinton-on-Sea. But while St. Mary's had the tang of salt and mansion polish, the comfort of dusty corners and thistles in the graveyard, B-by-the-S was clinically litter free, close cropped, clean and orderly. Inside it was cool and a bronze plaque gratefully recorded the benefactor who donated the air conditioning. I was grateful too, as I was going to a wedding there and felt uncomfortable as I arrived in my city suit of winter weight worsted avoiding pony-tailed, satin-shorted roller-skaters weaving between the zimmers. The service had the familiarity of the James I edition but the ritual was different. Groomsmen, cravated and close cropped to a man, lifted a left elbow to escort each female down the aisle. I had a card that said 'Pew 4 North' and concerned that I might get the elbow treatment too, I crept down the aisle in the wake of a dinner-jacketed video operator taking a panoramic shot of the Gothic arches and stained glass. After a procession of groomsmen, bridesmaids, flower girls and ring bearer each proceeding singly to form a sort of matrimonial wall of grey morning coat and cream seersucker, things got underway with a baritone solo. Half an hour later, hymnless and sermonless, we were squinting in the bright sunlight with a radiant, newly married couple anxious to get on with the fun and swig down Mimosas in the swankiest, most restrictive establishment of all the Southern states, The Everglades Club. In this WASP enclave, my hosts, a prominent local lawyer and his fourth generation Floridian wife, had scored a notable first by inviting a prominent local lawyer and his fourth generation Floridian wife; but they were black. Never before had this colour bar been breached. Not for nothing was Florida the last state to allow a coloured defendant a defence counsel in Belafonte v the State of Florida in 1936.

The Everglades Club lies at one end of Worth Avenue in dignified hacienda style, faced with coral blocks and clad in bougainvillea and poinsettia taking up 200 ft (60m) of some of the most expensive frontage in the world. Half the length of Bond Street, the Avenue starts at the ocean end with Cartier, Givenchy and Chanel and goes up from there. It stops at the Intracoastal Waterway where the marine equivalent of Lear Jet and Gulfstream float serenely indifferent to fishermen on the far side and poor side who are dangling a line for a supper supplement. These leviathans of gleaming white, trimmed with stainless steel and teak, rest on the swell, tied to land with umbilical cords of water, electricity, cable TV and fibre optics. Purposeful young men and women, uniformly bronzed and clad in well pressed cotton, daily polish inside and out in case the owner has a whim for salt and sea breeze.

Some of these smoothies (those of steel and teak) are supreme examples of marine engineering. 'The Other Woman', taking up 145 feet (45m) of the marina, carried aft two motor yachts of seemingly ocean going capabilities. Hank Zwarse (I got him to write it down), the Lacoste clad, just-missed-the-America-Cup-trials, Ring-of-Confidence crew member arranging the potted philodendron at

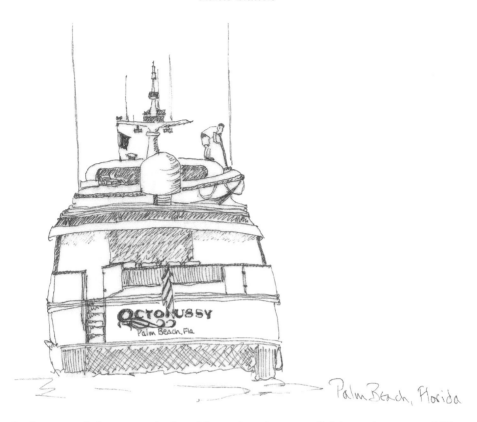

Palm Beach, Florida

the bottom of the gang plank, told me that the cost of this opulence was $45m; enough to fill a decent sized cargo ship with rice and bound for Somalia.

Turn towards the land and things are only a little more real. Police cars honk like pelicans (sirens would offend), rubbish bins are hidden in clipped hibiscus and aged skin is stretched as far as ambitions for youthfulness will allow. Tiffany's has a mid-season sale (eighteen carat Snoopy brooches are on special offer) and The Banana Republic has cotton chinos down to $60. But there is not a black skin nor a coloured postcard in sight.

Nambia and Botswana

August 1995

'Tourists know where they have been; travellers don't know where they are going'
— Paul Theroux

There is only one corner on the 250 mile (400kms) single-track, dirt road across the Namibian Desert and I missed it. In an instant of terrible confusion stones rained on glass, rubber burnt, metal was forced against metal in teeth-aching desperation, and there was the clear-headedness that comes with adrenaline, pressure pumped by fear and then a huge, all-enveloping and total silence.

We were alive and alone with a wreck of a car in a landscape stony and desolate to every horizon, under a sky where the evening star was already bright and with a temperature that would drop to freezing within the hour. Here were a father and daughter, two Capricornians, bizarrely stranded within a mile of the Tropic of Capricorn (we had passed the rusted sign a few minutes before), wondering at the clarity of the stars and thankful for the mercy of God. We lost no time in unpacking our bags and wearing everything they contained – three pairs of trousers, six shirts, a sweater and a sun hat. Then we divided a banana and three digestives for supper.

Near to midnight there was a glint in the mirror from a small beam of light that rose and dipped as a vehicle approached down the undulating road like a lifeboat's masthead in heavy seas. Suddenly it crested a brow, turned the fatal corner and lit up our two waving figures. A small rusty truck slowed to look, passed, stopped and reversed. From the cab stepped a swarthy, dungareed middle-aged man.

"You have a problem?"

His thick German accent could have been Gabriel's. He took in the smashed windscreen, two tyres shredded on their rims and a radiator hanging loose.

NAMIBIA & BOTSWANA

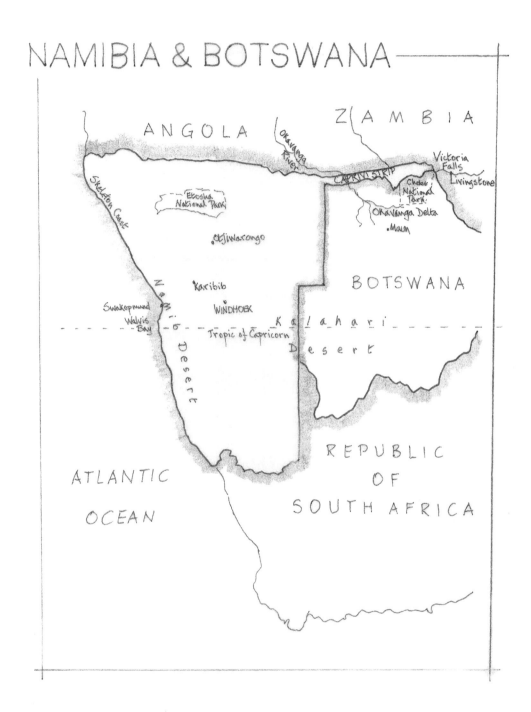

"You are British? Empty the car, put your luggage in the back and climb in the cab with Suzie while I find the spare wheel."

Suzie? We could see no one; a granddaughter perhaps? I opened the cab door and there was Suzie. The Germans breed Rottweilers, the Asians the Aveda and the Americans the bull mastiff; by some quirk of immigration and genetics, Suzie was a close cousin of them all. The wet lips of this huge hound were drawn back and quivering, her canines moist, her tongue glistening and her brown and bloodshot eyes were bright with anticipation as they stared straight into mine. She leapt at my shoulders, floored me in the dust and pinned me with paws the size of dinner plates. As she opened her mouth I gazed at rows of yellow teeth vanishing into a dark throat from which came a warm sticky breath, like wind blowing over the fires of Gehenna. Then, pausing only to ensure I was secured beneath her fourteen stone, her colossal tongue gave my face a wet and welcoming wash.

The journey to Walvis Bay was reassuring to the mind but retributive to the body with Suzie grumpy at two strangers sharing her berth. Constant grunts, heaves, bad breath and worse from the other end had trimmed our gratitude to this slobbering mastiff. Hans, our saviour, said little but performed like a saint as he took us to his house that sat on the shoreline. In the garden, weird shapes of sinuous driftwood cast shadows in the moonlight and seemed like the roots of a giant tree; I expected a Hobbit or two to appear. Instead, there came round the corner an attractive woman wearing a green skirt, a red jacket and blonde plaits that reached almost to her waist. She was followed by a seal.

Heidi had been crushing nuts for the *apfelstrudel* to be sold in her bakery the next day. The seal had been rescued as a pup, abandoned in the huge Cape Cross grey seal colony nearby and left to die with a badly damaged eye. It now had a home in a rock pool made by Hans and, as a treat from its fishy diet, had grown fond of pastry. While Heidi kneaded her dough and Hans sang lieder in the bath we listened to breakers pounding the West African coast, smelt the cinnamon and spices and regarded a one-eyed seal finishing an apple pie.

The morning, made damp and grey by a saturating sea mist, later disclosed a clean, tidy, balconied, clap-boarded town of parallel streets, dapper people, cafés called Edelweiss or Schwartz Moran and shops selling Bavarian lager. Miles of flat sand with holiday cabins placed at precise intervals showed the attractions that summer would bring to breeze-seeking holiday makers from Windhoek and South Africa. At Cape Cross, the colony of 10,000 grey seals clamouring and grunting in an ammonia-stenched air attracted day sightseers and inland, the lead mines and railway museum of a previous colonising century appealed to those tourists who lasted into week two.

Shamefaced we told our sad tale to the car hire people and endured their reproofs.

"You left it *where*?"

"It's probably had its engine stolen by now."

"That's the straightest road in Namibia."

But by the next day the little Golf had been rescued, re-tyred, patched up and cleaned up. After sending whisky to Hans and biscuits to Suzie, we set off at a more cautious pace with *strudel* and *bratwurst* in our tucker bag and a case of Becks in the boot.

At the end of its journey from the highlands of Angola, the Okavango River (the third longest in Africa) comes to rest in myriad tributaries in northern Botswana forming the largest inland delta on earth. Where the river dies in the desert, a paradise is born. The intervening 50,000 islands, lush with palm, acacia, sausage tree and wild sage, host a huge animal population in search of food and water in the dry African winter. Along the streams and broader channels fringed with reed and the feathery heads of papyrus, birds continually fish and forage.

"Stop that baboon, it's nicked my knickers!"

If you are travelling light (one worn, one washing, one waiting) and staying in the tree house of Oddballs Camp in the Okavango Delta, baboons are public enemy number one. Returning after a morning's excursion we found our bags unpacked, our clothes scattered and the bed clothes more rumpled than an energetic Casanova could have achieved. Here was the realisation of childhood dreams 40 ft (12m) up a biloba tree, reed thatched and oil lamped with a few sticks of furniture and a huge bed. To the Swiss Family Robinson this would have been the Presidential Suite since the remainder of the camp simply offered a patch of ground in a grove of fig trees on which to pitch a tent. We were woken by the light of the dawn, the cry of a mockingbird and the squeals of excitement as a warthog mother and her four babies rootled around the base of this lofty hotel room. Nearby was a bar with a range of bottles that would rival The Ritz (no filter cigarettes since filters do not biodegrade), a levered machine for squashing cans and a large black cat. Next door, the kitchen produced tasty food cooked over charcoal, with fresh bread baked in a clay oven.

Oddballs had a sister camp – Delta, separated by half a mile of grassland and served by the same airstrip. After two nights at Oddballs, having been double booked with a German lady with a vast bust, a bark of a voice and a worse temper, we were offered the luxury of the much more expensive Delta establishment which we grateful accepted. Ungenerously, we hoped that the baboons would make a special raid on the Wagnerian *hausfrau*.

At Delta there were eight individual chalets of stout timber and reed walls, each with jumbo sized beds, cool linen (hot water bottles on request) and hot

Chobe National Park

showers – my soap rested on a bleached kudu shoulder blade. Each new guest was made welcome by Bob, black, portly, with a watermelon smile under a Rajput moustache and Binky, the manager for four years, who presided over the whole establishment with the easy charm of a hostess at a country house party. Drinks were on a help yourself basis, dinner was around a great table of polished mahogany railway sleepers and on the sideboard there were jars labelled 'Coffee', 'Earl Grey' and 'Birdseed'.

A night in the bush was offered and we eagerly accepted this. Others were similarly setting off and we scoffed at the amount and range of equipment they drew from the store. Mattresses, pillows, stools, kerosene stoves and lights, canvas basins and mountains of blankets. We needed none of this excessiveness; the British know a thing or two about expeditions and a tent, a couple of tins of beans and a packet of biscuits would suffice. At dusk our mokoro poler cooked up an appetising meal for himself as we opened our cold beans and by midnight the cold had so chilled the day's warm earth that we spent the remaining miserable hours clasped together like foetal twins as we sought each other's heat.

First light, with its soft pink shadows, was the time to set off in a mokoro. Half a tree trunk and probably chiselled out personally by your poler, it was just wide enough for a well-fed figure and long enough to sit one behind each other, just above the water line. Point an arm at a passing saddle billed stork and the whole log tipped precariously. The poler, standing at the back, instantly adjusts the balance with his stick against the shallow bed of a water-lilied pond and stability returns before further enthusiasm, cries of alarm or laughter start another roll. In between, slipping through nature, there is still, silent magic. On the islands graze elephant, impala, kudu, reedbuck, giraffe and buffalo.

As the mokoro was poled away from the sandy shore, there suddenly appeared out of the reed and papyrus a huge bull elephant. Balanced in half a leaky tree trunk, just above the water and within yards of a five ton irritable elephant, places one in a scale of vulnerability close to a walnut shell in the Roaring Forties. An immediate squirt of adrenaline makes some reach for a camera and others for their God but as we back poled into the reeds, it became apparent that the elephant was simply demanding clear passage across the stream and in a few measured splashy steps of undeniable authority, he had crossed to a juicy patch of ilea palms on the other side. The nuts of this palm are a favourite but being out

Chobe National Park

Treehouse at
Oddballs Camp.
Okavango.

of reach, an elephant leans his forehead against the tree and in a series of quick heaves brings down a dozen or so nuts each the size and weight of a cricket ball in a fusillade that bounce off his armoured skull and on to the ground. The nuts have about the same density and flavour as a cricket ball but they apparently aid the elephants' digestion as they rattle around inside and the nut itself benefits from its enzyme ridden journey so days later, when it drops to the ground the other end, its germination has been given a useful start.

The sudden failing of tropical light brought a cacophony of grunts and croaks from the reed frogs. Occasionally they were all in unnatural unison, but then nature's conductor set the usual erratic beat and night jars, boubous and chattering quelea joined in. Cicadas provided the continuo, and fortissimo passages were managed by a trumpeting elephant, hippo grunts and a lion's distant roar. Later, there was sublime quiet through which the rustles of the smaller nocturnal rodents were caught by a weary ear.

Moving east we admired the Victoria Falls – The Smoke that Thunders – before indulging in a little rafting fun. Well, that was how it was put to me. I had not rafted before and thought that floating down the Zambezi would make a pleasant afternoon trip. Later, on the sandy shore, equipped with a life jacket, a helmet and listening intently to a muscular South African describe the emergency drills for roll-overs, flipping, and righting a Zodiac I realised I had been daughter-duped. The journey was terrifying, the walls of water were as tall as a house, the boulders vast and the current overwhelming. Had I known this was a Grade 5 ride (one less than that for professionals), reason and sense would have ensured that I never entered the rubber monster but since these were both absent, I had an exhilarating, enlivening, thrilling and rip-roaring ride.

Vietnam

February 1996

'Life for him was an adventure; perilous indeed, but men are not made for safe havens'
– Edith Hamilton on Aeschylus (The Greek Way)

Saigon was hot and humid enough to dampen a shirt in minutes and airport immigration was unusually trying – five forms to complete and each studied and checked meticulously by a fellow in a uniform of bilious green with four stars on his epaulettes; it took almost an hour and a half to reach him at the red line on the floor. When it is apparent that the wait is long, the scrutiny thorough and the officials tired, there comes upon the lines either a resignation (British and Americans), an anxiousness (East Europeans) or a competitiveness (Germans, French and Italians). The Japanese have no idea what is going on and stand smiling in hot sun throughout the day but all will push their luggage along a few more inches than might normally be civil. It is always the case that one's own queue has at its head the illegal immigrant, the illiterate or the ill- educated. Sometimes an interloper approaches – he pretends to be unaware of the procedures and has a stupid and sly grin. The queue, which so far has subscribed universally to individual competition, immediately assumes a mutual solidarity. Few looks are exchanged but there is a common broadening of shoulders and a shuffling forward of bags to close any chink in the defences.

In the morning I took a cyclo tour to the extraordinary temple of the Cao Dai sect; they combine Hindu, Buddhist, Confucianist and Catholic religions and their saints include Joan of Arc, Victor Hugo and Winston Churchill. Unique to a small area of Vietnam, they maintained strict neutrality during the war. I went to the Viet Cong tunnel complex at Chu Chi with its labyrinthine series of claustrophobic rat holes, some down to 65 feet (20m). The Museum of Foreign Aggres-

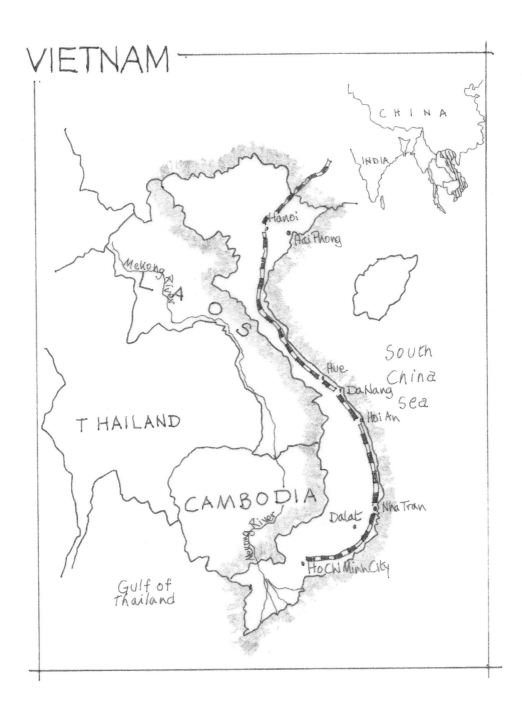

Hanoi resident

sion and the Ho Chi Minh Museum both appalled in their depiction of atrocities but they reminded me that Saigon fell to the Vietcong over 20 years ago on 30th April 1975. I hoped we would be able to leave the war soon – it is dreadful and depressing to have these reminders thrust upon one. I kept my toothless, whiskered, stick-like peddler to go on to the market in Cholon in the Chinese Quarter. For a country previously brought to its knees in economic ruin, there was now nothing you could not buy. Everything was geared to commerce and here was a frenzied, frenetic, fast moving, weaving, ducking, hurrying, bargaining orgy of activity.

At cross roads, there appear to be about 17 cars, 7,000 bicycles and 70,000 mopeds – all Hondas. These cohorts charge at each other from all four directions simultaneously; additionally, there are spectacular intersections of six roads. If you are in the middle, in a cyclo for instance or, God help you, on your feet, there is little you can do but pray to your maker and quickly too, for what remains of your life can only be measured in seconds. But moments later, at a time when you should be strawberry jam, a miracle occurs; you are out on the other side painlessly and noiselessly. How this feat is accomplished hundreds of times a day by countless popping motors, rickshaws, cyclists, walkers, carts, porters, trolleys and 17 cars seems a miracle. Part of the miracle may stem from a mutual social attitude, engendered by Buddhism, where individual survival is subservient to the paramount concern for others. To the westerner nurtured on a largely selfish diet, this selflessness is assumed to be primitive and naïve – it is exactly the opposite.

The Ides of March came with clear blue skies and the coolness of the hills. At 4,500 ft (1370m), the hill station of Dalat was a charming surprise with pine trees and large areas of cropped grass. It is to Vietnam the Darjeeling of India or the Cameron Highlands of Malaysia. The houses are sturdy and colonial with stuccoed and elaborately timbered façades, steeply pitched roofs and steps that lead up to the front door, like an oriental Le Touquet. Previously the haven of the families of the administrative French, it had now been taken over by communist officials eager to avoid sweating it out in Saigon. The people here are a little different too; Montegnards from the mountain tribes, fuller in the hips with high cheekbones and darker skins. It was cold and there was a blazing fire in the hall of my little hotel; I had to put on a shirt and sweater in the middle of the night, bringing my mosquito net down on top of me like an animal trap.

The road up from Saigon passed through plantations of pineapple, rubber, tapioca and banana. Sugarcane was being harvested and a belching diesel engine drove a giant mangle from which syrup was drained into seven successive boiling vats so that its viscosity ran from juice to glue. Much of the hillside would have been thick jungle had it not been slashed and burnt for plantations, cut for timber or destroyed by the toxin Agent Orange in the war. Coffee grew at higher altitude and in cafés it was served in a little metal perforated cup that sat on top of a glass and filtered down on to a teaspoon of sweetened condensed milk. Tea grew here too and was in every restaurant – green, coarse and pungent. Taxi motorbikes ruled the roads and at every crossroads there waited grinning youths who invited you to climb aboard then roared off laughing. I seldom knew where I was going (the language barrier is insurmountable) so I gestured left or right from behind – the roundabouts were terrifying.

Breathless from fear and altitude, I arrived at the summer residence of the last emperor, Bao Dai who was deposed in 1954. It was an appalling and sprawling sort of post-modernist, art deco dump, brimming with kitsch of the worst kind. Dalat is a honeymooners' town and the whole house had giggling couples in every corner taking photographs of themselves playing the gilded piano, hanging on to elaborately painted wrought iron screens or lounging on furniture that looked like 1940s Maples – it probably was. In the gardens, amongst hydrangeas, roses, agapanthus and arum lilies, photographers each had their own props. These included cowboy outfits and horses with wild-west saddlery, Mickey Mouse, Donald Duck, a prancing Pluto and Father Christmas. The brides were dressed up to the nines and looked as though they were off to another wedding in their high heels, gold lamé, the brightest lipstick, dayglo taffeta in every shade and raffia handbags. I hoped they were having a good time but it seemed hard work. In the evening they flocked to little cafés around the lakeside and pushed off into the water in pedalos shaped like hearts or pink clouds.

Later on I called on a Buddhist monk who lived in a mini pagoda he had built himself. He was perfectly charming, spoke a number of languages including excellent English, kept seven dogs and laughed a great deal. He was very interested in my camera and extremely knowledgeable in spite of his own being an elderly and basic model with which he kept taking photographs all the time, convulsed in giggles. He was an artist and thought it amusing that what he sold for $10 here, he charged $500 for when he exhibited in America.

A seven hour drive down to the coastal plains was spectacular, with pine giving way to market gardens of neat and carefully tended rows of beans, tomatoes, grapes, potatoes and melons. In turn these changed to the dazzling green of rice paddies, picture postcard scenes with white egrets, women in conical hats and small boys leading great, grey, lumbering water buffalo. I stopped for lunch at Cam Ranh Bay which had been a huge American port but nothing remained except the detritus of war – rusting military trucks and a million miles of barbed wire. Sitting close to the sea and vulnerable to the inshore wind, I lost my entire fishy dish to a freak gust that blew it westward off the table.

On the beach at Nha Trang three Vietnamese women, a mother and her two daughters, operating under a sign that said 'Massage $5' and on a mat laid on the sand, pummelled me for an hour causing me such pain I cried out but my pleas were ignored. When I said that I had a cold they squirted camphor oil up my nose where it stung for two days. Feeling black and blue and probably looking like a half ripe blackberry, I went off to a Confucian temple. There were no formalities, not even the usual abandoning of shoes. Huge coils of smouldering joss sticks were suspended over three inner courtyards and fantastic decorations of gold snarling dragons curled around every lacquered column while more joss sticks (bought in multiples of ten), burnt pungently in great bronze urns. In front of the 'altar', a lavish affair swirling with every shade of gold and scarlet and with more fearsome, open jawed dragons and elaborate friezes of reticulated devices, stood a long stainless steel counter of the kind usually found in a self-service restaurant. Here, just out of reach of hungry dragons, a small parcel of rice or bowl of fruit could be purchased, to be then offered for redemption or favours or a choice of animal in the return to the next life. Special requests required a few dongs of the local currency and this brought two thumps on a great wooden drum and a clang on a bell. I sat in the cool of a courtyard to gain relief from the heat and all who entered, clasping their smoking sticks, smiled benignly at me. When a poor market porter smiles at a fat traveller with pen and pad and a big camera, here must be a religion of universal sufferance and tolerance. Outside, the street litter bins were shaped as penguins.

Moving on, a hotel at Hoi An, a small historic town on the banks of the Thu Bon River and near the sea, had been the U.S. army officers' club and reminded me of the officers' mess at Ipoh – large, spacious and cool with lazy fans, dusty potted plants and elaborate but unattractive wooden decorations. My bedroom was huge – enough for one army officer, two tourists or three Vietnamese fam-

Ho-Chi-Minh tomb. Hanoi

ilies. There was a fridge well stocked with 7 UP and an inventory of the room's contents read: '*1 Chinese glass, 2 plastic slippers, 2 spoons, 1 tea set ....*'. This is followed by the instruction that '*all the equipment listed above must be kept in constant use*'. The laundry list included shoes, hats and ties with separate columns to indicate if you want them washed, ironed or both. In the morning I ordered four silk shirts – I cannot think why, as I have more shirts than I can wear, but at £7.50 each made to measure in 24 hours, I was seduced. I also made an appointment with Dr. Phuc (I just called him 'doctor') as I was so bored of my cold with its aches and pains; however, when my eleven o'clock appointment came and I was having a baguette and coffee overlooking the jetty where the fishermen came in with mud crabs and wicker baskets of shrimp, my cold suddenly felt better. Tonight I may regret the missed diagnosis.

One of the wonders of this country is the complete lack of pretension and the attractive openness of its people. The war ended 20 years ago and there is a new generation but even the over-40s are charming, friendly and without bitterness. Some world weary cynics might call it naïve but it is so universal and so clearly well meant that it must be firmly rooted in the culture. Children abound, as inquisitive and talkative as any worldwide but not once has a hand been held out and my pound and a half of Woolworth's mixed humbugs has been untouched.

At 6ft 2in (1.9m) a broad-in-the-beam Englishman does not fit easily in to the Lilliputian scale here. Doors are 5ft 10in high, beds are as short, it is impossible to get my knees under any table and the plastic stools arranged around a restaurant table seem to come from a playgroup. The stature of the Vietnamese belies their strength and they seem made mostly of tensioned rubber and reinforced steel. Huge bundles of sugarcane, great sacks of firewood, baskets of cauliflowers and barrels of water are handled like candyfloss. The market traders, boatmen, farmers and street vendors all wear the winkle-shaped straw hat that is fastened under the chin with a broad ribbon but the schoolgirls and all other women wear wonderful hats. From four years old upwards, black, straight, shiny hair is topped by every variety of hat that aims to please. Broad brimmed, cloche, peaked, flat, beret, flopping, stiff, straw, wool, denim, lace, velvet and raffia; always set off with a band, bandanna, flower or bow. They are jocular, frivolous, pert, provocative, smart and sassy and the prettiest hats I have ever seen.

Wishing for a boat trip to the mouth of the river, I made arrangements with a swarthy, cheeky fellow in baggy pants and with a couple of gold teeth. We went through the routine six times: four o'clock, down river, big boat, big motor, $2 and we shook hands. It was rehearsed this often on the presumption that my own disbelief at the modest price equalled the reassurance Two Teeth required as to his luck in earning $2. At four o'clock there was Two Teeth but not the 50 foot (15m) sea going launch I had sat on to make the bargain. With uncharacteristic brazenness he pointed to a rowing boat but my angry shout of, "Big boat and motor," deterred him further. He beckoned me to follow him to the far side of the fish market where, still muttering, "Big boat, big motor," I was rowed to a larger boat manned (sic) by a pretty helmswoman wearing spotted trousers and a winning smile; another rowboat picked up my guide whose only English words were *"good"* and *"OK"*. At the mouth of the river great nets, each the size of a tennis court, were suspended by bamboo poles the thickness of my leg. The net was let into the water and later winched up from a rickety platform. I never saw this happen (they fish at night) but it looked as though the weight of more than a dozen fish would have brought the whole contraption tumbling down.

Hiring a bicycle with the misplaced ambition of 'Mercedes' written on its crossbar, I pedalled to the beach which was backed by casuarina pines and coconut palms and edged by the froth of a mild surf. Palm thatched shelters were arranged in two long lines and as an early comer at 9.30 am, I secured a semi-detached model at the end of the front row. A few coins bought two deck chairs, a table, shelter from the sun, peace of mind and thoughts of home for the whole day. Small boys offered pineapples, hard boiled eggs, peanuts and shell necklaces and when I trotted out the well-worn, "Maybe later," they implored me to remember their name in case I changed my mind. By the time I reached my chair, Fang, Fung, Phoo and Sing, Sang and Song had all merged in my mind like a twanging tune from a broken banjo. Later Fang – or was it Fung? – peeled a pineapple into a spiral and I ate it like a lollipop, juice colouring the sand at my feet. Sing – or was it Sang? – miffed that I had promised to buy from him was placated by the sale of a baguette stuffed with Laughing Cow Cheese Spread, onion, cucumber and fresh mint and I winnowed a bag of peanuts in the off shore breeze.

A fishing fleet was beyond the surf. Long sleek boats with long curved bowsprits that arched up into the gentian sky, each with two men in coolie hats crouched in the stern. With an eye painted on either side of the bow, the boats looked rather menacing, like a swordfish on the prowl. On the sandy side of the surf, bicycles drew temporary lines. Had General Westmoreland seen the determination of a Vietnamese riding through sand, he would have kept his marines at home. In the afternoon, I bicycled into the countryside for photographs of laughing boys riding lumbering buffalo and later attended a Vietnamese cooking lesson. Based on noodle soup as a starter, stir fried fish or meat with vegetables followed. Intense competition in the markets produced the peak of freshness and the highest quality. Menus were long but all were variations on a theme that used peanut oil, garlic and shallots and all or some of mint, basil, parsley, coriander and plenty of lemon grass. The oddity of the language showed up in the menu. I did not find a word that was more than four letters long but there were seven accents that acrobatically sat over and under letters, sometimes three high. There seemed to be no logic so: *Canh thit cât heo nâo cai* was Pork Soup but *Gà sa ót* was Fried Chicken with Lemon Grass, Chilli & Vegetables. My favourite was fried eggs: *Gà ôpla.*

The old part of Hoi An had a distinctive Chinese flavour, although from time to time it had been garrisoned by Portuguese, Dutch, French and English. Only three colours were used to daub the stucco façades: yellow ochre, prussian blue, and turquoise applied in soft Provençal dilution. The old imperial capital carried its heritage well with wide streets lined with tamarind and mulberry and solid prosperous villas, with double mansard roofs, green shutters and a short curved driveway off the street, as though the original owners were simply replacing what they had left behind in the *banlieu* of Marseilles. The serenity of these streets was disturbed by music that blared out from cafés all day long. Morning coffee was drunk to a Nashville 'I've Got a Black Magic Woman' and 'Mary's Boy Child Jesus Christ' in Vietnamese.

The railway station at Hue mixed coloured twinkling lights around the bar and a three tiered crystal chandelier with the same lack of inhibition and taste that was so apparent elsewhere in the country. A notice in the waiting room read *'No spitting or explosives. If you break anything you will pay for it. All these regulations must be carried out seriously, sufficiently'*. Graham Greene knew about tropical rain when he wrote that 'it descends like a burden' and here it hunched the passengers as they waited with their heads cast down under a heavyweight onslaught. The dreary sky spat in anger, smearing whatever it hit and fouling the oily track. The Reunification

Coracle ferries at Nha Trang

Express arrived at nine o'clock and I scrambled aboard to find the 'Soft Sleeping Carriage'. 'Soft' was one layer of plywood on each of four berths while 'Hard Seating' was a two layers of plywood and a slatted back. It was hot and steamy, far from clean and the loo, a hole in the floor through to the tracks, buzzed with mosquitoes. I drank most of the half bottle of whisky I had bought at the station for £1.50 – Royal Whisky, 'A blend of Scottish malts'. This ensured a reasonable night's sleep in spite of station announcements piped through at high volume and great frequency. Rust stained and sticky with grease this monster shook from its clanking pistons and vibrated from rattling over 1,000 bridges. Adjacent to my carriage was the engine; opening the end door one could step straight on to the footplate. To the rear stretched 11 coaches of progressively deteriorating condition and reducing fares but conversely, progressively full of life and interest. It was as though the street had taken to wheels. Chattering families huddled together, chopsticks snapped and clicked, cards were shuffled and piglets squealed. Packages, sacks, parcels and wicker baskets were piled in abandon. Hammocks were slung between seat backs, smoke from coarse cigarettes hung like acrid smog at luggage rack level and tea and noodles were awash on the floor. An unavoidable factor of rail travel is the proximity of strangers, their stinks and unfamiliar smells, eating their food and enduring their habits but here, in the luckless end of the train, the appearance of a foreigner was ignored in the serious business of surviving. Here there was anonymity as too many were gathered to enable any interest in an individual. Even a large westerner wandering through this crush of busy humanity did not engender a glance and no one moved to ease my route. All tickets included breakfast and this was served by a troupe of laughing girls in grey dresses with white pinnies. Red and blue plastic containers of noodles, beans and pork were served up with a ladle from an insulated bucket; it was delicious.

Hanoi was reached at noon. The rain had stopped but it was chilly and the people were in several sweaters and fur hats. Things seemed more disciplined and orderly than in the south, although the electric and telephone wires were still strung in wild abandon and the pavements were as cracked. There seemed a rather serious, studied approach to living and a drabness of dress but there were flowers at every street corner and gladioli and chrysanthemums were sold from rusty cans whose water was replenished from underground cisterns beneath the pavement. Conical hats had given way to olive toupees (I had thought they were only for the tourists).

A sleek, slim, soft-life liner was tied up in the port of Haiphong discharging bewildered tourists. The ship stood out like Linda Evangelista in a back alley, as she shared a quay side berth with coal barges and the rusting tramps that hustled their way around the South China Sea. From an adjacent quay, I embarked for Cat Ba Island on the local ferry – as crippled and decrepit a tub as you would never wish to travel on. It was 'Hard Seating' over again but with added chickens, groaning, creaking machinery and black diesel smoke. It was also extremely cold. I was unprepared for this and had to unpack on deck for a T-shirt, two further shirts and a sweater but I still shivered during the three hour crossing. At my single storey hotel I had three beds in my room – each with a little pink satin pillow decorated with lace hearts. I went to bed in my four shirts and under the blankets of all the beds with the alcoholic salvation of a bottle of Apricot Liquor, being the only name I recognised in the neon lit bar.

In the morning, a dozen motor cyclists had assembled with their Russian bikes, all offering a trip to the forest. After much negotiation, I found myself hugging a youth with one earring, a few gold teeth and a leering smile as I perched precariously behind him on a terrifying ride through the steep and jagged hills, each bend pot-holed and sprinkled with loose gravel. We climbed through thick bamboo forest and spectacular scenery, he laughing and myself silent with fear. As I gripped him with my thighs at each bend and hugged him as protection from the cold, he interpreted these involuntary gropings as signs of enthusiasm and urged his machine to greater speed.

The phantasmagorical limestone outcrops that form the 3,000 islands of inspiring beauty of Halong Bay would have been stunning had it not been for the persistent cold that kept me huddled in the lee of the wheelhouse of the pseudo junk as it made its daily cruise round the most popular of these. I returned to seek warmth under my blankets and the comfort of the remaining half of the bottle of Apricot Liquor. They were using dynamite to blast rock for a new road nearby and huge explosions shook my glass. These competed in decibels with the karaoke bar next door. 'I've Got a Black Magic Woman' had turned up again as the current favourite.

The town serving the festival of Quang Am at Chua Huong Tich, the Perfumed Pagoda, attracted traders from every back lane. For two months it had milked visitors from all over Vietnam but it was on the river, the only route to the pagodas and the central shrine, that the cream was skimmed. Many hundreds of small boats, rowed almost universally by women, sought passengers for the hour long trip. Larger boats took several families at a time – children, grannies, forgotten cousins, firm friends and all the paraphernalia of a day's outing. On these, there was a rower at each end standing on the boat's edge and leaning their bantam weight against long slim oars, with a coolie hat fastened by a bright cloth strap that added to the gaiety. Flags fluttered and umbrellas were raised against the sun as this flotilla glided over limpid water towards dramatic little steep hills that receded to a horizon of darkening shades of grey; it was as though those islands from Halong Bay had been dumped inland. The passengers were tipped out into a mini town of bamboo snack bars, souvenir stalls and hustlers, each one awash with red banners and glitter. The stone path that led up to the cave had been oiled with the mud spread by 10,000 feet and children did brisk business selling three foot long bamboo canes for the precarious climb. Being cut for the Vietnamese, mine was a foot too short, so I hobbled along like a 90 year old with a broken back. The jungle steamed as the sun melted the mist but no one had warned me of the length of the climb. For two hours I sweated, hung about with the discarded sweater and two shirts that I had put on in chilly Hanoi. But there was jollity and expectation amongst the crowd and as we climbed further the price of water, fresh pressed sugarcane juice and walking sticks got steeper too. I had no real idea of what lay at the end of this trail and considered giving up on a couple of occasions, so arduous was the route.

Round a bend masked by giant bamboo, the path suddenly dipped to reveal the mouth of a gigantic cavern, its roof dripping with huge stalactites and its floor covered in a multitudinous sea of pilgrims. The view was obscured by the smoke of a thousand cooking braziers and a hundred thousand joss sticks. It was acrid, pungent and exotic. Huge paper lanterns, once white, hung from the roof like discarded cocoons. Blackened by decades of incense smoke, their red calligraphy had bled into the tattered paper: words turned to wounds. Hundreds of trays were held head-high piled with offerings of fruit, rice, chickens and brightly wrapped parcels as worshippers jostled their way to the inner sanctuary in the depth of the cave and the glittering statue of a female Buddha. For many, this had been the destination of many days' travel and for some the culmination of a lifetime's ambition. As on the river, there was a palette of bright colour in costume and flags. Some of the banners at the entrance of the cave were of huge proportions and were highlighted by the sharply defined rays of sunlight that sparkled on gold decorations and polished brass. The coolness of the cavern contrasted with the heat, the tropical vegetation, the religious passion and the holiday cheerfulness. Worship here was mixed with a good slug of festive spirit and refreshing drafts of jollity.

The two mile (three km) journey back down the hill was treacherous with 100,000 pilgrims packed ten abreast, half struggling up and half slithering down. As I was rowed back, the soft light of the setting sun slipped behind the serene grey hills and more boats, brimming with jolly and expectant worshippers, were being paddled towards the final destination of that magical cave.

Postcard Home

The Quiet American has long left Saigon
But still there lingers on the silhouette of Phong.
Within this city of the South, now Ho Chi Minh,
Five million mopeds move with discipline.
The girls who ride, straight backed with model figures,
Belie their years of hardships and life's rigours.
I've been by plane, boat, rickshaw, horse, cart, train,
And junk in drizzle, humid heat and rain,
On mountain, sea and river — so now to Laos
To rest, recuperate, to dream and drowse.

Peru

July 1996

'I have just been round the world and have formed a very poor opinion of it'
– Sir Thomas Beecham

I wrote this by the flame of a candle around which, and tragically occasionally through which, there darted and fluttered many moths and other winged insects that live beside a river flowing fast and noisily over great boulders, deep in the cloud forest and high on the eastern side of the Peruvian Andes. With me were 19 travellers, two naturalist guides, a Peruvian driver, a general factotum and his cook wife. Eight of the party were German for whom solid seemed to be an appropriate description whether applied to girth, conversation or mutual togetherness. They balanced on benches whose native manufacturer did not expect to have to accommodate bottoms so broad, and the legs of the benches were set too far towards the centre so that the bum at the end relied on several others further up to maintain its place at the table. The single narrow plank was bending to a degree that caused them alarm and myself eager anticipation. The others in the party, at 11 numerically greater but in aggregate lighter, were an English engineer, his wife and three female Danes in their 20s who were writing theses for a botanical masters degree in the genus *passiflora*. They were under the tutelage of an elderly man who seemed to be a sort of professorial chaperone. There were also an Austrian, a Swiss and two Americans hung around with techno devices of many kinds.

My journey had been long and tiring and with an interim disaster at Lima. Like anybody who has ever watched those bags ponderously make their way around the conveyor belt of airport luggage anxious for the first sight of one's own bag, that anxiety for the first time became dreadful reality with the absence of my luggage.

PERU

COLOMBIA

ECUADOR

River Amazon

Iquitos

BRAZIL

PACIFIC

OCEAN

LIMA

Cordillera Occidental

Cordillera Oriental

6426

Parque National Manu

Machu Pichu

Cusco

6344

6423

Lake Titicaca

Arequipa

BOLIVIA

CHILE

Reserva de la Biosfera del Manu

River Manu

Manu Camp

Puerto Maldonado

River Madre de Dios

River Marcapata

Machu Pichu

Cuzco

River Urubamba

Manu Tours rode to the rescue as best they could. One of the guides, John Arvin – tall, craggy, grey-bearded and with a silver earring – came to the hotel to size me up and generously lent me a thick shirt and two sweaters. A couple of hours around town secured a pair of bikini pants, socks, toothpaste and a razor and after much searching, a pair of trousers. Peruvians average 5' 4" (1.6m) and are giants at 5' 9" (1.75m) and I was squeezed into some black jeans that made my voice suitable for a descant and which ended well above my ankles. My new wardrobe was packed into a bag of striped *campesino* cotton (I paid over the odds for one I was assured was antique) and I was already beginning to think that I needed nothing else. Unusually, the altitude made me thick-headed and dizzy and I wandered around town under clear skies and in crisp air seeking salvation for my predicament. For a short time it was found in a charming small church where evening mass was accompanied by two wizened violinists, a pianist and a tenor, strongly singing Gounod's Ave Maria. I was moved to tears but this moment of emotional succour was stopped short by violent explosions in the small, flower-filled square outside. None of the devout blinked but I ran to the door, alarmed with thoughts of Sendero Luminoso and then, seeing the small boys who had let off fireworks, had to return sheepishly and caught the eye of the pianist who smiled kindly.

In the gloaming of 4 am, just bright enough to reflect off the damp cobbled street, I joined my fellow travellers and slumped into the one remaining seat. As dawn broke we were lurching down through the grasslands of the eastern side of the Andes on a rough track that eventually made its way through dense vegetation and forest. Breakfast was coffee and buns beside a pre-Inca burial ground (somehow it seemed appropriate as I still nursed a sick head and worse, a queasy stomach) and dawn revealed my companions. I was not too dismayed as they looked as dishevelled as I – but their trousers were longer. The Germans were already active, advancing like a Panzer brigade on an unfortunate mountain finch. Gradually the forest thickened around us but not before a pit stop at 13,000 ft (3,960m) in thick cloud, where I temporarily lost my bearings and might still be herding alpaca if the bus had not hooted long and loud. I was feeling better and my Austrian neighbour turned out to be companionable and intelligent.

The road to this first camp was full of wonder. Imagine a track as narrow and deep as a Devon lane, snaking along the contours of a near vertical hillside; smother it, stack it high, spread it thick with lavish abundance and lushness so dense you could swear you saw it grow and breathe, meld in the delicacy of ferns and bamboo with the loutish bully boys of *gunnera*, *ficus* and *philodendron*; splash colour, not too liberally but occasionally upset the paint pot on an 80 ft (24m) scarlet flowering *anthryna* and then continue this lane bouldered, pot holed, rough and makeshift for 200 miles (320kms), dropping from a freezing 11,000 ft (3,350m) to the humidity of 300 ft (90m), wriggling through trees so encrusted with lichen that the trunks seem constructed of sponge and past leaves the size of cartwheels. Torrents of water fall into and across the lane sometimes sweeping it away. Regulate the traffic to two trucks a day, scatter birds in all directions (but curiously almost no bugs or butterflies) and then, give or take a forest giant or a honking toucan, you have the main highway from Cusco in the Andes to Maldonado in Amazonia.

The staccato of rain on the roof of a raised platform where the tents are nailed into the plank floor woke me at 5.30 am and dawn came quickly after. The night had been cold and I had twice searched my secondhand duffle-bag for a hat – a large woolly affair more suitable for the Alps than for the forest and which I had scoffed at when first offered. Delicious large, airy pancakes, miraculously inflated and tossed over a kerosene flame, made a wonderful breakfast. Liberally garnished with juice from a lemon, with an insulated skin so thick you needed a bayonet to open it up, and dribbled with wild honey, it seemed a kind of jungle nectar. Eliana, our Peruvian guide, appeared with a fluffy scarlet-chested chick sitting contentedly on her palm looking around as though it too was expecting breakfast. It had fallen out of a tree and seemed quite unaffected by its sudden change of habitat.

After bumping further down the overgrown track the crowded forest gave way to a different vegetation, higher temperature and brighter skies. A settlement or two was passed and a small village, started by the road builders in the 1930s/40s. There were typical shacks, with roofs of woven palm or rusting corrugated iron, dirty, ragged, waving, cheerful children, a pig or two and a clutch of chickens pecking for grubs in the dust. Then lunch by a broad river with bright water cleansed by the grit of the bed and a shoreline bordered with boulders, a further drive to a riverside settlement, a long boat – leaking a little (it turned out they all do), a short walk, a longer ride in a Landrover so battered it would have been long abandoned by even the most pecuniary Scottish hill farmer, and then Amazonia Lodge appeared like a sanctuary. It was surprisingly solid with cut lawns, a flowering shrub or two and noisy, yellow tailed dusky green oropendulas constantly building their weaver nests in the palm trees, chattering like wives on a Grimsby dockside. The birds had a delightful call, like water plopping into a bowl followed by a little giggle. The male builds the nest while the female looks on and if she is not satisfied with its design or construction she scolds her mate and tears the nest apart. I shared a shower with a very large spider that looked angrily at me from a corner as I listened to the cicadas starting their evening trilling. The walls are constructed of planks with wide gaps between them, so as you sit on the pan (a proper flusher but no seat) you look onto the green, wet, tangled world and hope that not too many pairs of eyes are looking in – so undignified sitting on a loo with no seat.

A thunderstorm during the night left the ground sodden and myself tired; the gutter outside my window discharged onto an empty oil drum and for four hours this Maxim gun fired into my left ear, but the forest at dawn (we left at 5 am) was wonderfully fresh. The croaking, the calling, the cackling and the chaos of waking seems especially exuberant after rain. We bundled ourselves in the mechanical mongrel of the Landrover to drive to the river bank where it takes an hour to evenly distribute loads between three long boats. The river is very low and every extra inch of clearance is important. There is a great pile of stores – 50 gallon (190 ltr) drums of kerosene, groceries, chickens in woven baskets and trays of eggs. It would be a long day, 12 hours at least on the river. Each boat had a bowman with a long pole to probe the depth and to signal dangerous tree trunks or large stones unseen by the propeller man 30 ft (19m) aft. Often we grounded over the bouldered bottom and sometimes shot rapids. The Altro Madre de Dios is not a wide river, being about 500 ft (152m) between its pebbled banks, but later it broadens considerably as it joins the Manu River, which in turn runs into the Madre de Dios – one of 15,000 tributaries that serve the Amazon, that liquid master of South America. Herons skimmed across the water and kingfishers sat poised for breakfast. A family of peccaries watched our progress from the bank and a capybara, apparently rare around here, seemed rather amiable as it turned from the river and waddled back into the forest.

At 5.30 am in the Manu Camp, I was angry at the giant percolator, bubbling, hissing, steaming and roaring outside my window – a family of howler monkeys that lived behind the kitchen block had just woken up. Later, as the sun rose, we went out on a lake as smooth as glycerine. The mist lifted off the surface, lingered in the trees, rose like a veil of billowing organza and vanished by 8 am. Spider monkeys, hanging by a long leg or longer arm and tail, draped themselves over the branches of a huge cieba tree. The fluffy seeds were each the size of a football and hung from the leafless branches like Christmas decorations. These footballs are kapok and were once used to make lifebelts. Back at the lodge, I sat by the bank of the lake and tried to photograph Clotilde – an 18 ft (5.5m) black caiman that lived on the edge waiting for scraps. Turtles, the size of soup tureens, hauled themselves up on a log to enjoy the sun. Ponderously and very slowly they came out of the water in a line and shuffled along the length of the log. If the leader is bolshie they cannot move along and stick their heads out of their shells just above the water, wagging them to and fro like irritated shoppers delayed in a checkout queue. In the afternoon the techno anorak, the German lady and I went off to the 'canopy climb'. I had assumed that this was genuinely a climb but we were to be hauled to the top on a rope. This was an optional extra and the 'extra' was to pay all the men at the lodge to haul on the rope: one at the top and five at the bottom. I elected to go first, thinking they would need all their strength for me (though the *hausfrau* ran me a close second in the weight stakes). They heaved to a chant and strapped into mountaineering harness with many clips and buckles, I gradually ascended in a series of rather alarming jerks to a rickety platform 100 ft (30m) up. Above the canopy the view was astonishing but few birds came by. The platform was about ten feet square secured into the tree with rusty nails and quite unprotected by rails; I sat in the middle keeping an eye on a colony of ants – each was an inch (3 cms) long. We watched a glowing sun disappear into the forest over the leafy horizon and then I trusted my life to a wizened Peruvian who shouted to his invisible mates at ground level that El Grande was coming and I zoomed down, hoping I would not run into the monster ants on their way up.

The plan was to leave early to get to a lake two hours away by 7 am where a colony of giant otters was fishing for their breakfast. They are known locally as Lobos del Rio – Wolves of the River. Like so many things here, plans go astray a little and any departure time was certainly suspect. I listened to the bullfrogs by the side of the lake until the light was sufficiently bright to send them snuggling into the mud for the day and watched the dragonflies dry out the dew of the night. An hour and a half late we were off, led by the delightful Eliana, our hard working guide who organises everything, reminds us of all the things we have forgotten and has eyes sharp enough to spot a parakeet in a palm tree at 50 paces in poor light.

We set off across the lake on a raft so flimsy that Huckleberry F would have discarded it but with a paddler on opposite corners we made our way well enough, squatting around the edge with the baskets of our packed lunch stacked in the middle. The inhabitants of the lake, a family of eight giant otters, were sunning themselves on fallen trees. They are about five feet (1.5m) long, weigh in at about seven stone (44kgs), have twelve inch (30cm) whiskers and I fell in love with each one of them. In the blistering sun, floating on a lake surface unruffled by a breath of wind, we watched these wonderful creatures swim, porpoise and eat fish. They hold a fish vertically in their webbed paws and crunch down, starting with the head. There are only 50 recorded in the million acres of the Manu, so seeing almost 20 percent in one day was something of a coup. Back at the lodge, there was my bag. I did not know whether to welcome it as a prodigal or scold it as a deserter but I had no need to unpack except to find my Mefloquine pills – now five days overdue. In spite of a liberal dosing with Deet, my arms and ankles were covered in a pointillism tattoo of bites.

The Swiss, two Austrians, two Americans and myself were off on a separate trip to the Macaw Lick which is six hours up river. We slalomed through the fallen trees on a great, grey, greasy surface with the banks hung about with fever trees and much else. The volume of the water of the rainy season carves off 60 ft (18m) from the outer edge of each bend every year – hence the trees that are brought down;

but this is compensated by the inner edge expanding 60 ft (18m), first by a sand bar and gradually, over 20 years, back to jungle. Suddenly the bowman spotted a large animal on a wide pebbled shore and we all leapt out to give chase. It turned out to be a giant anteater, one of nature's most bizarre creatures with its two feet (60cm) long nose and six feet (1.8m) bushy tail. Just as we caught it up, it plunged into the river, clung to a passing log and floated with the flow to the far bank, clambered up and disappeared into the forest. It is something of a triumph as one had not been seen there for five years. An hour

Woman in Colcha Valley

or two further on, we made landfall at a small camp that serves the clay lick. Our destination had been billed as a ranch and I had in mind a solid, whitewashed building; a courtyard with a great tree casting its shadow, substantial timber entrance gates, a shady interior with a lamp burning before a baroque Madonna and lovely girls in boots strumming guitars. The cluster of huts under a palm roof with planked floors raised as protection from termites did not fill this cinematic ideal. One hut contained a dining area with a crude bar at one end serving local rum and beer and a crackling radio link to other scattered camps. There was a local Indian family who cooked, a couple of mestizo and a tame young spider monkey who was the constant friend and companion of the cook's little daughter. When we arrived, we saw the monkey creep up behind his human friend and whip down her trousers. We laughed until we ached. There was a large roofed platform with about 20 beds arranged open plan like a dormitory and all this gave a pioneering feel to the place. Colonel Fawcett, dripping with sweat, plastered with mud, clothes ripped and pierced with arrows might have burst in any time. As I dropped off to sleep, a potoo called from across the river – a low wheezing like a whoopee cushion with a puncture; Guido the Swiss answered with the snore of a man tired and contented.

The clay lick was a mile down river and a large palm thatched hide was moored to a log mid-stream. Ingeniously, the anchor rope was wound around a capstan and this allowed the 'boat' to drift down with the current or be wound back depending where the best action was. The birds only eat the clay from a narrow strip about 50 ft (15m) long and although the reasons for this strange diet are not yet proven, it is thought that they not only benefit from the minerals but also the alkalinity that counteracts toxins and acid from the fruit they eat.

The first shaft of sunlight, filtered by the forest canopy, ricocheted off 100 leaves lustrous with overnight dew and hit the bank of the River Madre de Dios at 6.05 am. Then, out of the sun and into its light, cackling like glass through a coffee grinder, glowing like a thunderbolt forged in the furnace of a tropical Vulcan, there glided in on wings three feet (1m) wide the Peruvian rainforest's most exuberant inhabitant. Gorgeously apparelled in colours that would make Joseph sulk, a rainbow macaw had arrived. After this advance guard, flocks of blue headed parrots two or three hundred strong swung and turned, squeaking and screeching. With lime green bodies and cobalt heads they covered the bank as they pecked the clay. They were joined by green headed parrots, yellow crowned parrots, dusky headed parakeets, iron cheeked parrots and mealy parrots, the latter looking as though they had fallen into a bag of flour. After the brave foray of the single rainbow macaw, others gathered in the trees; scarlet macaws, blue and gold macaws with huge beaks and dozens more red and green macaws. Gradually the junior parrots disbursed and their larger but more cautious macaw cousins took their turn. Occasionally something stirred to frighten them – a camera flash from the hide or a caracara landing in a nearby tree and then, in a dazzling kaleidoscope with much noise of rasps and cackles, the whole chorus line took off. The scarlet and the blue and gold macaws left the bank first after about two hours and then, in a finale of precision flying, 70 or so red and green macaws flew along the bank wing-tip to wing-tip, wheeled into the sun, turned and in a glorious final fly-past showing their scarlet undersides, they zoomed downriver and were gone. This is one of the world's great avian spectacles and I had had a front row seat.

Six huts make up the only street in Boca Manu together with a few grubby children, a couple of dogs and a bar; such is the main town for 50 miles (80kms) in any direction. We picnicked in the bar, fed one of the dogs and watched the vivid green amazoniensis moths that come for the minerals leached from the ground. At the airstrip, the two-engined Beechcraft looked in reassuringly good condition and a brass plate on the bulkhead showed that it was licensed for eight passengers. Eleven of us crowded in and when the seats and the aisle were full, then came the cargo. Baskets, boxes, small machine parts and piles of pamphlets tied up with raffia all sat on our laps. Unusually, the seats faced each other like benches. The co-pilot, was in charge of the loading – rather like one of those white-gloved pushers on the Tokyo underground. He scrambled over all the paraphernalia of the assorted cargo sweating and smiling, whether in fear or in welcome I could not tell. Since I had no safety belt – there were not enough to go round – I was sweating too but I was not smiling. Finally, two huge valves from an oil drilling operation were heaved aboard. The aisle was so crowded that some passengers had to sit with their legs stretched out resting on packages or propped against steel wheels. Had the end of the runway not been the open space of the river rather than the wall of the forest we would never had made it. As we skimmed the river and grazed the trees I made a note to thank the Beechcraft Corporation of Kansas for my life.

Arequipa, at 7,500 ft (2,280m), has 300 days of sunshine and a temperature that is never more than 75°F (24C) nor less than 50°F (10C). The lack of rain has scorched the earth as far as the three snow-capped volcanoes that provide an alpine backdrop to the town. The highest is Mount Misti and another, Chachani, erupted in 1970 flattening part of the town. My small hotel was a curious, long, single storied affair and built into the bank of a fast flowing river. It is not called Posada del Puente for nothing. The bridge is the main entry to the town and my room was practically under the first arch. The noise of the river competed with the traffic and worse, a wedding party had danced till dawn. Sleep deprived and altitude-dulled, I opened my garden door to find an alpaca – it looked even more surprised than I. It was the resident mowing machine and fortunately disliked roses, nasturtiums and chrysanthemums.

In bright afternoon sunshine the older buildings of the town dazzled my tired eyes with their brilliant white stone. A scattering of important colonial 17th Century churches were extravagantly adorned with altars of beaten silver and arrayed with plastic flowers. In the dim light, suppliant locals were lighting candles. In one church, a confessionary box had a plate saying Padre Fred; it gave a friendly touch to the otherwise churrigueresque decor. The cathedral has the largest organ in South America – it was built in Belgium and the pulpit was carved in Lille. Strangely there are Moorish touches everywhere and another bridge into town (the world's longest in 1882), was designed by Eiffel. This is the centre of the alpaca wool trade (started by British merchants) but I resisted buying a sweater even though I had been warned that it would be cold in the Colcha Valley.

My guides to the valley came at 8 am. There was Patricia ("call me Pat"), short and dumpy, and the driver Mestor, huge for a Peruvian and with two front teeth missing. He spoke no English but smiled a lot and drove the little Toyota minibus

ploughing & sowing maize

like a demon. We climbed for five hours through dry and arid country on dusty roads that were frequently churned up by great Volvo lorries carrying cement from a huge plant that belched smoke like another volcano about to burst. When they passed, the air was as impenetrable as a Saharan sandstorm and a fine grey dust entered every crack and crevice; the road was invisible but unfortunately nothing deterred Mestor. Having climbed the long steep slope of the Chachani volcano, the road flattened across the Aguada Blanca National Reserve. It was desolate but scattered tufts of ichu – a spiky grass that grows on the puna – and low growing cactus support small herds of vicunas. Every now and again a lonely and isolated dwelling served beer, Inca Kola (an unattractive greeny yellow concoction that smells of aniseed and tastes of oil) and Maté de Coca, a tea made from the leaves of the coca plant which elsewhere, in hidden jungle retreats, would be distilled and chemically refined to produce cocaine. Although I chewed vigorously on the unpalatable leaves, no buzz came my way. A little further on, a rock cliff had been sinuously shaped by the erosion of the wind and beyond, crossing the pass at 17,000 ft (5,200m), small cairns of piled stones witness the passing of travellers who, thankful that they had come this far without mishap or a radiator bursting, gave thanks for their salvation. There was snow beside the road and curiously, a bog inhabited by Andean geese and puna ibis. At this altitude even the spiky grass had given up but great mounds of a curious lichen called azorella moulded itself over the scattered boulders. It is bright green but as hard to the touch as the boulder itself and is chiselled off and burnt as fuel by anybody unfortunate enough to be stranded there. Descending the other side, there were large herds of alpaca bred on isolated and primitive farms. The wool can only be shorn every three years, so in a herd some are shaggy and others smooth as they shear only a few at a time. The wool is taken to Cusco every month or so to trade for vegetables and although Arequipa is much nearer, the market there perversely does not cater for the food these Indians like.

Although twice as deep as the Grand Canyon, the Colcha Canyon does not have its sheer sides but is the longest, widest, deepest valley on the South American continent. Its slopes are terraced with thousands of tiny plots of land created by pre-Inca people and on which peasant farmers now grow maize, wheat and alfalfa and graze goats, sheep and cows. Women in their bright multi-petticoated skirts waddled around like flowery pyramids and all had plaited hair and attractive embroidered hats – a different hat for each of the 14 villages. The houses are built of mud bricks with roofs of grass thatch and each village has a squat white painted church dating from the Spanish colonisation. It is a volcanic region and although the mud houses are strong and flexible, the churches are continually cracking and most have been patched and mended to such an extent that there is hardly a straight line of masonry left. At this high altitude growth is slow but the terraces are feathered with young grass and a froth of emerald corn is emerging from the stoney, russet earth. There were glimpses of villages isolated and looking forlorn with only a rock path for access. This far side of the valley is a little warmer and avocados and apricots grow there. Scattered chimneys had balanced above them veils as thin and blue as uninhaled tobacco smoke and slow threads from distant bonfires rose swaying, expanding and then vanishing as though Mohicans were signalling. Alpacas, each with coloured, identifying ribbons in their ears sauntered arrogantly past and the sonorous sound of a single bell mournfully summoned the noon mass. At night it was several degrees below freezing and under six alpaca blankets I listened to the silence of this ancient valley; it was heavy, restful and completely absorbing.

By the light of a candle, I was reading Dervla Murphy's book Eight Feet Through the Andes. She writes: 'There are times when we need to be close to, and sometimes subservient to, but always respectful of the physical realities of the planet we live on. We need to receive its pure silences and attend to its winds, to wade through its rivers, sweat under its sun, plough through its sands and sleep on its bumps. Sitting in the moonlight it frightened me to think of the millions who have become so estranged of our origins that many of their children believe architects make mountains and scientists make milk.'

It was only 20 years ago that a road was made into the valley; before that access was by mule or by foot. Few tourists make this long detour but this is another of those rare places destined for change in the name of progress. Isolated from the world, the land has been worked in the same way using the same tools for hundreds of years. In places the terracing was the steepest I had ever seen and at some points it was as though by a miraculous geological quirk, a whole mountainside had been hewn into a giant staircase. Partridges, doves and occasional deer crossed the pathways between the villages and groups of parakeets chattered in the eucalyptus trees. The villages have euphonic names like Cabanaconde, Pinchollo, Chivay, Yanque, Tuti and Mata. The churches were all locked which was disappointing as I was told that they are the least plundered in Peru; the sacristans who hold the keys are elected to hold this heritage secure. We drove to Cruz del Condor, a lookout point where the valley dramatically narrows into a defile. The

River Colcha snakes 1,000 ft (300m) below glittering in the sun and 10,000 ft (3,000m) above are the snow-capped peaks of the Cordillera de Blanca. A few sightseers were gathered and four peasant women in elaborately embroidered costumes sold fruit and prickly pears. They were from the southern part of the valley and wore a white pork pie hat with a band of coloured lace and rosettes on the side as though they had won a prize at a pony club gymkhana; one rosette for those still single and two for those married. An older woman wore black rosettes: she was in mourning, although the flowers on her skirts and the closely worked thread of her waistcoat seem appropriate for a fiesta. The condors rose on warming thermals, circling upwards in slow loops with never a beat of a wing, although their flight feathers constantly twitched and adjusted.

We looked in on a couple of villages and at one, Maca, a small earthquake a year before toppled the church tower. This had the principle church of the valley and behind it was a convent run by two truly remarkable women – Mother Antonia and Mother Sarah. I had asked to call on them having heard of their good work and caught them at lunch, weak soup and biscuits, but they were instantly welcoming. Madre Antonia was in her eighties, a New Yorker who spent several years in the Bronx, then in the slums of Lima and for the last thirty years in the Colcha having learnt quecha. She was doctor, friend, counsellor and universal aunt to the whole valley. Disarmingly dressed in an outsized sweater, baggy trousers and local sandals that show her cracked feet, she exuded warmth and goodness. Madre Sarah was Indian, a little younger and wears jeans, an anorak that said Bronco Braves on the back and a fluffy sweater. They organised a communal lunch each day for 1,000 – yes, 1,000 – cooked within the convent. I saw the huge pans. So many men had left the valley for the towns that there were many poor and old women who struggled to eat. We had our photograph taken by Mestor – I on my knees so as to equal their height. I could not speak for a while afterwards as I would have choked on my words.

At lunch in Chivay, the main town in the valley, the restaurant owner had rescued a vicuna when its mother had been illegally shot and at three months old and standing four feet (1.2m) high it wandered around the restaurant begging scraps. The local market was full of women squatting by sacks of maize and potatoes – many different kinds of each – and I bought a kilo of maize for roasting; it had been delicious scattered in the tomato soup at lunch. And then we left this lost valley with its smiling people, its fruit, its alpacas, its scattered emeralds of alfalfa and its diamond river for the climb again into the lifeless high Andes and through the churning dust to Arequipa where the setting sun coloured the volcanoes with splashes of carmine and crimson.

In sombre mood I went to the Monesterio del Santa Catalina, a glorious

building and a place
of great peace and
tranquillity; I had it
to myself. A convent
from 1580 to 1970,
there were a dozen
or so nuns still in resi-
dence. It was almost a
small town with little
internal streets and
squares all painted
in peeling and fading
ochre, purple, tur-
quoise and prussian
blue. Scarlet gerani-
ums abounded in old
pots. I was given a
map the size of a bis-
cuit to find my way
around but discarded
it as useless within a
few minutes. Life for
the nuns was clearly
hard but nevertheless

Scarlet Macaw

each had a little apartment – a room to sleep and pray, a kitchen and in what was no more than a cupboard, space for a servant.

In the evening, I called in at a travel agent to book a later plane to Lima. There are three airlines, all of which seem to fly half full on identical schedules – Aero Continente, Faucett, and Americana. Flying in on Continente, the stewardess had crossed herself on take-off and landing; and on the presumption that she knew more about the maintenance of the plane than I, it did not seem wise to trust them with my life again. Faucett had engine trouble and so Americana it was. Taking off on a runway so short that passengers gripped their armrests until their knuckles were stretched white, it rattled a bit and a piece of the ceiling fell down during take-off; a pity since it rather spoilt the new interior paint job where white gloss had been liberally coated over everything except the seats – and some on them too.

Writing this under grey skies in the depressing surroundings of a drab hotel at JFK Airport, the parrots, the peasants, Amazonia and the Altoplano were already a continent away. But hurrah! I was on my way home.

Singapore to Bangkok

November 1997

'The only way of catching a train I ever discovered is to miss the train before'
— *G.K.Chesterton*

Almost all the ghosts of the colonials had crept away and my own memories had vanished too. Changi, Neesoon and Kranji had fallen victim to high rise suburbia although the Tangyi Club still held up its head in defiant exclusivity and token buildings such as Stanhope Road, the National Museum and Raffles, of course, remained. This '90s city was sweaty, tropical and vertical but with none of the frenzy of Hong Kong nor the individualism of Manhattan; it was a kind of eastern Miami swept of vice and rollerblades. Spitting, long hair and fire crackers were an offence and possession of just 200gms of marijuana brought mandatory death. Clinically clean and accountancy dull, its people were cardboard cut outs of respectability. Taxi windows were so covered in regulatory notices on insurance, tyre pressures and inspections that it was hard to see out. Chewing gum was prohibited, few smoked, Playboy magazine was banned and, in a society that has little privacy since the xenophobic state continually controls and regulates, foreigners were regarded with disdain and seen as being disorderly and a decadent influence. In a humid 90°F (32°C) only the snowmen and Father Christmases were not melting. Feline women with skinny arms and fragile bones were stockinged and dapper men in Armani suits spoke earnestly into their mobiles. No one was fat, no one was poor and no one was badly dressed. Like hothouse flowers, the inhabitants bloomed in ordered seasons, the overprotected products of a manipulative government. Street underpasses were air conditioned and served by Schindler escalators, M & S (the largest in Asia), Gucci (three of these) and all the world's top fashion names had bullied away the street vendors and limos

46

SINGAPORE TO BANGKOK

Pilgrims on way to Pilgrims Pagoda

had stolen the road from rickshaws. The great harbour remains but even so, the wharfs, godowns and fleets of packet boats have yielded to huge container ships continuously pecked by huge cranes. But there was redemption too: the giants of marble and stainless steel stood guard over little pearls of Christian churches – Armenian, Catholic and Protestant – that were scattered around, painted white and standing on emerald napkins of grass. Prolific planting of trees and shrubs succeeded in greening the streets and although they were continuously shedding leaves, these hardly touched the granite pavement before they were scooped up in the name of order.

A modest £5 for 'eat all you can' around the pool was as attractive as the dishes on offer. It was only when a gas cylinder was connected up to a cast iron plate on my table that I realised that £5 did not include the chef. Oil – sesame, peanut or palm – was spread on the griddle and then it was DIY. Since the choice was raw chicken or pork, the gas kept going out in the breeze and the poor light made it difficult to judge the degree of singeing and further, as the food passed to the mouth via chilli sauce whose scale of searing started at agony, it would not be until the next day that I would discover whether it was salmonella or myself who had survived.

Ah! The triumph of an old Asia hand, I was alive! Overnight rain had cleaned the streets and cleared the skies and I walked to the station to board Express ER2 for Butterworth departing at 7 am. Once the busy terminus for all traffic to the north, the station was now forlorn with a single train per day. Nevertheless all the carriages were full; full too of blaring music which I hoped was not going to spoil the ride. A clerk used a bicycle to deliver forms to the guard at the end of the long train. Parked on a long curve, one end was invisible to the other and a series of flag wavers passed the all clear round the bend.

Crossing the island was like slicing through Metropolis. Not a kampong, chicken or buffalo to be seen; no rows of papaya, no grubby, smiling children and not a sarong in sight. Blocks of flats built or being built were divided only by concrete roads. The northern side of the island seemed to be scrap yards but even here the wrecks were neatly stacked. It will not be long before the island sinks. But cross the Causeway, pull away from Johore Baru and hurrah! for rusty roofed shacks, bananas, old bikes and brown backs hacking into red earth. Here there was life.

On board, drinks arrived brought by a young Malaysian woman who balanced cups and glasses with circus skill as the train swayed and jogged. The radio had been replaced by Tom Hanks on a video in a corner. Individual rubbish bags were distributed and a small fellow with cracked teeth and a bent back came through from time to time to sweep the carpet with an old Ewbank. Here, the view was of palm oil acres and smaller plantations of rubber trees which were fringed with rows of avocado, mango, coconut, papaya or banana. Occasionally there was durian and jackfruit. Sunbirds and pied kingfishers perched on the telephone lines, there were white egrets looking for frogs in the storm ditches and small stations had platforms filled with potted plants. At each station the guard went through the same routine in three languages. "Mind the step, don't leave anything behind and thank you so for the pleasure of travelling." He had a strange singsong voice with a refined accent which made him seem like an effete dilettante – perhaps he was.

Kuala Lumpur went by in a flash – a pity, as its domed and crenellated Moorish exterior make it the best looking city in Asia. Just a glimpse of the Petronias Towers (the highest in the world) and a host of cranes that were completing the competition. No longer was K.L. 'Kuala L'Impure'.

I had forgotten the hills that surround Ipoh, some with dramatic sheer cliffs, others great limestone lumps standing isolated. Strange that such significant and dramatic features could have slipped my memory, even after 35 years. But from the train, the town seemed familiar; the single storey buildings with painted corrugated roofs and the taller buildings down the main street with tiled roofs, all stained by neglect and the rigours of the tropics. Then, as a lieutenant in a cavalry regiment that was limited in its activities by the need to keep its Saladin armoured cars and Ferret scout cars on the roads, there was time to explore. Dinners in the mess were up to the standards of the UK, with the regimental silver shining with a polish that came from hours spent at camp rather than in the field. Tropical mess kit of starched white cotton jacket and skin tight blue serge trousers was accompanied by the accoutrements of patent leather boots, silver spurs, chain mail epaulettes and medals. We felt and looked smart and proud but there was no contact with any educated Malays to discover their opinions; perhaps just as well. In any case, two years later in August 1963, Malaya received its independence and we were gone.

Fourteen hours later, under a sky whose lightning competed with the neon of George Town that shimmered across the Straits of Malacca, we pulled in and I hurried to catch the ferry. It was hard to simultaneously carry a suitcase, shoulder a heavy bag and hold an umbrella and so I had had my bath by the time I arrived at the hotel. At dinner, the revolving restaurant made me giddy, and moving away from the glazed perimeter I found myself closer to a band whose only solution to the unfamiliar notes of western pop was to pump up the decibels.

Mr Teh was dapper, two days older than me and drove a stretched limo. Had I known about the car I would not have booked the hotel room. A family could have lived in it; in fact, judging by its condition they might have only just left. It was a Proton, one of three in the country and when I asked how old it was, Mr Teh dodged the question. The string around the boot rather let it down, but who needed a boot when you could fit a cabin trunk inside? At first, we drove through plantations of oil palm but in Thailand these changed to rubber trees planted in precision rows for mile after mile, each tree with its little cup collecting a few tears from its scarred trunk. Sometimes, a tapper's hut had a few sheets of dried latex hung out on a line to dry like a row of pillow cases after a weekend house party. In the towns, stinking lumps of latex from the bottom of the curing vats were laid out on the road. Looking like pumice rocks they were bought to stuff chair seats. Along the roadsides young teak trees had been planted – hundreds of miles of them. Whether this was a gesture towards replacing the robbed forest or a cash crop for the future, I did not know.

Mr Teh was keen on retaining British names for roads, strict parent control, English as the primary language and the death penalty.

"The only way to do business don't you think, Mr Chilton?"

He was very formal and used my name in every sentence. We got along well. When he talked he slowed down and since talking was what he liked doing best, we took longer than planned to reach Pattani – or perhaps he was just nursing the limo.

The town was predominantly Muslim, mostly of Malay origin; the men wore little skull caps and the women covered their heads. The remainder were Hokkien Chinese. It was a beach resort with an old and attractive fishing port – very photogenic and very smelly but away from the sea it had gone in for high rise (that meant four storeys in this part of the world) and my hotel was an early model. Many of the houses and shops had delicate bamboo bird cages hanging in the shade. Most contained singing doves, mournful little grey birds that were expected to sing their hearts out in a competition held all over southern Thailand each October. I whistled a bar or two of La Paloma to a few but their pink, beady eyes never blinked nor their throats opened; in November they had probably had all they could take of encouraging whistles.

I shared the dining room with a pair of lovers and seven waitresses. The menu was written in unintelligible Thai, so I asked for chicken as the safe option but a scrawny leg and a slice of cucumber were not what I had in mind. Extravagant Billy Bunter

Building site at Pattani

gestures produced a whole farmyard of boiled beasts and asking for a little more rice, the whole prodigality was repeated. Had Werner von Braun discovered the chilli sauce, he would have cancelled his experiments. Dinner was accompanied by a series of chanteuses (eight before I left) clad in mock tiger or shimmering chiffon who sang sad songs that seemed to be about lost loves. I could not make out whether they were in a competition all singing the same weary tune or whether the fact that the lovers had drowned or jumped off a cliff made for sickening similarity. In any case, I was busy chewing through the farm yard. At breakfast, my request for an omelette and bacon arrived as fried eggs and chicken sausage and each request for a cup of coffee came accompanied by a cup of green tea.

Mr Teh tightened the string on the boot and we set off to Narithawat 40 miles to the south. He was reluctant to stray off the main road but I had the map and the money so he was persuaded to make one or two detours. On one we came across a fish drying factory housed in a shack beside the muddy shore. Piles of fresh fish, mostly small sharks, were filleted, put into great clay pots of brine for a week and then laid out on huge bamboo trays to dry in the sun. The smell was terrible. On one side two men cracked open oysters and patient cats sat by for the rejects.

Narithawat was not quite the 'small pretty fishing village' the guide book had promised but it was rural and pleasant all the same. A scruffy, elderly man with a deferential manner and ill-matched shoes shuffled up and in good English told me he had obtained a degree at Cairo University, gone to London to teach but had 'lost his mind' and returned. He had certainly lost his teeth and most of his hair but otherwise he seemed pretty sane. Beside a wooden quay, a small girl was making a boat from folded palm leaves and, filling it with frangipani blossom, she gently launched it as her offering to a river god. Other palm boats had been caught in the detritus that accumulated in eddies; I hoped the prayers they carried were received before they got parked in this aquatic rubbish bin.

At noon in Yala, Mr Teh announced that he had to drop me at 2 pm. Since my train left at 5 pm, I was angry and made it plain that if he could not find me a good hotel to spend three hours in, he would have to keep driving around. Much to his surprise and mine there appeared like an apparition, at the end of the dirty and dismal main street, a brand new, air conditioned, ten-storey palace of comfort and coolness. Most of his tip was saved and he set off on the eight hour drive back to Penang. Being lunchtime and wary of the small portions served, I tried to order a double amount of nasi goring with the result that two places were laid and two plates served. So courteous were the staff, they showed no surprise when I followed my own meal with that of my absent friend.

Joining another train for the final leg of my journey, my compartment was fitted out in grey formica and polished aluminium; it was efficient, clean and as soulless as a home to a dead sardine. But the air conditioning worked well, I could turn off the music and I had it to myself; my plan to travel on a Sunday seemed to have paid off. As we left, the door of the carriage opened and a charming boy handed me a fresh orange juice and a menu that ran to four pages – heaven knows where they cooked it, perhaps they telephoned ahead. When my choices arrived, the tom yum soup was spiced with coriander, ginger, chilli and lemon grass and burdened with shrimp, crab and octopus. It was in a special metal bowl under which a saucer of oil was burning. Had the train suddenly stopped, I should have got a gallon of boiling soup over my chest and the carriage might have caught fire.

The scenery was unchanging for a thousand miles. Paddy fields were dotted

Mr Teh and his limo

with lonely sea coconut palms and wooden houses each with a TV mast. Ditches of lotus and tufted water rush made for a weary landscape that was flat to the horizons from the South China Sea in the east to the Andaman Sea in the west. Train travel carries with it the voyeur's fascination of prying unseen into the lives of others. A hundred years ago, Ford Maddox Ford summed up rail travel: *'One is behind glass, gazing into the hush of a museum, seeing little bits of uncompleted life.'*

Sleep was fitful. My carriage was next to the engine and the driver had a whistle blowing phobia that needed attention. The rail lengths differed too, so The Emperor kept changing to the Radetsky March and then to Honeysuckle Rose.

Bangkok is an unattractive city, sprawling and dirty, crammed with humanity and sectioned by clogged klongs. But like Singapore's Christian churches, little jewel boxes of temples were dotted around so that suddenly, between the car breakers and the washing-hung tenement blocks, a little oasis of cool contentment appeared shimmering in gold and crusted in shining ceramics. In one of these, I fell into conversation with a young Buddhist monk. Asked if I knew about Buddhism I muttered something about reincarnation and hoped I might return as a dog. "Could I choose?" I asked. To return as a Chinese chow rather than an English setter would be an unfortunate error. He gave me the contemptuous look that such a facetious question deserved.

In the afternoon, I took a long boat down the Chao Phraya River and through a few of the wider klongs. The boat's 40 ft (12m) of length and four feet (1.2m) of beam were propelled by a six cylinder motor that was wrestled by a teenager. Had the engine had a silencer, it would have been a more pleasant way to explore the back waters. I was back at 6 pm in time to hear the National Anthem broadcast over a school playground beside my hotel; rather a catchy number, it also made a jolly start to the day at 8 am.

The Floating Market of Bangkok now sells only hats, carved elephants and bags of wooden fish but I had heard that the water market at Damnoe Saduak, thirty miles away and on the road to Kachanaburi and the River Kwai, was still authentic. I was wrong; charter tours seemed to have reached there years ago. Marshalled by barriers, the paunchy and patronising, squeezed into local sarongs or sweating in 'Thailand Loves You' T-shirts, stumbled into long boats that left at fifteen second intervals. Like safari jeeps around a lion cub, a dozen of these boats circle a lone floating greengrocer and twenty-five shutter clicks later they zoom over to Handicrafts (MasterCard and American Express accepted). I fled for Kachanburi.

The River Kwai is 1,000 ft (300m) wide, brown, benign and fringed by bamboo, liana and many floating restaurants. The celebrated bridge, black-girdered and on concrete supports streaked by age and algae, seemed menacing and sinister and a rather tacky museum displayed many pictures and mementos of the brutal treatment and dreadful conditions of POW slave labour, but it was at the cemetery that my emotions spilled over. It was so neat, so well ordered and so dreadfully poignant. I sat down and cried in the shade of a spreading acacia tree beside the brave rows and the cross with its wreath of poppies.

Back in Bangkok, Patpong, the city's Chinatown, is a wide, short street whose edges were occupied by girlie bars. Leggy but listless girls were clad only in what decency and the law required – this was satisfied by a single cardboard star. Extravagantly priced beer was topped up frequently by other less leggy but more active girls who offered something more than mere companionship. The centre of the street was taken up by stalls selling fakes and very good they were. I bought a Cartier 'Santos' for £9 (in Bond Street it would have been £2,000); I hoped it would still be going when I got to the airport.

With Ton and his tuk-tuk, we puttered off to Wat Po, home to a Buddha weighing in at five and a half tons of solid gold (5,600 kgs) where I was buttonholed by a stout English matron clad in several layers of frilly pink cotton; she continually complained of the heat to her insipid companion. When waiting for buses, boats and trains I had been compiling a list of characters from Saki's short stories. These two filled my image perfectly of the alarming Mrs Packletide and her drippy companion, Loona Bimberton.

At 4 pm as the sun just started to dip, I took an Express Boat with Ton and we went to Nonthaburi, a suburb half an hour away, zipping past coal and rice barges, tourist cruisers and varied commercial water traffic. Each stop was an exercise in precision by passengers and crew alike. The skipper was in a little glass hut in the bows and the passengers got on and off at the stern. Coming alongside at each stop was controlled by a series of whistles from the man at the stern and another at the bows so that the skipper was a sort of marine sheepdog. It took an average of nine seconds at each landing point, which was exactly the time that slack was achieved between full astern to bring the boat to a halt and full ahead to zoom off again. In these critical moments, a crowd leapt on and a crowd leapt off; it was not an operation to be undertaken by those weak of limb or lacking courage, nor the tight skirted.

Just before our final landing point, a buckle from a girl's rucksack got hooked onto my back trouser button. The boat was swaying, passengers were pressing, the shore approached fast, I had a plane to catch and here we were, back to back, inextricably connected. Just as I was thinking we had better get introduced, we were free and I leapt the yard to the landing stage. I waved to my ten second friend and she vanished into the spray and the sunset.

Thailand, Cambodia and Laos

February 1998

'Stop worrying about the potholes in the road and celebrate the journey' – Fitzhugh Mullan

In Bangkok's Luphini Park, dawn breaks at 6.00 am and by then all the best picnic spots are taken by the geriatric fitness clubs, each separately distinguished by coloured shirts. As the light comes up with tropical urgency, the yellow shirts are ballroom dancing, the reds are being schooled in theatrical grimaces and in blue, 90-year-olds are on their backs bicycle pedalling. At this time in the morning, it is the sanctuary of the elderly and early rising Chinese community, and solitary individuals battle in slow motion against an imaginary assassin in T'ai Chi. Breakfast picnics seem to be largely of women gossiping amongst great thermoses of green tea and wicker baskets of rice cakes and dried fruit. By 8.00 am they are packing up and on the hour, as the national anthem is broadcast over the city, they respectfully stand for a minute or two and then shuffle off to lonely flats and memories, passing the first of the office workers taking a short cut to crowded blocks of glass and steel.

A day trip to Ayutthaya was a disappointment. This tourist destination 40 miles north of Bangkok is billed as the ancient city of Siam, a UNESCO World Heritage site, the cultural, religious, political and trading centre of Indo China for four centuries. But all that I found were weedy ruins scattered over a large area within a town that had spread over and around them. Only one great monument of the thirteenth century remained impressive. Wat Phra Si San Phet with three great chedi (the Burmese influence – they attacked the city 24 times with their war elephants) is set in a great, peaceful, grassy park dotted with trees as gnarled as old olives and scented with pink and white frangipani.

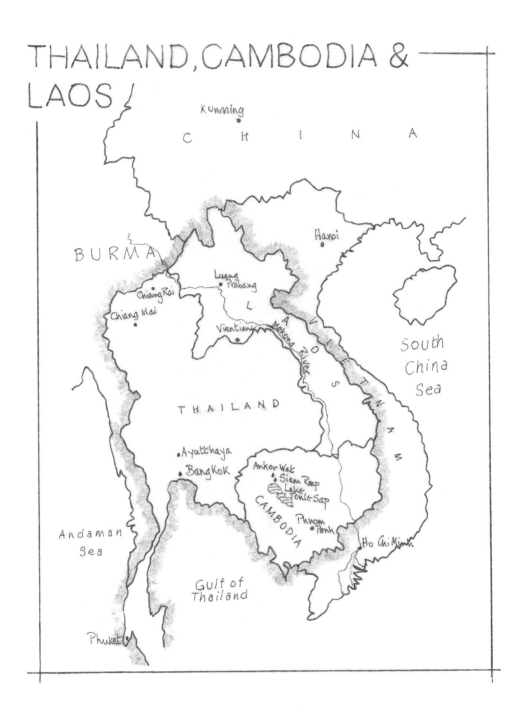

THAILAND, CAMBODIA & LAOS

To this archaeological bystander, an exception to crumbling piles was Wat Yai Chai, built to celebrate victory in an elephant duel. A phallic 80 feet (24m) of carved sandstone with an alarming post-prostate tilt, it is surrounded by trim lawns, potted bougainvillaea and topiary. Restored for daily use, there squatted at its base a group of Buddhist nuns packing joss sticks in tens, wafers of gold leaf into fives and stripping lotus blossoms of leaves. However, two contemporary images unsettled the antiquity and contentment of the place. Around the base, 100 images of the Lord Buddha formed a guardian square – each identical and each a clone of Barbra Streisand. Similarly, the great benign golden Buddha in the inner sanctum seemed modelled on Mr Neal, my prep school Latin master – it was the squint that gave him away. A fishy lunch beside the River Chao Phraya outside the old walls and near the old Portuguese colony brought reality home again.

There were just six on the flight from Bangkok to Siam Reap in Cambodia: two and a half pairs of back packers and a grandfather. I hoped the airline, new in the last two months and with a single aircraft, would last long enough to bring me back. At the airport we were outnumbered two to one by officials in identically styled uniforms with green for immigration, grey for customs and brown for police, but all with the same hat. The five green men took care of the visa formalities. The first applied the stamp, the next the seal, the third the date, the fourth signed and the last entered the details in a large book and took the money. The grey and the brown men chalked my bag, smiled and indicated my waiting guide and driver. At the hotel, everyone smiled. The door mat said 'Welcome', so did the bath mat and 'Hello Welcomes' was embroidered on the bed cover. The manager smiled the most when I brought him a cockroach from my room – flat on its back fortunately – and complained that my room was airless and that although it had curtains, they framed a window artfully painted on a white wall. His smile was as wide as his supplicating hands as he assured me that when the tour group left I would have the room with the biggest real windows. As for the cockroach – his smile stretched further, "You know how it is," and a well-practised flick sent the beast into the bin.

On the edge of the town are the Killing Fields where tens of thousands of innocents were slaughtered or worked to death by the ruthless Khmer Rouge under the infamous Pol Pot. His influence seemed to lurk in the shadows and his guerrillas are said to be still in the hills to the north. In a country the size of England with a population of only 15 million, he ordered the city dwellers into the fields and the farmers into the city murdering two million on the way. Land mine clearance teams are still at work – mostly Vietnamese attracted by the high wages that compensate for a lost leg.

Chea Bunat was an excellent guide. His father and mother had been killed by the Pol Pot regime and he worked freelance as he had neither the relations nor the

money to bribe the man-
ager of the travel agency to
employ him on a full time
basis. A guide was important not only for informa-
tion but also to make sure
one did not stray to mined
areas. In 90°F (32°C), the
sweat that poured into my
eyes would have prevented
me seeing a mine even if
I had stepped on it. Bunat
was keen to improve his
English. We both got con-
fused with mind, mines
and mined and we got into
giggles with gaggles, gog-
gles and gurgles. We rode

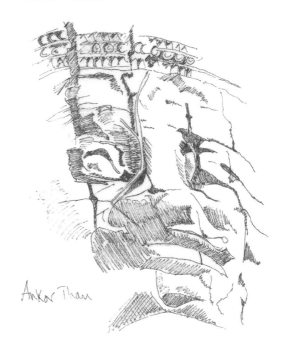

AnKor Thom

around on bicycles, taking alarming short cuts over single plank bridges and
weaving our way through little back gardens neatly planted with onions, radishes
and pak choi. Pot-bellied pigs wallowed in mud as black as themselves. Resting
under an old mango tree, Chea admitted to a passion for ballroom dancing and
reeled off the names of big bands. Joe Loss, Victor Sylvester and Count Basie
were his favourites.

Of all the 290 temples built between the ninth and twelfth centuries by the
great Khmer empire around Siam Reap, Angkor Wat is justly the most spectacular. Seen in a setting sun across a wide moat, with a line of monks in marigold
yellow walking across the causeway, is the iconic picture postcard view but the
temple itself it is an extraordinary monument to the labours of a million men
over 30 years. Soon it would have as many tourists in a single year. But for me the
temple of Ta Prohm was the best. It seemed a model for a schoolboy adventure
story, the set of any jungly film or as the backcloth of a romantic legend. Tarzan
might have hollered from a crumbling tower or Indiana Jones dashed across a
courtyard of tumbled boulders pursued by angry natives. But there is no conflict
here, only peace, occasionally punctuated by cackling parrots or a toucan's hoot
against a continuo of cicadas. The temple's 1000-year-old stones had been prised
from their original positions by the roots of a dozen fig trees. Smooth and grey,
some torso thick, they poured down walls, snaked over the floor, spread through
the masonry, strangled Vishnu images, garrotted a dancing girl and girdled a

door. A Buddhist monk, holding his saffron robes over one arm, was caught in a shaft of sunlight. I caught him too, in my lens.

Ton Le Sap is the largest lake in South East Asia and controls the floodwaters of the rainy season when it extends its surface area 10 times. It irrigates the rice paddies and a unique form of rice grows ten feet (3m) high to cope with the depth of water. The lake is extraordinarily fertile and supports a fishing industry around its shores. A floating town had grown up with a school, a hospital, a police station and a range of shops with floating houses from single shacks to large houseboats which are scattered randomly over its surface. Some had little floating vegetable plots, chickens coops and even pigs. We stopped by a catfish farm, where the fish were in a frenzied turmoil when fed baby versions of themselves. A tethered pet monkey was eating a fish – meticulously picking out the bones and three bedraggled pelicans in a cage were waiting the knife of a festival meal. As we chugged up the channel to a land based village, we passed a cumbersome barge stacked with beer being poled with great effort by a man and two women. It had been loaded from a small steamer moored in the lake. It was cheaper to bring the beer from Phnom Penh by boat rather than road; sweated labour was still exploitable. The stench of drying fish, eels and water snakes was appalling, the rubbish dreadful, the heat oppressive but the whole malodorous scene bustled with activity.

On the road back I passed a tree nursery irrigated by a great water wheel. By an enlightened law every citizen has to plant two trees during his lifetime. Leaving the nursery, a roadside policeman offered me his badge for sale; on graduation each policeman was given two, whether the second was to boost a poor salary I never found out – perhaps he had a suitcase full. My horoscope in the newspaper read 'Be in touch with recalcitrant relatives. Gifts will add to your wardrobe; people will say, "You look spiffy"!'

The Secret War, when the CIA established a base against the Pathet Lao (Kurtz the crazy colonel in Apocalypse Now was modelled on the real life green beret Tony Poe), seems to be still running, although its cover was clearly blown. My immigration card at Vientiane airport had a space for 'pseudo name'. I put in Bond. The town was in turmoil; the airport half constructed, new drainage being laid city-wide, dirt roads paved and the electricity off 8 am to 5 pm – the last being the most inconvenient with no air conditioning and drinks light on ice. The buildings were low rise, the streets full of cashew trees, palms and frangipani and there were even rice paddies in the centre of town. Traffic was sparse and made up mostly of mopeds and much patched tuk-tuks. After two obligatory temples and a dreadful concrete national stupa, I watched the sun sink into Thailand on the far side of the Mekong River.

A bit of dirt and dust outside the front door seemed inconsequential when at lunch, the lamb was pink and garlicky, the prawns were fat and the asparagus thin; eels from the river had been salted and smoked and were accompanied by crispy baguettes and fresh butter: give me an ex-French colony any day. If La Cage aux Folles came here the waiters would be first in the audition line; in tight white shorts they wagged their little bums and giggled a lot but were delightfully helpful and attentive – well, to me anyhow!

The currency changes have been confusing. The Thai baht fluctuated 20% a day; in Cambodia they used the dual currency of US dollars and riels and here I changed 50 dollars and got 128,000 kips in a stash of notes as thick as a brick.

Nothing much moved in Luang Prabang – the old capital of the Kingdom of Laos. A single set of traffic lights was stuck on red, there were chickens in the main street, no wind rustled the bamboo, and dogs lay around and snoozed. My hotel, the Villa Santi, was once the Villa de la Princesse, the home of the last king's sister. Since the revolution in 1975 such names have been politically incorrect, nevertheless, it took until 1995 to get around to the name change. (The princess still lived in town but rather more modestly now and had to do her own shopping.) With just ten bedrooms, the hotel was cool and airy with much polished wood, stone floors and rattan ceilings woven in herringbone. I established my table on the first floor veranda and looked out on life ambling by, waving to the children across the street as they struggled with a mangle that extracted juice from sugar cane.

I hired an old fashioned 'sit up and beg' bicycle and for reasons that neither the lady renter nor I could work out, it was hard to turn to the right. Consequently, I devised an anti-clockwise route around town but dogs, chickens and stray children were at risk. It squeaked from every moving part and as I passed, people looked up and wondered where a pig was being slaughtered. Monks, with shaven heads and robes in a variety of orange tones from public park-marigold to forest-cinnamon and with a long cloth bag slung over a shoulder, were everywhere. It was as though a cargo plane had jettisoned a ton of orange lollies. Most were novices doing a mandatory three months or more and some, for personal reasons – the death of their father perhaps – sign on for another three months. Considering they were up at 4 am for their first mantras and lived on rice they had to beg for, they were a cheerful lot. Buddhism is deeply integrated into the culture of daily life and in Luang Prabang, the religious capital of the country, there seemed to be a wat on every block and sometimes four in a row.

The women have fine-boned features and appeared delicate and dainty until you saw them heaving a sack of rice onto a lorry or carrying a hod of bricks up bamboo scaffolding. They wear long skirts of woven cotton or silk, banded at the bottom with coloured stripes of gold and silver. There seemed to be a single size that fitted all so at the waist the fabric is folded and tucked in as necessary. The

Doorway - Xiang Temple. Ankor.

town typified the laid back life of the Lao. It lies at the confluence of the Mekong and Nan Khan rivers but there was little boat traffic and the water was mostly enjoyed by cheerful children playing with inner tubes around the sandy shores. It was a languid, listless and loveable place with a lot of laughing and a little work.

It was the dry season and there was a haze over the hills from smoke which rose from the slash and burn of the hill tribes. Many move their villages every two years and need new ground to cultivate. The Hmong originally came from Northern China – some say Mongolia – and live rather aloof from other tribes, growing a single crop of rice which they plant on the hillsides. Having slashed early and burnt late they had little to do. Children played in the dust with fat, contented pigs, chased turkeys, (chickens are for the valleys) and were cuddled by mothers wearing elaborately embroidered costumes. These were a long skirt, bright with coloured beads around the base, a loose shirt with white sleeves, the waist wrapped in a scarlet sash and an intricately embroidered square of cloth hanging over the shoulders. Their heads were usually covered with a sort of crocheted cap whose little balls of wool at each corner bobbled around their back. The men were universally clad in black shirts and baggy trousers and looked like stereotype Viet Cong. Their windowless long houses rested on stilts like arks washed up by a flood. They had palm woven roofs (renewed annually) and underneath were stacks of wood in Swiss precision, together with pigs and maybe a loom. The rice was winnowed laboriously by being pounded in a great mortar and was then put into sacks to be carried to the roadside slung over the back of a surefooted horse. A few men carried a homemade rifle which I judged as being more dangerous to the hunter than the hunted. The gun has a slim barrel about six feet (1.8m) long into which is stuffed gun powder and a pea sized lead ball and then everything is set off with a hammer blow from a child's cap gun. They used much the same method at Edgehill in 1642, although I doubt whether the soldiers there could have hit a starling sitting 30 ft (10m) up in a mango tree. Small boys used catapults with similar accuracy; no wonder birds were scarce.

On the wall of a village house were posters that showed the candidates in the forthcoming elections. There were ten and each was represented by a domino. Since few people could count above five, any candidate numbered above six had little chance. At the end of the village and enclosed by a stout fence were the poppy fields. Xiao, my guide, explained that these were 'medicinal'. I was told that the sale of opium was illegal but no one would bother about a small field or two and besides, it was too far up the mountain. Since a stout Englishman had got there in three hours, I believed none of this. As we climbed, strands of bamboo, with stems as thick as a thigh, grew 50 ft (15m) up in the sky before their tips arched back towards earth. Sometimes high winds, or perhaps overenthusiasm to outgrow their neighbour, caused stems to crack and twist and then the whole great clump fell in confused agony.

I abandoned my two day boat trip up the Mekong. I was to have travelled on the M.V. Pak Ou, sailing on Tuesdays and Thursdays. I had imagined a river steamer of two or three decks with an awning stretched aft, commanded by a cheroot-chewing, stubble-chinned captain twirling a mahogany wheel and possibly a boy in the bows probing the depths with a pole or swinging a lead. A sharp whistle before a bend would have announced the arrival to a waiting crowd who would swarm up a narrow plank with vegetables in wicker hampers, chickens in coops and babies swaddled in braided shawls. Hammocks would be slung and charcoal braziers lit and there might be dancing when the rice wine flowed and perhaps a fight would break out on a lower deck. But never have the dreams of a romancer been so thoroughly crushed. The boats that catered for passenger traffic were no more than 40 ft (12m) long, five feet (1.5m) wide and sat only 18 inches (50 cm) above the water. There were ten rows of rattan doll's chairs, set two by two and tight for a Lao bottom let alone mine. Under its metal roof, being slow roasted in the heat, there would have been no food, no fizz and no fun. The alternative was to take a speed boat.

And what a boat it was: bright yellow with a red stripe, flat bottomed, with a snub prow and square stern and lying on the damp sand of the shore. The naked engine was being fuelled for the seven hour journey out of a plastic can marked 'Best Cooking Oil' and its exhaust was gathered into a single cannon that sloped backwards and upwards. Settled on to the floor with a rough board at my back, I pushed in my BA earplugs, donned a motor cycle helmet of kaleidoscopic colours, pulled down the visor and we shot off with rocket speed and thunderous noise for Thailand. Had we hit a log in this timber-planked bomb, the Bisto-brown, languid and viscous waters of the Mekong would have swallowed me up in moments.

For the most part the river was benign, broad, with sand banks at the low water level of the dry season and bounded by hills, part slashed and part forested. Solitary giants, up to now spared the chainsaw's execution, having established their sovereignty by the denial of light to others, stood guardian of their territory. Occasionally the flow quickened through rocky narrows and here drift nets were cantilevered out on bamboo poles, often using mosquito nets donated by an aid agency. Other speed boats coming downriver passed like angry wasps and we hit their wake with bottom numbing thumps. At other times, the water rippled over stony shallows and for miles the boat shuddered like a Citroën 'deux cheveaux' over pavé until it seemed that every joint would have loosened and one's body would collapse like a marionette at the close of its show.

At about the time store holders were opening up for the afternoon's business, we slid onto the sandy shore of Huey Say. Transferring to a leaky dugout, I crossed over to Chiang Khong on the Thai side and at a spot where Burma, Laos, Thailand and China joined, the strings of my limp skeleton were once again tautened as I stepped onto land and drove to join M who had manage to endure the lavish luxuries of the Regent Hotel in Chiang Mai.

¤ ¤ ¤

The Andaman Sea brushes the west coasts of Burma and Thailand and near the peninsula of Phuket, Phangnga Bay shelters some of the most dramatic scenery in South East Asia. At its southern end lie Phra Nang, Rai Leh, Koh Phi Phi and a number of other spots whose geological drama belies their little names. Islands of limestone dot the sea like crumbs scattered on a bowl of Crème de Menthe. Some habitable, others no more than rocks but all covered with a fuzzy topping of vegetation and many with sheer cliffs up to 200 ft (60m). These karsts have been made by a slice of the island cracking away and often at the base, there is a great pile of bus sized boulders which themselves have developed a leafy tonsure. Magic inland harbours have been formed, approached through narrows slits in the sheer cliffs and a strip of talcum white sand separates an azure sea from the flourishing vegetation. Sometimes, as though such absurd picturesqueness was insufficient, a thatched hut and a fishing family with hammocks swinging in the shade of a scattering of palm trees has been added at one end of the beach. If Jason had come this way, the Argonaut would have been beached in a trice: the Aegean is tame stuff compared to these idyllic seas.

In a great cave, scooped out of one of these cliffs, stalactites hung from an invisible roof and the air was full of the flutterings of brown rumped swifts that build their nests in tens of

Buddhist monk

thousands. Clutching our nose against the ammonia arising out of droppings that lay thick and crawling with cockroaches, we were led to the back of the cave where a rickety series of bamboos lashed with creeper disappeared into the damp darkness and muscular men with calves like steel hawsers, shinned up with a torch in their teeth and a pronged fork in their belt, to prize off the saliva secreted nests. The gourmets of Taiwan and Singapore would pay £25 for a bowl of boiled swallow spittle.

Our hotel was a collection of little two storey mushroom lodges dotted around a coconut palm plantation, surrounded on three sides by water and on the fourth by impassable cliffs. Arrival and departure was to the timetable of the tides and if this coincided with low water, a tractor drove through the surf carburettor high, towing a trailer as a jetty. The mushrooms had sprouted rather too prolifically and many seemed occupied by pairs of lean men who may well have sent post cards saying 'Having a gay old time'. But paradise can spoil if lingered in too long and after a week blinded by reflections from a turquoise ocean, browned by a tropical sun and brim full of grilled lobster, we dodged falling coconuts and limp handshakes on the way home to the glories of daffodils and March winds.

Madagascar

October 1998

'I have found that there ain't no surer way to find out whether you like people or hate them, than to travel with them' – Mark Twain

The capital Antananarivo was noisy at night and a hubbub by day. Before dawn people moved in to establish their street patch. My window looked on to weighing machine alley – five in row. A two-toothed grandmother, wrinkled as a prune and with only one shoe, swept the dust from the pavement, set down her bathroom scales, moved them to the right a little then to the left, flicked away the falling frangipani blossoms, edged the scales back an inch, spat on the glass indicator and polished it with her skirt; nudging the scales a final fraction, she waited for business. Presentation is everything. Why the passersby, universally lean and bony, should want her custom I never understood; perhaps they were anxious to put *on* weight.

There was a dog on the balcony of the house opposite. It jumped on to the rails and hung there with the elbows of its front legs over the top bar. It seemed as interested in the passing scene as I was. A street market was nearby and a continual stream of goods was carried by on heads of black curly hair. Stacks of old sacks, woven panniers of bruised bananas, dirty plastic jerry cans of oil, a brief case as a shade, a chipped enamel basin full of offal, bundles of firewood, second-hand bottles stickily overflowing with wild honey, a calabash of wine, a crate of rum, trays of eggs, oranges shiny and waxy glowing in the sun like embers, piles of bones, a hundred baguettes brown with crusty anticipation, newspapers, a carpet, brushes, pots, cots, mats and hats.

The hotel was by the railway station, a grand affair with turrets capped in weathered copper. No passenger trains were running (they were short of spare parts) but families were gathered with piles of packages, hoping to catch a ride on

66

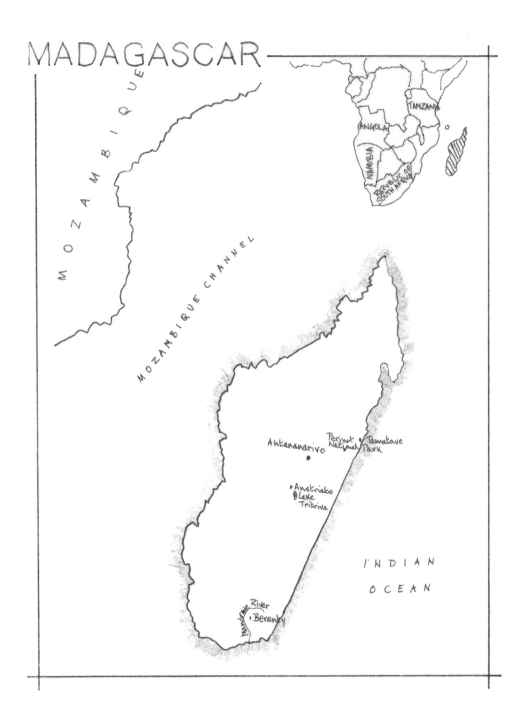

one of the two goods trains per day. Boulevard Marachel Foch, colonnaded on each side, was the pickpocket pitch and unsavoury youths sat around in groups like black widow spiders. I felt uncomfortable and unsafe even in the middle of the road.

Leaving the city we climbed up the hills, past road side stalls of locquats and pineapple and woven baskets spread on the red earth that covered the island like a spilt can of terracotta wash. Everywhere there were brick makers; clay was thrown into wooden moulds, dried a day or two and then piled in great ziggurats covered with a layer of mud and straw. The hollow interior was packed with wood and roots which was then lit to burn for a week. The plot, now conveniently dug a couple of feet deep became a paddy field. Barricades of spiny euphorbia, blooded with scarlet flowers, kept out the humped zebu cattle and inquisitive neighbours. It was chilly in the early morning and villagers wrapped to eye level in blankets of grey and brown, squatted by the road selling tomatoes.

Anstriabe, built by the French to escape the summer heat, sat neat and provincial at 5,000 ft (1,500m) amongst pine trees, myrtle and eucalyptus. The Hotel de Termes – turreted, veranda'd, gabled and balconied – sprawled amongst clipped cedar and polished gum trees and would grace any European spa. I got a key with a large label attached saying Chilteren Jam and a small map showing the route to the west wing. An over-amplified band on the terrace was playing and a chanteuse was belting out, "Let's make love, get it up!" while I had dinner with my companions – seven widows. As the band went into the next number -"I wanna have sex on the beach, come and move your body," I caught the suspicion of a raised eyebrow and the glimmer of a smile from the Yorkshire grandmother of seven.

The third day was a day off. Others seemed content to laze by the pool but I booked a car and a driver.

"Today is super wonderful," enthused Racine. "Yes, thank you suh, spiffing."

His friendly features and Rastafarian locks were profiled against the pale violet light of early morning that softens the Central Highlands. With a smile that cracked the silhouette wide open, he leant on the bonnet of his car. And what a car! A 1947 Chevrolet, hand painted with many coats so that the present peach barely masked the previous plum. It was when I was handed a watering can that I suspected that its mechanical excellence fell short of its exterior perfection. As we groaned and creaked over rutted tracks, I sat with this two gallon (10ltrs) recycled tin between my feet and at a regular fifth mile the boiling radiator was topped up. The starter was out of action too so when I went to photograph women fishing for frogs or a cart of carrots hauled at snail's pace by a yoked pair of zebu cattle, Racine had the dilemma of deciding whether to keep the engine running, expensive for a four litre monster, or finding a slope to park on.

Lake Tritriva, a sheer sided lozengey volcanic crater – the shape of Madagascar itself as each of the five boys who tagged along pointed out – was ringed with casurina pines, mimosa, myrtle and orange flowered buddleja. I blew my whistle to test the echo, refused all the pea sized 'sapphires' offered by the boys, offered them two biros and a pack of chewing gum and then we steamed off down an exquisite little valley, bordered on each side with napkin-sized terraces of wheat and barley (all at different stages of growth), which supplied the local brewery.

'carpet' sellers, Betaso

The town of Betaso had been recommended as an architectural gem: it was not. But it was market day – crowded, colourful and odorous. From the northern end of this commercial melée came a large and extravagant funeral with flags flying, hands waving, bare feet stomping and with clarinets, drums and dented bugles leading the way. By the time this band of jolly mourners were crowding into the market square, from the southern end came the First Minister on an electioneering tour. He was accompanied by 15 cars, two trucks of gendarmes, an army escort and a helicopter. Each procession met nose to nose roughly where I stood. Hat stalls were on one side, many yards of cloth draped over a line just to the right and nearby were six pigs each with a back leg tethered by raffia rope. Behind, a street restaurant was preparing lunch with blackened cauldrons of boiling rice and teapots of hot coffee that sat in a *bain marie* of hot water.

Since the minister's entourage could go no further, a gendarme jumped out of his truck to move the mourners and in doing so his rifle butt caught one of the pigs on its rump. The rope holding the pig snapped and the five other pigs, frightened by the racket of sirens, klaxons, horns, drums and clarinets got tangled. The loose pig upset the coffee, got scalded and ran off through the army escort with its owner in pursuit. The down draught of the helicopter swept up several lengths

1947 Packard and Racine

of cloth so that an outrider was suddenly dressed in floral cotton and one of the coffin bearers, on a crucial corner of the litter, was blinded by another length of pink nylon picotee. As he stumbled, the coffin slid towards the minister's car and the lid, together with its accompanying wreaths of plastic roses, slid further. Confusion closely encountered Chaos but in a surrealist few moments the outrider, now free of his unwelcome frock, steadied the coffin, a dusky hand snapped back the lid, the pigs were untangled by two small boys, the helicopter rose in the sky and the buglers, with inspired spontaneity, changed their metre from polka to pomp. The band then took up a cheerful beat again, the cook stirred the rice and refilled the coffee pot, the gendarmes cleared a path and the market swung back into business. The minister, clearly delighted by the unexpected large crowd, stepped out of his car to wave a grateful hand and the vote-seeking entourage moved off to speeches and lunch. I patted a pig to check on reality and went off to find a '47 Chevy parked on a slope with Racine snoozing at the wheel.

"Welcome back, suh," he said. "Sleepy place this I'm thinking."

The flight to the south was cancelled; apparently locusts had got into the engines. There were huge swarms around causing the locals dismay but there was an alternative story that the President had demanded the aeroplane to take him to South Africa for a holiday and that the other plane in the 'fleet' was still on the way back.

At any rate, one could not fault the generosity of Air Madagascar, known locally as 'Air Mad', as it put us up in the Hotel Colbert, the best in town, and provided a dinner that proved the equal of any Parisian four star establishment.

Back in 'Tana', I walked up the steep, cobbled and tree shaded streets past the terraced houses of the old part of town. Neat comfortable villas showed their French architectural origins. Often they were protected by hedges of clipped *spirea* and hung about with wisteria or jasmine. Where else would one see a banana tree alongside a flowering peach, a little pot of violets beside a bristling *agave* or *drasaena* in the company of heather? School children giggled at me good-naturedly as they stopped at a corner stall for banana fritters or a sweet beignet on their way home. The top of the hill, cooler and with a view that reached to four grey shades of distant hills, was all convents and churches. Like Club Med, the missionaries always seem to get the best spots. There was no way of telling whether the smaller churches were Catholic or Protestant but all were refreshingly simple and in each one (I tried four) there was jolly revivalist music; a piano and four men, a choir practice with white-smocked school girls, or two guitars and a double bass. As is so often the case in countries shackled with poverty, music and worship provide succour for the spirit and a lift to the heart.

There are 8,500 Malagasy francs to £1 but in the market most purchases are made in coins, the largest worth 5p and the smallest less than a farthing. I could not find a bag of peanuts with more than 25 nuts in it and they are grown here! Small wonder that the few tourists are pursued by those taxiing, selling, begging, cleaning or just hoping. When two screws in my camera sheared off and I had to contemplate buying another, only cash would have been accepted. The notes are the most worn, torn, soiled and sordid that I have ever encountered and smelt of old bones and rotten cabbage. If my budget had run to the five million Malagasy francs required for the camera (more than twice the UK price), my sack of malodorous notes would have had dogs and pigs running behind it.

In the country areas, Fana Fody is practised – a rather toxic mixture of tradition, religion and herbal medicine. Like most traditions it moves with the times and the ceremony of circumcision, known as Le Savatee, has adapted accordingly. After a day of ceremony involving special food, particular presents and the attendance of the poor lad's senior uncle, the operation is performed by a visiting health worker. The resultant redundant scrap of flesh is then stuffed into a shot gun and blasted to oblivion.

Berenty, beside the Mandrave River in the Southern province of Androy, has as much rain as Paris but all in one month. It was here that I met the first of the lemurs to capture my sentimental heart. Gentle and enquiring, wide eyed, long fingered and friendly, each seemed to wear a label that said 'Be My Friend'. They

71

come in almost fifty varieties from sun loving to nocturnal, brown, polar white, pied and variegated, with combinations in between. The smallest, the mouse lemur, is the size of a hamster and the largest, the sifakas, can reach up to your waist on their dancing legs but all have a tree climbing agility to shame a monkey. Hold out a banana to a Ringtail and a dozen will shin down a trunk quicker than firemen, hesitate as though too hasty an approach might betray bad manners and then with great courtesy, stretch forward a furry arm and gently take the banana with hands that seem moulded of neoprene and wearing gloves of the softest chamois leather.

The rain forest of Perinet National Park, half way down the Central Highlands as they slope eastwards towards the Indian Ocean, was a total contrast. Steep terrain divided by clear streams, reputedly full of crayfish, is densely covered by lush subtropical trees and plants; nothing giant, but cool and glistening in the daily rain. Three hours of walking were rewarded by the rarest Malagasy bird, the pigmy kingfisher and several chameleons including Parson's chameleon, the world's largest at 18 inches (45cms) nose to tail tip. Its eyes, each independent and swivelling through 180 degrees, scanned me around the compass as I offered it a grasshopper. It declined (perhaps it liked to catch its own dinner) and then coiled up its tail, shut down the two search lights and carried on its snooze. It is the only species that does not change colour, its size being enough to deter the hungry. Earlier, another species when moved on to my hand, changed rapidly from *Crème de Menthe* to Baileys and curled its tail around my finger thinking it had landed on another branch. With more than five thousand different species of flora it could be forgiven thinking that a warm brown arm was simply one of the many that had yet to be identified.

Perinet is the home of the Indri lemur, the largest and most elusive of all the lemurs. Family groups establish their territory vocally and their glass shattering cries mixing a wail, a howl and a bellow, echo through the forest canopy as though the Spanish Inquisition was ferociously at work. I found a pair and their adolescent offspring clinging one above each other on a slender tree trunk and they looked down with the shocked and surprised expression that seems common to all lemurs; as though someone had exploded a fart in the Royal Enclosure. Not wishing to be associated with tourists, they bounded off through the forest leaping with wonderful gymnastic agility from tree to tree.

Sunday was a day of rest and Sunday best and the small town of Andasibe had a Caribbean feel to it as churchgoers, men in T-shirts and jackets, women in straw hats and girls in lacy white cotton dresses, meandered to church exchanging greetings as they went. Around them on the red dusty road, children played with a stick and hoop, a stone dragged on a piece of string or a small wheel nailed to

Pirogues on l'Pangalanes lakes

the end of a bamboo. Chickens and chicks pecked amongst the poles of the stilted wooden houses while geese and goslings paddled in muddy pools.

The Catholic church was stone-walled, solid and pew-packed by the suited and straw-hatted. On the other side of town, the Protestant church, wooden walled under a rusty roof, was less well attended but for me carried away the singing prize as with much clapping and occasional stamping, the praise to the Lord rocked through the rotten rafters. This choral fervour drowned the harmonium where the player's knees squeezed the bellows with such enthusiasm that I was anxious for the short fourth leg of his chair as it balanced on a bible and a brick.

The electricity failed one night. It chose an awkward moment as I was left in underpants and a flannel-sized towel halfway between my wooden hut and the shower. The horned gecko by the light bulb would be deprived of dinner this evening. Dressed, I made my way by torch light to the Hotel de la Gare hoping my dinner had not also have been abandoned. M. Joseph, *le patron*, immaculate in a double breasted white suit (a pity about the flip-flops), beamed a smile of matching dazzle and waved me into the beamed railway booking hall that glowed with candles propped in the bottles of yesterday's dinner. After a meal to rival any on the Rive Gauche, the coffee, locally grown, freshly roasted and crushed was all the more authentic for the accompanying Nestlé sweetened and condensed milk that oozed from a sticky punctured tin. As I paid the £3 bill (and that included the beer), *le patron* apologised profusely for the inability of the cook to produce a better dinner: "He has tried his best but the charcoal was damp."

The road to the coast twisted through fields robbed of forest and left to the scrub of wild *rubus* and *grevillea*. In a small local town all but two of the many stalls sold fruit. Bananas were in several varieties – large plantains, pigmy 'ladies' fingers', stubby over-ripe red ones and sculptural green ones; here were custard apples, jackfruit, papaya, mangosteen and others I could not recognise. The exceptions were a table piled with the blackened hoops of smoked eels and one where wine was being poured into little bottles through a paper funnel – this had the longest queue. We turned off the road down a track heavily fissured by previous storms and now turned to toffee by the present rain. Réné, our driver, kept the bus going with safari skill but at a wooden bridge where only two rows of single planks were provided, a front wheel slipped off to wedge in the gap between the beams. The seven widows, giggling with fright or the adventure of it all, crept off the bus while the three men lifted the wheels back and as cameras were held ready to catch the moment I fell into the mud of the river.

Verreaux's Sifaka

At our thatched beach hotel, rum punches in three kaleidoscopic layers that matched the sunset were served up on the house and I added a few extra on the bill. How quickly a damp, dull evening can be brightened by a punch or three! The shore of the Indian Ocean is unfriendly here, with great breakers, a fierce undertow and sharks. Our sand bar, only 300 ft (90m) wide, keeps the ocean from swallowing the fresh water lakes and canals of the Pangalanes that run north south along the eastern coast. Along the sand bar there is a railway but the trains stopped five years ago, abandoned for lack of mechanical expertise and spares and the booking halls of the little stations now provided homes for families of brown babies, black chickens and green geckos. Tropical weeds cracked open the platforms. The track of rusted rails was now for foot traffic only but the stones were sharp and the rotting sleepers irregular, so the locals walked along a rail like brown skinned Blondins; if you spend your life carrying your possessions and your shopping on your head, balance requires little effort or concentration.

I had a visitor as I slept. Four biscuits left on the table for tomorrow morning's early tea had vanished and two tomatoes bought in one of the colonised railway stations had been nibbled. Opinions around the breakfast table varied from tenrecs (a type of hedgehog) to hypogeonys (a giant jumping rat). Our leader, David Sayers met a spider as big as his hand and when he squashed it, it bounced across the wooden boards like a rubber ball; I was rather apprehensive that its vengeful brother might have come and demand a retribution ransom of Butter Osbornes that night. I had my Swiss army knife ready.

The roof of my hut blew off; the rain was a degree off horizontal, my bed lifted in each gust and the sea surfed through the door and swept me out of the back window. I awoke from my dream to find that the downpour had discovered convenient spots in the palm thatch to drip onto my pillow and camera. But with the storm past, the diamond studded skies of indigo velvet, the dawn, the chattering of wild life waking and the surf marking the rippling boundary of the warm ocean, all gave the island the romance so exploited by tellers of tropical tales.

In the early morning we pushed off in the African Queen, a wooden boat from which weevils had had several good meals and with a patched canopy to shield the sun. It seemed the perfect way to chug through the inland waterways, hung around on either bank by eucalyptus, palms, elephant leaves and strands of strappy grasses. Our sinewy boatman with three teeth and a poor razor sat on the outboard motor while his friend in the bows spotted for stray bamboo logs and propeller clogging clumps of water hyacinth. Fishermen in pirogues hollowed from a tree trunk were out tending fish and eel traps or wading with a weighted net near the shore. After four hours the activity on the river and the banks increased. Wooden planks lashed haphazardly together and topped with a makeshift shelter were being laboriously poled and there were pirogues loaded with wood, some with a pathetic sail patched from sacks.

The landing at Tamatave, beside the oil refinery with its sour and shiftless water of a curious green and dense viscosity, was reached after six hours. Our transport had not appeared – *plus ça change* – and I took a *pousse-pousse* rickshaw to the Hotel Joffre, the hangout of the ex-pats. The journey was hazardous as my sweating 'driver' negotiated truck sized pot holes, cars that drove on the pavement to avoid them, piles of rubbish and the familiar assortment of fritter fryers, chickens, children and now, in this important regional town, a colourful scatter of smart young women and demure nuns. The town was devastated by cyclone Geraldo in 1994 and on many roofs of corrugated iron, tyres or bags of sand lay in anticipation of the next big blow. The *pousse-pousse* had a twisted wheel and a loose shaft and the strange corkscrew movement brought back a memory lost for 40 years of riding a lame camel from Bir Fucquum to the town of Aden. At the Joffre, the biggest crevettes are known as 'Coriande' and I had half a dozen swimming in garlic and served on white china and a less than white table cloth. The hotel provided the salvation for all those returning from a few days in the bush – a hot shower.

On the forest road a convoy of *taxi-brousse* and vans waited to cross a river on a pontoon poled across with sweating effort by two boys. At the centre of the river pirogues were tethered while divers with scoops and buckets gathered sand from the river bed six feet (2m) below. When full to the water line, the pirogues were pulled to the shore and the sand shovelled up the high steep banks in four separate stages to await sale by the track. At other places, women hammered at boulders to reduce them to walnut sized pieces for use in concrete. Clumps of arum lilies grew on the margins, each throwing up 20 or more waxy white trumpets and in the forest, *methonia* ablaze with scarlet and orange flowers, lit up the canopy, its petals scattered on the ground like tropical confetti. The peeling bark of eucalyptus was caught in sunlight and wild cinnamon spiced the air.

My neighbour on the returning Air France flight was short and hairy with a Neanderthal jawbone and clad ankle to wrist in scarlet robes embroidered with intricate patterns. I took him for an Ethiopian bishop. Silent for an hour, he suddenly asked to borrow my two week old Economist, checked the bond prices, uttered disapproving tut tuts and then, putting a thumb in each ear, hummed for an hour or two. Whether in prayer to ease a private fear, to lessen the pain of falling financial futures or as a composer I could not tell. It seemed an appropriate farewell to an island where the unexpected was the convention and the only surprise was a day that lacked surprises.

Burma I

February 1999

'The Burmese are a curious crew;
The girls wear skirts and boys do too.
The boys wear hats but girls refrain
And view such fads with much disdain.'
– U Myint Thein (1900-1994)

The plane from Bangkok to Rangoon seemed full of old walnuts – smiling, nodding and for the most part spectacled walnuts. A Burmese Buddhist contingent was returning home, probably from their last monkish convention judging from the wrinkled faces that melded by colour, crease and crinkle into the brown robes wrapped around them. Searching inside his cotton shell, one venerable pulled out a packet of sandwiches which were chomped between two rows of gold teeth and each had a fan in an embroidered zippered cover – monks too collect souvenirs.

Arriving at the country of my birth 55 years later was not quite as nostalgically thrilling as I had expected – "A bit of a wet firework?" Johnny my guide remarked later. The airport was too large, too clean and too imposing for memories nurtured on family albums half a century old but later at the Hotel Pansea, nostalgia returned. Converted from an old merchant house the hotel attractively combined teak, stone, flowing water, flowering plants and noisy birds and in the cooling day, on a huge shady veranda, amongst rattan furniture and potted plants, I drank tea brought soft-footed across teak boards by sweet smiling boys skirted in longyis. For a moment the Old Burma of faded photographs and family tales surrounded me and close at hand, my mother laughing and my father calling his bearer.

A search for my infant haunts was both frustrating and fascinating. With my guides, Johnny, Joshua and George – oddly all Anglican Christians, we questioned

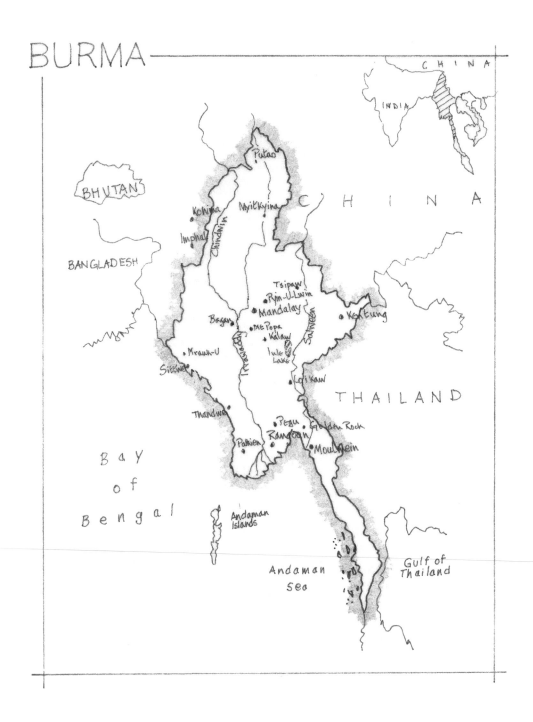

old inhabitants and searched older maps to identify English addresses renamed in a post-independence burst of nationalism. A copy of my birth certificate from the Corporation of Rangoon drew a big smile from the superintendent of the Dufferin Women's Hospital; one home remained undiscovered but another, in an idyllic spot beside Inya Lake, was intact. Trees taller, a swimming pool added and secured by guards and high walls but otherwise exactly as the little photograph I carried. When it turned out that this was the home of President Ne Win's daughter, Joshua turned pale. Telephone calls and the story of my family's occupation opened the gates, I took new photographs, left a note and returned to my greatly impressed guides.

On my last day, just as I was packing for the third time a basket of cabin trunk proportions to fit in my purchases, U Moe Zaw, Dr Win's husband telephoned. "We live on the way to the airport as you know, so why not just pop in?" He and his wife were charming, interested in the history of the house and offered egg sandwiches and tea of a strength usually found on building sites in cold weather. Although there were two large black Mercedes in the drive, the house was simple, plain, airy but without air-conditioning. "It was an absolute wreck when we came. We had to do it over top to toe." I felt I might have been visiting a friend showing off a newly restored farmhouse. I showed them the old photograph and we chatted about our children, travelling in the countryside and congestion in the towns. I made a wide detour around politics, a neighbour came to call and then it was time to go. Considering I had been entertained by one of the most powerful and influential couples in the country – a president's daughter and the president of several of the country's largest companies – my visit was remarkable in its normality. Johnny was ecstatic with the story he could tell and the driver almost hit the gatepost his hands quivered so on the wheel.

Lack of paint and the rigours of tropical decay have left grand old colonial buildings in downtown Rangoon looking forlorn and unloved. The exotic, bustling images from the family photograph book were now fractured, abused, frail, shabby and weary. It was a city sad and skeletal. Old Burma hands might shed a tear but many buildings are preserved by the present regime so that new money from Singapore and Hong Kong, intent on new offices and hotels, must leave exteriors intact. Ochre wash, fretwork balconies and dormers, wooden window frames, classical façades, turrets and brick to match the medium roast complexion of the passersby, remain to mask the air-conditioned interiors. Many multi-storey blocks of flats were under construction and their lower floors were at a premium since the absence of lifts and the lack of water pressure make the top floors attractive only for the fit or impecunious. In the streets, crowded buses dating from World War II jostled with Japanese cars and pedalled rickshaws. Isolated

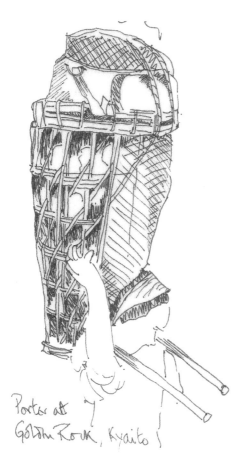

Porter at
Golden Rock, Kyaito

by a military dictatorship, Rangoon was helpless. There was no bounce or buzz; instead it was a city without ambition which, like a family dominated by drunken parents, had succumbed to despair. There was no challenge and no defiance.

The ferry to Twante was as rusty a hulk of dented metal as ever had the miracle to float. Oozing oil into the Rangoon River with every riveted plate complaining in buckled protest of labouring on decades after a visit to the scrap yard would have brought an honourable end, the double-decked tub turned into the rising sun, swung north on the ebbing tide and headed upstream. On the decks, amongst the fumes of diesel, the stink of old fish and pungency of chilli and spices from the stern kitchen, squatted farmers, monks, giggling teenage nuns draped in cherry pink, dour soldiers, cheroot-smoking grannies and an assortment of children. Smaller cross-river ferries rowed or powered, darted about like gnats and later on, as we belched between the banks of flat land, barges, lighters and all manner of river traffic universally overburdened with goods or humanity hooted as we passed as though in mutual recognition of the good fortune of surviving this far. I shunned the first class section, distinguished only by a table and a slatted bench, and sat down with my back to the funnel to watch the early morning mist rise off the dry paddy fields where families were already busy winnowing rice.

Any piece on Burma cannot avoid mentioning that formidable and defiant champion of the people, Aung San Suu Kyi. I could not get closer than a couple of hundred yards (180m) to her house as the street was blocked and a guardhouse was built at each end; to have walked down the street would have meant certain arrest and probable deportation. Johnny summarised what he felt was the national mood.

"In people's hearts, Suu Kyi is already elected. We are simply waiting Ne Win's death and the subsequent revolution."

He needed patience; Ne Win was then eighty-eight and reputedly booked into a Singapore hospital each year for a full service including, disgustingly, a total transfusion with teenagers' blood. Johnny, thirtyish and intelligent, was a Karen whose people were something of a thorn in the sensitive flesh of the government (and all previous governments) since they sought autonomy. A different view of The Lady was told to me over dinner with an English businessman resident in Rangoon for four years and about to give up the unequal struggle of international communications.

"Suu Kyi is worshipped by the people for sacrificing for them her children, her husband and her life but in practice she is dogmatic, arrogant, has few substantive policies and maintains a stubborn insistence on non-negotiation with the military."

The views of both guide and businessman may have been exaggerated but the problem was clearly complex when you tossed into the political wok the further ingredients of 135 different tribes – some of which had secessionist ambitions – ill-advised western sanctions, powerful drug barons in the Golden Triangle, succession squabbles amongst the governing 20 generals (some with surprisingly liberal views) and the country's relatively unimportant position on the geo-political map.

A tide of souls searching for salvation flowed around the great Schwedagon, the most sacred pagoda in Burma and the world's largest. Small groups constantly moved in and out of shrines special to their cause bearing candles to light or gifts of money and flowers. They prostrated themselves or squatted for a while, their hands held out in supplication, before leaving their offerings and then, their moment of individuality gone, they were swallowed by the surging crowd. Strong currents of laughter, fun and festivity added a froth and sparkle to this great inspirational river of humanity and its vivacity was contagious. It was also bizarre: coloured neon encircled one Buddhist image, flashing lights surrounded another and mirror and pastel paint turned others into replicas of seaside ice-cream parlours. A bust of Bo Nin Guang, a celebrated wizard (the guidebook's word not mine) was continually pressed with cigarettes since, as a heavy smoker, it was thought that this would help him cope with the afterlife. If the cigarettes did not account for his demise in this life, the seven smouldering fag ends and two cheroots stuck in his mouth and stuffed up his nose will certainly finish him off in the next. Everywhere there were brown robed monks, some joking, some praying; a group of novices in a corner were listening to the radio. Nuns, with shaven heads and wrapped in pink with an orange sash over their left shoulder were more serious. Every minute of every day of every year, these episodes of individual pleasure, devotion, redemption, hope and enlightenment pass around the Schwedagon. As the sunset emblazoned the gold leaf of the stupa and warmed the whitewashed walls of the monastery buildings, my initial impression of a fairground turned to one of magic and mystery and took on a more intense spiritual quality.

The vicissitudes of the Burmese are many but beneath their languid and ever amiable exterior there clearly resides a resilience that has enabled them to overcome a poor standard of life and centuries of hardships. The Buddhist philosophy is central to this exterior charm and inner strength. In Pagan, in a monstrous act of bullying, the government cleared away the old village and bulldozed the homesteads of generations with the excuse of letting an archaeological excavation take place; it never did and the reality was an obsessive anxiousness that the villagers might talk to the many foreigners who visit this area of great historical importance. In compensation, each householder was given one dollar, a bag of cement and three sheets of corrugated iron roofing. Having sold the roofing on the black market, they established a new village which now exists largely off tourism and appears relatively prosperous. If ever there was an example of the tenacity and determination of these charming people, there it was.

Our visit to Pagan coincided with the two months of the year that *shyn-po*, the novitation ceremony for young Buddhists to the monastery takes place, and propitiously, there was also a full moon. *Shyn-po* ceremonies are expensive and elaborate affairs with several families clubbing together and in the late afternoon one such group of participants was gathering. Six dancing girls, with much flicking upwards of palms and *jete* of feet pointing downwards, moved graciously in unison to lead the procession, followed by several loudspeakers blaring music painful in both harmony and decibel. The stars of the show came next: eight young boys on horses, gorgeously dressed in white with an array of costume jewellery banded around the chest, wrist and ankle and so heavily made up with lipstick and rouge and wearing such pretty earrings that I had the unsettling thought that they were some paedophiliac prey. Their mounts, led by turbaned syces, were caparisoned in colourful harnesses and each novice had an attendant holding a golden umbrella. Behind the riders, 100 or more girls graded with the shortest in front shuffled through the dust in a long line in their best clothes, with blossom in their hair. Several were incomparably beautiful. At the monastery, the dancing girls went into their routine again and the riders, all looking rather dazed and solemn, sat before a venerable abbot who, suffering from Parkinson's disease, added some anxiety to the proceedings with the expectation that his spectacles would be shaken off his nose. In the evening there would be singing and dancing in the elaborate and dazzlingly colourful tent that had been erected, and a feast for the whole village. Outside caterers had arrived that morning, dug pits for their fires, unloaded sacks of rice to be steamed, peeled a mountain of onions and pre-pared six great three foot (1m) wide dishes of lentil soup. The dozen cooks showed well-rehearsed efficiency and were expecting to feed 1,000.

From the central plains, the land rises to the east and here is found Inle Lake lying limpid and languid, mirror surfaced and framed by the Hazy Blue Moun-tains of the Shan State. As we arrived, chugging along the length of the lake, a glorious farewell of the setting sun in the west was met by a full moon rising over the mountain ridges to the east. Lotus and water lilies covered its margins and in the next morning's early morning mist, I watched a couple of fishermen in their flat-bottomed boats slap the water to scare the fish into their traps of great conical bamboo baskets. If unsuccessful, they stood in the prow and, curling their right leg around an oar row with a gondolier's corkscrew motion, moved to another spot. Later, on another day, sitting in a bamboo chair on the deck of a stilted hut with an iced G and T, a cheroot of *cordia* leaf, mosquito free, with rising fish occa-sionally rippling the calm water, Nirvana seemed to have been reached rather sooner than expected or deserved.

We journeyed around the lake in a long boat powered by a noisy engine stamped Shanghai Water Pump Company and equipped with yellow life jackets marked Thai Airways. Umbrellas of various origins were provided for sun protection and a line of passengers flying these fully extended looked like colourful toadstools. Water buffalo took obvious pleasure from walking along the bed of the lake just showing their nostrils and small boys standing on their back seemed to perform a miracle of walking on water.

The Burmese have some of the most attractive bodies on the planet. It is the lack of hips that make their silhouette so smooth and their walk so supple. Torsos start at the shoulder, pinch very slightly halfway down and then continue to the ground. The longyi emphasises the smooth vertical line as it drops from a knot at the waist to earth. Arriving in the country still smarting from Mr Cooper of Savile Row's remark, "A

Kalaw – Boys at play

Ox carts returning home

little winter thickening, sir?" such beauty was both a delight and an irritation. Teenage boys, hipless and skirted, are almost indistinguishable from teenage girls. The boys have a flawless complexion, teeth that outdazzle pearls, eyelashes that generate a breeze with a single blink and long elegant fingers. An occasion of gender guessing occurred when I had to endure not one but two nights of traditional music and dancing. Since the hotel staff were the performers, I was trapped between the soup and the noodles while they went to do their bit. The first night's performance was helped by votes taken around the table as to the sex of the gorgeous dancer got up in a tulle bodice, baggy trousers of silver brocade and a silly hat. The answer arrived the next morning in the shape of Huang the breakfast waiter with long greasy hair parted down the middle. The second night he performed an extraordinary dance holding two lighted candles and went into contortions that would have earned him a place in a travelling circus. He was again draped in several yards of nylon filigree and the patience required for sitting through this number was helped along immeasurably by the knowledge that a single miscalculation of writhing limbs would result in self-immolation.

The great, golden, balancing boulder at Kyaikto sits on a small rocky outcrop and, by legend, two hairs of the Lord Buddha. At 4,000 ft (1,200 m) it looks out over the jungle clad hills to the Andaman Sea. Leaving town, pilgrims and visitors alike are packed into an open truck to squat on rows of matchstick-slim planks raised on brick high blocks. On a road that makes the Big Dipper seem like an amble over the Malvern Hills, the driver, possessed either by demons or more probably high on betel, shot off and then accelerated through the hairpins. On crawling out battered and almost speechless with fear, several dozen boys with large wicker panniers strapped to their forehead then clamour for the custom of carrying your crushed luggage another vertical 400 ft (120 m) to the salvation of the hotel.

The path to the celebrated boulder was steep, hot and dusty. Along the way stalls provided walking sticks, drinks and assortments of herbal remedies from monkey guts to seedpods; prices rose relative to altitude. At the top, the Pagoda Precinct Dispensary was handily placed and a plaster group of Nats (spirits that embody human form and foibles) were comforting a fellow Nat laid out horizontally; I knew how he felt. A huge flat area was covered with a random selection of colourful tiles that seemed to have been salvaged from Victorian bathrooms and on one side were various buildings of tasteless design in shades of bright yellow and green. Here were happy family groups, pilgrims young and old, the penitent, the psychotic, the perspiring, a few curious tourists and a bus-sized boulder balanced on a hair of Buddha and covered with an inch (2.5cms) of gold leaf. A monk with a bad cough intoned spiritual words over a loud speaker as families squatted down for picnics. In a money-making wheeze, a replica of the mountain had little pockets around it to throw money into as it revolved under bright lights; the whole ill-repaired scene was noisy, gaudy and tacky. The famous rock was smaller than I expected but it shone nicely in the setting sun as more gold leaf was applied by the devout.

Two hundred and fifty miles (400 kms) northeast, another revered geological oddity is Mount Popa. An upturned cup of volcanic rock, it is topped by a turreted monastery painted bright viridian and sits like a child's sandcastle decorated with flotsam. I stopped to pay my respects to the Nats to ensure a safe journey. A dozen or two fashioned in their human form by plaster and paint were dressed as though for a fancy dress ball and were arranged in a line for supplicants to offer prayers or leave small gifts. One was hung about with bottles of gin and turned out to be the same fellow that in the Rangoon Schwedagon was pressed with lighted cigarettes; his first preference was apparently booze but this was deemed inappropriate in religiously austere surroundings.

Kalaw was reached late and in the dark. Weak bulbs and kerosene lamps threw thin light over the cluttered interiors of the small shops and their proprietors were wrapped in thick sweaters and woolly hats. My short sleeves and shorts raised no eyebrows in the restaurant where a few dusty bottles of Merlot and an Australian Chardonnay were as unexpected as the poster on the wall of a Ferrari against an Amalfi backdrop. At the Pinehill Hotel an old dog lay before a blazing log fire, there was polished wood on every surface, a vase of old fashioned sweet peas scented the air and eager dark and sinewy hands unloaded the dusty luggage. On the beds were thick blankets woven with giant roses in colours of hallucinating brightness, there were soap bars of Imperial Leather and Thermoses of hot water. It seemed the perfect journey's end.

Rudyard K. never travelled the Road to Mandalay. Neither flying fish nor the thunderous sun of this ridiculous poem are to be seen; just a tarmac strip straight, flat, paddied on each side and full of huge trucks moving slowly north to Mandalay and crawling south, diesel-stinking logging lorries with their immense loads of teak and ironwood from the forests of the Bago Hills. Indian communities, descended from those who built the railway at the turn of the century, live along the roadsides and add flashes of colour with saris in kaleidoscopic patterns. There is no speed limit on the roads and although the state of the surface and the age of most vehicles effectively set a maximum of 50 mph, hazards abound in stray dogs, pigs and water buffalo which continually cross with no regard to traffic. Amongst unprecedented chaos and accidents, driving was changed to the right in 1964 and since vehicles are still right-hand steered – even the new ones – they have to pull out from behind the bullock cart, trishaw, cannibalised lorry or taxi bus loaded seven layers high. Killing somebody means five years in jail regardless of whose fault it is but this seems no deterrent to speed or daring.

As we rattled northwards towards the teak forests the sawmills multiplied progressively, so that at Taungoo, 100 miles (160 kms) from Rangoon, I thought I might have come all this way just to view a mountain of sawdust. Turning off the highway, we bumped along a switchback forest road with precipitous slopes either side covered in bamboo and young teak. An hour later the forest camp was reached, clad in quisqualis, bougainvillaea and jasmine. It was quiet, windless and oppressively hot. I was in one of six rattan huts and Onido Suchi, a Japanese photographer, was in another; don't mention The War! He was big in teeth, short on eyes, had a camera lens the size of a howitzer and an 'assistant'. She was demure, giggled a lot and confided that she went to language school in Dublin; whatever course she enrolled in, it was not English.

In the cool of late afternoon I set out for the forest with Aung, the local naturalist guide. "We go for a little amble," he said and pausing only to shorten his longyi and tuck his curved knife into its waistband, he set off at a tremendous pace. I stumbled along behind with camera, binoculars and carrying my shoes – we spent a lot of time crossing rivers. Aung could spot an ant bending its knees at a hundred paces and two hours later we returned in the setting sun having seen green pigeon, woodpecker, hornbills, bee-eaters, sunbirds, egret, owls, rua, hawks, jungle fowl, brown and red squirrels and a wild boar. We had also slurped tea with a Karen local who demonstrated his astonishing accuracy with a catapult and chatted with another who had shot, killed and eaten three bears in the last year. Then I knew what the knife was for.

In the dry season, the elephants only work early in the morning as they find the day too hot but for a few hours they tugged and heaved with great effort and much grunting, while their mahouts (they stay with them for all their working life) instructed them by working their feet behind their ears. After a bath in the river the elephants ambled off with shackled front legs to forage in the forest. Trees are felled and extracted from the steep slopes by elephant (there are 1,500 working in this forest), sectioned by handsaw, loaded on trucks and taken 100 miles (160kms) to the saw mills (those that are not 'lost' on the way). 10,000 trees are cut each year and 10,000 planted; those being cut now were planted by The Burma Teak Company in the 1920s.

The barbecued barking deer for dinner was tough but tasty, the mosquitoes buzzed all night but the calling of birds at first light as the mist lifted performed its usual magic. Onido was in gumboots and a sort of sou'wester as he opened his bag of macrobiotic breakfast and Cho, my driver, tucked into a hearty curry. Onido fired off 100 shots, was amiable, impressively knowledgeable on trees, the assistant thought the elephants 'vely stlong' and none of us mentioned The War.

Images that settle in the mind later are pretty standard stuff but real nevertheless. Banyan trees, delicate ponies and traps, bullock carts stirring dust against the sun, stilted houses, bougainvillea, bicycles and bamboo; water buffaloes with small boys legs akimbo, cinnamon monks, sugarplum nuns, ice-cream coned pagodas. Winnowing rice, school children everywhere in green longyis, bodies of balletic grace and the strength of mules. More lasting is the spontaneous generosity of the people, their apparent indifference to social advancement, their care of animals (it might be their grandmother!) and their tolerance of the inevitability of divine consequence.

Postcard Home

Here in the jungle tigers roam
And apes and peacocks call it home,
While pachyderms push through bamboo.
I'm back to make a rendezvous
With friends of old and places new.
But on the road to Mandalay
Trudge those caught in the tourniquet
Of poverty and government
That rules by threat of 'prisonment.
When will this yoke be hurled aside
And this great race retrieve their pride?

Brazil

September 1999

'Not all those who wander are lost' – *J R R Tolkien*

The Varig in-flight magazine had a full page advertisement for armoured cars – effective against a .44 magnum. While South American politics have a reputation for turbulence, I had thought that truces were breaking out regularly. The implication that this might be premature added piquancy to the trip as I landed at Sao Paulo to change planes. Broadcasting the departure to Rio de Janeiro, the female announcer stroked the last four syllables with such mystery and sensuousness that anticipation for adventure oozed from the speakers; she followed up further flights to Recife and San Salvador with equal intrigue and excitement. Here, it is Mata Hari at the microphone breathing sedition and scandal.

The flight west passed first over Sao Paulo's shanty towns of rusted sheeting and then across grey-green, moisture-starved land, dotted with patches of ploughed red earth. No woods, no forest, no pockets of equatorial lushness, only a million acres hacked, burnt, harrowed and sown to feed the millions in their urban tin huts; then came the great coiling ribbon of the Parana River, ragged on each edge with fissures that reached far into the parched land. Near Campo Grande, areas of woodland appeared in strange irregular shapes like pieces of a scattered jigsaw and plumes of smoke rose where the arid picture was completed in charcoal and ash. The town sprawled over the flat grasslands and since the roofs of its suburban margins were tiled with the same red clay of the earth, it seemed smaller from the air than reality proved on the ground. At the airport, an incongruous mix of rotten wood and aluminium, there were public telephones concealed in giant plastic wood storks. Dark, tall, craggy men in worn jeans and scuffed high heeled

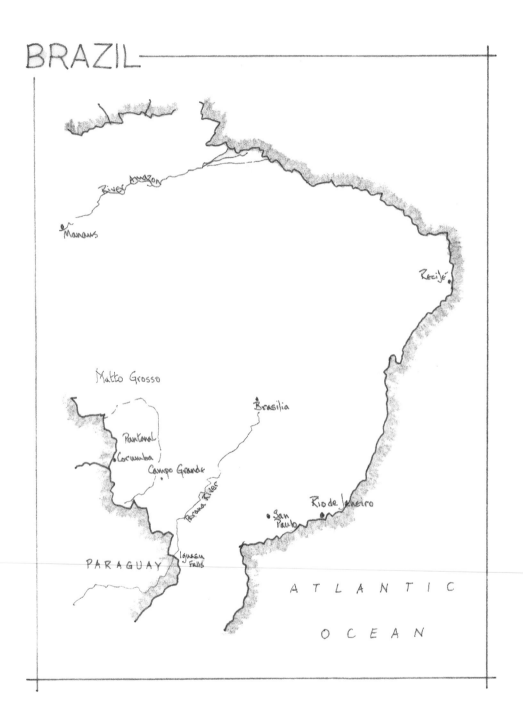

BRAZIL

River Amazon

Manaus

Recife

Matto Grosso

Brasilia

Pantanal

Corumba

Campo Grande

Parana River

Rio de Janeiro

San Paulo

PARAGUAY

Iguasu Falls

ATLANTIC

OCEAN

boots, strolled around with self-assured swagger, their legs bowed from lives spent in the saddle, and gave a whiff of romance and ruggedness.

"The bus should be here in an hour." After the weariness of 16 hours of continuous travel, to arrive with a hunger unsatisfied by that curse of long distance westerly travel – unceasing breakfasts – one of Brazil's national characteristics had already appeared. The country's motto, *Order and Progress*, sits unhappily beside its habitual lack of punctuality. You can try and excuse it – the climate is hot and what else is there to do anyway; psychologically examine it; rage over it; threaten all manner of menacing consequences if it continues; but you never get resigned to it. A party of Brazilians delayed us further, apparently unable to climb aboard until they had finished their conversation – another national affliction.

And then we were off on the road to Corumba – yes, Corumba, by golly! A single track narrow gauge railway snaked alongside the cracked tarmac. Electricity poles, each a slender twisted tree, gave a vanishing perspective to the road. For three hours, we swooped up and down the gradients, the surface sometimes scarred and holed and great trucks full of cattle packed sideways head to tail thundered past. Sometimes we swept down an avenue, at other times the scrub stretched to each hazy horizon. Many small wild animals lay in the roadside dirt, victims of the scurry across the man-made divisions of their territory. Later, rocky outcrops with flat tops like the tepuis of Venezuela appeared, circled by turkey vultures languidly riding abundant thermals. The road was edged with charred strips of land burnt by the Indians to encourage new grass growth, much as keepers in Scotland burn the heather but here it seemed that part of Brazil was perpetually in flames.

This was cattle country, sparsely dotted with grey zebu that moved slowly over the yellow grass making for the little shade that existed. Grand gateways on the road announced Estançia Jesu Maria, Fazenda Cordoba, and Poussada Paradiso. At some, well fed horses mingled with the bony cattle. Having passed through the roadside entrance of Estança Caiman, my destination, it took an hour to reach the ranch house (there are another three hours to drive out the other side). The estate of 150,000 acres (60,000 hectares) looked like Hampshire with palm trees.

"Oi!" said our guide on arrival. I looked around. "Who, me?" but in Portuguese it is not, "Oi! – You there," but, "Oi! – Hello." Our small party of eight included two chain-smoking Koreans whose only language seemed to resemble that of the family of peccaries that rootled around under the stilted lodge, two Germans and six Brazilians. One Brazilian was a singer (in high heels and a pint of Chanel), and another the president of Avon Brazil. "Ding Dong Avon!" he proudly and cheerily admitted. In the case of the Koreans, there was some initial difficulty in establishing their nationality. Carlos, a dentist from Sao Paulo, said they were

Mongolian, apparently deduced from their easy horsemanship and preference for lamb at every meal. The German couple (who, after they left, turned out to be the German Ambassador and his wife) insisted they were from northern China – he had once had a spell in Urumqui. As it turned out, I took the prize by drawing from a random selection of eastern countries and suggesting, "Korea?" Great smiles of recognition split their faces accompanied by much nodding and bowing. The tricky thing was then to discover the relevant half of the peninsula. While thumbs up indicated the top half, it simultaneously implied friendliness to dictatorial communist regimes. Conversely, thumbs down tended to show a disapproval of cheap televisions and computer assembly lines. I followed up with, "Daewoo?" whereupon they each shot out a hand to shake and with more beaming nods I found I had made two friends where the only word between us was a car whose name I could only ever call to mind by humming the Jamaican farewell, 'Day-o, Dayay-o'. Korea, England and the Caribbean were thus surreally united on the Brazilian pampas. To myself, I named the German ambassador King Kong (he was broad and hairy), the Koreans Ping and Pong, the entertainer Sing-Song and the Avon chief was, of course, Ding-Dong.

The tropical wake-up call is one of life's most exciting and satisfying pleasures. To lie in bed as an interloper on nature watching the sky brighten and the mist lift while howler monkeys whoop, macaws cackle, hornbills honk, chacochocalades have their first squabble, emerald ibis screech and mocking birds mock, is as wonderful a half hour as any I know but the rising sun soon exhausted the ritual and wonderment was rudely reduced as we went out to meet our horses.

"These are cowboy horses," said Adriana, broad of beam and smile and long in leg and patience. She added, "They are well trained, tough, nimble and like exercise. Don't pull on their bit as they get angry." I trembled a little at the thought of an involuntary exploration of the Pantanal on a beast that yearned to stretch its legs, simmering with an anger that might turn to violence as I pulled harder on the bit. "Keep a good distance since some of these horses like to bite. They enjoy riding through thorns, it scratches off dust and ticks. And one more thing, if you let your horse go into water, it may lie down." Added to this alarming advice was the juggle with a large camera, the binoculars around my neck, a note pad at the ready and a whip – for goodness' sake, what did I want with a whip! The boyhood envy of the Lone Ranger's carefree life vanished with the reality of the rigours of the saddle.

In the event Tonto, as I charitably christened my bay gelding, was a friend from the start. I daresay my weight gave him second thoughts about exercise but he patiently braced himself as I heaved myself aboard and he responded instantly to the slightest touch of the plaited leather rein on his neck. A little practice showed that there was only a gram of pressure between pull for stop and pull more for reverse. We ambled through the prairie grass, avoided thorns, gave a wide berth to water and three hours later with a patronising pat to his rump, I slid off and with a John Wayne gait returned to base for embrocation and to offer a prayer for deliverance.

The Pantanal oozes life from every pore and I had favourite animals; the ringed coati was one of these. It is a large racoon that saunters in a dégagé manner with its long banded tail held vertically and several together look like a furry hula-hoop stall. They are gregarious creatures and small groups shuffle along in single file with the dominant male leading. When ousted from his kingpin position, this male

a campiero of the Pantanal.

remains alone and relieved of the responsibility of care and protection, becomes a slouch – fat and lazy and spending most of the day snoozing. Armadillos, on the other hand, incessantly scuffle around searching for bugs and worms. Poor sight but keen smell mean that they can be approached up-wind but within a few yards they sense something is amiss and trundle off, blundering through the grass like a miniature tank. The native cowboys catch them with a long pole and roast them, the unfortunate animal making its own self-immolating oven.

At this start of the dry season the dwindling pools known as *baias* and the connecting *corixo* channels force caimans to come together. Normally solitary individuals, a fish diet attracts hundreds to the same *baia*. "Never lost a guest yet," Adriana jokes for the fortieth time. I wish that the two Brazilians, who had spent the last two days laughing at each other's jokes with much back slapping and complete indifference to nature, might be the first exception to this unblemished record. In the hope of not only removing an irritation but also providing a sensational photographic scoop, I offer to take their picture and urge them closer to jaws that had opened

93

Fisherman on the
Rio Paraguai

an inch in anticipation. The fun is spoilt when the alert Adriana, no doubt equally irritated but anxious to return to base with the same tally of limbs as she started with, shouts a warning. Roseate spoonbills gather by the last waterholes glowing like candyfloss against the sun. Jabiru storks – white, with a fleshy band of scarlet around their neck – pace slowly and gravely along the sand on slim black legs, their heads bowed and shoulders hunched like trainee philosophers in thoughtful meditation. Hyacinth macaws, the largest of all the parrot family and as deep a blue as a tropical midnight sky, fly past in pairs cackling like old fashioned football rattles. Ornithologically they are *araca azura* which perfectly describes their call and their colour.

In the evening, the trees on the margin of the rivers and *baias* provide refuge for countless egrets, herons, cormorants and spoonbills. In the twilight they squabble for the best bed in the dormitory but at lights out, when every branch seems double booked, the chatter stops. Capybara and giant anteaters with large bodies to support continue to munch away through the darkness.

The Aquidauana River translates in the local dialect as 'Water of Yellow Fever'. I double checked my vaccination certificate and persuaded Ding Dong, Mrs Ding Dong and the two Koreans to take the trip. The former packed a small suitcase of lotions and anti-bug preparations and the latter an extra carton of Marlboroughs. Expecting something akin to the Limpopo but with extra fever trees, I took a flask of whisky. The trip did not start well. First, Ding Dong had to wait for a fax (although I had come 7,000 miles (11,200kms), to those who live out their steamy life in a Sao Paulo suburb, four days in the Matto Grosso is akin to leaving Fulham for a long weekend in the Lake District); the Koreans got into trouble by throwing stones at the cattle to make them stampede and then the truck had a flat tyre. On the way, several miles from the lodge, we stopped to look at turkey vultures feasting on the carcass of a dead cow and the truck would not restart; pushing was the only option. Whatever preconceptions one might have of the Brazilian economy and the resultant frequency of truck breakdowns, Mrs Ding Dong made it clear that in her back yard pushing five ton trucks was uncommon and undignified but Ping and Pong from the land of Daewoo took to it like professionals. Miraculously, although we only heaved it along a few feet, the engine fired. Mrs D.D. sat in the shade a while to recover and the Koreans each opened up a new pack of cigarettes. Thirty miles from base and beside a rotting carcass almost invisible with greedy vultures, I measured how many tots remained in my bottle of whisky.

The river turned out to be benign, beautiful and bordered by flowering trees of yellow *Putrea* and purple *Ité*. Nothing bit nor buzzed and not a fever tree in sight. We pottered gently along in an aluminium dingy slowing for caiman, capybara, herons, macaws, curassows and howler monkeys and then the Great Event occurred. In an uninteresting stretch where each bank was thick with tall grass and taller reed and several of us had taken the opportunity to nod off, the small boy sitting beside me in the stern suddenly bellowed, "JAGUAR!" If he had yelled, "INDIANS!" the effect could not have been greater. The boatman went instantly into reverse, heads swivelled like spinning tops and the Koreans shouted, "WOW, WOW, WOW," and kept shouting until sat upon.

There on the bank, lying relaxed and somnolent with one front paw over another, indulgent of noisy Koreans, disdainful of a boatful of breakfast and indifferent to any activity that might spoil a snooze, was a large male jaguar. Beautifully spotted, whiskers catching the sun, head up, ears pointed and with a coat that seemed woven in velvet, he exuded an air of arrogant supremacy. Fourteen rolls of film later and videos exhausted from hyper drive, he was still posing and then, stretching a limb or two, he turned his head to the boat, indicated the audience was over (I swear I saw him nod), scratched his nose and casually wandered off. The boatload broke into spontaneous applause.

The jaguar is secretive, rare and habitually nocturnal; to have seen it at all was exceptional, to gaze at it for 15 minutes extraordinary. We had urged the boatman to get nearer to the bank (the Koreans would probably have jumped off and hugged it) but he would not move from mid-stream and it was only later that he sobered the excited chatter by explaining that a jaguar can clear 20 ft (16m) in a single bound and we had floated to within 15 ft (4.5m). The encounter was the talk of the guides and the guests and a note to me from the Director asked if the Refugio Ecologico could have my photographs.

After three days, my new friends departed and I moved to another lodge and another guide. My room rested on stilts on the edge of a lake whose surface was carpeted with water lilies and in whose crystal water swam small pink fish and large, black, whiskered catfish. My new guide Mauricio was dark, handsome, seldom out of a T-shirt and shorts whatever time of day and, like Adriana, could identify most things that grew and everything that moved. Against the sun this was by gait or wing beat, in the forest by sound and when these were absent, he knew the tracks left in the sandy soil and dug around in dung and droppings to explain diet and seed dispersal. His enthusiasm went straight into top gear at breakfast and his accelerator was then set for maximum revs all day. In three languages he identified, explained, joked and encouraged. But he never patronised and was eager to learn from others with specialist knowledge. If he had been able to find an alternative for 'beautiful' that described every bird and 'wonderful' for every mammal, I could have tagged along in his tracks for weeks.

Manuelo, a local *campeiro* born and bred in the Pantanal, came with us one day. He wore a battered hat and had a *facoes* − a great knife that could slice hardwood like salami, stuck in a decorated leather sheaf in his trouser waistband at his back; his eyes could pick out a pigmy owl in a cup sized hollow or snails' eggs in a lake of hyacinths. He was only happy in a saddle and as with all *campeiros*, he liked a spirited horse to show off on. After riding at barely more than a trot for the day, he suddenly spurred his horse as we approached a village so that he could arrive at full gallop, the horse's mouth lathered with foam, its hocks sweating and create a small dust storm as he pulled up his steed and dismounted. With dark skin tanned to a walnut brown and cracked by the rigours of a life lived under the sun and stars and with a smile that split open his leather face like a pod about to shed its seeds, he was a character straight out of the pages of those books which librarians once classified under 'Travel and Adventure' and which I used to read with a torch under the bedclothes long after lights out. On the fifth day I said goodbye with warm handshakes and they waved until the dust blurred their farewells.

Back in the urbanity of Rio de Janeiro, there are few birds but many dogs, and early on Sunday mornings these are taken on slow preambulations by women with thin legs and flabby waists who then retire to flats with balconies from which they watch the later surfers, rollerbladers, bicyclists and joggers before they in turn give way to the hedonists of the beach. I looked on for a while too and then went to Petropolis with William. This was not the centre of Brazilian oil refining and William had no catapult or short trousers. The town was the early 19th century centre of the imperial court of Don Pedro de Orleans Bragança and William, bearded and bald and speaking not a word of English, gesticulated enthusiastically as he drove round the hairpin bends of the busy road which wound up the hills to the north of Rio.

Petropolis had once snuggled duvet-deep amongst forested hills but now a blan-

Jaguar on bank of Rio Paraguai

ket of urban sprawl reached up the sides, sometimes to the top, spreading modern clamour over previous tranquillity. On this particular Sunday, the cathedral was shut as was the Palacio Cristal (a poor and small replica of the Palm House at Kew) and the Palacio del Isobella was under repair but Don Pedro's palace introduced an insight into the stiff formality of the Portuguese ruling power. They had a useful wheeze there; on entering, each visitor steps into huge padded slippers with which you slide over the marble, terrazzo or wooden floors – a trick that English country houses might usefully adopt. In the stables, an English Merryweather fire engine, badly needing a polish to its brass equipment, incongruously sat beside an exquisite and dusty 19th century nobleman's landau.

Contemporary horse-drawn carriages clattered along the town's cobbled streets and the older houses had steep pitched roofs, painted stucco façades with timber decoration, and sat behind high walls and solid metal gates. Substitute the tropical vegetation for pine and remove the smell of sewage from the river and it might have been an alpine canton. William seemed unconcerned that the doors to history and prayer had been locked, possibly because his long frame needed one of its daily top-ups of meat. Food in this country comes in huge portions and apart from every meal's staple accompaniment of *feifao* – rice and beans – it consists of meat, meat and quite a lot more meat; well done or overdone. The prince of all eateries is the *churrascharia* and William hurried to what his excited gestures indicated was the best, the largest and the meatiest *churrascharia* he knew.

In these carnivorous establishments there is no menu in the conventional sense but a list of veggie side orders; deep fried potatoes, battered onion rings, sautéed cassava, fried beans, bread soaked in garlic butter and cauliflower with dripping. William ticked them all. Waiters continuously wove in and out of the tables, each with a sword of skewered meat. Grilled on an open fire, they drip juice and smell divine. Baby beef, rib of beef, neck of beef, haunch of beef – a small break for a skewer of chicken hearts, chicken feet and crispy pork fat and then beef steak, breast of beef, shin of beef, tail of beef. As an example of carnage and gluttony it has no equal but half a cow and several poultry dented my pocket only a tenner.

The downhill journey to Rio was slower and weightier. At every other bend or so it seemed, William exulted me to take a picture with accompanying *oba! cho-cante!* or *tudo bom!* In the heat haze, the smog and the failing light I might as well have photographed the interior of a Loch Fyne smokery; in any case I was too busy picking from my teeth rib of beef, tail of beef, neck of beef, shin of beef…

Ethiopia and Eritrea

November 1999

'Do not follow where the path may lead. Go instead where there is no path and leave a trail'
– Ralph Waldo Emerson

I chugged across Lake Tana in the Northern Ethiopian Highlands nursing a heavy cold I had brought from England. Sitting in the stern of a small passenger boat under a patched pink canvas canopy, I watched the pelicans, African darters and swallows skim the olive surface of the waters that feed the Blue Nile. All western Mediterranean civilisation that was rooted in the culture of ancient Egypt owed its existence to Lake Tana. We were coming back from Kidane Mihiret, a 12th century monastery constructed like an African roundel under a grass roof with four great pairs of doors, each leaf cut from a single plank of cedar. A young monk with a ready smile, a yellow robe and holding a key to a rusty padlock had put his shoulder to one of these planks and sunlight had poured in to light floral chintz curtains. These twentieth century garlands of roses were drawn back to reveal the bright colours of the Christian story naïvely and sometimes brutally depicted. Jesus and his family were, of course, black.

I had come to Ethiopia for its extraordinary Christian culture, its bird life, its dramatic landscapes and its people. I had come with some urgency believing that its current political stability in a corner of Africa hardly discovered by tourists needed to be savoured quickly; I was mistaken, there was no rush. The Ethiopians are proud (they are the one country in Africa that has never been colonised) but they are hopelessly, desperately poor. This was fundamental poverty exacerbated by a civil war; it will take a generation just to provide sanitation.

"You!" The finger pointed straight at me. "You, out." The battered bus had stopped by a barrier of multi-coloured ropes knotted together at Wondo Genet,

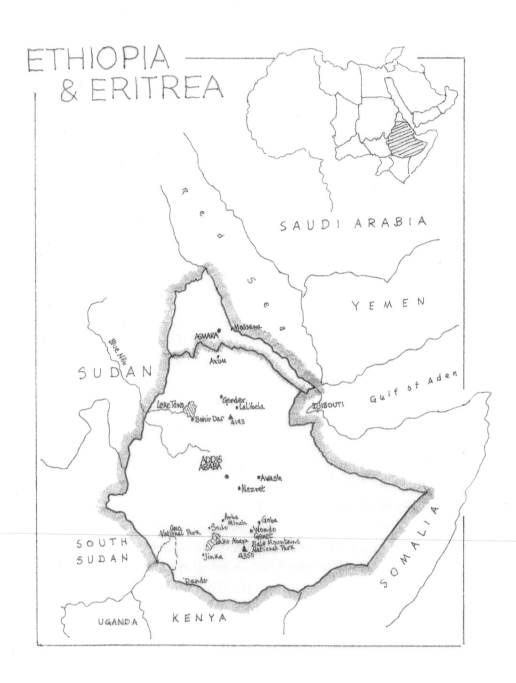

ETHIOPIA
& ERITREA

SAUDI ARABIA

YEMEN

SUDAN

Blue Nile

AGMARA •   • Massawa

Axúm

Gulf of Aden

DJIBOUTI

• Gonder
• Lalibela
Lake Tana
• Bahir Dar   ▲ 4143

ADDIS
ABABA
•
• Awash
• Nazret

Omo
National Park
• Arba
Minch
• Sodo   • Goba
• Wondo
Genet
Lake Abaya   Bale Mountains
National Park
• Jinka   ▲ 4350

SOUTH
SUDAN

SOMALIA

• Dande

UGANDA   KENYA

a small town in a fertile valley of Southern Ethiopia, cut into the escarpment of the Rift Valley before the ground eases gently down to the lushness of the Omo Valley and Lake Turkina. The customs post monitored the sale of chat, the mildly hallucinogenic leaf of a shrub whose young growing tips are plucked and chewed occasionally by Ethiopians but are almost part of the national diet of the Yemeni. It forms an important export trade through Djibouti. The shoots are packed into round nine-inch long bundles, wrapped in banana leaves and secured by strips of acacia bark. The customs officer, distinguished from other villagers by a leather jacket and undarned trousers, had seen me photographing the loading of the morning's consignment but it seemed he only wanted to assert an authority quite disproportionate to his official duties. A little while later he had taken my photograph, I had taken his, a few birr had changed hands and all was well.

Wondo Genet lies half way up a thickly forested mountainside and its attraction, apart from the lushness of its surroundings, is its thermal pools. These are owned by a small hotel, which included a separate and far better appointed bungalow previously used by Haile Selassie. A smaller, shallower pool had been constructed for him since at 5' 3" (1.3m) he was a foot shorter than his fellow, long-limbed countrymen. The water comes straight out of the mountainside at 90°F (32°C). On our previous two stops, hot water had been unobtainable but here, typically in this country of inconsistencies, it was cold water that was unobtainable. The overnight dew lay heavily on small plantations of bananas, papaya, coffee and pepper. Higher up the valley it was maize and tefe, the small-grained wheat with which the Ethiopians make a solid, tasteless bread. Hornbills honked in the fig trees, a hooded vulture (that disarmingly grunts like a pig) stared with shrunken shoulders from the frangipani and a troop of colobus monkeys, trailing their white tufted tails, looked down inquisitively from the tamarind trees.

In a country as poor as Ethiopia, clothes are an important indication of status. Elderly men invariably had a jacket, a hat and either a walking stick or a rolled umbrella, although I never saw one opened. Women, on the other hand, often used an umbrella against the sun and wrapped a long cotton shawl with a broad embroidered border around their bodies and over their heads. Sometimes these were brightly coloured but were always white for church. Laundry lists invariably listed petticoats and aprons. Urban teenagers wore the discards of a richer world and there was a thriving second-hand clothes market where savvy dealers knew the value of designers' labels whether counterfeit or genuine.

The Ethiopian Orthodox Church has its own seat on the World Council of Churches and in a remarkable line of religious conformity, dates back without interruption to the 12th century. At Axum, by legend if not in fact, lies the Ark of the Covenant and in almost every church St George is depicted slaying a dragon

Hermit

and St. Michael and the Angel Gabriel – each with black curly hair – guard the doors. The Sunday congregations that fill every church would make an English clergyman pack his bags for orthodoxy and this in spite of a service so long that special sticks are provided with a T-piece that fits under an armpit and allowed one foot to be rested on the knee of the other leg. Thank God those missionaries were never sent forth in this country to reap their destruction of local culture and ethnic customs. Here, uniquely in Africa, Christianity was firmly in place before St Augustine and the Ethiopians have remained religiously unblemished.

I had started at the agricultural southern half of the Ethiopian highlands. Wheat, maize, sunflowers, tomatoes and potatoes grew from soil tilled with a single timber plough behind a pair of oxen. This was also cattle country and brahmins, longhorns and zebu were herded by small boys with long sticks. This country has water to spare, but it is nevertheless back-breakingly hard to move from source to user and involves donkeys strapped with old jerry cans, probably left over from the civil war, lengths of inner tube tied each end or more often, huge clay calabashes balanced on the head or tied to a stooping back.

Around Nazret, the land was divided between five different tribes – one of which, the Danakil, required a young bachelor to kill a male from another tribe and as proof, cut off his penis and hang it around his neck; he was then sufficiently manly for marriage. As we drove through the villages, every man seen with an ornament on a thong around his neck caused hoots of excited recognition.

Although the country was almost self-sufficient in food, anything requiring manufacture needed to be brought in and that meant containers and their recycling was a business of its own. In Addis Ababa, half a shelf was taken up by peanuts sold in bottles – curiously all Johnny Walker Red Label. Barrel ends were cut and lipped for cooking pots, small saucepans were made out of tins and stalls whose sole business was to provide containers of every kind, shape and material were in every market. On internal flights with Ethiopian Airlines, plastic cups were gathered in carrier bags, paper napkins were torn into quarters and plastic spoons often washed between courses.

For a week spent in the less visited south, hot water had been unavailable with sanitation inevitably suffering in consequence and it was often smelly (of Dettol if you were lucky). But now, moving into more discriminating territory inexplicably no cold water was provided. There is something quite alarming the first time you see steam coming out of the loo cistern. Having manufactured a bath plug (the cap of a deodorant spray fitted nicely), I ran a bath and came back in an hour and a half after it had cooled to a temperature that left the body *'à point'* rather than *'seignant'*.

One of the southern stopping off spots was the Awash Gorge where the camp sat perched on a rocky rim 1,000 ft (300m) above the muddy but fast-flowing river. The accommodation was in caravans which were labelled 'Lindwalt Corp., Indiana'. Perhaps at the time they were bought, at least 30 years ago, they were bankrupt stock or an end of line bargain. The caravans provided adequate accommodation and were rather cosy, but it was disappointing that local materials had not been used which would have at least blended against the background of Ethiopia's premier wild life park. This was one of the places where hot water was unavailable and arriving late I read the notice pinned to the inside of the door: 'To call room service, please be to open the door and call "Room Service".' I duly bellowed into the dusk but no one came. In the morning, I saw that the staff quarters were out of hearing range and reading the notice more closely found additional words on the bottom. 'Please do not call loudly as others may sleep.'

The Amharic language is a joke. If you took the alphabets of Arabic, Cyrillic, Sanskrit and Greek, broke them up into pieces tossed them in a calabash, randomly glued together the legs and curly bits of this entomological stew you might get something that was close. There are 216 letters which are then arranged backwards for reading right to left. Many small boys would attach themselves like a leech at the various tourist spots to give you their address, written on a small piece of paper and ask you to be their 'letter friend'. You might distrust their ability to write a Roman script but they do so with an easy flow of capital letters. I suppose if you had to grapple with Amharic, this was something of a doddle.

Moving north, the mountains grew sharper and the tourists increased tenfold as they followed the Trail of Historic Cities. This is a well trampled route that takes in Axum, Gonder and Lalibela. This last tethering post is in the central highlands and has secured a UNESCO commendation for its unique churches. Sliced into the soft rock there would be no sign of them were it not for the flotsam of tourist tack that surrounds them.

With a sturdy horse and its bearded owner, I trekked one day up to Ashetan Maryam where there was a celebrated church cut into the cliff face. The way was steep and stony, the views (the church lies at 10,300 ft (3,150m)) stupendous and the caretaker monks persuasive with their plea for alms. I walked up and back, no doubt to the relief of the horse, but to the consternation of its owner who was clearly anxious that his tip might be in jeopardy. I had secured carrots from the hotel kitchen before setting out and at the end of the trip prepared to give these to my untried and possibly undeserving steed. At first, its owner thought the carrots were for him but then with much grumbling he took off the bridle so that I could offer up my vegetarian gift. The ungrateful beast chewed them once and then spat them out.

Returning to my hotel down the dusty track to the village, I came upon a teenage girl laden with school books; I had passed her school earlier. Two weeks in Ethiopia develops an immunity towards teenagers in multi-patched trousers and discarded tee-shirts. They tag along and engage one in conversation with words that seem to originate from an identical text book. They are soft words and are usually effective, since they come with friendliness rather than grabbing opportunism, but are seldom rewarded since a gift to one requires gifts to a dozen. This teenager had disarming frankness, her continual chatter and her tee-shirt emblazoned 'Chicago Bulls' were probably responsible for the fact that it had not crossed my mind that she had clearly spotted a middle-aged, male and affluent European and chased after him. But Zed was different; she was a girl – sixteen she told me – and a girl had never fallen in step beside me; they were too disciplined by the morality of a peasant society that is severe on any hint of female promiscuity. "Just call me Zed," she said breathlessly, "everyone does." Her full name was Zwedtu Genanu, so Zed it was.

Her parents had died in the famine of 1985 and her elder brother now had useless withered arms as a result of malnutrition. She had been brought here by one of the aid agencies and later had been able to recover a little of her parents' money. Not that this information was volunteered since she prattled on about her school, her teacher, her friends, her wish to become a guide and her worries about her brother. Any questions I asked as to her circumstances were answered promptly and then she set off on a different subject. It seemed that she accepted her orphaned status, her dependant brother, her prospects of continual hard work and no money, simply as the rather trying and irritating facts of life. Here the harsh realities of survival were linked to a likeable honesty.

We reached the centre of the town, circled a baobab tree, stepped back to allow mules to pass laden with a great heaps of dried haricot beans and retraced our dusty steps down the hill. "Please come and see my house," Zed said, "I would like to show it to you." I was wary and apprehensive of a monetary or honey pot trap. Also, it was getting dark and a cold beer and a shower beckoned. "Look, it is just there." She pointed down a small path that wound over a stream beside a patch of potatoes. It sounded interesting, genuine and intriguing. "Well, just for a few minutes." She led me over the stream, past the potatoes, round a huge boulder which had hidden the view of two small girls who herded their goats to the evening safety of a thorn enclosure and up a few steep steps cut into the earth. For the equivalent of £10 she had bought 800 sq ft (25 sq m) of this hillside, dug into it to

provide a level space, terraced below it for her garden of maize, tomatoes, cucumbers, beans, potatoes, squash, marigolds and a pink rose. Then she had built her round house out of wattle and mud, roofed it with dried grasses and secured the door with rusting corrugated sheet. She invited me to sit on a log of wood, placed with other boxes and logs on a spotlessly clean earth floor and introduced me to her disabled brother. Her whole life and all her possessions were here; some of these, such as school books and a jar of oil with a string wick for a light, were tucked into hollows in the wall. In an area half the size of my English country kitchen she had built a house, a garden and her life.

She collected water for her plants from the stream in a huge clay calabash, balancing this on her back bent double and with a woven strap around her forehead. She was also growing wheat so that she could grind her own flour and bake her own bread and was largely self-sufficient except for charcoal, oil, meat and clothing. As I got up to go, I asked her how much these things cost each month; 20 birr she said, with the expression of a worried housewife and the tone of voice that made it clear how outrageous she felt this was. I gave her 50 birr (about £5) which would support her for two months and she dropped to her knees and burst into tears. When she had recovered a little, I asked her what she would really like and she said some files for her exercise books since they were badly made and kept falling apart, and an English dictionary. I promised to send these.

As I stepped down the earthen steps, past the pink rose and the lines of vegetables and climbed back up the hill to my bath and beer, I felt I had made a good investment in Ethiopia's future. (Back in England I dispatched a large parcel via DHL but I never heard back. I had to draw a map on the outside; I hope it was understood.)

Turning east, past the stylae at Axum and then through a parched and stony landscape, I crossed into Eritrea. Here was a country that had spent 20 years

Lalibella
Bet Giorgis (13ᵗʰ

fighting an enemy ten times its size, and yet, only two years after winning, there was prosperity all around. Asmara, the capital at 7,400 ft (2,400m) in the Central Eritrean Highlands, was spotlessly clean, its people well dressed, not a beggar in sight, new Opel taxis cruised the palm lined streets and prices were half those of Ethiopia. In a country about the size of Britain, it offers dramatic mountain scenery, harsh desert, miles of white sand along the Red Sea and above all, a delightful and tolerant people. No doubt this toleration stems from Muslims and Christians (the latter being the Catholic Church and the Ethiopian Orthodox Church) living side by side for almost 1,000 years and the huge determination of a people united in rebuilding their country. The debris of war was still there and rusty Russian tanks lay in unexpected places – the middle of a corn field, at the bottom of a chasm or stuck through the wall of a house; six wheels of an upturned APC were now garlanded with bougainvillea and thousands of strategic hill tops were fortified look out posts. But mountain roads, severely damaged by the tracked vehicles of an Ethiopian army half a million strong were being rebuilt, hotels had been repaired, cinemas were opening and public services functioning.

Solomon Abraha of Travel House International beamed excitedly. "You have signed the first American Express ticket ever in Eritrea. I will blow it – is that right? – and hang it on the wall." He introduced me to my driver, Belai Haile Mariam, one of five brothers. The oldest was a distinguished resistance fighter partly responsible for the huge underground hospital built into the mountains and who was now governor of one of the five provinces. Two brothers had died in the war and another was at Frankfurt University. They seemed to exemplify the struggles of the past and the hopes for the future.

The road to the Red Sea port of Masawa must rank as one of the most dramatic on the continent. Dropping 8,200 ft (2,500m) in 55 miles (80kms), it twists through three different climate zones and countless geological formations that range from huge boulders to shale and a palette of rock colours that change through red and orange to black and white; sometimes in vertical stripes, sometimes in horizontal layers. Acacia thorns give way to hillsides dense with cacti, giant lobelia, eucalyptus and the scrub of the desert coastline. Herds of goats and sheep were everywhere and groups of camels, carrying salt from the evaporating pans along the coast, were a continual hazard. Most of the camels were on the way to the Sudan, 250 miles (400kms) to the north and the main road was their most convenient way up to the highland plateau.

Masawa itself is two linked islands joined to the mainland by a causeway constructed during the Italian colonisation. Here was some of the fiercest fighting of the war – not a building was unscathed. Much of the damage has been made good but my small beach hotel was still riddled with bullet holes. I was the only guest but the tables were laid for 20. I shared the dining room with six cats and my bedroom with several families of geckoes. Typical of the air of optimism and enthusiasm, the owner was extending already and Italian beach parasols and chairs were arranged in anticipation of brighter days.

The influence of the Italians was still strong. The infrastructure was their real achievement and this included an extraordinary cableway up from Masawa and at 46 miles (75kms), the longest in the world. This had not worked for years and had recently been dismantled and sold to Pakistan. That distinctive *fin de siècle* typography of the Italians was on many administrative buildings (along with Amharic and Arabic), *"ciao"* and *"cappuccino"* were part of everyday language and pasta was on every menu.

The Keren Hotel in Asmara was not the best but it had the faded charm of happier days. Built by an Italian at the turn of the century, its dining room walls were peeling off a layer of raspberry colourwash to reveal the previous mustard ochre. There was much rococo plaster work, mostly of satyrs and bunches of grapes. Leaving the hotel early on a Sunday morning I needed a taxi and this was a problem. The Ethiopian Orthodox church has just begun their two hour services, the Muslims had been called to prayer and the Catholics were at mass. The porter had a badge on his lapel which read 'Hall Porter on Practice Duties' but his initiative deserved a row of medals. Pausing only to bring me a croissant and a cappuccino, he called his father who drove a bakery van and I rode out to the airport amid the sweet smell of doughnuts and brioche.

At the departure gate I put my last birr in the box marked 'Contributions to the Children of the Martyrs'. It will undoubtedly reach them and they certainly needed it but I have never found a country where common cause and universal endeavour has been so apparent, so uncontaminated and so worthwhile.

Oman

January 2000

'We travel not to escape life but so that life does not escape us'
– written on a hostel wall in Amsterdam

As corrugated and rutted as a crocodile's back, the mountains of Jebal al Akhda lie across northern Oman, jagged, lifeless and cruel as though in retribution for the cataclysmic thrust that brought them from deep within the earth's mantle. But from the air, in the dawn light and with a mist that wrapped the wadis and lower slopes like gathered tulle, their aggressiveness seemed tamed.

Seed Airport was so lacking in formality with its absence of customs, immigration or form filling and so pleasantly efficient with luggage off-loaded and waiting by the clean, cool bus that this novelty of international arrival seemed like an invitation to visit a neighbour's new-built house.

The road to Bilad Said – at 9,186 ft (2,800m) the highest mountain village in Oman – ranks amongst the most dramatic in the world. Forget the Karakorum Highway and put to one side the corkscrew track down from Cusco to Maldonado, this route has the steepest gradients, the sharpest bends, the roughest terrain and the narrowest defiles. No snow-capped mountains, not a torrent of white water in sight but a switchback that curls, doubles back, wraps around and cuts through the highest mountains of the Arabian Peninsula. A geologist's textbook passes by in bewildering variety; shale like stacked sheets of veneer, splintered rock heaped like crushed bark in great ramparts, a sheer wall of 2,300 ft (1,300m) in glistening oolite. Around another bend and then into sinuous shapes like coiled entrails that meld into courses of red sandstone, finishing with black rock imprinted with the underwater ferns and waving grasses of a Jurassic sea. Bus-sized boulders, veined like northern faggots with a net of white quartz, are superseded by granite slabs

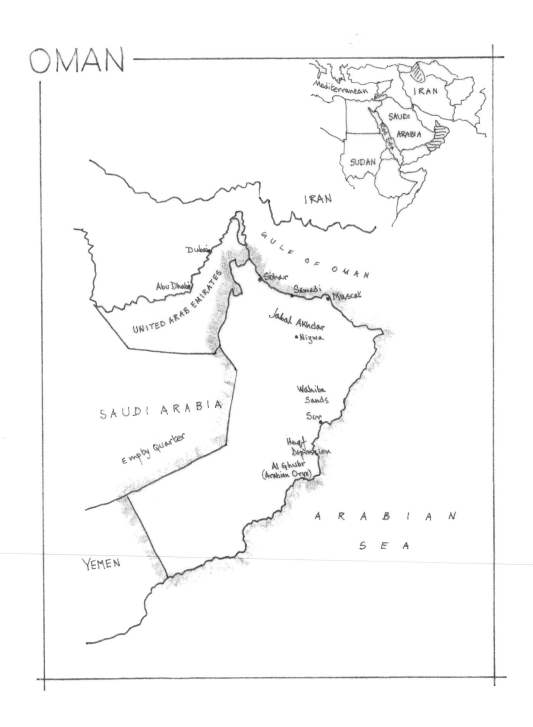

OMAN

IRAN

SAUDI ARABIA

SUDAN

Mediterranean

IRAN

GULF OF OMAN

Dubai

Abu Dhabi

UNITED ARAB EMIRATES

Sohar

Saradi

Muscat

Jabal Akhdar

Nizwa

Wahiba Sands

Sur

SAUDI ARABIA

Empty Quarter

Huqf Depression

Al Ghubr (Arabian Oryx)

ARABIAN

SEA

YEMEN

one moment, mica dust another; then a delightful interlude of a cool oasis of date palms with cheering children of the mountain bedouins before the road plunges to the bottom of a ravine and claws its way up the far side. Below the dispassionate peak of Jebel Akhda, Snake Canyon has opened a deep wound between grey and red granite in a sinister slash 400 ft (120m) deep. Rumpled, crushed and stretched in the tectonic conflicts of a hundred million years, the rocks appear thrust out of the earth's womb in convulsive agony. Thesiger came this way describing: *'A chaos of twisted ribbon rock, the debris of successive cataclysms, spewed forth molten to scald the surface of the earth'*. Just as my stomach muscles had been tensioned to a point where they could only snap and my heart had quickened to the pace of a Tonto drummer, there appeared the little village of Bilad Said. Calm and contented with terraced viridian patches of wheat and alfalfa, its serried features clung to the rock face with the nonchalance earned by 1,000 years of undisturbed exclusivity. Then, when the eye could not encompass that vertical scale any further, the heart could not bear any further shots of adrenaline and the lungs had been stretched to gasping in the thin air, it was time for a second helping on the return journey.

The beehive tombs at Al Alyn have stood sentinel along a stony ridge since 4000 BC and were silhouetted in the setting sun against the great rock face of Jebel Mischt as we camped below on a dry wadi bed amongst *tamarisk* and *acacia*. Six beehive tents of 2000 AD sprang up and the Landcruiser roof racks exploded with coloured bedrolls, patterned blankets and striped sheets. Ali, our local guide, factotum, jack-of-all-trades, bustler and hustler, was everywhere, rattling off orders in Arabic and English and no doubt cursing to himself in Hindi. He placed tents, organised the dining area, directed the cooking, supervised fires and chopped the garlic. Mohammed carried bedrolls, eight at a time, Ibrahim peeled potatoes and scattered groceries over the sand, lit a fire, cut his finger and spilt the sauce. Sayed tended the pots, put up the tables, filled the lamps and unfolded the chairs. Heide Beal, calm at the operation centre, chatted to her guests and directed her team with an efficiency that was the product of practice, Swiss precision and team loyalty. Hurricane lamps lit the tent entrances and marked the corners of the matted dining area while a fire crackled under a pot and smoke and steam rose to a tropical sky of indigo velvet, studded with stars of astonishing brightness. The day's journey was recalled, an autopsy performed of each wrong turn or missed sign and each wonder discussed; whisky was sipped, then gulped, laughter rose then fell, embers shed their glow, there was a curse from a toe caught on a peg, the zip of a tent flap, a weary goodnight and under the vigil of the tombs, silence enveloped the wadi like a shroud.

Mohammed, our driver with the orange turban, brown eyes to shame a Jersey cow and a smile to capture any heart, had invited us all to his home. He was a

Bahla Fort.
Jabal Hallat Mountains

desert bedouin living on the edge of the Wahiba Sands – a sea of sinuous dunes scattered with *euphorbia* and *protopsis* trees. As we left the stony desert, the boundary of the Wahiba was suddenly upon us and the flat, grey gravel turned to great waves of tawny sand. Here were camels, the bedu, the tracks of Thesiger, the exploits of Lawrence, the romance of Beau Geste; this was what we had come for. The track required as much skill as crossing a frozen lake and we skidded along from side to side passing an occasional hobbled camel and a bedouin encampment. After several miles, Mohammed pointed to a huddle of ramshackled huts in the distance and perched on the eastern slope of a dune; his smile broadened in anticipation. Flicking the Landcruiser into low gear and high ratio we roared up the slope churning sand like a side-paddled steamer. Home was an enclosure of palm fronds stitched together with fibrous strands. There were two rooms – for a kitchen and a bedroom and more palm fronds roofed a matted area. Sacks of barley for the animals and rice for the family lay in a corner, a pile of old tyres shielded a sick sheep from the wind and a great studded dowry chest filled another corner. Six tame rabbits scurried around – pets now, the pot will claim them later – and there were five, shy, clean, healthy children with beautiful teeth, dark eyes shining like ripe dates and skin as smooth and perfect as polished *crème de marfil* marble. We removed our shoes (being careful not to point our bare soles at our hosts), ate grapes and dates crushed with turmeric and drank weak coffee spiced with cardamom from tiny china cups. The smallest children kept close to their mother, peeping around the kitchen door at these aliens and giggling with the excitement of it all. I dished out lollipops to eager hands and then we left them to their endless horizons, swirling winds, driven sand and open skies.

The livestock markets of Barnard Castle or Banbury could take a tip or two from the animal auction at Nizwa. There is no less shouting, arm waving or bargaining but here it is the seller that sets the price. In the dappled shade of acacia trees of great age, a circular sandy track of about 100 ft (30m) in diameter, forms the viewing ring. At the hub and on the outer boundary, squat or loiter the buyers and spectators. Universally clad in dishdashas of a white dazzle that Persil PR men have only dreamt of, men outnumber women a hundred to one, the latter in colours to rival a rainbow and with layers of fabric that sparkle with metallic threads. Goats, some with kids that can barely walk, are led or dragged around the circle while their owner shouts out the price required. After a couple of circuits he drops his price until a bargain is reached, riyals change hands and the beast and bleating kid are lead off to be lifted into a pickup truck or the back seat of a car and comforted by a bundle of alfalfa to munch on. Sheep get similar treatment but calves are sold from trucks brought 600 miles (960 kms) from the south by dark skinned, scornful, black-turbaned cattle drovers from Salalah. I asked Heide, our tireless guide, if I could photograph them. "Not if you value your life," she replied. Behind the lens, not only etiquette but survival itself has to be carefully checked here.

Leaving the parched interior, the moisture of the coast was as welcome as a cool beer on a desert dune but at the Sur Beach Hotel there was disappointment. "So very sorry sir, I forget. It is Friday and with regrets, no beer before 2 pm." The Pakistani waiter was obsequious in his apologies, having already offered me a choice of three German lagers. Perhaps because it was Friday, I sat alone in the huge domed first floor dining room, watching the azure Arabian Sea lather the beach in a tumble of surf while a team from India and beyond hovered around their only customer.

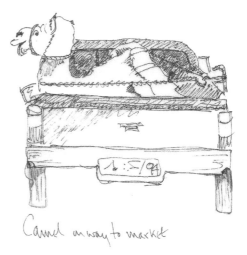

Camel on way to market

Sur had little of merit or interest, although the extravagant villas of the *nouveau* and *trés riche* provided some diversion, but in the old part of the town there is Oman's only dhow shipyard; a sad reflection on a nation whose sea-faring skills had enabled it to colonise Zanzibar and sail at will over the Indian Ocean. Nevertheless, a couple of dozen dhows were being built or repaired, propped up on a beach littered with the off-cuts of a thousand previous ships. Spars and ribs are roughly shaped with an adze and teak planks from India fixed with six inch nails as thick as a finger, their heads recessed into the timber and sealed with what looked and felt like pink chewing gum. Like the bones of beached whales, previous generations of these marine adventurers lay discarded on the grey sand usurped by fibre-glass, aluminium and outboard motors from Yamaha. Behind were the decaying homes of shipwrights, ship-owners, brokers and fishermen. All these homes had been abandoned leaving behind intricately carved but sturdy doors weathered and bleached with salt, latticed upper windows with creaking shutters and crumbling mud brick walls flayed of their protective plaster and lime wash. But a few new shoots of regeneration sprouted where houses had been restored for weekend homes. It will not be long before the last dhow will be anchored in concrete for conversion to a coffee house and the debris of the beach cleared for jet skis and ice-cream sellers.

In the soft shadows of early morning the high dunes on the coastal edge of the Wahiba Sands curve in seductive sweeps of silver sand, some honed by the wind to a knife edge, others rounded and voluptuous. Driving in sand soft enough to cover your ankles as you walk requires a special skill that the bedu have become particularly adept at and seemingly none more than Sayed and his brother Ahmed. However deep the tyres in the sand, however bellied the fuel tank on a ridge, Sayed 'the specialist' extricated any vehicle. Speed and momentum were essential and as Sayed flicked down, through five gears, selecting four wheel drive in high ratio then low, the $4\frac{1}{2}$ litre engine roared then screamed, the rev counter hit maximum and we hit the bottom of slopes at 60 mph before riding to the ridge where we hit the roof too. White-knuckled on the grab handles, anxiety turned to exhilaration as the wheel spun full lock left and right, sandaled feet moved between clutch, accelerator and brake with lightning co-ordination. Scattered sand flew high enough to obscure the windows as we raced up a slope oblivious as to what lay beyond. Twice we almost rolled, a dozen times every muscle was tightened taut to exhaustion and 100 times every nerve was stretched to its limit. And then, viewing another drop and another crest, Sayed let out a whoop and nerves and muscles were extended to cracking point once more.

We had given a lift to a bedu woman and as we dropped her off in a spot unmarked by any feature and clear to all horizons, she raised her right arm and with a hand tattooed with henna and with fingers extended, she gave a graceful flick of the wrist that seemed to indicate in a single gesture, "Thank you, goodbye and now go."

'The boys' were giggling loudly at breakfast and Ali, crouched over a pan of eight frying eggs, looked less than his usual effervescent self. Apparently Ahmed, knowing that Ali would climb the dune for his early morning constitutional, had positioned himself behind the crest naked but with a face painted with powdered milk. Just as Ali reached for his flies, Ahmed

rose up arms outstretched, against the rising sun and grotesquely masked. In our tents at the foot of the dune, we had heard the shouts of panic, the cries of rage and then the laughter as Ali fell backwards down the slope terrified that the demon Jigu had come to claim him.

It is disconcerting to sit on a thunderbox with one side open to a deserted and distant horizon looking at a vulture looking at you. There is little else that comes quite so close to humiliation and helplessness as being hobbled by your trousers, at a time that a very large bird with a beak designed for tearing flesh may well be celebrating its good fortune in finding enough food for a week tethered and semi-naked, already partially prepared for dinner. With the intention of redirecting any salubrious thoughts it may have had as to whether a start should be made on my eyes or my heart, I threw my left shoe at it and it grumpily flew away. I had arrived once at Leeds railway station on a rainy February night tired and hungry to find that the chip and pie shop had closed a few minutes earlier, so I knew how the bird felt.

From Muscat in the north to Salalah in the south, 628 miles (1,028 kms) of flat tarmac dribbles across the flat, open gravel plains of central Oman:

'...boundless and bare, the lone and level sands stretched far away.'

Midway, if you turn towards the sea, there is a track whose potholes are filled with sand as fine as talcum powder and which crosses the Jidat al Hararis. At the edge of this escarpment, the bouldered way leads down to the Huqf Depression.

Saline pools, white rimmed with the crystal crust of salt still being leached from the ancient sea bed, added a forlorn and lifeless emphasis. We camped here to the displeasure of seven brown-necked ravens whose home it seemed to be, in a spot scorched by the sun, polished by the wind and with the earth's bare bones lying around us. Apart from the ravens, there were also sand grouse, bustard, wild donkeys, gazelle of balletic daintiness, hares with huge ears, hedgehogs, small pale foxes and scurrying lizards, all seemingly placed here by uncaring fate to adapt as best they could.

But above all it is the Arabian Oryx that has made this dry and desolate place its own exclusive domain. Its sturdy but elegant body has a fine head from which grow two horns of rapier precision and extraordinary length. It is even more capable of surviving without water than a camel. Its hide is a colour that paint salesmen call 'Buttermilk' and is marked by a black triangle on its forehead, two black eyes and black legs. Those properly brought up on the stories of that Edwardian vet Dr Doolittle, will remember the Pushmepullyou. Leaving aside awkward questions of physiology, that novel beast was simply two oryx for the price of one. Why a creature of such intelligence and exquisite features should wish to live in these desolate surroundings defies sense and evolutionary theory. Shot almost to extinction, revived by foreign zoos from the requirement for stock and then poached again to the limit of viability, they are now being nurtured under the patronage of HRH Sultan Qaboos. With only about 400 in a sanctuary the size of Belgium, the chances of finding one were less than slim. However, we had underestimated the skill of the bedu rangers and to our intense excitement a group of six – a male and five cows – were found within a two hour drive with the additional bonus of a three day old calf.

In the evening, under the stars, a quarter moon and the light of a blazing fire our bedu team danced in celebration of our success. Sayed was lead drummer on a plastic jerry can, Mohammed accompanied on washing-up bowls, Ahmed waved a stick and whooped, Ibrahim yelped and kicked the sand and Ali, the impresario, shouted encouragement as his feet beat out the rhythm on a truck's bonnet.

A few days later in Muscat, leaving the extravagance of the Hyatt hotel, our airport departure coincided with the arrival of the President of the Maldives. Four helicopters hovered around two huge Hercules cargo planes that had brought in the President's entourage and whatever the Maldive Islands could offer to a land whose rocks and desert have seen tens of millions of years go by and whose culture, several thousands. As I climbed the aeroplane steps with a knapsack of frankincense and myrrh, I wondered how many coconuts you could get into a Maldive cargo plane.

Antartica

January 2001

'I have not been everywhere but it's on my list' – Susan Sontag

The Piaf sound-alike was still there at Sao Paulo Airport. Hidden from view but vocally calming the late boarders and informing the packaged, criss-crossing, sweating travellers. We had last met a year ago when she guided me to Campo Grande and the Pantanal; now, a little hoarser it seemed, she guided us towards Santiago.

With the South American backbone of the Andes forming her eastern flank, Santiago sprawled over a plain with the River Maipo, grey and turbulent with summer's melting snows, rushing through an urban forest of glass façades. Apartment buildings dripped little gardens from multi-layers of balconies and the streets were lined with sycamore, mimosa and palms. Herds of yellow buses thundered along downtown high rise ravines where skyscraper banks jostled for domination. Streetside booths were bright with Christmas wrappings and Jingle Bells, in Spanish, blared from shop doorways.

The 17th century church of San Francisco, built of great blocks of masonry, now stands beside a central urban artery. Its parquet floor has been worn into ridges by the feet of the penitent who still seek solace in its cool interior, light candles and attach messages of gratitude around the altars of favourite saints. Elsewhere, a few grand buildings from colonial times remain: the opera house, the cathedral and several museums but nothing domestic or vernacular. At least nothing seen on a day's visit before heat and weary feet drove us back to the 19-storied Hyatt with its ocean-sized pool.

Despite the city's civilised and prosperous appearance, a warning from a passerby to remove a gold chain necklace and hide a large camera shook our confi-

dence; morality here does not march with commercial success. Later, in the hotel where dark suited and swarthy security men were intentionally conspicuous, we dined among a respectable looking bunch of fellow guests. Leaving a bag on her chair to graze along the buffet, M was shocked to find on returning that it had been strapped and shackled to the arms. We never discovered whether this was a gross overkill by management ensuring that they were never troubled by any complaint of a straying possession or a sensible precaution against endemic kleptomania.

We lunched in the fish market, where endless rows of shining scales on shapes as long and as thin as a pipe or as round and flat as a plate lay in mortuary precision on the marble slabs in filleted shades of pink, white and grey. Prawns, so red they seemed bred in a sea of blood, reached our plates within a few hours of death; anointed with garlic butter and lime juice, they did not die in vain.

At Gate 17A, the other 98 passengers for the Falkland Islands, the MV Explorer and the frozen south eyed each other up. Suddenly we were aware of our own youthfulness and fitness. The brochure's description of steep stairs, narrow corridors, precipitous and icy gangplanks had seemingly gone unread by those who now waited leaning on a stick, checking a pacemaker or breathing heavily from the strain of standing. Not all of course, but as we marvelled at the spirit of those who might be rather closer to salvation than ourselves, we were also anxious as to the possible task of supporting them.

Mount Pleasant military airport on East Falklands was as small and efficient as it should have been, considering its post-war construction. Several good looking women soldiers in camouflage and big boots guided us through with warnings of 'No photographs please'. A sign stated 'FOD hazard. Please remove your hat'; we never discovered the hazard, but we all removed our hats. Another sign told us that the Alert State was 'Glacier White' – this seemed reasonably stable, although not entirely static. An hour's drive over the *campo* was wall to wall peat, 'rock rivers' and large sheep, each with ten acres (4 hectares) to graze. Jim O'Callaghan, an ex-engineer sergeant, "demobbed, liked it and stayed", gave a commentary in the single sentences of the parade ground. "Minefield on right." "Settler farm on left." Port Stanley, twinned with Whitby, was compact and single storied, with painted tin roofs and timber façades that spread along the waterfront like lines of naval flags. At the Upland Goose Hotel there was a huge tea of cucumber sandwiches, scones laden with jam and cream, slabs of fruitcake and tea the colour and consistency of the Amazon estuary. We strolled past Thatcher Drive, cottage gardens blooming with lupins, fuchsias and marigolds – it was high summer after all – and then reached our floating home. The Explorer, 'The Little Red Ship', was newly provisioned, freshly painted, the brass shone and the crew were welcoming. We had come halfway across the world, leaving on the northern hemisphere's shortest

Black browed
Albatross

day and arriving on the southern hemisphere's longest day and now we were off on our frozen adventure.

After two days around the outer islands of the Falklands shining in sunshine and peaceful with calm waters, we headed south to enter Drake's Passage, the stormiest waters of the world where, at the Atlantic Convergence, the planet's largest seas battle for oceanic sovereignty. Friendship increased with the familiarity that comes from grabbing the same stabilising rail or the shared apprehension of waves that washed the windows of the boat deck, thirty feet above the Plimsoll line. Universal inebriation seemed endemic as we swayed, rolled, pirouetted and twirled in involuntary choreography into the arms of an unexpected partner and waiters performed extraordinary feats of acrobatics. Most passengers stumbled along on half bent knees like one of those illustrations that show the ascent of man from an anthropoid ape but they may have been descending to pray. Cutlery and china set up a chattering rhythm in the dining room, suckling pig with rich gravy went untouched, jellies become animated and the soup tureen, in a mini ocean of its own, developed a froth of cresting waves. At the stern, slate grey skies met granite grey sea and southern giant petrels, black browed albatrosses and storm petrels revelled in the spray and updrafts of the element they were bred for.

Those of us accustomed to the warm and familiar feelings of Christmas in England tend to remember those that do not follow the traditional arrangements with particular clarity. If, after 54 Christmases in a tangle of family, wrapping paper, an oversized turkey and seven pints of bread sauce, one finds oneself anchored NNE off the Antarctic Peninsula with a carolling Filipino crew, the sight of 1,000 Magellanic penguins and a sea broken by the grey and white flanks of Connerson's dolphins, then that clarity is indelibly etched into the memory bank. Captain Ulrich Demel ("Feel free to call me Captain") was the archetypal seafarer with straight back, spade beard, steely eye and dreadful jokes. Before the festivities began he introduced his officers: English first officer (jolly good), German first engineer (jawohl), Polish radio officer (possibly, but how is his English?), American doctor (maybe), Austrian chef (hooray) and Scottish expedition director (three cheers).

New Year's Eve started grey but ended bright. Blued hued growlers like cast offs from a Murano glassworks, drifted benignly *en flottant* in front of a meringue horizon topped by a cloud of whipped cream. The cry of, "Whale, 2 o'clock starboard," started a frenzy amongst the camera crowd. Mart, our steward, got flattened in the bodily onslaught; there were bodies on board so broad that they filled the corridors completely; light was momentarily excluded and a vacuum created before the bulging frames swept each wall and exploded onto the deck.

Some New Year Eve's parties come and go, stuffed with food and blurred by champagne and the kisses from those to whom you have not even extended a hand. Others remain vivid and this was one of those. We sat with the Captain and Chief Engineer for seven courses that any Ritz would have been proud of before the entertainment began. Edna Everidge, aka the cruise director (ex-Coronation Street), poured into bulging blouse and sequinned skirt, tried his best to warm up an audience too bashful to enter into the spirit of the evening and was followed by the individual talents of some of the Filipino crew. The upper deck steward, bizarrely dressed in a towelling robe with a tablecloth turban, dropped all his conjuring cards; the female purser, brave but tearful, stood smiling for a full five minutes as successive inept hands struggled with the amplifier; an engine room hand, unaccountably togged out in pyjamas with a floor mop on his head, gave up his much rehearsed guitar number but with admirable spontaneity, belted out We Wish You a Merry Christmas. And as a finale, seven waiters in an enthusiastic number with much arm waving that resembled a desperate semaphore message stripped off their shirts to reveal tattoos and lacy bras. We forgave all the technical problems, cheering and clapping them on before we trooped out to the fo'c'sle for the oldest passenger to ring out the old year and the youngest to ring in the new. Stopping for a last glance at the rippled ocean, a humped back whale sublimely displayed its flukes as it dived into the grey depths.

"All landings will be wet," instructed our charming, female, 30-plus expedition director in her gentle Scottish brogue. She did not explain at the time that riding in a zodiac inflatable over cresting waves at full speed in weather notorious for its unpredictability in practice meant a thorough soaking. Clad in several layers of wool, Polartec jacket, scarlet waterproof parka, two pairs of trousers – the outer pair waterproof – topped by ear protectors, a hat pulled down to eyebrows and a neck warmer pulled up to nostrils, thick gloves, a life jacket and a backpack, we looked like dirigibles. To then waddle down a ship-side gangplank

Chinstrap penguins

swaying in the swell and step into a rubber dingy that corkscrewed off a launching platform momentarily disappearing in a grey froth required an agility that had not been adequately described in the brochure. Some bounced, some fell, many hands reached out but we all laughed. In any case we were, of course, all in the same boat. Ashore, in a magical transformation, penguins, seals and nesting petrels removed all sense of the cumbersome, the biting wind ignored the layers of Merino and the eyes and mind went into full alert. This is what we had come for.

It is a strange anomaly that four tons (4,000 kilos) of blubber with a bad attack of dermatitis can have charm but an elephant seal, beached on a sandy spot, looking at you through eyes like two tumblers of amontillado, is a heart melting experience. But look away from an individual soft face and a group takes on a different aspect. Bunched together like a pan of giant sausages, grumpy, grunting, belching, bloated, farting, itching, sweating, snorting and stinking, they seemed wedged together in obese discontent like a band of bad tempered bachelors. Snowy sheathbills scavenged around the perimeter picking off pieces of moulted skin, while chinstrap, gentoo and rock hopper penguins waddled along on their pink flippered feet in a continuous trek between sea and nest. The chinstraps became my favourite; the thin black line under their chins gave them a permanent smile and an expression of continuous surprise that their hat may have blown off. Bold and inquisitive, it seemed as though it was they rather than ourselves who were doing the sightseeing. Arms akimbo, head tipped to one side and swaying slightly as they balanced on the rocks, they regarded our intrusion with interest. When south polar skuas on their continuous patrol for unprotected chicks swooped overhead, penguin necks stretched vertically skyward and a raucous chorus began while their little wings flapped in alarm.

Icebergs floated in the open sea; the smallest like a cathedral, the largest county-sized. Under clear skies and bright sun they were majestic and would retain their sovereignty for up to ten years but in the great storms of the southern oceans, they become a serious hazard. The bones of many thousands of whalers, sealers and seamen lie on the seabed, their moaning souls frozen in perpetuity as a result of fatal collisions with these polar giants. Inland, where explorers have struggled against the coldest and most fearsome weather on the planet, the icy hand of death has grasped other souls. No wonder the names along the coast echo cries of desperation and sorrow: Cape Longing, Exasperation Inlet, Deception Island, Cape Disappointment.

Then, at the point that this polar wilderness might become addictive, we headed back North. Drake's Passage was kind and Cape Horn magical in the dawn light. The Beagle Channel, with its shores edged by *northofagus*, led us to Ushuaia – the world's southernmost city. And then on to Buenos Aires, suffering a heatwave that had its ten million people perspiring in 104°F (40°C) under a smoggy sky.

For a day we wilted and then took a bus tour where the air conditioning and the microphone collapsed in a premature siesta at 9 am and a distraught tour leader paced up and down the aisle calling out the city's sights in four languages: the presidential palace, painted pink on the façade where Eva Peron rallied the underprivileged, several grand avenues named after dates that commemorated revolutions and several more named after generals who either started or suppressed them, the Italian quarter of La Boca painted in a pallet of primary colours, the old docks now reclaimed for upmarket housing, the Palermo district of great grassy parks and trees scattered with picnicking *porteños* and professional dog walkers and finally the fashionable Recoleta area where we de-bussed and where, in a maze of marble mausoleums of the country's rich and powerful, we sought out the resting place of Eva Peron.

Elephant seal

Tango dancers
Buenos Aires

In shaded squares and by street cafés, impromptu tango dancers animated those sepia photographs that we thought were simply romantic ideals. Absurdly handsome men in chalk striped grey suits, scuffed shoes and fedora hats tilted over black greasy hair and dark brooding eyes clasped slim women dressed in colourful frocks cut low in the front and generously around the hem. Moving with passion and precision with arching backs and nimble feet to the toe-tapping music of an accordionist or a scratchy record of Carlos Gardel, they put on an exhibition for the surrounding voyeurs of fully clothed, open air, vertical sex.

Later we escaped across the dark brown estuary waters of the Rio Plata to Uruguay and its charming riverside town of Colonia. Whitewashed cobbled streets, shady fig trees, bougainvillea and a languid attitude to life gave the town great charm. We lunched outside a small restaurant with check tablecloths, low beams and a piano player who, in his braces, hat and drooping cigarette, came from the same faded postcard album as the tango dancers. From a menu, stuck inside two driftwood planks, we ordered *'Chivito'*. The brief description seemed to suggest a kind of *salade nicoise* or perhaps an antipasti of sorts, not quite the spicy sausage we expected. The reference to fries seemed a little unusual but a plate of these on the side might well have been welcome if the salad was a little meagre. There was additionally the description as 'A typical Uruguayan dish'. All in all, just the thing for a light summer lunch for a first time visitor.

When we enquired of a young American at the next table who looked as though he had worn out a backpack or two, what the dish comprised, he simply said, "Gaucho's Breakfast." M thought that this probably referred to the gauchos working along the Piranha River estuary who enjoyed a bit of fish now and again. We should have smelt a rat, particularly when the young American's companion added, "It's a nice meal." In retrospect, remembering his door-sized shoulders and his whale of a waist, this was another clue that passed us by. But M was looking forward to this snack; something to keep her going for an afternoon stroll before a more substantial meal back at Buenos Aires. Our table in this cosy little restaurant was small but solid and our final hint that something that did not quite fit the menu's description came with the removal of the restaurant trivia. In fact, the table's entire surface was the subject of a short but sustained programme of land clearance.

Held aloft on a pewter charger of cartwheel proportions came the morning morsel. Uruguay's gauchos might well be hungry at daybreak but this was not just breakfast, it was lunch, tea and dinner all on the same plate. I don't know how large gauchos grow, they may all be direct descendants of Goliath; but to anyone who regards themselves as near to the human average, this plate of breakfast was a whole bingeing weekend.

At the foothills of this food mountain and spreading out to most points of the compass was Russian salad, tuna with onions, calamari with capers, octopus in batter and assorted chunks of tomato and cucumber with boulders of olives arranged in a mayonnaise lake. The fries gave the base its bulk and the stability to support in successive layers, a paving slab of beef, rashers of bacon, ham and cheese and then, at the peak, flowing down the ravines and crowning the crest, a pierced fried egg. The summit was suitably acknowledged by a flag with the enigmatic inscription 'Free Drammer'. We never discovered who Drammer was or why he should be freed. We were only halfway up the north face of these mountains of meat when a rainstorm of an intensity that only Noah could have previously experienced, tipped out of the sky. To her credit, M had demolished base camp and got half way up the south col when the klaxon blast announced our ferry's departure and denied her the final push to the summit.

Back in Buenos Aires, the urban millions had traded sweat for squelch. In a bar of chatter and polished mahogany, I struggled with indigestion and shivered from the air conditioning that cooled my soaking wet clothes and I remembered my chinstrapped friends, the carving glaciers, the heavy swell and the white silence of the uttermost end of the earth.

India I

February 2001

'There is no moment of delight in any pilgrimage like the beginning of it'
– Charles Dudley Wilson

I left a frosty Oxfordshire at dusk with a sore throat, a bad cough but with high hopes. Ten hours later, at noon, I was clattering through the heat, haze, dust and clamour of the southern suburbs of Delhi in a battered Ambassador, in the company of a young guide with a bad lisp and a driver with a scowl and the looks of a brigand, to be dropped at Tikli Bottom. In this oasis of tranquillity I swapped notes on mutual friends with my charming hosts and then, after a restless night and a short flight, lay down in the last available room in Varanasi. The plumbing was being dismantled with sledgehammers, a chanting gang of Tamils were pick-axing up the road, the adjacent lift lobby was a children's playground and the television next door was being watched by a family who seemed to suffer from congenital deafness. I collapsed on a bed whose mattress would have been hard to penetrate with a nail, took another swig of cough mixture, sucked on a Fisherman's Friend and wondered at the changing scenes of travel and the waywardness of a wish to experience them.

But back to that oasis. At the head of a small valley and gently nurtured in the embrace of the Aravally Hills, Tikli Bottom lies like an architectural jewel of Delhi's imperial past. Reproducing the classical style of Lutyens with lofty rooms, a shady courtyard, joinery of oiled teak, floors of polished stone and country house furnishings, Martin and Annie Howard have built themselves an extraordinary home. To have had the energy, foresight and imagination to create this in such an isolated rural area is astonishing. To then share it with strangers seemed perverse. To a gardener from a windswept Cotswold hill, an arboretum that shoots up three

126

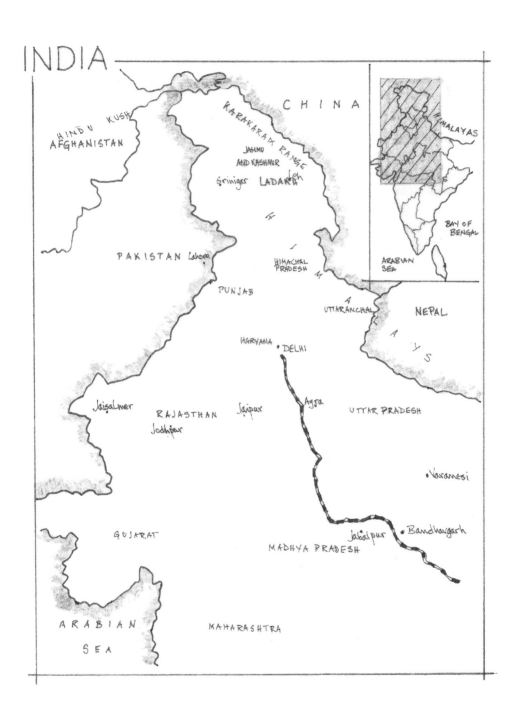

feet a year (with teak and poplar four feet and *bombax malabarensis* six feet), this was the stuff of myth and envy, but then the Oxfordshire Uplands do not have families of porcupine that ravage through the gladioli crop or herds of nilghai antelope that munch through the young growth of mango and guava orchards.

Pre-dawn, the streets of Varanasi that border the banks of the Ganges are bustling with rickshaws, sizzling samosas, sweepers and sellers of flowers and plastic bottles. In this holiest of Hindu cities – Kashi, the City of Light – the devout come to immerse themselves five times in Mother Ganga to seek redemption for their sins and wash away the wrongs of all previous lives. They pour water from the sacred river in devotional thanks and those that are pilgrims from outside the city will fill a plastic bottle to take home. The ghats terrace the city for two miles (three kms) and each has its own devotees. The young are largely absent – who wants to be reminded of mortality when life is for living? The bathers are elderly and several steps nearer the need to cleanse the soul in anticipation of salvation. Men strip to underpants or a loincloth but women duck down in their saris and emerge clinging and clammy in yards of printed cotton. This seemed a particularly uncomfortable penance.

Sadhus, many bandy legged with skeletal frames and wrapped in orange blankets against the dawn chill, gave blessings; others, grey-bearded and turbaned, handed out marigolds and words of comfort. Young girls with panniers garnished with flowers sold little lumps of wax in a paper container which were then floated on the still waters so that 1,000 prayers sparkled in the dim light.

At the southern end smoke rose in twisting spirals from the Mari Karnikh ghat where bodies, shrouded in white or red, were placed on burning pyres; their souls to rise to another life, their bodies to return to earth. The mourners of the rich bought fuel of sandalwood, the poor made do with roots. Many great stacks of timber piled square and high surrounded this crematorium; it seemed that they were ready for a plague. The northern end was dohbi territory where lines of dohbi wallahs scrubbed, rinsed and flogged the washing brought to the shoreline by donkeys. *'A Hindu is a man who spends his life breaking stones with wet clothes.'*

The narrow alleyways behind the ghats were grimy, clogged and claustrophobic and the stone walls had been cleaned and polished by the shoulders of a million pilgrims. In tiny niches, betel leaf sellers squatted and in larger alcoves cauldrons steamed with spicy stews and smoke blackened the vaulted ceilings. From other gloomy niches were sold marigolds, powdered sandalwood, shrouds and incense. The air was thick and pungent, the crowds pressing, the atmosphere heavy with smoke and spirituality. An unfamiliar religion pervaded and oppressed. I felt that death crept around each corner but the crowd was lively; I could not square this anomaly. It was wonderful but disturbing; there was a spiritual force present but I could not grasp it; there was vitality but an uncompromising harshness – both were too concentrated. The acceptance of death and the liveliness of life were intertwined. I needed sweet air, long horizons and time to reflect. I needed to escape.

Heading north to Sarnath down dusty, tree-lined roads, I bumped into religion again, but this time it was cushioned by the smiles and gentleness of a Tibetan Buddhist colony. I spun a prayer wheel, helped a granny up steep steps, pulled a child to safety from the traffic and felt refreshed.

The road to Allahabad forms part of one of the northern arteries of India. National Road No. 2 starts in Calcutta, skirts Varanasi, rumbles through the centre of Allahabad and pushes on to Delhi and Pakistan. Along its way it pumps out life and vigour. Between the towns and villages, broad avenues of tamarind, eucalyptus and mango fringe each side and shade potters, brick makers, brick breakers, stone masons, rag sifters, metal merchants, tin can gatherers, cardboard collectors, wool dyers, carpet weavers, sari sellers, basket makers, wood splitters, tyre menders, tea shops, farmers with neat haystacks and piles of alfalfa and dusty white chickens with bright red feet and cockscombs. All the way, piled in their tens of thousands were pancake mountains of dung fuel. What a buffalo takes in, it gives back in abundance but not to the land where it is needed.

Grossly overloaded Tata trucks thundered through villages hooting incessantly and children, dogs, buffaloes, cream coloured cows, the lame and blind idly crossed the road each with a death wish unfulfilled. Tomorrow there is an important festival to the god Shiva in Varanasi and along the verges individuals and groups of young men clad in bright orange and yellow walk and sometimes trot towards the city. Carrying a pole decorated with tinsel, they will walk barefoot for two days and a night carrying small copper pots or plastic bottles to fill with the sacred water of Mother Ganga. "They will go to Varanasi," said my driver; "They will go bananas," I thought. The less pious, less fit and less bananas rode in convoys of Mahindra jeeps decorated with flags and plastered with slogans; they were happy, in festive mood and drove dangerously. The pilgrims who walk on bleeding knees to Santiago de Compostelo, the penitent who crawl on their stomachs up the steep slopes of Mount Bohadapur and these young men sweating in the sun for 150 miles (240kms) humble the traveller in his comfortable car. I was content to be humbled.

The Finara Bungalow at Allahabad ("Four rooms, very clean, all meals extra") sat squat and comfortable with a style that managed to satisfactorily mix Corinthian columns framing the porch with Moghul decorations around the frieze. It fronted a busy street opposite the huge High Court complex, the largest in India. I had a lunch of bony chicken at one end of a long mahogany table; I could have had Fish and Chips with Dark Gravy and Rich Plum Cake with Thick Custard.

Sadhu by Ganges

Rajput man

Ramnagar Fort
Varanasi

130

My driver, the cook, the manager Mr Saxena (ex-Caledonian Insurance), the owner Mr Ghandi ("Ravi Ghandi is my second cousin") did not eat but sat looking at me. My room, just off the porch and at the pavement edge was shared with a family of geckos and, it seemed, with the traffic and hawkers. Junior barristers in striped trousers and black coats missing a button or two and worn through at the elbows tucked into snacks at the roadside café just outside my window. If I had opened the French doors from my bathroom, I would have stepped into a garden of dahlias, daisies and gladioli; the sweet smell from the blossom of the kumquat orange trees filtered through the fanlight from the outside and helped leaven the liberality of the carbolic on the inside. In the evening, as I was lying prone on my bed after an unsatisfactory session under the dribbling shower, a fellow of fierce looks but charming manner gently opened the door.

"Many sorries, sahib," he said, "but I have come for buggers."

This service had not been on the menu and besides, we had not even been introduced.

"No worry," he continued, "no need to move, I will attend to everything."

As my consternation and curiosity grew (but nothing else), he produced his enormous weapon – a Flit gun with which he enthusiastically sprayed the room with clouds of insecticide. I coughed all night.

I sought solace from the clamour of the streets in the cool and dusty interior of All Saints Cathedral. Like an overgrown English parish church it sat in a carefully tended garden. Inside, worn hymnals rested on the pews and brass plaques on the masonry walls remembered judges, officers of the 3rd Brahma Horse and two army medical officers who had died of blood poisoning in the course of their duties. A pigeon had started a nest in the reredos.

"The best Indian food is in London."

Gubhan Kakkar, MD of GN Pharmaceuticals was insistent. I agreed, the trouble with food in India is that it looks a lot worse than it tastes. Along a buffet, the colours are two shades of brown, two of khaki and one like chewed seaweed. Poking around in the murky pots, the chunks you find all look the same. Could be fish, could be mutton, could be meatballs stuffed with cheese. On the *a la carte* menu there is little difference except for a dribble of yoghurt on top and a reasonable expectation that chicken ordered will be chicken delivered. The tastes of course are subtle, spicy and mild but even in the top establishments, presentation, that essential message the eye sends to the slavering tongue, has been ignored. I got talking to Mr Kakkar at a roadside stop for tea and cake. He swaggered in accompanied by two henchmen, one small and thin with an immense moustache and the other very tall. Weedy had a rifle and Lofty a shotgun – they were Mr Kakkar's armed guards. "You never know around here," he said enigmatically. I hope he never got to know as the lack of ability of his minders was obvious to a sparrow.

"Keep it safe!" he called as I drove away.

Where the River Jumna meets the River Ganges and the invisible River Sawasrati rises from its mythical underground course, long low sandbanks break the flow before the Ganges doubles its volume and pace. This is fortuitous, as upstream of the confluence and spread over 8,800 acres (3560 hectares), seventy million pilgrims had gathered over the last six weeks for the Kumbh Mela. Held every 12 years, this Hindu festival is the largest gathering of mankind on earth but on these last two days, only 250,000 were left. They were a happy bunch, probably glad to have the place to themselves as they stripped to their underpants in preparation of bathing, offered rice and marigolds to the sacred rivers and scooping up water in a pot, poured it back in a symbolic cleansing of their sins.

I chatted to a smart Indian army captain in polished riding boots, jodhpurs and a swagger stick. His whole regiment had been camped here for three months. "It has been a most efficient operation," he said proudly, "not a single moment of trouble." He was right to be proud. A huge city had been constructed in six months together with a separate town for 11,000 officials. Nine pontoon bridges had been laid across the great river; sewage, water and lighting installed to serve six million each day; 155 miles (250kms) of metal plated road laid down; a hospital built. Forty trains a day brought the people in and returned them, 1,500 frogmen patrolled the river and the world's largest public address system continually broadcast for the lost and found. Many wives were never found, deliberately abandoned in the immense throng by husbands who sneaked out of the back gate. In a country where a westerner cannot understand how even the simplest task gets accomplished and despairs at the lack of maintenance of every utility, this organisation was a miracle in itself. Nothing of it would remain within a month of the festival's end.

I had not been prepared for such a concentrated mass of humanity and this was just the remnants of what had been there a week or two before. It stretched to every horizon. It ate, danced and wept with the emotion of a lifetime's sins purged and laughed with the joy of salvation attained. It was as though half of India was on a long spiritual picnic enjoying the sideshows, enough coloured lights to crown a Bombay skyline, tented restaurants of every kind and a multitude of striped and caparisoned enclosures. Huge pots steamed, charcoal glowed, rice cones were piled four foot high on copper platters each the size of cartwheels and piles of sweet meats dripped with honey and sugar syrup. Such plenitude in a land of hunger but this was a festival to end all festivals and all who attended would remember it for their lifetime.

From time to time, a group of devotees from a particular sect came to the river with much fanfare and ceremony. Some wore orange turbans and yellow robes and were surrounded with garlands, others wore green or white or red and some wore nothing at all. These were the Nagas who were smothered in a paste of dung and ashes and carried a stick and a pot and nothing else, although I spotted one in trendy sunglasses and another carrying an umbrella. Emerging from their isolation in caves and forests, the multitude that they now found around them must have been intimidating. There were families from Rajasthan with women in bright colours and the men with bushy moustaches, loosely wrapped head cloths and proud handsome faces. And there were dark skinned groups from the south with saris of purple, green and brown shot through with gold thread; there were fat business men with fat wives, sadhus, seers, swamis and gurus some with long flowing beards others completely shaven and young men and women with small children who yelled as they got ducked in the sanctifying waters. On the fringes, commercialism intruded with a giant inflatable Colgate toothpaste tube, a scarlet clad stilt walker dropping promotional leaflets and a group bizarrely costumed as bears, whose message was as incomprehensible as their furry attire.

There is no monopoly on the highway to faith. Many paths lead towards Nirvana but those routes that reach that final goal are the rockiest and the steepest. At this great gathering there was no time for meditation; all were in celebratory mood, although some explored these alternative tracks and there were plenty of distractions along the way. From dozens of tented pavilions loudspeakers blared out the philosophies of the alternatives on offer. Brahmins, Hari Krishnas, Pandas, Sadhus, Shramanas and Akaras – the original militant caste of priests – all had their followers and sought to inspire by myth and decibels adherence to their particular path. In one temple of bamboo and canvas, 100 fires were lit and smoking, each tended by a robed priest; it looked like St Pancras in the blitz. Dante would have been moved to a dozen more stanzas. But the sampling of these many spiritual menus was accomplished in piety, good nature and curiosity and all under the umbrella of a universal faith. An intense aura of spirituality and happiness was all around.

As we drove back along National Route No. 2 through the reckless traffic and the lumbering and slumbering cattle, I regretted the imprudence of failing to fill a pot with the blessed and protective water of Mother Ganga. At least it might have helped the cough.

St Petersburg for the Weekend

February 2002

'Tourists wander for distraction, travellers ramble for fulfilment'– Hilaire Belloc

You do not see the bones of the 40,000 slaves buried in the foundations of Peter the Great's city, nor the 100,000 timber piles of Siberian larch that were cut sunk into the marsh of the River Neva delta, but as you walk the elegant straight streets with their classical façades washed in lemon yellow, pale blue or ochre, the turbulence of 18th century Russia and the legacy of the Romanov dynasty lies all around. In February, any colour however muted gave a little warmth to the grey sky, the grey snow and grey complexions of the inhabitants of Russia's second city. This sombre mood seemed emphasised by the granite expressions of its people, the frozen canals, the huge scale of its principle buildings and the bitter climate of a city on the same latitude as Anchorage. Not for nothing is St Petersburg known for a yearly tally of 30 days of sun, 120 days of snow and the remaining days of rain. Gaiety and lightness of touch are not part of its character, but open the doors of its great palaces with their stifling heat, thaw the hearts of its people with a friendly gesture, throw down a shot or two of vodka (available at every meal and at any time in between) and a warm smile breaks out. But there is a darker side to the city too. Venture through an alleyway, peer in some trepidation into a shaded courtyard and you will find double-bolted doorways of steel, rusting vehicles and curtained windows from which corners may be anxiously drawn back. It is a dispirited world of poverty and in winter, cold and hunger. We looked into several of these darkened corners but retreated discombobulated with the aggressive stares of those lingering in shadowy corners, fearful that a foreign smile would not only be unwelcome but angrily rejected. But here is opulence on a staggering scale, culture of world class, learning and history are all in abundance and friendliness and humour are there if you look for them.

Our own private chatelaine Elena Koshutskaya had all the keys to all the doors. Chunky, bow legged, croissant fingered, blonde hair piled in an untidy hayrick on top of her flushed face, in her squirrel skin coat she looked like a furry brick. In faultless English, though sometimes slipping into German or French, her other fluencies, she mothered her flock through private entrances and across icy roads pouring forth information like a gatling gun whose supply of ammunition was infinite. Given the chance, she would never have stopped talking and this flowing stream was often sidelined into eddies of dry humour. "I give you choices but you must come with me – this is democracy!" Her little eyes,

Peterhof Palace 1750

darkly made up, twinkled with fun. "I interrupt myself," she would say without a change of pace or tone pointing out a statue of yet another Alexander or Nicholas in between a discourse on the merits of a restaurant or the poetry of Pushkin. "My dear ladies and gentleman, can you imagine… it's amazing!" Her enthusiasm kept us going at breakneck speed through seven imperial palaces. She was candid in her approach. "The Hermitage has four million exhibits, the National Museum three million, the National Library one hundred and thirty million. I know everything but you must choose. Shall I inform or shall I navigate?" By some miracle she seemed to accomplish both and in between obtained the best seats for the opera, spirited taxis for the tired, obtained tables at restaurants fully booked for a month and opened doors that museum directors were probably unaware of. This whirlwind carried our band through three centuries of Russian history and seemingly through every room of every palace (thankfully not in practice – there are 600, palaces that is) and left us not only breathless and happy at the end of each day but most miraculous of all, eager to greet her the next morning.

The auditorium of the Mariinsky Theatre is a magnificent horseshoe of gilded balconies surrounding rows of uncomfortable upright chairs that make up the

C19th Church of Peterhoff Palace

stalls. *Eugene Onegin* is long, soulful and full of Russian sadness and despair and it was a pity that each of the two bars was staffed only by a single lady so that the queues snaked around the narrow corridors of the Tsar Circle, even for intervals lasting half an hour. Those who did not try or gave up waiting promenaded in a clockwise direction around the strip of carpet that was the perimeter of the Grand Hall on the first floor. At Act III, Scene II, an uneasy shuffling and head turning indicated that most had become aware of the smell of smoke that seemed to come from the foyer. Perhaps the conductor had too since the volume seemed to increase and the tempo quicken as he too considered his route to the nearest exit. Whatever the cause, it was some relief when the pathetic Onegin was dismissed to passionless oblivion by the faithful Tatyana and the curtain of embroidered gold and silver thread descended for the last time. We scrambled out into a street fresh with snow and lit by the amber glow of streetlights. We had a second bite of entertainment to see *Raymonda* with the Kirov ballet on another night – the fire had been extinguished by then. Reckoned against the Royal Opera House, the

Metropolitan or La Scala, the performances had not reached the highest artistic peaks but it was enough to have been close to the boards trodden by Tchaikovsky, Rimsky Korsakov, Borodin, Glinka, Diagalev, Nijinski, Pavlova and all the other stars of the Russian musical and artistic firmament.

The mafia and *nouveau riche* have been socially assimilated without rancour; they are the new entrepreneurs and are largely welcomed. A few were evident at the opera. The women were young and good looking in glittering jewellery but clothed in tasteless or poorly made dresses as though a last minute invitation had necessitated re-modelling the spare room curtains. Their men were stern and serious in olive green or black suits usually with matching shirt and tie. In the street, black leather jackets and fur hats were universal – at least amongst those walking. Amongst those incapable of standing on their feet were the vodka-sodden or pathetic elderly women – far more of the latter. At the Metro entrances huddled in blankets, perhaps with a small dog (all the better to prick a passing conscience) they held up a selection of home knitted hats or scarves. Widows' pensions are pitifully small. Food takes 38 percent of the average budget and heating accounts for another 20 percent; there are few pleasures available on the balance.

We had not come to St Petersburg to eat well but nevertheless the purchasing power of these *nouveau riche* and the recent taste for foreign travel has spawned restaurants of world class with commensurate prices. We were content with the likes of borscht, herrings with dill and potatoes, beef stroganoff and delicious pancakes filled with redcurrants and covered in honey. Caviar of course was available at every meal; the prices seemed on a par with Belgravia.

We did not risk the Metro; not because it is the deepest in the world (needing to clear the beds of 68 rivers and canals), nor because it never surfaces, but because a previous subterranean excursion in Moscow had left us on the central line equivalent for six circuits before we recognised the right chandeliers.

On a Sunday, a few attend one of the many churches and several cathedrals of the Russian Orthodox faith. At 7 am, trampling up a snowy path, we went to St Nicholas Cathedral. In its low vaulted, icon hung, dimly lit interior, salvation was offered to a congregation who were largely poor and elderly. There was no formality of seated rows – chairs are not provided in a Russian Orthodox church, but a slowly moving tide of the penitent entered with frosted breath to bend a knee or buy a taper or two to offer to a favourite saint in one of the many side shrines. A bearded priest in heavily embroidered cope intoned comfort from religious texts while a middle-aged choir, muffled, fur-hatted, great-coated and warm-booted sang *a capella* in that incomparable harmonic so distinctive to a Russian Orthodox service and which brings such spiritual warmth. We understood not a word, comprehended nothing of the liturgy, were confused by the congregation as they knelt, prostrated or crossed themselves extravagantly but the cold, the delayed breakfast, the sense of intrusion, the incense from the smoking, swinging censers all had a powerful effect. We left uplifted and humbled.

On our only bright and sunny day we headed west along the edge of the Gulf of Finland to the Peterhof Palace. In a cloud of unpleasant exhaust fumes, we passed similar ill-maintained vehicles on the road to St Petersburg's summer residences. Old dachas, clapboarded, snowbound and broken-fenced, were interspersed with the brick-built, clay-tiled dachas of the affluent new generation. But what romance there seemed to be in the broken bones of the original buildings! I pictured a booted father in high-buttoned linen shirt, a vase of daisies on a scrubbed wooden table, a balalaika hanging on the wall, carefree children, a smiling long-frocked mother and a shaggy dog. Such is the banal inheritance of Dostoyevsky or the films of David Lean. The palace itself stood two storied and immensely long, its terraces that overlook the Gulf inhabited only by lonely statues shielded from the rigours of winter by straw filled timber enclosures. The fountains were frozen, the canals drained, the cherry trees and larch bare. Nevertheless, it was easy to imagine the delights of summer, of sparkling water and illicit liaisons in pavilions of pleasure. A trio of musicians with a bugle, basset horn and clarinet, wigged and costumed in eighteenth century dress, played a Mozart minuet, stamping their feet to the metre as we slipped on the felt slippers to skid over the intricate parquet floors. Gilt, ormolu and marble were in accustomed abundance but somehow this palace had a lighter touch reflecting perhaps its summer use. At the Pushkin Palace we came upon the extraordinary, unique and overwhelming opulence of the famous Amber Room. The room glowed with the translucence of a million polished globules of pine resin set on the wall floor to ceiling in between rococo mirrors and flamboyant torcheres. It was not art or even attractive but it was designed to intimidate a visiting diplomatic dignitary and reinforce the dominance and wealth of the Russian court. It certainly knocked for six two 21st century visitors.

A piece like this on St Petersburg should mention art. Art in all its variations should be at the beginning, the middle and the end – there is no other sensible reason to visit St Petersburg and if you want to know about the city's art and architecture, take a tour and buy a book or 20. But the really remarkable story, the one so extraordinary and unequalled that it will probably never be attempted again, is the prodigious programme of restoration carried out by a communist government starting in 1953 and now almost completed. During this time it has occupied the talents and energies of the most skilful artists and technicians of the Russian republics and consumed 90 percent of the government's cultural budget for the whole nation. As remarkable is the voluntary effort of tens of thousands of local residents who shifted bricks and rubble, dug and dusted and worked all their spare time to restore their national heritage. The opulence of palaces of the 18th century imperial courts have been recreated from the roofless, smouldering and collapsing ruins left from the longest military bombardment in history and the 872-day siege of Leningrad from September 1941 to January 1944. What has been achieved is a miracle.

Mali

November 2002

'My favourite thing is to go where I have never gone' – Diane Arbus

"I am going to Mali."

"To Bali, that will be wonderful."

"No Mali. It's between Burkino Faso, Mauritania and Guinea and twice the size of France."

"Oh! That will be... interesting."

At Charles de Gaulle Airport, smothered in a north European fog on a November morning, those at Gate 41 looked as though their trip might be interesting too. Chinese businessmen in dark suits, Malian business men in billowing robes of embroidered white cotton and wives draped more colourfully with a yard or two of matching fabric around their heads, a party of fit professionals with a mountain of bags tagged 'humanitarian aid', an assortment of tee-shirted twentysomethings in expensive trainers and efficient rucksacks and a few young Malians in sandals and bin liners. Some of those returning home recognised friends and embraced them; there were never fewer than six kisses.

The market at the Malian capital Bamako, spread its tattered stalls over a wide area of potholed streets and filthy drains, but no trader seemed too keen on business, preferring to squat on a ragged sack and swat flies. If there were any sales at all, aluminium cooking pots seemed the most popular and were sold in family sizes: the smallest was for a family of ten. The museum provided a cool retreat from the dust, sun and insects and a taste of the country's anthropological jigsaw. Figures, masks and fetish symbols showed cultures that clearly lived in harmony with nature and had respect for human foibles. A two-faced headdress represented our public and our private face; carved chameleons showed hypocrisy and

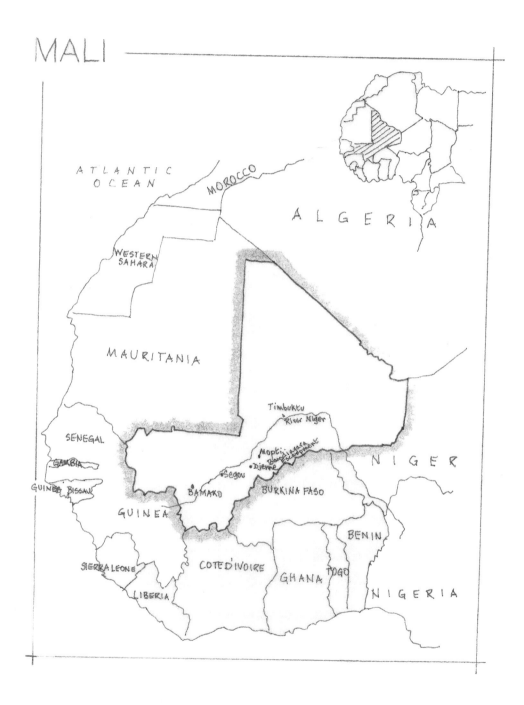

snakes, with their constant changes of skin, were the changing values through life. There were male fertility statues grossly well hung and women with breasts firm and pointed enough to be battering rams. Alarmingly our female guide, herself something of a siege weapon, told us that male circumcision was a job for a black-smith and for female circumcision, his wife.

Before daybreak and by the light of torches, my group squeezed themselves into Landcruisers overloaded with camping equipment. Our guide was called Yaya, a giant of a man, whose looks were so primal that I expected him to drop suddenly onto his knees and knuckles. He was gentle, amiable and intelligent but neverthe-less such was his wish to please that almost any question was answered true to his name – Ya, ya. The local team was completed with Mena the cook and two drivers. Our party was small and I looked them up and down with some apprehension. There was a hairy sack of a Scotsman, short on words in a shirt too tight and trousers too loose, who was inclined to range independently in search of birds with binoculars raised permanently to his eyes. As a balance, Brian from Essex had an answer for everything, usually uninvited or in the absence of enquiry he raised the question himself. Bearded, sandaled and multi-zipped he constantly drummed his restless fingers. He was the archetypal birder and carried four volumes of ornitho-logical reference to check on legs, mandibles or scapular plumage. At breakfast (hibiscus tea and bullet hard eggs) he had finished the jam before others had even sliced the bread and regarded his wife as a porter. However, entirely self-effacing and fully aware of his image, he had a ready wit and was the fall guy every group needs. His wife Mimi, when not on portering duties, wrote up her diary on a minute by minute basis. It would have been hard to choose a less appropriate name and it was not her fault that she erupted in livid spots with each insect that bit her (and there were very many) but who was to suggest that shorts were available longer and singlets looser? Ray was the sparrow of the party and at a sprightly 73, he darted around helping with chores. "I do all the cooking and ironing at home you know." And there was Christine, a large and capable lady from North-ern Ireland. But stepping out ahead, arm occasionally beckoning us on, was our leader, Sinclair. Portly, labouring heavily up a steep slope on short legs, he was far removed from the usual professional guide. Carrying two suitcases and wearing a tie, I had mistaken him at Heathrow for one of those ill-equipped tourists whose only previous foreign holiday had been at Alicante, out of season. The suitcases turned out to include a full length tartan woollen dressing gown, a Churchillian boiler suit (mosquito proof) and a bath towel of tent proportions. He shouted at small boys who tried to sell him beads, conversed with the locals in good French, had a huge fund of stories, good and bad, and quoted chunks of Yeats, Houseman and Auden. During the day he carried a stalking telescope, a leather clad bottle of water (well, that's what he said it was) and an Army surplus haversack full of books.

The road was straight and flat, the scenery dull and dusty, the inside of the Landcruiser cramped and sweaty and after a couple of days I contemplated the wisdom of the trip.

The Dogon people have a remarkable history. Originally pasturalists on the plains of the North, they resisted the pressures of Islam and resented its interference with their culture. Persecuted in the 16th century, they moved south across the flat, baked land to a point where the plain suddenly drops dramatically at the Bandiagara Escarp-

Gold earrings
Mali princess at Mopti

ment, 650 ft (200m) high and 150 miles (240 kms) long. The erosion of this great sandstone cliff has caused huge slabs to fall off and among its boulder-ridden base, the Dogons made a new and impregnable home. Anthropologically unique, they have changed little since that great exodus 500 years ago. Self-sufficient, they grow millet and corn, herd goats and sheep and live in the harsh terrain in peaceful co-existence with nature, other neighbouring tribes (including Bongos, Bozos, and Troglodytes) and increasing bands of tourists who come to wonder at their strange houses and their way of life.

The Dogons are a sociable lot, have strong family ties and time on their hands. As they pass each other, "Hello," is never enough. The standard greeting goes something like this:-

The eldest: *"Aga po."* (Hello) *"Seo."* (How are you?)

The other: *"Seo."*

The eldest: *"Oumana seo."* (How is your family?)

The other: *"Seo."*

The eldest: *"Ounou seo."* (How is your wife?)

The other: *"Seo."*

The eldest: *"Yahana go seo."* (How are your children?)

The other: *"Seo."*

The whole routine is then repeated with the roles reversed. There are no short cuts or abbreviations. If there are more than two in the group, each needs the full greeting, so that two women passing two others on a narrow path block the way until all the obligatory pleasantries have taken place. That is before any discussion on the price of fish, the health of a friend or the group of westerners that have just walked through their back yards.

Their animist beliefs give rise to frequent ceremonies, employing much action and many masks. At Tireli, a village protected by the status of a World Heritage Site, the chief, with an entrepreneurial spirit that has been absent from his people for centuries, organised performances of these ceremonies. We caught a Thursday matinee. In his full length boubous, fluorescent green plastic sandals and pink tinted spectacles, the chief waved his fly whisk to urge on a couple of dozen villagers on an area cleared of stones and surrounded by huge boulders usually used for winnowing millet. Backstage right sat a number of elderly men who chanted like a Greek chorus and rattled various cans. Two goatskin drums at front stage left thumped out a syncopated rhythm and extravagantly costumed men and women, some on stilts but all grotesquely masked, stomped about in the dust. It was a good show. Whether this commercialisation of a 500 year old heritage will diminish its significance or produce dancers rather than millet farmers, remains to be seen. But in the meantime, the village might earn enough for a new school, their culture will be more widely spread and traditions will be kept extant. I congratulated the chief as I left and he beamed. "I think it went well today, don't you?" Lloyd Webber might have said the same. An earlier visit to the celebrated guitarist Ali Farka Toure was not nearly so entertaining. From his bar in a dusty town, he handed out poor quality CDs in a listless fashion and charged extra for an autograph.

The River Niger rises in the highlands of Guinea 400 miles (650 kms) from the Atlantic Coast but eccentrically ignores the short route to the sea and flows off

Maisons des Femmes - Bozon Escarpment

in the opposite direction, widening into an inland delta on the flat plateau of central Mali before realising its mistake and making a long curving sweep back to the sea through Nigeria. The river is already half a mile wide with 100 miles (160 kms) yet to go. Its slow moving and benign progress is reflected in the people who occupy its banks and several long and languid limbs steadied my steps along the slippery path to board our river vessel.

The mud Mosque at Djenné

The *pinasse*, for that is what passenger boats are called here, was about a tenth of the size I had expected. In a single glance there vanished hopes of gin and tonics on the afterdeck, a snooze in a mahogany cabin or a deckchair by the rail with a *citron presse*. Secured to the muddy bank by a rope knotted in several places and approached by a gang plank whose two boards moved apart with the rhythm of the waves, was a brightly coloured craft with four rows of wooden seats, a cooking area aft and a hooped roof of woven palm. In size and design it was the sort of craft that might have been hired from just south of Magdalen Bridge for a pleasant afternoon with a jolly girl, cucumber sandwiches, a bottle of Bollinger and a tartan rug but as presented, Bogart might have been content to tug it through a swamp. As a vessel to travel up one of the great rivers of Africa it seemed entirely inappropriate. Nevertheless its hardwood construction seemed robust and barnacle free, the freeboard clear above the water. Two 50 gallon drums of petrol were secured in the bow, a mountain of provisions was strapped to the roof and the red, yellow and green flag of the Democratic Republic of Mali flew confidently in the breeze. Bogart would have been content to tug it through a swamp or shoot the rapids. On the raised stem, with the word 'LAVATORY' hung upon it, was a small enclosure that served to secure the modesty of the occupant; there was a hole to the water and I noted that accuracy would be vital. As a teenager, I had once spent a week with a Norwegian family whose house in the forest was served by a three-seater privy. With the fear that my hostess might arrive mid constitutional, I was constipated for a week. I expected to be similarly concreted for the next three days. Nevertheless, it looked as though it would be a breezy but enjoyable trip. But then I spotted the crew. The captain, or so he was addressed (an extravagant title for one whose only job seemed to be an ability to have one hand on the outboard motor), had a right leg twisted and scarred as though it may have been mangled in machinery, two fingers were missing from his left hand and a genetic defect to his mouth and nose gave him the unfortunate appearance of having unintentionally encountered a brick wall. One eye suffered from river

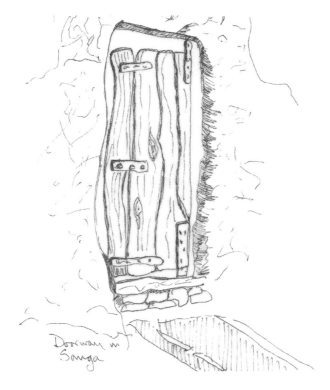

Doorway in Songa

blindness. His name was Halith and since the 'h' was silent, his bizarre appearance was compounded by being called 'Alice'. However, the maxim of never judging on appearances proved correct since Alice was skilful, helpful and resourceful and he was also the cook. He was accompanied by two boys whose job turned out to be that of continuous baling.

The shallow margins of the Niger were policed by pied kingfishers who took up station every few yards, undermining the banks with their nests. Herons stood patiently before lifting off with an insouciant slow wing beat for another less disturbed breakfast area. Harriers, goshawks, falcons, kites and the occasional African fish eagle patrolled the skies and sandpipers, stints, godwits, terns and plovers occupied the shoreline.

We stopped occasionally at a Bozo village whose people depended on fishing for a living. Medicine was frequently requested for a malarial child, river blindness or a suppurating sore but we could seldom help. The women had rings through their nose and coloured string tied through their ears. All day long they pounded rice or millet, washed clothes and pots, cooked and cleaned. There was little other river traffic, although occasionally a pirogue, heavily laden with firewood, was poled with great effort along the shallow river edge, or the twice weekly pinasse from Bamako to Gao (six days and nights, God help them!) and heavily laden with a commercial and human cargo, cast its bow waves to rock the fishermen. These were wearisome days, hot and dull, with a plank of a seat less comfortable than that of a third class railway carriage and I was paying a price that could have hired a whole steamer.

Suddenly our soporific progress stopped dead in the water. It was lunchtime and plates of food tipped into laps, the kettle toppled, fuel drums were dislodged and there were cries of alarm; we had run on to a sandbank. Le Capitaine looked distraught, no doubt from the dual concerns that his seamanship might be questioned or that his tip might be jeopardised. He and the two boys jumped into the water, as did I and help was summoned from fishermen whose poles were employed as levers amid much conflicting advice. Eventually we floated free, lunch and leisure were resumed and I for one looked forward to the next *desastre*.

Approaching Mopti, a large town at the confluence of the Niger and the Bani rivers, we passed through Lake Donde where the grey of the sky melded into the grey of the water with bare distinction. I have never seen ten square miles (25 square kms) of water so universally calm. The whole lake held its breath not daring to ripple less it expend unnecessary energy. Cormorants occasionally crossed our bows flying east to west just above the syrupy water and here at last was a lushness of reeds and plant life. Perched upon the tallest stems were groups of carmine bee eaters, Abyssinian rollers and paradise wydahs.

Going on to Djenne we reached what was once the country's most prosperous city with far reaching traders bartering Saharan iron, copper and stone but now trade was listless – just like the rest of the country. We had come to look at the mud buildings of which the much photographed mosque, with its turreted corners and crenulated walls, is the biggest in the world. I should have been impressed but it seemed like a larger version of those that are annually patted into place on Weymouth beach. Here they were also patted but by teams of boys who scrambled up the precarious scaffolding with buckets of red mud from the banks of the River Bani in a continuous programme of repair. The buildings may be centuries old but the open sewers were too and I was anxious to leave this mud pie of a town for the warm, clean winds of the desert.

'Is the rumour of thy Timbuctoo
A dream as frail as those of ancient time?'

In a word, Mr Tennyson, yes. The rumours may well have once had substance but in Timbuktu now all there seemed to be were thin goats, ragged children and an air of dusty despondency that swept around every corner: there was much dust and there were many corners. We had flown there in a Russian aircraft of Air Mali, known locally as Air Maybe, and at the airport, Tuareg men, wrapped like mummies in blue indigo cloth so that only dark, bloodshot eyes were vulnerable to swirling sand, gave a hint of authenticity. The golden years were in the 16th century when the city was the hub of the trans-Saharan trade routes travelled by merchants from the south dealing in gold, ivory, ostrich feathers and slaves and from the North, salt, copper, cloth and horses. Out of this prosperity grew the greatest centre of learning and religious thought in the western Sudan. The tales of fabulous wealth attracted Mungo Park, who never reached the town, Gordon

Laing who did but was slaughtered by Tuaregs as he left and Rene Caillie, who got there in 1827 only to write home describing *'a mass of ill-looking houses built of earth'*; and so it was.

Late one evening I found Sinclair robed in his tartan dressing gown on the roof top veranda of the Hotel Colombe. He was having his hair cut by a prim and pencil moustached barber who had the words 'Maurice René – Paris and Timbuktu' embroidered on his white tunic. Waugh and Durrell would have rejoiced that such scenes could still be real. The shower had dribbled and the bed was harder than the tiled floor but after a dinner of rice and river fish on the hotel roof, I looked up from reading the tales of Beau Geste to the sparkling canopy of stars in their infinite number and for a moment thought I could hear the welcoming shouts of a camel train as it approached from the great dunes of Sudan and caught a hint of frankincense on the warm wind.

"I've just been to Mali."

"Oh really? Dogons, Timbuktu, the Niger and all that; it must have been wonderful."

"It was... interesting."

Postcard Home

I'm an ingenue in Timbuktu.
It's so damned hot I think I'll rot!
My group loves a bird to a point that absurd;
"Hoopoo at 4 o'clock" one of them cries
And six pairs of binos are raised to the skies.
(I've seen the odd mammal but each one's a camel)
But when all's said and done, I'm having quite fun.

Sabah

August 2003

'One of the pleasantest things in life is to go for a long journey' – William Hazlitt

Singapore was 73°F (23°C) and drenched with rain. En route to Sabah, Kuching, the capital of Sarawak, was even wetter. A large party of jolly young Malaysian men were there to play golf. They wore co-respondent spiked shoes, many were dressed in tartan trousers and most were chattering into a mobile phone. These rang constantly, each playing a different jingle; a dozen or so might be calling at the same time. A tin marked 'Horlicks' and slices of Swiss roll by the tea urn and something grey labelled 'Beef Pie' revealed that the past still lingered. It could have been Perth airport for the Gleneagles fortnight.

Kota Kinabalu, the capital of the Malaysian state of Sabah, was a smaller version of Kuching but still about seven times larger than I had imagined or had wished. There were high rise buildings, an urban sprawl in all directions and scars of red earth where new industrial estates and more houses were planned. Evidence of older houses only appeared on the fringes where coloured tin roofs clustered together in kampongs. The town was largely destroyed by the British in World War II in an attempt to deny it to the approaching Japanese and it was then comprehensively flattened three years later as they were being driven out. Rebuilt in the '60s and renamed from its previous name of Jessleton, it was long on function and short on charm, had little appeal and I longed to leave. By now it was 10 pm and with a two hour mountain drive ahead, fast food was called for and there it was, glowing in red neon – Double Cheeseburger and Chips.

My prayer for departure was clearly garbled in transmission as a tropical storm of great intensity broke out. As we wound laboriously up the mountain, often axle deep in floodwaters, I pondered the omens. After a 25 hour journey from

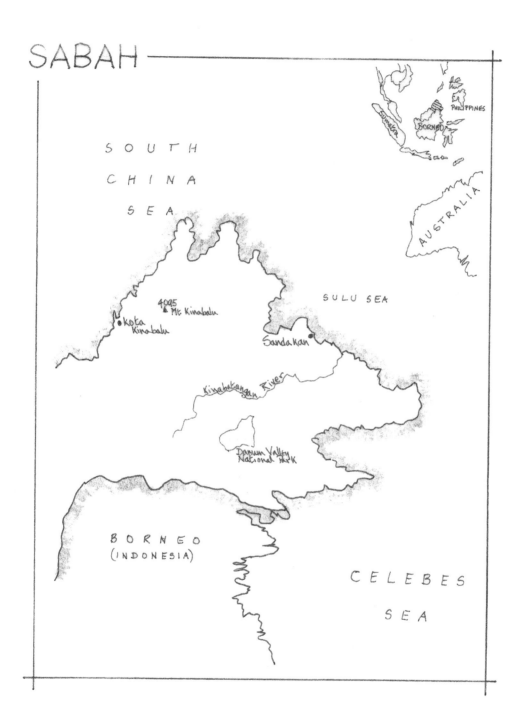

a parched Oxfordshire landscape, I had arrived to a waterfall of rain to eat at McDonalds with a male Chinese guide oddly called Jessie and who had spent his teenage years in Borehamwood and a driver with one ear (as I noticed in the almost continuous forked lightning) and unaccountably known as Captain Julius. I judged the omens good, if only on the basis of improbability.

Mount Kinabalu pokes its granite nose out of the rainforest on the northern tip of Borneo and for many is the sole reason for visiting Sabah. The summit at 13,400 ft (4,095m) is the highest in South-East Asia, with tropical vegetation up to 1,000 ft (3,200m). It lies at the centre of the Kinabalu National Park which has World Heritage status and one of the most remarkable of all nature's paradises with reputedly the richest diversity of flora in the world. With 6,000 vascular plant species, 1,000 different orchids and 780 ferns, it seemed a likely claim. It also has an annual drenching of 15 ft (4.5m) of rain and most of it seemed to fall on the morning of my climb.

Rigorous procedures at the park headquarters ensured that I had a coded yellow plastic label to hang round my neck. This was principally to check that I returned but more likely so that my corpse could be identified if I strayed off the path. I felt like a heifer with a tag in its ear. Guides, or more truthfully helping hands, were compulsory. The system allowed these guides – stocky, wiry, mountain men with bulging calves and cracked skin – to barter for their clients, so as the tagged heifers milled around, they made their bids. Single, fit young men were the cheapest; plump Japanese pricey and families sky-high (the children might need carrying).

The route was steep, sometimes vertical and the steps high (there were 2,800 to the summit). The rock was slippery, washed by mountain streams, and the mud sticky. But there were no bugs, good shelters every half mile (.8kms) and there was the camaraderie engendered by those who know that they are engaged in a challenge. For me, the challenge started at the gate and continued in increasing stages of difficulty for the next four and a half hours. I saw one other of bus-pass age but so intent was I in following one secure foothold with another that I might have missed a few. I made it to the tree line – an uphill two and a half mile route. My knees were jelly, my legs wobbled and my heart pounded; only bravado and the spirit of empire builders kept me moving. I celebrated the point of no return with my packed lunch of cold chicken sausage, fried bread and an 'energy bar' that looked and tasted like Old Bruno Ready Rubbed pipe tobacco. From 9,800 ft (2,980m) there was perpetual cloud whose drizzle made a scotch mist seem like a puff of aerosol and this suddenly gave way to a tropical storm – another one! Climbers slithering up or sliding down stopped at our corrugated roofed shelter and soon a polyglot, multi-lingual, international, dripping but cheerful group were crowded together, confined behind the heavy bars of rain. National characteristics were displayed in their wet weather gear. The Japanese were fully equipped for Cape Horn, the Dutch and Italians were in proper waterproofs and sturdy rucksacks, there was a Spaniard in an anorak and guides in tattered trousers, flip flops and charity t-shirts. There was also an Englishman in split boots, shorts, a muddy shirt, carrying a Peruvian shoulder bag and sweating under a cheap plastic poncho.

The downward journey was heavier on the knees but lighter on the heart and there was some enthusiasm for handing back my tag and a great deal more enthusiasm for my bed. The whole trip to the top would have been ten hours, with a cold and wet night in a hut on the way and then six hours down the next morning. Limping back to my bungalow, I passed a sign that listed the time of the winner of the last annual Climbathon Race to the summit and back: two hours, 41 minutes. Some men are not human.

Sandakan, Sabah's second town, lies on the east coast. The flight across the state showed the rainforest sprawled across the heavily corrugated landscape with the highest trees and the widest canopies in the valleys. At 7 am mist and low cloud had settled in these warmer valleys but would burn off soon. Occasionally a patch of red earth showed through where there had been logging but in this part at least, the damage looked minor. However, where the land flattened towards the sea, over 250,000 acres (one million hectares) had been cleared and oil palm in blocks of neat rows had been planted over the last 30 years. Rivers writhed through the flat land carrying silt whose colour matched the terracotta of the roads – the latter only distinguishable by their straight path.

On the aeroplane I was reading *A Parrot in a Pepper Tree* by Christopher Stewart and my suppressed laughter made tears pour down my cheeks. I was interrupted by the woman beside me wearing a *baju kurung*, a white Muslim headscarf. She might have been a nun but at any rate, she was clearly a kindly and caring soul and she put a hand on my knee and gave me a tender and compassionate smile. On a later leg and similarly convulsed, my companion, this time short and hairy (and big in cement he told me) seemed to assume from the book's title that I was reading an agricultural text book; he must have thought me either deranged or was using the cover to mask something lascivious.

Sandakan was clean and conforming and its urban vulgarity spread along the shoreline to where the stilted houses of the fishermen and sea gypsies took over in a tangled town of timber boarded, tin roofed shacks linked by planked walkways and all hung about with the domestic decoration of washing, potted plants and plastic utensils. The rows of white villas in cul-de-sacs and squares of urban propriety were soulless and abandoned but in these offshore communities chil-

Rafflesia — largest flower in the world.

dren giggled, women chatted and life throbbed. The products of the fishermen's labours were spread out through a huge fish market. Slippery under foot with guts and scales, the night's catches were piled in heaps for wholesalers and housewives. There were huge rays three feet (1m) across, snapper, parrotfish, grouper, eels, crabs, conch, flatfish, tube fish, yellow finned tuna, mountains of little jacks, white-fleshed shark and red fleshed tuna. Great slabs of ice covered in hessian arrived in pick-ups and were slid over the market floor, lifted by toothed prongs and then pushed on to the boats down narrow wooden channels where they were crushed with sledgehammers for the next night's fishing.

A mile offshore but in shallow water, bungalow-sized bamboo fish traps with great square nets were anchored in the sand to catch the fish swept in by the tide and these were serviced by smaller boats that continually chugged out almost obscured by their diesel smoke. We looked at these nets on the way to Turtle Island, an hour away in a high speed boat. There, a conservation project attempted to protect Green and Hawksbill turtles that find their way back from the ocean to lay their clutches of between 80 and 200 eggs in the sand. The jetty had been rammed by a misguided military boat the day before (there was a small contingent of Malaysian police on the island to patrol the seas against Filipino illegal immigrants, the border with the Philippines being only ten miles to the north) and so we ran aground on sand as dazzling as snow and in azure water waist deep. We had not been warned of this type of arrival and for a little while there was confusion. Two of our party, Val and Ian Hales, a middle aged Australian couple, he a pumpkin she a stick, unpacked their bags and attempted to change into swimming clothes. Not an easy matter in an open boat rocking in the surf while maintaining modesty in front of crew and strangers. I shunned decency and stripped to underpants and the other traveller Bas van Steegeen, a 6'6" (2m) tall pigtailed Dutchman, whose whole wardrobe was contained in a rucksack so small it might have been sold as a female fashion accessory, jumped in with shorts and singlet. My suitcase, heavy with cameras, books, boots and 'things to do if it rains', got laboriously passed from shoulder to shoulder as we stood in the warm water. It would probably have floated but I had an anxious few minutes.

The whole purpose of this lengthy side trip to these pleasant islands in the Sulu Sea was something of a disappointment. A mother turtle – in this case a Green (the Hawksbills having come ashore earlier in the year) – having reached sexual maturity after ten or sometimes 30 years at sea and its pea-sized brain having being guided by ocean currents, moon phases and magnetic fields, hauls itself up with great effort onto the same beach that gave it birth. Highly susceptible to heat, she does this at night. Under pain of island expulsion no camera flash was allowed, so loaded with the fastest film available and a torch, I sought to capture this intimate occasion. In the event my torch was banned and by the dismal glow of a guide's torch and standing four deep like students in a labour ward, we just made out the plopping of one hundred and eight rubbery eggs. After laying, the clutch was immediately gathered up by the rangers for reburial in an area safe from rats, monitor lizards and raptors and mother turtle skilfully but pathetically covered over a now empty hole with her back flippers. The highlight of the eve-ning – by now it was midnight – was the release of 100 or so hatchlings (three would fit in one's palm) back to the sea. They were tipped out from a plastic bucket at high tide level so that their lungs could be exercised before their swim and they scurried over the sand, their little flippers whirring like a wind-up toy. The laggards were urged on by the crowd and when the last one was safely afloat, a cheer went up and there were some sobs too. Within three hours of birth, in the darkness, alone, uncared for, unguided, unfed, vulnerable and lonely, these hatchlings were embraced by the warm water of an immense ocean.

The Kinabatangan River is Sabah's largest and rises in the hilly interior and empties itself on the east coast in a muddy soup that extends far out to sea. At this eastern end and hemmed in by vast oil palm plantations (Sabah produces ten percent of the world's cooking oil and chippies in Bolton could not do without it) are wetlands that support a high concentration of birds and mammals. The forest dwellers include Asian elephants, Sumatran rhinos and various cats, rats, squirrels and many monkeys – gibbons, macaques, langurs and the bizarre proboscis. One of nature's jokes, a male proboscis monkey sports a belly that might have been fed on beer and has a great floppy, extended and inebriated nose. Its tight, biscuit-co-loured fur improbably has a band of white around its bottom to give the impres-sion of an elderly drunk clad only in his underpants. Bas, the pigtailed Dutch-

Buffy's Fish owl

man, had appeared again and as we shared the backseat of a longboat, he roared with laughter whenever a group of these drunkards appeared. Oriental darters and many kingfishers – pied, blue-eared, black-backed, rufous-backed, stork-billed and banded and imperial green pigeons, egrets and many raptors, including the white billed fish eagle and the magnificent crested serpent eagle, inhabited the riverine margin. Pairs of hornbills continually crossed the river calling raucously like old fashioned football rattles. The rhinoceros hornbill is another freak, with a great extended casque welded on to the top of an already impossibly unwieldy beak. Like the Brabazon, aerodynamically it should not be flying.

The rains have so swollen the river that it covered the base of the tree trunks on either side and it seemed as if the forest is draining into it. The current was swift and carried a great assortment of logs, branches, floating islands of hyacinth, an oil drum or two, bamboo poles, planks and the plastic detritus of humans further upstream. On one such pile of flotsam there was a monitor lizard three feet long that fixed me with a dinosaurian eye before swimming away and overhead, a brahminy kite flew so low I heard the rush of air through its primaries. It then circled overhead, its pale brown flecked belly white in the sun and mewing a shrill call before it soared away. Occasionally egrets sat perched on a log and they seemed to enjoy the ride as they swirled into whirlpools. The water, beige coloured with the silt that was washed from the riverbanks and hillsides stripped naked by logging activities, mixed with darker earth in the eddies so that the whole river resembled a huge helping of Caramel Delight. The egrets, when not riding the river rollercoaster, stood sentinel and silent to catch a fish or a frog. But no self-respecting mammal enjoys the rain, and the monkeys vanished to the shelter of broad leafed trees.

The rain followed me to the Danum Valley where a fashionable eco-lodge had been built at the end of a three hour drive on a switchback rubble road through a logging concession of one million acres (404,000 hectares). Taking a 'get wet and be damned' attitude and protecting my camera in a lodge laundry bag, I strode out down a forest trail in shorts and a tee-shirt. I should have known about the leeches. Some unpleasant weeks at a Jungle Warfare School 40 years before, lugging a bren gun through drenched undergrowth and splashing through jungle streams, should have reminded me of the guile of these silent and stealthy parasites. Painlessly, they clasp on to warm-blooded mammals as they flounder by and hang on till they gorge themselves. They can take onboard six times their weight in blood and live off it for months. Enthusiastic for the lushness of the jungle, I walked the trails for an hour or so and returning damp and muddy stripped in the shower to find half a dozen of these blood suckers. A lighted cigarette dispatched them but three had climbed to the tenderest and warmest part of my male anatomy. These clever and insidious creatures inject an anti-coagulant which ensures that blood runs for several hours. The dinner gong had sounded and I had only a pair of cream trousers to wear. The manufacturers of sticking plaster do not seem to have properly researched the adhesive properties required in this particular area of the male body and as the blood flowed, I contemplated the alternatives. An embarrassing stain getting steadily larger, the use of a plastic bag (I only had one and that crackled), missing dinner (I was hungry) or tightly tied handkerchiefs. I chose the latter and walking as though in a wet nappy, I timidly headed for the dining room sporting a bulge like a family bunch of bananas.

Botanically, the jungle here is Lowland Dipterocarp Forest. Commercially it is a loggers' dream with hardwood trees two or three hundred years old, up to 260 ft (80m) high and with a girth of 1.5 ft (4m). For the forest inhabitants it is disastrous and the orang-utan population was down 50 percent in the previous 15 years. Like all primary forests it was benign, with few thorns or bugs, but full of sound; monkeys crashed through the canopy, birds called, cicadas screeched and deer barked. Palim, my naturalist guide, was born in the forest and started out as a hunter relying on the forest for food but now he spoke Malay, English, Japanese and Chinese and he led our band along damp and shady forest trails. One glance at the dark green wall of forest took in a millipede in the floor litter, a medicinal plant or a flying squirrel 160 ft (50m) up. Droppings were minutely poked about and identified and after three days I found I knew more than I might have wished about the digestive systems of civets and what a langur had for lunch.

After a day in such a place, one acquires a misplaced possessiveness that claims exclusive rights. Those joining a small group are treated with some indifference and even resentment. I was the interloper who dared join an established team of two Nipps, two Swedes and two Brits. This stew, made up of rather bland and respectful national ingredients, seemed to work well. The addition of a couple of Yanks might have added body, but a Wop or two would have been far too spicy and to have thrown in a handful of Micks would have had the pot boiling over. After the pleasantries of mutual Good Mornings, each kept to their own until some occasion provided an opportunity to offer a better viewing position or a steadying hand over a rocky river bed. The flavours slowly intermingled and simmered. And so it was for two days and a night – Koshi and Hourima, Petra and Sven, Tom and Annabelle plus James; a pretty successful recipe.

On my last evening I sat on a boulder by the river for an hour or two and was visited by a family of wild pigs rootling in the riverbank and a timid sambar deer coming to the edge to drink. A black hornbill called from the far bank with low growls that gathered speed and ended in swift cackles as though he was delighted in his own joke. A troop of maroon langurs crashed around before returning to the forest for the night. Gibbons sang their sunset songs and a pair vocalised to each other over a three octave range. The bugs of dusk came out too; Keats remembered them (although beside a Scottish loch).

'Then in a wailful choir the small gnats mourn
Among the river sallows, borne aloft
Or sinking as the light wind lives and dies.'

In the dusk, I made my way back to find I was the only guest. I sat in the great first floor dining hall with six waiters, two barmen, a kitchen full of chefs and with maids and flunkies eager to please but lacking commands. By some freak of booking mismanagement, this 20-bedroomed lodge with its stockpile of rattan furniture and sitting in a million acres of jungle was all mine. Simultaneously I was all powerful, somewhat disconcerted and rather forlorn. Some might have relished this opportunity to act the pasha in his palace but this armchair Tarzan, lordly but lonely and missing his Jane, called for another beer, paused on the veranda to catch the sounds of croaking frogs, the squeaks and whirls of myriad insects, the trill of a flycatcher, the ripple of the river, wondered at the stars, the trails of fireflies and the lightning of a distant storm silhouetting the forest canopy and headed for dreams.

Lahad Datu was the face of modern Sabah that I had sought to avoid. This provincial town on the extreme border of Malaysia showed up the prosperity of the country as a whole. Car scrap-yards, depots of mechanical diggers and logging lorries grinding their way to the port with oil palm tankers in their wake. Along the road were new army barracks, a huge new hospital (although short of doctors I was told), new power lines from a hydroelectric scheme and a university campus for 1,000 students. Japanese 4x4s, mobile phones, TVs and techno gadgets were in every shop and showroom. Identical residential boxes with no gardens but plants in all types of containers sat in sullen rows and scattered across this urban landscape were an assortment of evangelical churches and extravagant domed mosques. And all this was inhabited, driven, worked and regulated by a mix of Malay, Chinese and Indians, all speaking their own languages (with a universal fall-back of English) and worshipping their own gods in a harmony that prejudiced parts of the world should envy.

I stopped over in Singapore for a change of planes and a gulp of nostalgia. Every arriving passenger was thermodynamically screened for high body temperature as an indicator of the SARS epidemic allegedly raving at the time. Singapore takes everything seriously and all school children took their temperature daily. The female taxi driver had two mobiles and an electronic screen, all of which bleeped or spoke. She thought I was under 50, which somewhat compensated for a boatman in Sabah who had thought I was 72. Torrents of rain filled the storm culverts and dimmed the view; was there a message somewhere in these buckets of water that were upturned wherever I arrived? When the rain cleared it revealed a city unknown to me; refreshingly green and remarkably clean and with every car seemingly driven out of a showroom that day; even the school buses were polished.

I took a taxi with a driver of low intelligence but high spirits and an incessant gabble that might have been English if only night school could have honed his pronunciation into something intelligible. Unfortunately, he did not think much of my pronunciation either and in a lay-by we studied a map of my objectives. Neesoon, where I was happily stationed for a year in 1962, was a vast housing estate, the Goodwood Hotel and Raffles recognisable only externally and the Tanglin Club, once the haunt of arrogant young cavalry officers, had a long waiting list for would-be members of the business noblesse. The Singapore Tourist Office would, no doubt, have wanted to tell me about the old fashioned charms of Geyland Serai, Arab Street or Little India but to me they were sanitised history. Memory lane had been turned into dual carriageways, although road names were unchanged and familiar. My last memory of Orchard Road was one of driving down it in my yellow, two-seater TR3 with six brother officers in the back. We were going home then and it was time for me to go home now. Besides, it had started to rain again.

Shangri La

June 2004

'The world is getting such a dangerous place, a man is lucky to get out of it alive'
- WC Fields

It seems a pity to start with a complaint but I need to clear away an irritation that arises from the dawn arrival of each of the last four flights I have taken. Why, oh why is breakfast served so early? Sleep is scarce enough and each wink is precious. Prior to a 6 am arrival, to be woken for a foam rubber omelette and a leather sausage at 4 am and to have this cleared away only for the lights to be turned off again is a special kind of long haul torture. I said as much to the senior hostess: "Royal Thai Orchid Class should treat its customers better; after all they are the ones that make you money." She smiled a charm school smile, dipped her knees just sufficiently to put a tiny crease in the back of her silk skirt and said that she would note my comments and hoped that I had had a pleasant flight. I had thought that she was human, she was certainly pretty and it was a shame that she turned out to be simply an automaton. However, a signal had gone out, as later the purser arrived. He pursed his lips, went down on one knee and listened intently. He then thought for a while and said he would note my comments and hoped that I had had a pleasant flight.

The flight of Southern China Airlines from Kunming was far noisier, considerably more crowded and a lot more fun. I thought I was going to miss it as 43 Taiwanese golfers queued in front of me on their way to The Sunshine Golf Tournament. When I realised that they were queuing for my own flight, my anxiety was reduced to wondering whether there would be enough room left for me.

To a westerner the Chinese are small and so are their airline seats. A six foot

160

SHANGRI LA

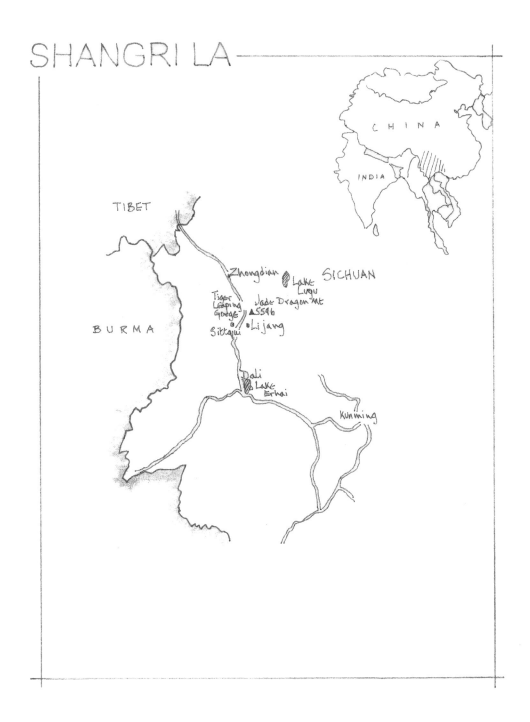

New Zealander had his knees around his ears but I was fortunate being by the emergency exit; the captain came to say, "Pleeth no touch." My smile of acknowledgement was confident but should the moment have come when I should have been required to touch, 43 golfers, a tall New Zealander and 159 assorted Chinese would have been kicking my bum to be the first to escape. I asked my Taiwanese neighbour if it was difficult to enter China. "Oh no!" he laughed. "We are the ones who lend the money." He chuckled about this absurd question until we landed an hour later.

The old town of Dali oozes charm from its tree-lined, stone-paved streets busy with local shoppers and groups of Chinese tourists gathered up by flag waving girl guides. Here, the Bai are the majority tribe, the women wearing a single coloured vest over a blouse with an apron falling over black trousers. Confusing in name but not in dress are the Dai who filter through the market adding bright splashes of colour with their striped sarongs and fitted jackets – resembling their tribal cousins in Burma's Shan states. Lahu also come down from the hills to shop, distinctive in their black turbans with a long back flap. They are Christians and in a small chapel, a picture shows Christ floating ethereally above the Great Wall. The Bai, on the other hand, are Muslim but all seem tolerant of each other's religions and customs. This tribal cocktail gets the occasional addition of Wa women puffing away on home grown tobacco stuffed into long silver pipes. Having paid the obligatory visit to the ninth century Three Pagodas (they looked 19th century to me), spent two nights in a vast hotel of ghastly gaudiness and fished with trained cormorants in the rain, I moved on.

Like a ribbon thrown against the mountainside, the road to Lake Lugu winds around the steep sides of valleys several thousand feet deep that a millennium of snow and flood, rock falls and crashing streams has vertically scarred. The road is partly metalled, partly cobbled and in between are sections of rutted dirt. The echoes of the tramping feet of Kublai Khan's armies resonate all the way. Like ants toiling over a ploughed field, his weary troops climbed 100 mountain ranges and crossed the Yangtze and Mekong rivers before eventually garrisoning the Lijiang district in around 1250. As we dropped 4,000 ft (1,200m) in two hours, the scrub pine gave way to alder and birch and then, at the base of deep valleys where the sun is trapped and the wind filtered through 1,000 subsidiary glens, bananas, lemons, pomegranates and oranges grow in terraced rows. Small areas of pasture had been cleared to graze a few brown and black cows, and grape vines growing in ordered rows and originally introduced by French Catholic missionaries for sacramental wine.

As we climbed again, the flash of sun on moving water far below gave a first glimpse of the River Yangtze. These glimpses came more frequently as the road descended the next valley via 100 hairpins and then brown water, swiftly moving amongst the sandbanks, rocks and cascades, was squeezed between concrete buildings that intrude like a proletariat wart on the natural grandeur. Crossing the river by the bridge that is anchored by these buildings (the only bridge for 90 miles (144kms) north and 80 miles (128kms) south), the opposite side of the gorge had another random ribbon of road along which overloaded lorries slowly inched their way, belching enough black exhaust fumes to darken the sky. These were not the brightly coloured glittery vehicles of the southern Himalayas and the Karakorum but in the nature of the Han Chinese, plain and conforming. We made long detours to the ends of side valleys, past little settlements where the wooden houses are built alpine-like with interlocking trunks from the pine that cover the hillsides. The almost vertical slopes were sometimes cleared of stone boulders and planted with potatoes or maize, both introduced by missionaries in the early 19th century and now staples of the local diet. Why these crops were not washed away by the rain is a mystery; perhaps they are, but an occasional loss is presumably preferable to the labour of terracing such steep slopes. Down once more, the switchback road was then surfaced with a zillion small pieces of granite individually jig-sawed into compacted clay that left my bones rattling like a laboratory skeleton. The bus often had to manoeuvre over and around landslides, each time coming heart-stoppingly close to the edge. There were lacy patterns of goat trails over the hillsides and far below rice paddies, in varied stages of growth, made a patchwork of viridian, emerald and jade.

Up again, this time into the territory of the Mosu people and on the fringe of the Yi. Married Yi women working in the fields were wearing two foot (60cms) wide canopies of black velvet on their heads – a more impractical and awkward headgear it would be hard to devise but in case this was not handicap enough, this was coupled with eight inch long earrings of semi-precious stones, a heavily embroidered, brilliantly coloured coat and weighty silver jewellery. The Mosu, like the Naxi whom we would meet later, follow a flexible form of co-habitation before marriage known as *ashu* – literally 'good friends'. We have heard that one before! Sexual activity often begins between teenagers and needless to say the incidence of sexually transmitted diseases is frightful. In 1957 Peter Goullart, a Russian-born Frenchman who wrote extensively of this part of China, recalls an encounter with a Tibetan trader returning from the Mosu region. Asked to treat the man, Goullart quickly recognized the symptoms of gonorrhoea and proceeded to suggest a suitable course of treatment. But the man protested that he only had a cold. "How did you get the cold?" asked Goullart. "From riding a horse," replied the man. "Well," said Goullart, "it was the wrong kind of horse."

Descending again for the fortieth time, I regretted the breakfast of bracken shoots and crunchy chicken feet. Here was another change of architecture where the wooden houses had stone bases up to the first floor and were grouped around a courtyard. Black faced sheep appeared together with Mosu women this time wearing turbans of black knitted wool covered in silver and gold beads, embroidered tunics and long, white, pleated skirts.

My first impression of Lijiang appalled since I had fond and vivid memories of an outstanding TV documentary of the late '80s, called 'Beyond the Clouds'. I had longed to see this wonderful town – the genuine, untouched, medieval, cobbled, cool, stone-bridged, clear-streamed, willow-hung, single-storied and timbered-fronted and dotted with charming squares full of magnolias and camellias of venerable age. Unfortunately, the Chinese Office of State Tourism seemed to have been watching television too and had other plans. After the devastating earthquake of 1996 that destroyed many of the Naxi homes, the state poured in money to clear, gentrify, sanitise and reconstruct. UNESCO then added a World Heritage Site stamp of approval. Ancient, sleepy little alleyways became busy with souvenir shops and internet cafés, cobbled lanes were transformed by the brash and the tacky and all were filled with crowds bussed in and flown in to experience the 'Real China'. Many shops sold old domestic items of dubious authenticity and age. Like their counterparts worldwide, their sign might well have read 'Bric-a-brac bought, antiques sold'. However, strolling the lanes and back alleys in the angled sunlight of early morning (even Chinese tourists don't get out before 9 am), there was still a quiet magic to be found. There were vendors at street corners with fresh, newly peeled, water sprinkled vegetables and dumplings steaming, dogs stretching, children yawning, neighbours chatting, thresholds being swept, cobbles being watered and wooden shutters being opened; all the indications of a prosperous market town starting the day. But post 9 am, these townsfolk, some descended from the garrisoning armies of Kublai Khan, were engulfed by some of the three million tourists a year (99% Chinese) that stay for two nights in the 75 hotels or rent one of the 3,200 self-catering apartments that have been built in the last five years.

Wandering around the town, I came upon the Cultural Museum; the sign at the entrance read: 'The Tired and Over-Sixty are Free'. I walked in, doubly eligible. The museum seemed to be staffed exclusively by women reflecting the matriarchal society of the Naxi. The women own the house, the lease of the land (all land in China being state-owned) and have custody of the children. As strong as Greek donkeys, they work the fields and run the businesses. The husbands look after the house, the potted plants and the children, write poetry, play musical instruments and gossip.

I had injured an old and trusted friend, a big camera lens made by those clever people at Canon which allows me to take in a panorama and then zoom to a local character unaware that an intrusive foreigner believes their face would look interesting in his picture book. I should have known better but as the shack at the corner of the hotel had a hand-painted sign saying 'Camera Repairs' and since the Chinese are ingenious in their repair of western technical wizardry and the lens seemed ruined anyway, it was worth seeing what could be done. The youth inside with a blond streak in his greasy black hair recognised that his apprentice-ship had not gone beyond 'point and shoot' models and took me through a dozen alleyways and up a dark wooden stair to an older man with long fingernails who rummaged in his drawer for a suitable cross-head screwdriver that would deal with screws scarcely visible to the eye. This seemed a good start but a large padlock was then produced to bash the bent connecting plate and when this had not sufficient clout it was superseded by a plumber's Stillson wrench to really get down to deal-ing with the highest grade of Japanese stainless steel. A vital lug careered off and landed in my shoe. The technician, if that is what he called himself (there was no means of questioning him as to experience or ability), seemed quite unconcerned. Returning to his worktable, one short leg of which was propped on two cans of tuna, he fashioned a new lug with solder and vigorously went into the attack with assorted rasps. After digging further into the electronic bowels, opening another pack of foul smelling cigarettes and kicking the faulty bench light for the twenti-eth time, the scattered entrails of cogwheels, springs and delicate copper wash-ers were miraculously reassembled. The lens still did not work but curiously I had enjoyed the show, a kind of triumph of pragmatism over technology. Later, recounting the tale to the camera specialist in London, he told me that but for a single cog put in upside down it should have worked perfectly.

Following the brown swirling Yangtze, we drove north to Shangri La – yes, really, the Shangri La of myth and legend – but here it was covered in mud and drenched in drizzle. The state tourist machine hijacked this evocative name and formally applied it to a wide area of south west China with Zongdian at its centre. Peter Goullart in *'Forgotten Kingdoms'* started the rot calling it 'A paradise of nature and humanity' and James Hilton continued the dream in *'Lost Horizons'*; later transferred to celluloid by Frank Capra in 1937. (Niether Hilton nor Capra ever set foot in China.) The PR slush of the film studios has one reaching for the bucket: 'A dream and a reality – a land of eternal enchantment for those seeking and yearning for the perfection of human community.'

The Gyalthang Dzong Hotel in Zongdian was both a surprise and a disap-pointment. Surprising for its interior designed elegance, its fully working mechan-ics and its level of comfort; disappointing for the exact corollary. I was looking forward to the homeliness of hewn pine, an intermittent shower, an open stair

Draughts players in Lijang

Lijang.

Street musician

Yi woman

to the first floor and possibly (and even preferably) the warm smell of cattle and the honk of a black pig. What would never have been in doubt in either circumstance were the smiles and the helpfulness of the Tibetan staff. As our little bus drew up the whole staff of eight appeared through the overlapped, thick felted, ochre yellow and crimson trimmed curtain that served as a front door. All were gorgeously costumed, each different and everyone handsome. It could well have been the final curtain call of Turandot. The speech of welcome from the tall, heavyweight young Dutch manager (he could have lifted a Tibetan with each arm to shoulder height; what was he doing here?) was followed by a cheerful song from the chorus line and we were ushered in for a five night stay.

On reflection, the wish for rustic simplicity went out of the double-glazed window. Perhaps one night at the local inn would have satisfied the search of authenticity but I am clearly something of a fraud, for if a hot bath and a cold whisky are on offer, I am first in the queue. However, before I condemn myself too harshly, I object to the grotesqueness of out of place, self-indulgent luxury – the candelabra on the safari dining table, the six course dinner as a train rumbles through primary rain forest or the cruise ship that swamps a fishing village and its culture with six air conditioned coaches of gawping, camera clicking, medallioned, bermuda-shorted trippers. And while I am letting off a little steam of my personal prejudices, I am reminded of a holiday that M and I had in Thailand in 1998. I had come up the Mekong from Laos in a boat akin to a walnut shell propelled by a jet engine to join her at the Regent at Chiang Mai – an elegant hotel with a reputation amongst travel softies of producing the best of comfortable lazing and jolly nice it was too. But then we went on to the Rayavadee at Krabi that was so over the top in inessential luxury that I found it simultaneously obscene and a giggle – M in particular giggled a lot. Each round two-storied villa was wonderfully positioned but who on a seaside holiday, even if their name was Branson or Beckham, wants separate bathrooms, a dining area, an 'entertainment room' and for heaven's sake what do you do with a butler beside the beach? Ours was charming, attentive, keen to unpack suitcases and keener to pack picnic baskets, arrange a dinner for six, press clothes, ensure the maids had polished every corner and 'be of service'. While my shorts and torn tee-shirt for the cocktail hour clearly disappointed (M fortunately salvaged a little of our reputation with a slinky silk number), he brightened considerably when asked to arrange a day's outing to some sea nomads. However, having done that and explained the buttons for the blinds, lights, air conditioning, the exquisitely veneered panel that slid back to reveal a monster TV, the racks of movies, the music system, the workings of the juice extractor, ice maker and microwave, he outlived his usefulness and had to go.

But back to the real Shangri La. This came with a thumping headache and a foul cold. While others went off for a Tibetan hot pot in town, I sank a whisky or three, wallowed in a foaming bath, sipped onion soup as good as that from the Brasserie Lipp in front of a fire crackling with incense cedar and finally, on a moderately soft mattress, gratefully pulled up a duvet of exceptional warmth and prepared for a slow death. In the morning I was better and the others worse. The hot pot was so fully authentic that they had had to grapple with grizzly meatballs, boiled bones, slices of pigs' liver, hunks of pork fat, chunks of cabbage, chopped tubes of varying diameter, slithers of yak cheese and turnips, all of which floated around in grey and greasy broth.

This is not the place for a treatise on botany but any piece that mentions Yunnan must consider the extraordinary diversity of flowering plants, trees and shrubs that grow there. Yunnan means 'South of the Clouds' (referring to its position South of the Sichuan rainbelt) and its high altitude grasslands not only feed the great yak herds of the nomadic Tibetans but are the natural habitat of magnolias, ancient camellias (in Lijiang there is one reliably recorded as being 600 years old), and over 650 varieties of azaleas. In all there are about 18,000 different botanic species – Europe can muster around 3,000. No British garden or park could possibly bloom so prolifically, for such succession and with such variety, if seeds had not been brought to this country from this botanic wonderland. The 19th century legends of the plant world -Vietch, Farrow, Forest, Wilson, Rock and Ward explored, identified and collected and this continues with today's entrepreneurs – Lancaster, Kirkham et al. As we travelled, I was reading Kingdon Ward's *'Land of the Blue Poppy'*, passing through the same towns and seeing the same plants (including his famed discovery, *meconopsis wardii*) but did not have to endure the rigours of his solo journeys. At Yuhu, I sat for a few reverent moments in the lodgings of the eccentric and cantankerous Joseph Rock; a single first floor room where he lived for 15 years until he died having collected over 1,000 plants new to the west. But if I mention plants by name, a few hundred more will clamour for attention so these will have to remain in my notebook and my memory, but I was conscious that every foot I travelled was across one of the great botanical wonders of the world.

The Shangri La Horse Festival was something of a highlight of the trip. Not only for its local colour and excitement but because we had a chance to be on our own feet instead of riding on Chinese wheels. A half hour walk over red clay, thoroughly wettened by days of rain to a glue as effective as Oxfordshire plough, brought me amongst hundreds of jolly Tibetans. All entrances to the substantial grandstand were heavily guarded to ensure that neither tourists (there were only a couple of dozen) nor locals mixed with the military and government bigwigs. Almost entirely male, they sat in glum rows each with an identical arrangement of lilies, *stellera* and juniper between them and facing the crowd camped on the sweep of hillside partly covered with birch and stunted pine that overlooked the arena. For the three days of festivities many of the onlookers had erected tents. These were mostly of white canvas and covered in intricate interwoven designs in black but some (including those stencilled with a Coca Cola logo) went for the multicoloured look. Inside were laid mats of woven yak hair and outside, braziers of charcoal smoked continually giving off spicy smells from pieces of meat of strange shape and colour.

Tibetan women are a colourful lot; like most of the minority peoples we met, it was the women who were in tribal dress and they wore it every day. On special occasions such as this they glitter and shine, weaving into their braided hair heavy ornaments of silver, malachite, turquoise, coral or bone. Giggling groups wearing shocking pink turbans and white pleated skirts made bright spots of colour on the hillside. A few other Chinese tribes were present: Yi, Muso and even Dai who had made the long journey from Dali. The men, in drab suits whose jackets seldom matched their trousers, seemed pre-occupied with gambling or shooting at balloons with an air rifle at five paces and seldom succeeding.

The first entertainment of the morning was exciting. Small, wiry mountain ponies galloped at top speed while their riders, trailing coloured streamers and dressed in tunics of a loose white jacket wrapped across the chest and wide, plus six trousers tucked into leather boots, stood on the ponies' swerving backs, leaping from one side to the other, leaning out at right angles and sliding off their rump. At breakneck speed, slipping on the mud, nostrils flared and lathering under a single rein, these game little horses bolted round with their acrobatic riders to huge applause. And then on to the stage show; it was magnificent – apart from the screeching singing bit. On a raised dais, to amplification that could probably have been heard in Lhasa, 60 or so dancers, extravagantly costumed in many changes of highly coloured cloth and metallic thread, went through an elaborate and energetic routine. There were drums, symbols, trumpets, Buddhist horns ten feet long, conch horns, banners, streamers and flags, 200 waving children and a grateful crowd.

Formality over and BBQs dampened, the afternoon's racing began. For myself, but clearly not the crowd, this was distressing entertainment. Four at a time, more of these brave ponies, bred to be nimble footed on mountain paths and steady under a load of wood or panniers of vegetables, were whipped around the arena by large and amateur riders, many riding bareback or at least on a gaudy blanket; some riders pulled back on the bit at the same time as thrashing a flank. Some ponies came near to total exhaustion. Next were the yaks; lumbering, shaggy, two-toned, long-horned, ill-tempered and obstinate. Completely unsuited for moving faster than an amble, they lined up to great applause, whistles and clapping. A tall yak herdsman, a practised poseur if ever there was one, delayed the start while he strutted around and stood with a hand in his belt for the cameras. And then they were off. For 30 ft (ten metres) they went into a spirited sprint and then, true to their stubborn nature, they spread around the course in several directions, one of them backwards. Riders and herdsmen tugged their noses, whacked their rumps, tugged their manes or lifted their tails – all to little effect. The crowd went wild yelling advice, clapping and stamping their feet and crying with laughter. This was animal entertainment of a high order and I laughed loudly too. But it was cruel. The poor beasts were probably terrified and an hour later when I saw a couple tethered behind the stand, they were still hyperventilating. However, this was exceptional and wherever we travelled, the ponies were well fed and in good condition, dogs – most of which seemed to be descended from an inappropriate marriage of a Corgi and a Pekinese – were happy and yaks grazed contentedly in rich pasture-land amid a patchwork of *primulae* and iris.

On my way home I stopped off in Bangkok to visit a friend. On the traffic-stalled flat road to the unsavoury suburb of Pattaya, the eyes are assaulted by huge bill boards, lungs are damaged by diesel smoke and sensibilities are dulled by drab developments of commercial concrete. In Pattaya itself, sullen, fleshy, scarlet-lipped girls anticipated the wallets of tattooed, paunchy, hairy, middle-aged, mid-European men. I longed for pure high altitude air, vertical valleys, peasant smiles and a yak with a bone through its nose.

Dubrovnik for the Weekend

October 2005

'No vacation goes unpunished' – Karl Hakkarainen

I never saw them but sometime during the night 100 maids with 100 mops must scrub the Old City of Dubrovnik until it shines. I have never seen such cleanliness. Not a toffee paper, not a dripped ice cream, a cigarette butt, debris in dusty corners nor weeds in careless cracks. And this in a town whose arms are always wide open in welcome for anyone who has the word 'Adriatic' written in their itinerary. The limestone that covers the streets wall to wall in precision cut paving is polished by 10,000 tourist feet each day.

Our first view of the old town was against the setting sun and the massive fortified walls stood stout and solid like a sumo wrestler crouching defensively in the ring of the much larger modern city. There is nothing refined about these walls; no crenellation or embrasures, no fancy stonework to relieve the areas of great limestone blocks. The gates north and south are protected by squat bastions and that's about it. Muscle seemed to be the order of the day when the main construction was carried out in the early 13th century, when fear of Ottoman expansion was at its highest. This immense perimeter protection surrounds a city whose stone buildings are almost universally roofed in new clay tiles since terracotta has been so vulnerable to earthquakes (1667 disastrous, 1989 bad) and artillery shelling (1991 awful). The wall has been an effective deterrent to any intending invader and there have been plenty of them. Slavs, Venetians, Hungarians, Turks, the Pasha of Bosnia, Emperor Napoleon, Austrians and the Yugoslav Montenegran/Serbian Herzegovina/People's Army joint forces. When Balkan alliances get *that* complicated, all hope of understanding these regional politics are lost. The latest invaders come in shorts and trainers seeking the history that

171

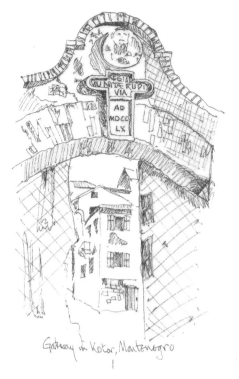

Gateway in Kotor, Montenegro

these aggressors have left behind and are met by 500 smiling, apron-clad waiters each of whose establishments offer identical choices: fish, fish or fish.

We stayed at the Villa Dubrovnik which was built into a vertiginous slope with each part at a different level. Like an extravagant club sandwich, there were eight layers from roadside reception to waterside terrace, each one room thick. With bedrooms at level two, a book forgotten at crispy bacon level six effectively exercised legs and lungs. Every item from pillows to sugar packets was elaborately monogrammed with the hotel's initials producing an unfortunate epidemic of VD.

One morning, drawing back the curtains of our shoreline bedroom, there was the alarming and intrusive sight of a huge cruise ship moored, so it seemed, against our balcony. Ten stories of identikit rabbit hutches as high and as long as an aircraft carrier, the *Costa Mediterranea* began disgorging its inhabitants into a fleet of orange-roofed tenders that then sped to and from the harbour all day. Meeting a boatload of chattering, arm-waving, holidaying Italians in sequinned tops and Lycra bottoms as you walk the narrow path along the perimeter walls turns a pleasant stroll into a *scusi*, squeezing, squealing experience that is tiresome and tiring (a sequinned top or two excepted). It was time to leave town.

The Dalmatian coastline recklessly casts islands into the sea so that over 1,000 are scattered offshore. One of these named Lokrum was opposite the villa and we escaped the Italian hordes to wander its pinewood paths. Not just pine but black berried myrtle, arbutus laden with red and orange fruit, arboreal heathers, rosemary, pittosporum, ruscus, broom, dainty little autumn cyclamen and others whose identity showed up my botanical gaps. There were lovely, woody, wild scents, clear clean water, privacy and peace. Apart from these island charms, Lockrum's history was a typical cocktail of Balkan excess and eccentricity. Reputedly the island where Richard the Lionheart was shipwrecked, it suffered the same indignities of the chain of invasions as Dubrovnik itself and was then bought by Archduke Maximilian of Austria (a Hapsburg and Emperor of Mexico) who chucked the Benedictines out of their monastery to make a summer retreat. Sub-sequently, on Maximilian's murder by Mexicans, a local businessman turned it into a health spa; this failed and the island was bought back by Emperor Franz Joseph (he whose assassination started WWI) to pamper his son Rudolf's bronchi-tis (he of the ballet *Mayerling*). Now a retreat from noisy tourists, it is also home to a botanical garden and an impressive Napoleonic fort; the Benedictines are back and a nudist colony has bagged the only sandy beach within 100 miles (160kms).

Leaving Dubrovnik in a hired car only slightly larger than a dustbin, we dar-ingly set out for Herzegovina and Montenegro with a Croatian map on which not a single name corresponded with any in my guide book. For additional confusion, many names were in Cyrillic script. Winding down the coast road precipitously cut into the rough hillside and cowering past the 14-wheeled monster trucks coming up from Albania and beyond, we veered off at Gruda to the celebrated restaurant Konavoski Dvori (celebrated, that is, by coach drivers for the cruise ships). However at 10 am on a Sunday morning, its abundant charms were just for us. A waterwheel, powered by the purest of chalk streams and linked to huge millstones, was grinding corn, whole lambs turned on a spit above charcoal onto which a branch of wild rosemary was thrown from time to time, rainbow trout awaited the grill, seats were shaded by walnut trees of great age and woodland walks were aromatically spiced by bay trees. We sipped an espresso or two while serving girls changed from tight jeans to flowing national costume and left before a dozen coach parties destroyed the sublimity.

The mountains of Montenegro are as bare and rocky as those of Croatia with stands of Italian cypress punctuating the skyline like groups of guardsmen called to attention. Along the roadside there was an impression of colourful plastic, sacks of potatoes, lines of laundry and strange architecture – usually in concrete. But there was elegance and style too from earlier times and at Perast, a small village at the head of a saltwater inlet, buildings lining the waterfront were of ashlared stone, of classical proportion and idiom, finely detailed but sadly much neglected. In the handsome Bujovic Palace (six windows square), Peter the Great sent his admirals to learn their craft. The sun reflected peace and serenity off the 18th century walls and although our lunch of smoked ham, pale pimentos, glowing tomatoes and an omelette as bright as saffron was not as refined as the buildings, the silhouette of an island monastery, the smell of the casurina pines, the blessed absence of tourists and the attention of two puppies all accounted for a perfect stopover. We were served by a girl as thin as a broomstick who sat on her boyfriend's lap in between attending to orders from ourselves and those of a large and corpulent policeman (who did not appear to pay a bill). Later, driving through towns, there seemed to be many broad and burly men in sinister black leather jackets, but perhaps leather is in this year, or I have seen too many cold war films.

Kotor, another historical and architectural jewel, was also deserted. Within the walled town we wandered along narrow streets paved in multicoloured polished stone. In alleys, balconies reached across from either side – what fun lovers must have had, but it was impossible to appreciate the finely detailed façades from an oblique view. Venetian lions, sometimes raised, sometimes in relief, an Austrian prison, churches with domes and foreshortened naves (sometimes with a campanile) and elaborate stone dressings around windows and doors all told tales of different foreign occupations. As we left, the latest insurgents stepped ashore from the Hebridean Spirit (registered in Glasgow) crisply laundered and straw hatted, but these were culture seekers from Virginia Water and Cheltenham and the city gates opened wide. Driving back in the dusk, the Montenegran border policeman took time to finish his internet game of patience and stretched our own patience accordingly, but sensible travellers do not argue with border guards.

On another day, driving north (with our headlights on in the bright sunshine as Croatian law requires), the fastigiate cypresses mysteriously disappeared and gave way to scrub oaks and sage. There was no sign here of the goats and sheep with floppy ears which thrive on this type of land elsewhere around the Mediterranean. All along the Dalmatian coast great, grey mountains of pockmarked stone rising to 1,280 ft (4,200m) form a forbidding fortress for those who might wish to push inland. Sometimes the rock was striated from cataclysmic upheavals; the last earthquake in 1989 caused serious structural damage and that of 1,330 killed half the population. Tito's partisan guerrillas could have held out forever in such a landscape.

At Trsteno we stopped by the two champion plane trees of the world, a pair of *Platanus orientalis* believed to be over 500 years old. Beside their massive trunks two local women had set out their stalls of dried figs, burnished pomegranates and goat cheese that sat in a puddle of grass green olive oil. Their faces were so lined and fissured and their backs so bent that it seemed they might have planted these venerable trees themselves.

Many place names along our route were single syllabled. Split, Hum, Bol and Ston are easy enough but asking the way to Sbr, Crmp or Drn required an unfriendly grimace or pen and paper. At midday, via Grg, we reached the end of the Peljesac Peninsular which stretches a bony finger into the Adriatic where the sea turns aquamarine over the shallow shingle. Small children squealed when a ripple caught them unawares; little open fishing boats whose chipped paint showed many years of service bobbed at the end of mussel encrusted ropes. The branches of broad-headed pines leant out so far to the west that their cones touched the water and solid but stylish bougainvillea-clad villas of retired 18th century sea captains sat comfortably along the shore. In the shade of a trellised vine turning seasonally crimson, we lunched on bass which had left the sea a few hours earlier, fresh apricots and a tangy cheese. A shaggy, grey-muzzled dog whose eyes showed wisdom and whose manner affection, rested his chin on our table simultaneously welcoming and expectant. The outlines of the islands became blurred in shades of violet and orange before sharpening to silhouettes, I scratched an ear of our four-legged friend, turned our little car south and we headed for home.

Chile

November 2005

Once the travel bug bites there is no antidote and I know that I shall be happily infected until the end of my life' – Michael Palin

The traveller to Patagonia needs to be properly equipped – or so I thought from my Oxfordshire armchair – and so I visited Rohans in Covent Garden, a shop that is experienced in fitting out adventurers. A young man was courteous and helpful.

"Trousers? Certainly, sir. Will you be bivouacking at high altitude?"

Heavens, no.

"Any icework?"

I prayed not.

"You'll be trekking, of course?"

"Oh, yes." Hours I hoped, not days.

After further interrogation it seemed clear that I had disappointed him.

"Perhaps our recreational department might be more suitable?" and he directed me to Leisurewear downstairs.

First stop was Argentina.

Buenos Aires is the most cosmopolitan of all South American cities – *'Italians who speak Spanish and think they are British. Its history is written in its telephone book – Romanov, Radziwill, Rommel, Rothschild and that is only the Rs.'* as Bruce Chatwin put it. Exile, delusion and anxiety behind lace curtains. The *Buenos Aires Herald* (*'a world of information in a few words'*, so few in fact that it only just made eight tabloid pages) advertised the Annual Canasta Tea at the British Embassy and English practice at The Highland Heritage Society. My hotel, The Claridge, had bellboys with white gloves, a muscular security guard with a revolver in a holster whose strap was unclipped and an English Bar. Recoleta, a favoured residential address of the '20s

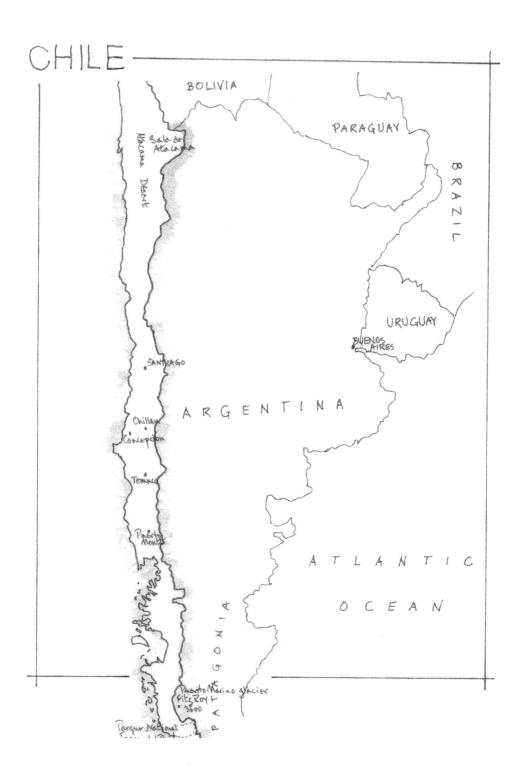

CHILE

BOLIVIA

PARAGUAY

BRAZIL

Atacama Desert

Sala de Atacama

URUGUAY

BUENOS AIRES

SANTIAGO

A R G E N T I N A

Chillan

Concepción

Temuco

Puerto Montt

ATLANTIC

OCEAN

Difficultices

P A T A G O N I A

Perito Marino glacier

Fitz Roy
3600

Parque National

and '30s, had been hijacked by tourists and exploited by antique dealers. Some sold bric-a-brac and others genuine quality but both gave a social insight into a better and more pretentious age with French furniture, marble statues by the score, hats, parasols, tailcoats and extravagant bits of brass plumbing. I walked there by way of the Avenues Venezuela, Bolivia, Brazil, Peru and Chile. I had only been here a few hours and had already crossed the continent. I was about to hail a taxi – *"Claridges, por favor"* when I collided with a lamp post that cut my forehead requiring a handful of tissues from a restaurant, a bowed head past reception and a dose of aspirins.

The route plan of Aero Argentinas' in-flight magazine still laid Argentinian claim not only to 'Islas Malvinas' but also South Georgia and The South Sandwich Islands. The TV national weather forecast included them too. Flying south across the billiard table plateau of Buenos Aires province, square boundaries drawn by eucalyptus or poplar, indicated cattle estancias with ruler straight dirt roads connecting them. Three hours later the view over La Pampas province was unchanged. Later, in the Andean foothills, lakes coloured in shades of pea soup, gooseberry fool and raspberry sorbet appeared each with a piping of sugar indicating a mix of minerals and salt deposits. And then, strung along the horizon like meringue beaten to peaks were the Andes themselves. Above, a sky of the palest and coldest blue; below, the gravel brown of the Patagonian pampa and then the lakes changed to aquamarine and turquoise and the land wrinkled, riven by erosion. From the air it looked magical and, best of all, I was going there.

El Calafate, with its high street of tree trunk façades, had a schmaltz of alpine charm fronting the concrete of the back streets. The few shops selling high altitude climbing equipment were outnumbered by 'genuine Patagonian crafts'. The beat-up pickups of out of town sheep farmers with big, tough dogs barking in the back will not rattle through for much longer. The middle aged, moneyed tourists (Spaniards and Italians this week), in cruise ship quantities, will soon add restaurants, jewellers and fur shops and backpackers will convert the side streets to bars, cheap sightseeing agencies and more 'genuine Patagonian crafts'. My Footprint guidebook recommended Sendarian as the best meaty establishment in town. Here, it was said could be found beef fed on alfalfa, grazed under the stars of the southern hemisphere and massaged by handmaidens (whoever they are). I had trained for dinner with a snacky lunch and read several menus to ensure that the juices were flowing and expectant but never before had quantity so overwhelmingly outclassed quality; brick size was not my size and the mixed grill would have fed Ethiopia. I left inflated and humbled.

The Perito Merino glacier is one of 47 in the Parque Nacional los Glaciares

Church at St Antonia – Atacama – 4500m

but at 200 ft (60m) high and 3 miles (5kms) wide, it is the biggest. Twenty eight tourist buses rather spoilt the personal visit I had planned but as it turned out, their passengers were like snowflakes in a blizzard, such was the scale of this great wall of ice that moved forward at six feet per day – a glacial sprinter. Following a boat trip that emphasised the stupendous height of the ice wall at water level, I watched from the myrtle-covered shoreline only a couple of hundred feet away and gazed into the deep blue of its visceral soul. Those watching were strangely silent – even the Italians; there was respect and reverence for this gargantuan lump of ice and the final moments of its 100 year journey. Along its wearisome way it had been beset by terrible events that had riven and crevassed its surface. On its contorted and twisted body it carried the scars of a life of torture. It cried out in cracks of agony, great sonorous grunts came from its unseen interior and at its edge, it roared in a final release of pain as it calved off an ancient limb. Was it dying or giving birth? But whether corpses or new born, they would only survive an unhappy month or so gnawed by the winds and waves of Lago Argentino.

It was springtime in the Southern Andes. Willows dangled their catkins, black faced ibis incessantly quacking as though they would rather be ducks were busy nesting in a Monterey cypress, and male guanaco stood on high ground ready to protect their harem from lusting lotharios. The Chilean Firebush (*Embothrium chilensis*) was ablaze on the hillsides interspersed with Ladies' Slippers (*Calcelarius biflorus*) in varied red and yellow stripes and *Mullinum spinosa*, known locally as 'Mother-in-Law's Sofa' looks invitingly soft for the unwary. Francisco was late: he came to say that he would be later still – a wheel needed fixing. When he returned, a straggly girl with thin hair and several painful looking pins in her left ear had spread herself comfortably over the front passenger seat. Her job (in the car that is) was to top up Francisco's *mate* pot with fresh leaves and boiling water. For the four hour drive across the steppe it was sensible to keep the wits sharpened.

"Do you like movie music?" Francisco asked.

"Well, some." Was he into cowboys, American wars or *The Sound of Music*?

As it turned out it was something of them all and the sound tracks of *Larimee*, *Gone with the Wind* and *Mary Poppins* carried us across the high, dry pampa. No vehicles shared the dirt road and only a gaucho with three long-legged dogs raised an arm. Here was the pampa of Julius Beerbohm:

'The seemingly endless plains akin to but grander than any ocean. The pampa is eternally silent while the ocean is noisy and restless.'

In this province of Magellanes, Chiles' largest but with only one percent of the population, the golden age ceased with the opening of the Panama Canal in 1914 and now even the sheep were reduced to one for every eight acres.

In the middle of nowhere (and in Patagonia, nowhere is as far from anywhere as you can get), we stopped at a three roomed shack of corrugated tin. HOTEL was painted in green across the whole façade; the paint had dribbled from the foot of each letter. The elderly proprietor lived there alone since a disastrous fire in 1968 had burnt down the previous little hotel, killed her husband and crushed her right hand. Literally single-handed and helped only by her young son, she had rebuilt the hotel (scorched, reclaimed timbers spanned the ceiling) and now she stood smiling with cracked lips, in a floral pinafore and frayed slippers exchanging jokes with the straggly girl. In winter the snow blocked the road and the wind reached 120mph. At a lonely border post that stood amongst in several acres of dandelions (*dentes de leones* locally), the Argentinian police searched my suitcase and wordlessly thumped an exit stamp into my passport. The Chilean civilian smiled and wished me a pleasant stay.

"Senor Chilton, *hola*," greeted the luggage porter alerted by the van's short wave radio. At the front door stood Marcella, slim, hair immaculate, in a cream silk blouse under a wool suit. She beamed with pleasure and enquired of my journey. "A cup of tea, perhaps? Or can I get you some other refreshment?" (She could do this in at least four languages.) Country house hostesses of such charm and savoir faire are rare but here, in the wilderness of Torres del Paine National Park, at the architecturally contemporary Explora Hotel, was an assured and genuine welcome; the combination was seductive and stimulating. The 1,200 ft (3,600m) Paine Grande was framed by my bedroom window, its severe granite sides softened by the dusky pink of a setting sun and reflected in a lake so turquoise its glamour was near to artificial. Over the next three days we hiked across rocks, marvelled at the blueness of the Grey Glacier, rode sturdy horses in armchair saddles and strode over the rolling folds of the Patagonian pampa but always looming over our shoulders was the stern and forbidding presence of the Torres granite peaks.

We saw most of the airports of Chile on the 1,000 mile zigzag north to The Lake District – Punta Arenas, Punto Montt, Concepcion and Tenuco. All modern and efficient, all with kiosks stocked by the same persuasive postcard salesman. Blurred, sepia photographs of Mapuche and Arucarian Indians in the late 1800s, their bodies painted in white stripes, full frontal naked, looking mournful and broken spirited. Four centuries earlier they had been the scourge of *conquistadores* and before that had halted the southerly progress of the Incas. A group of black African men boarded at Concepcion, each with a diamond stud in their left ear, a cross around their neck encrusted with enough cut glass to construct a chandelier and a wrist watch the size of Big Ben. If they were not costume jewellery sales-men, they were on an evangelical mission that, for only a modest down payment, would guarantee susceptible peons eternal salvation, immaculate conception and a bountiful life.

The road to Villarica (it rhymes with Billericay), sauntered past estancias whose wooden houses were set well back and were bounded by white railings and there were paddocks of thoroughbred horses alongside places set out for Chillan high-way racing – a straight 500 yard (450m) dash between two horses in a knockout competition. Ash and oak stood together in lush pastures, their base worn to bare earth by sheltering Herefords and Devon Crosses. There were rhododendrons and white azaleas in profusion and drifts of arboreal broom grew over dry river beds like generously spread butter. Pucon sits at the eastern end of Lake Villarica and at the foot of an active volcano. The peak of the perfect snow covered cone anchored its own cloud of steam and at the town hall, a clap-boarded, gabled, turreted and dormer windowed confection, a cluster of traffic lights on its façade served as the town's early warning system for the volcano's next eruption; happily it was showing green. Hotel Interlaken, Swiza Pizza and timbered buildings lent an alpine air. The pizzeria displayed elaborate cakes and served lavender custard with poppy seeds. In the heavy drizzle, damp dogs hung their heads and looked gloomily at small, stout men with leathery faces and sad eyes wearing straight brimmed sombreros and coarse grey ponchos. Avenida Bernardo O'Higgins was filled with election posters: Esther Contigo in rimless glasses was going for the newly emancipated and Xavier Pinero, with a pencil moustache, a piercing eye and a straight back, struggled to display the common touch.

In the gardens of Hotel Antumalal, there were camellias, pink roses and hydran-geas; *erigeron* had spread along every rocky crack like little flurries of unseasonable snow. The development of the hotel was an example of the pioneering and entrepreneurial spirit that has contributed so much to this country. In 1938, Czech émigrés Guillermo and Catalina Pollak arrived in Chile. Newlywed and enthusiastic, they fell in love with the beauty of Lake Vallarica and bought the damp, run down little Hotel Playa which they refurbished with their own labours. The eruption of the Villarica volcano in 1949 destroyed the hotel but they had already purchased a rocky and steep piece of land beside the lake considered only good for grazing sheep and here they built a small café. One day, the holidaying President Videla visited the café and with the brashness of a man with nothing to lose, Giullermo asked for financial help to build a work of architectural significance. He got the loan although the architectural qualities of his hotel may be questionable, even allowing for the vogue for Bauhaus severity current at the time. Nevertheless, fading photographs on the stone walls of the reception area showed its popularity; proud sepia rows of snapshots included Queen Elizabeth, King Baudoin and Jimmy Stewart. Its dated style no longer seem to attract European monarchs or celluloid legends – the least faded photograph was of Emma Thompson.

Heading north again, more buttery broom spread itself along the verges and later, little posies of pale yellow lupins took their place. Smallholdings with a single storied planked house, washing on the line, a few sheep and chickens scratching around an abandoned and rusting Chevrolet pickup regularly lined the road. There were stands of poplar, fir and eucalyptus and in between the shacks and the trees, long stretches of pasture with fat cattle and well bred horses. Stopping in a small town, we looked around; self-conscious and inquisitive travellers but arrogant too, poking our affluent noses over neglected picket fences through which privet had stretched itself like the desperate hands of prisoners. *Acanthus* had seeded itself into gutters and whenever a truck thundered through, dust hung over the streets to the point of invisibility. Despondency hung around too: over the town and on the faces of weary men but there was not hopelessness. The church was being repaired and a shack had opened up advertising internet connection although it did not look as though business was going to be brisk. Once painted in the shades of a 19th century palette – grey greens, soft reds, rich creams and gentle blues, the clapboarded houses had never had a second coat. On the outskirts, well away from the irritations of dust, shielded from despondency and at the entrance of a long poplar lined drive, a magnificent freshly varnished sign read *'Estancia Garcia'*.

Fundo Curanilahue had an English touch; there were geraniums in tubs, roses and jasmine wound around a shaded loggia and comfortable sofas were upholstered in Colefax fabrics. Red Angus cattle grazed in knee high grass and conversation with Louisa and John Jackson was of friends and relations back home. But a dozen horses and a dozen farm hands in sombreros, fields of alfafa, log fires in

Valle de Luna. Atacama.

Guanaco crossing river

the timber lined bed rooms, pisco sours before dinner, flowering paulownias and huge Monterey cypresses anchored the farm to Chilean soil. My diffident entry in the visitors' book read:

'Up from the granite south to travellers' rest,
I found a garden by sun and rain caressed.
Here was tranquillity and smiles of friendliness,
Laughter and all the seeds for happiness.'

On the previous page, John Julius Norwich had written of what a hopeless guest he had been.

Down a dusty side road skirting the whitewashed adobe walls of the little town of San Pedro de Atacama, one arrives at a tangled fence of acacia branches, a clump or two of pampas grass and a high white wall. No signs, no varnished railings and no flags. Rumbling over the stones of a stable yard, a chubby man with a shiny face and a broad nose raises a hand in recognition. Twenty three horses of placid temperament and in perfect condition watch from stalls shaded by a slatted canopy and then a strange building of sharp vertical and horizontal angles, blue shutters, narrow fenestration and white concrete is approached by two wide banks of steps. The façade dazzles, the contrast is clearly contrived but the effect is stunning. You have arrived at Explora Atacama.

Do not expect convention in the Atacama Desert, the world's driest and oldest, 700 miles (1,100kms) long and 70 miles (110kms) wide. There is little sand to be seen but volcanic turbulence has scattered rock from truck sized to pea sized and either corrugated, crumpled and crushed the landscape or, in the high altiplano, rolled it into great wide, soft undulations that stretch to horizons. The consequence of malignant winds and searing sun has sculpted monumental art from pillars of sandstone. Under its dislocated and contorted surface lie sulphur, lithium, copper and all manner of minerals brought up from the bowels of the earth. Evaporating vapour has left behind huge salt flats some crusted, some painfully surfaced in crystal shards. Where rain has fallen (for not all of the desert is infinitely dry), the torrents of millennia have cut deep gorges and steam hisses into the freezing air from vents slashed in the veneer of the altiplano. One day, perhaps tomorrow, another cataclysm will rupture the land.

Until then, there was life. Plants – fruiting trees, tough shrubs, spiny cactus and waving grass – colonised their own special band of altitude; birds – geese, ducks, tinamou, waders in profusion, finches and flamingos; a few beasts – llamas, vicuna, viscacha and mountaineering guinea pigs; fewer insects – a fly or two and occasional dragonflies; and least of all man – dark skinned from Indian inheritance, stocky and resolute. He has endured the capriciousness of nature with apparent resignation and astonishing cheerfulness.

Later, 1,000 miles (1,600kms) south, downtown Santiago had a painted plastic horse at every street corner, dark suited business men entered doors of glass and steel, balconies overflowed with little private jungles and Pablo Langueria, wearing jeans, a sweater and an eager smile was running for senator. His cardboard cutout had crumpled in the rain.

South Africa

March 2006

'For the born traveller, travelling is a besetting vice. Like other vices, it is imperious, demand-ing of the victim's time, money and energy and the sacrifice of comfort' – Aldous Huxley

The N3 heads south from Johannesburg and turning off at Vrede you come upon Volkrust and later Newcastle and Dundee before reaching the villages of Non-dweni and Nqutu. (Adding to this confusing transposition of towns, Heidelberg and Frankfurt are also on the route but no guidebook could explain why two north German towns should be remembered here.) These names reflect the for-eign encroachment that characterises the history of this country; here, in Kwa-zulu Natal it is the Dutch and the British trampling over the land. The uses of the land and the design of the buildings also mark the different nationalities from Dutch three-storied prosperity in neat towns where each had its own stone built church, to British colonial farms sheltering in stands of eucalyptus, through to the round thatched huts of the Zulus scattered in little groups over the great grazing grasslands.

Treacherously potholed tarmac changed to smooth rust-coloured dirt and then, turning left down an undulating narrow track, through acacia scrub and 12 ft (three metre) high aloe of great age, we arrived at a small group of buildings with timber walls and corrugated roofs all set about with an abundance of plants and mature trees. Here two smiling Zulu girls lifted our luggage on to their heads with Olympian ease (the cases still bearing a 'Heavy' tag from the Heathrow check in) and guided us down basalt steps flanked by canna lilies, heliotrope and solanum to a cabin of spacious rooms that looked out over the Buffalo River to hills hazy and lazy in the heat of late afternoon and whose slopes interlocked like clasped fingers. Further out still, just visible over a saddle of ground, the eye

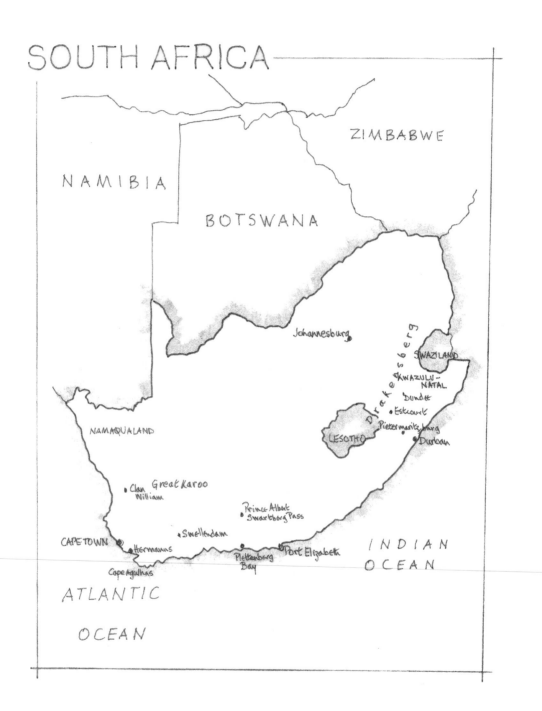

was led to a hill that stands alone and whose shape resembles a sphinx. We had reached the warm embrace of Fugitive's Drift and gazed on Isandhlwana, the site of one of the most terrible defeats in all of British military history.

The battles over the rolling plains where the British fought Zulus and Boers are all tragic; the product of political expediency, military incompetence, borders mistaken, ignored or deliberately altered, trusts broken and treaties torn up. But on the ground, in the hills and along a river, extraordinary courage and exemplary discipline were shown by each of the red-coated British, the black skinned Zulu and the bandoliered Boer. David Rattray, the master story teller of the Zulu Wars, describes events in such gripping terms and with such fluency that after two and a half uninterrupted hours you will swear that you have smelt the cordite, itched with the dust, dripped with sweat, heard the terrible cries of wounded men and horses and been paralysed by the fear of death in the ghastly jaws of hell. Should you not then have wiped away tears, your heart must be chiselled from granite. [*In a violent armed robbery at his farm, David Rattray was murdered in January 2007.*]

The polygamous traditions of the Zulus have meant that old men have sired sons by young wives and so tales of the terrible events of 1879 and 1880 have been passed down through only three generations. Whether today's great-grand-sons can forgive those authorities who currently order their lives and have turned the greatest sub-Saharan fighting force ever assembled into small time farmers and domestic help, I do not know but the history syllabus of the schools that are now state-provided recognise the distinguished exploits of their forbears.

As we drove south towards the Drakensberg Mountains, little swifts and white throated swallows perched in long columns along the telephone lines and flew off in fluttering clouds as we passed. On the country roads nothing much else moved and even the dust seemed reluctant to settle. The scattering of huts that from time to time formed a village were lifeless although once, a group of four schoolgirls, smart in their green skirts, yellow blouses and brown ties (it was 40 degrees!), giggled their way along the road to distant homes. The towns, however, buzzed and hummed with activity. Markets were served by taxi vans packed with large women and thin men that constantly rattled in; huge diesel-belching trucks lumbered through, tractors pulled trailers of pigs for slaughter and as always, a ragtag band of wastrels, unconcerned of where to go or what to do, passed the day in bored circumspection of others similarly vacant of thought. Occasionally, intent upon a different view of their world, they would wander across the road without warning and without a glance left or right.

We climbed up from the hot plain, turned west on to a steeper road passing stands of eucalyptus and pine that broke the silhouette of the shallow slopes of the hills and continued through lush fields as green as Tipperary with Devon Reds munching their way through succulent, knee-high grass. Lakes sparkled in the hollows. At 5,500 ft (1,680m), a herb garden of Elizabethan intricacy appeared and in a thunderstorm of epic scale whose lightning lit up the stone lips of Cleopatra's Mountain that sneered 3,000 ft (900m) above, we sought refuge in a room where a log fire crackled and a bed of large and luscious proportions invited immediate salvation. Outside the window, a scarlet chested sunbird indifferent to nature's raging, was intent upon sipping nectar from a fuchsia. We had reached Cleopatra's Mountain Retreat, an altogether different establishment from Rattray's guest house. Food was the watchword here and cholesterol only a word to prick the conscience. There were neither greying roués nor stick-like women in sight; the palate was king and the gut its servant.

Log fires, sunbirds and clean clear air aside, Richard Poynton is the lure that keeps twelve double rooms booked every day of the year. A living replica of those Escoffier caricatures, his short, rotund, pebble-glassed, grey-bearded body was wrapped up like a swaddled baby in starched, monogrammed white cotton. He resembled a decorated Easter egg. Before dinner he presented his menu – six different courses, not a salad leaf amongst them and no choice. When he was finished, I was torn between putting his rhetoric to the test ("We serve proper food here. We bake our bread twice a day and ice cream is 20 egg yolks and two litres of cream") or going to bed there and then uncomfortably replete simply on his descriptions. As it turned out, the food was too fussy for a simpleton like me but the cooking was of a very high order. A Hamilton Russell Merlot, at 14 per cent and darker than blood, helped to alleviate the disappointment of eating alone; M had buried herself in the foot thick duvet with traveller's tummy and a high temperature. After dinner this hirsute, short-sighted Humpty-Dumpty gathered opinions as he dispersed port. "You survived the onslaught?" he boomed. "It's all a lot of fun isn't it?" Here was an artist with a refreshing attitude to enjoyment; I warmed to him and looked forward to tomorrow's preamble and the gluttony that would follow.

While M lay in the warm embrace of duck down, I walked across the high veldt of grasslands in a warm drizzle and was astonished to find the true parents of plants in our Oxfordshire garden, growing in natural profusion. Here, at 7,200 ft (2,200m) were *kniphobia, dierama, artemesia, senecio, ligularia* and many others. Alpine lakes were home to herons, moorhen and duck and in the distance, six eland (the largest of all African antelope) grazed and a troop of baboons scuttled off. While the land on the summits lay in comfortable folds, the way up was steep and scattered with boulders of immense size, left there by retreating glaciers many millions of years before. I contemplated the huge difficulties of the Voertrekkers with their wooden wagons each yoked to teams of eight oxen, yelling, sweating, swearing and cracking their long leather whips. Where mud and rock required all available muscle, harnessed women and children heaved on ropes and men put their shoulders to the wheels.

The fanciful names in the Drakensberg such as Cathedral Peak and Champagne Castle (11,000 ft, 3,377m) give an unfortunate theme-park flavour to some of the most dramatic mountain scenery on the African continent. As we drove up a long wide valley between towering cliffs and precipitous over-

David Rattray
at Zulu Memorial

hangs, school lessons were finishing for the day in small villages and for several miles not only was it necessary to avoid the pot holes that made the tarred road slower than a dirt one but we also had to slalom around children wandering across the road in little groups on their way home.

I have toiled up the twisted trails of the Karokoram, the Tien Shien, the Alps and the Andes but the Swartberg Pass beats them all for drama, for the terrifying compulsion of vertigo and the skill that is required to maintain momentum through tight triple hairpins and dizzying spirals. With all four wheels skidding sideways on the loose gravel, M handled each of them with the aplomb of a seasoned rally driver. It was getting dark too and the descent had as many perils as the way up and so it was with triumph and relief that our little two-door, two-toned, too small Toyota eventually cruised through orchards of peaches, apricots and olives into the town of Prince Albert on the southern edge of the Great Karoo. At the Swartberg Hotel (1840), our huge first floor bedroom was enlarged by a wide balcony that overlooked Main Street – the only street. Next door was the Slaghuis Butchery and opposite, a garage which unaccountably housed a small jeweller behind the left hand pump but more usefully The Bottle Store behind the right hand pump; at six o'clock on a Friday evening it was doing good business. Grey eucalyptus of great age lined the street whose cottages, some with Dutch gabled ends, had corrugated roofs painted in pastel shades and whose owners, neat and tidy with straight backs and polished shoes, walked the gravel pavements nodding to neigh-

RORKE'S DRIFT
22 JAN 1879

24ᵗʰ Regiment of Foot Memorial
Battle of Isandlwana.

bours as they passed. A few cottages had thatched roofs but all had pretty little verandas with trellised corner pillars that supported bougainvillea and plumbago. The Dutch Reformed church was stone built in the style of English Perpendicular and next door the Anglican chapel cowered in its shadow.

We sat on our balcony overlooking the comings and goings of the Bottle Store and the street. Pickup trucks packed with black labourers were going home and white locals exchanged Afrikaaners chitchat and lifted a hand in greeting to men in shorts, paunchy and confident. They were the product of a tough pioneering race driven out of the coastal band over two ranges of mountains to rear cattle and sheep on the dry and dusty plains of the Great Karoo. In the hotel rooms, sepia portraits of these sturdy pioneering families hung on the floral wallpaper; the wooden floorboards creaked with every step, the brass work was polished daily and the dining room had dainty lace tablecloths on which was served Lamb Pie, Sticky Malva Pudding and ginger beer. Had an ox wagon lumbered by marshalled by dusty and bearded men, no one would have turned their head.

While the Swartberg Pass provided heart-stopping views, the way back snaked through narrow canyons whose rocky and contorted strata displayed the agonies of geological movement. And then we were out onto the wide open plains, with wheat stubble to each horizon and kori bustards and blue cranes scavenging whatever the harvest had left behind – Africa's largest birds reduced to the size of magpies in the shorn landscape. Wild thyme bordered the long straight road whose end, masked by the distortions of heat, seemed infinite.

'While barred clouds bloom the soft dying day
And touch the stubble plains with rosy hue.'

Plettenberg Bay (or Plett to the long-time resident or pretentious traveller) displayed its credentials with nine polo fields, four golf courses and three cricket pitches. Here was a community of crisp pressed linen, clubhouse gossip, Friday bridge, Sunday lunches, good deeds and old values. Fading god-botherers with all its implications: gardening, bowling, cricket-watching, churchgoing and jumble sales; Cheltenham aligned with Palm Beach. The rooms of Mallard River Lodge looked out incongruously over the Bietou River where an oxbow lake, fringed by reeds and bullrushes, harboured cloud cisticolas and yellow warblers. A hoopoe looked startled and disapproving as it strutted around the base of a cactus, probing for ants.

The town was in darkness when we arrived (the consequence of a spanner dropped accidentally into the turbine of Cape Town's nuclear power station), and searching for life in a community that had suddenly had to adopt a war footing, we came across an Indian family of six children wandering on the beach by the dim light of a waning torch. They had driven from Beaufort West especially to show the children the beach and the ocean. They were remarkably cheerful about this wasted four hour journey but in spite of this country's newfound tolerance, they would not have felt comfortable when daylight shone on the white formality of this South African Frinton-on-Sea.

Hermanus echoed Plett but was less sporty and more sedate and oozed the gentility that comes with the genes of old colonial stock. Afrikaans had moved in at the eastern end and some of them, driven out of their homes and farms in the Transvaal by lawlessness and refugees from Zimbawe, were adding to the shacks at the western end. This may have been a sanctuary for these refugees, but each permanent resident in their neat, tree shaded, shuttered, pastel painted, rendered house had a high wall and a high gate. In such a social environment, the walls were not there for personal privacy.

Kensington Place, true to its elegant name, came with elegant people. So discreetly was it tucked into the steep hillside of the fashionable, residential Gardens area of Cape Town that we circled around it for a while until, like a raptor waiting its moment, we suddenly swooped from a road above and arrived at a locked gate with an elaborate electronic entry system and a small brass plaque that confirmed our destination. Carefully stepping around beautiful people, we passed through billowing organza and suede pool side upholstery to find our room. Decorated in three shades of taupe, the telephone, TV and fridge were so artfully concealed and our experience of such places so limited that sheepishly we had to return to reception for instructions as to where to find them. But the view over the city was spectacular and Table Mountain rose sheer behind. So ultra-boutique was this place and so minimalist its design that the bathroom was strewn with fresh rose petals. Needless to say, candles glowed in every niche. What the two smiling, uniformed, round black girls who brought us our designer breakfast thought of this I

Arniston –
Southernmost house
of the African
Continent

do not know. Each day a different colour-coordinated composition of fruit, china and napkin. Hopefully, they giggled about it as much as we did. I wondered in which band of the city suburbs they came from, no doubt starting into work at first light. The outermost band was a recycled flotsam of shacks of beaten cans and splintered planks arranged in disordered profusion – a sargasso of drifting, dispossessed and desperate humanity. Next came breezeblock-with-single-room boxes set in ordered rows north/south and east/west like a cloth of grey gingham spread over the rise and fall of the ground. And then there was a mix of modern, low income, single design houses squeezed into the cleared ground of a previous leafy suburb which had succumbed to the seduction of commercial pressure and whose remaining bungalows now crouched under the last of the avocado and eucalyptus trees and slunk into the hypnotic shadows of industry and shopping centres. Further in, larger houses but still densely packed until at the inner band, surrounding the city core. Beautifully designed homes were ingeniously set into the hillsides and shoe horned between neighbours, ADT Armed Response notices were on every closed gate and very large or very small well-behaved dogs trotted unattended on the clean pavements.

Elegance of a different kind came 170 miles (273kms) north in the Cedarberg Mountains. I could not fault the billing of Bushmans Kloof as a 'wilderness retreat' but any suggestion of a vigorous regime of devotion and a diet of gruel should be immediately dismissed. This was a retreat from humdrum life and harassing schedules. Here was pampering on an industrial scale, comfort in voluptuous proportions and attentiveness where just a blink attracted staff to your elbow. I exaggerate only a little but do so to emphasise my minority view that excessive luxury in a natural environment are uncomfortable partners. Nevertheless, there was a waiting list of those whose idea of wilderness came with down feathers, starlit Jacuzzis and celebrity chefs (whoever they are). The guests seemed to come in two sizes, petite and gross; whether these two sizes cohabited elsewhere was not for me to ask, but it made for spicy conversation.

Taking a break from another round of signature dishes, we headed off to visit the Moravian Mission at Wuppertal – an hour's drive over a couple of craggy passes and across a valley verdant with peaches and almonds. At the end of the road, shaded by huge and ancient trees and watered by a wide stream, stood 20 or so single-storied, thatched, whitewashed, stone built cottages that lay along the lower contour of a little valley. This being Sunday, there was no work on the vegetable plots or sheep pens nor drying of onions or tying in of vines. This was the Lord's Day and little groups of the coloured community were dressed in floral dresses and straw hats or suits, ties and felt hats. They clutched their Afrikaans bibles and after paying their respects on bended knee to departed friends and relatives at the gate of the cemetery, they dusted off their clothes and entered their church – 1858, gabled, simple, wood-lined and cared for.

Staff at Bushman's did not have Wuppertal on their suggested itineraries and with good reason; innocent fundamentalism could not be allowed to prick the conscience or kick the bum of extravagance. Who knows, guests might return wanting only bread and cheese and a glass of water.

In the rush-hour traffic en route to the airport, buses and minivans were crammed with black faces, older cars with Indians or Coloureds and new cars with Whites. In our travels across the country we had been cushioned from political reality, the struggle of daily living that the black majority had to endure and distanced from conversation with any colour other than white. We did not visit a black township nor stoop through the door of a Zulu home. South Africa gives the privileged white population an uncomfortable conscience but looking at our fellow travellers, they all seemed reasonably content to be sharing the same road, chatting on the buses or, in the shiniest cars, calling from mobiles. Each may occupy their own band of The Rainbow Nation but, at last, at long last, most seemed to have a voice that was heard and a dignified place in a unified and prospering country – so far.

Ethiopia II

December 2006

'If you come to a fork in the road, take it' – Yogi Berra

Bradt puts it concisely:

'South Omo is a remote zone tucked against the Sudanese and Kenyan borders where a dozen or more ethnic groups live and decorate themselves in a manner that scarcely acknowledges the twentieth century. Travel is as tough as it gets: erratic and bumpy transport, lousy accommodation and indifferent food. Around Mago National Park, the black cotton soil is treacherously sticky and often becomes impassable after significant rainfall.'

I was going after the heaviest rainfall in living memory.

The airport bank was closed so a suburban bank was needed to obtain Ethiopian birr. I had expected that $100 notes would have been snatched out of my hand in gratitude, possibly the manager would have shaken my hand. I was mistaken. Of the six banks we tried, only one was prepared to consider foreign exchange. Outside each bank was a guard to frisk customers; some had a rifle which was handled with alarming casualness although the guards would in any case have been more adept at wielding it as a club. Most wore an attempt at a uniform, if that is what you call a matching jacket and trousers, and one had a hat that said 'Ritz' on the brim. Inside, customers sat patiently on benches in orderly rows clasping a numbered metal token. Foreign exchange, where it was transacted, was not so ordered. First, the dollar bill was minutely examined for tears, held to the light for a check on watermarks and its issue date and the number was noted (a pre-1996 bill is unchangeable). It was intended to be fed into a dusty machine that shone an ultraviolet light but the machine's cord was too short so it was taken to a teller's booth but the booth was locked, and to authorise it to be unlocked required an official to sign a form and pass it to another for counter-

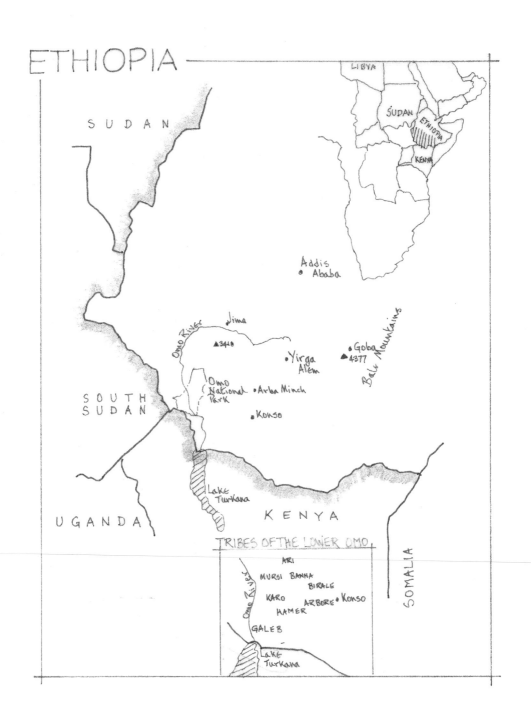

signature. Once this procedure was completed and the $100 notes accepted as genuine they went slowly down a line of other officials who, with another form, each added a signature. The last one examined my passport, added his own scribble and then it was taken to the teller's booth. But the teller's booth had been locked…! Throughout this charade, Melkanu (more of him in a moment) was magnificent. He shouted, waved his briefcase, his jacket and his arms, drummed the counter and urgently tapped his watch as though his express train was already hooting. None of this had the slightest effect. I stuffed the wads of notes into my pocket like a bookie at a northern race meeting and ran out past the guard – one saluted. Changing dollars at Chipping Norton post office was going to be tame stuff in the future.

Melkanu was a weasel. His arms swirled, his hands fluttered and his fingers twitched. Agile on his feet and quick in mind, he scurried around generous with his smiles and courtesy and anxious to inform. "These are pelicans, they eat fish." I hoped this enthusiasm could be tamed before I grew weary of it. His English was good but his pronunciation was obscure and his accentuation eccentric. Teckle, my driver, was older, larger, slower and steadier and seemed to be the only driver obeying the rules of the road. They would make a good team – provided they did not swap jobs.

Passing down an avenue of pepper trees towards Nazaret, we stopped at Dreamland, an unlikely lump of breeze blocks painted in two shades of knicker pink overlooking a grey crater lake. A Chinese man in a neatly pressed blue suit was busy negotiating with earnest Ethiopian businessmen. With smiles all round, they stepped into the dusty dirt street; another road to be built perhaps, another factory estate developed. Chinese money is now reaching into some small and remote corners.

My hotel dining room had a blaring television and seven unlaid tables. On a wall was an unframed print of an Edwardian lady in a ball gown who was either scratching her left ear or coyly shielding her face and looking uncannily as though she had just taken a call on her mobile phone. As I was to learn later, this is what all dining rooms look like. In the gloaming of a 25 watt bulb I contemplated the menu. 'Fryd fish. Fryd stake. Fryd veal (this was clearly a lie). Fryd liver.' I risked the fish with a 'mixt saled'. The starter of onion soup turned out to be a powerful brew composed uniquely of garlic: friendships would be scarce for a day or two. The local beer was St Georges and had a label of a fully-armoured, mounted medieval knight spearing a crocodile. As I tried to write up my journal in the dim light the waiter asked what I was writing. I replied, "The dinner is delicious and is served by an expert waiter." Not a muscle of his face moved and he slouched away. I slouched away too, leaving the room as mournful as I had found it.

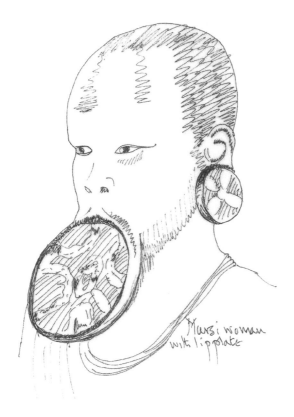

Marsi woman with lip plate

I have two words to offer on Ethiopian food: 'Eat spaghetti'. I ate the best food available and it was somewhere between awful and inedible. The meat would have soled shoes; the fish was overcooked, overbattered and always tilapia and vegetables were boiled – just. Ethiopians eat *injera*. To the uninitiated this rolled up, blotchy, grey, foam rubber mat can present a problem; do you put it under your plate, on your lap, clean your shoes with it, clean the floor with it or has it just cleaned the floor? It tastes as it looks, horrible. If you were an Ethiopian, you would unroll it, tear off a chunk with your right hand, scoop up some sauce or plunge it into a greasy stew so that it becomes a squashy mess, stuff it in your mouth with an urgency that suggests that the next meal may not be on time and then splutter half of it out as conversation continues uninterrupted. It is not a pleasant sight.

But amid mud, squalor and the detritus of a people careless of neighbourhood and with poor eating habits, the Ethiopian values the cleanliness of his shoes and his vehicle above all else. Shoeshine boys squat at every street corner equipped with a tub of water and a selection of jumbo sized tins of Kiwi polish. It is a competitive market but a brisk one. If shoes are not muddy, they are dusty and shiny black leather commands respect. Lorries, minivans, pickups and rusty wrecks are driven axle deep into rivers and lake shores to where the Ethiopian carwash is a dozen boys with empty tins and bare hands. In the midst of the inefficiency, the effort of daily life and the inability to maintain the simplest of equipment, there is universal optimism and a touching wish for friendship. Ragged fellow citizens will be greeted with the same warmth as a neat and clean *farangi*. To a starchy Englishman this is awkward rather than endearing (Ethiopians are embarrassingly tactile) but cast aside national characteristics and there are warm hearts to be found everywhere.

The time, as well as the day itself, puts the country somewhat at a disadvantage in any dialogue with rest of the world. Adhering to the Julian calendar, it persists in having thirteen months in each year and is seven months and eight days *behind* the rest of the world. The day is reckoned in 12 hour cycles so that on a daily basis it is six hours *ahead* of the rest of the world – breakfast is at 12 o'clock and lunch at 7 o'clock. But none of this matters much as no one has a watch.

Swaynes Hotel at Arba Minch sits on the edge of a forested escarpment look-ing out over the Bridge of Heaven – a hilly division between the two largest lakes in Ethiopia, Abaya and Chamo. Behind the lakes were three ranges of high hills, each higher as they receded and each a paler shade of violet. Thick tree cover serrated their silhouettes and to the south the growl of thunder was momentarily trapped in these enclosing hills before it ricocheted off the etched surface of the lake. A flock of red-billed quelea, hunting for seeds in the grass, fled up and away to safety but pied crows in the palms dropped to the ground. The rain fell like bath-waste. For miles around the roads became rivers, the desert a flood and every mountain a cataract. Where was the dusty, desiccated ground parched to a crisp that I had planned and packed for? The worst drought for 50 years had turned into catastrophic floods.

Leaving the valley, the fun began. Rocks and ruts bounced and twisted the car while my body groaned and my bones rattled. Chirpy goats, indolent cattle, and hurrying market goers slowed travel to a tortoise pace. From time to time short but drenching rain turned the road to oil and the riverbeds to cascades. As the road climbed, dipped and twisted through the mountains, small boys appeared gyrating their hips, bending their knees and waving their arms with such energy and abandon it seemed that they may well have stumbled into an ants' nest. This dislocated dancing was a local form of amusement and the boys had discovered that since it seemed to amuse travellers too, it could be worth a birr or two for a photograph. These writhings were accompanied by cries of, "Ireland," or so it seemed. In fact, they were shouting, "Highland," a variety of mineral water whose plastic bottles are prized as containers.

This is an active country of muscle and sinew, of walkers and of workers. The walkers are fast and purposeful but often they run (this is a country of marathon winners). The workers carry immense bundles of firewood, huge bales of hay, cal-abashes of water and young children. Donkeys strain in shafts of overloaded carts, ponies are whipped into greater speed and bullocks are yoked to wooden ploughs to turn dry and stony ground. Men direct these operations – or so they think.

Mission churches abound. Of utility corrugated sheet construction, they are scattered liberally. Gospel, Pentecostal, Adventist, Rastafarian, Children of God, Jesus Christ International Gospel Ministry, Believers in Christ. Believers in Anything if it brings with it a bowl of soup and a Sunday sing-along. In a country that claims the resting place of the Ark of the Covenant and traces its Christian heritage back to King Solomon, it is astonishing that such diverse offshoots from the root and branch of the Ethiopian Orthodox Church can flourish.

At Jinka, the last town before Sudan to the west and Kenya to the south, I looked forward to The Resort Hotel and all that the name implied. The reality was damp sheets (moderately clean), damp spirits (temporary), a dripping shower (all night) a flickering light (not for long) and a wickless candle. Over warm beer and goat goulash, I engaged the only other guests. They were a forties-plus pair from Edinburgh who had arrived by public bus. Unable to find a dry patch to pitch their tent they had checked into this £14 per night luxury establishment. "It's such a treat once in a while." I slunk humbly away. I was reading Robert Byron's *'The Road to Oxiana'* and he had just arrived at Herat after two days in a public bus and was suffering from dysentery. He had carried with him the 1834 Journal of the Bengal Asiatic Society and Dietz's two volume *Churasanische Baudenkmaler*. He wrote:

'Dawn like a smile from the gallows, pierced the drizzling, gusty night.'

If you write like an angel, pretentiousness and overweight luggage can be overlooked.

A group of 4x4s rolled in, suspensions groaning, with their roof racks piled with tents and jerry cans and weary women and bearded men stepped out and called for beer. They had come from the Mago River, my next planned destination and they made gestures of disappointment and difficulty. They were Swedish missionaries and told me that the rains had made the roads so impassable that they were stuck in mud for two days without food and water and walked seven and a half miles (12kms) to find a vehicle that could pull them out. The Mago River will not be my destination after all. The drivers boasted of their adventure and displayed that typical Ethiopian characteristic of broad smiles and cheerful acceptance of whatever life throws at them. If you have nothing, anything is welcome. This is bush country, untamed, little travelled, home to some of the most remote tribes in sub-Saharan Africa and there is a pioneering swagger about those who have ventured this far.

Evengadi Lodge sat in a grove of spreading acacia trees. The birds that called to each other all day were superseded by a generator that coughed and spluttered all night. This was not a lodge but a tented camp with a dozen patched, darned (or sometimes not), grey canvas homes creased with age, some with a plastic tarpaulin thrown over them where patching was no longer an option. Once, when zips had worked and their nets were without fist-sized holes, they might have deterred mosquitoes. They were probably bargain hand-me-downs from a refugee camp. Still, they were spacious enough for two iron bedsteads and a bamboo chair. I took the chair outside, poured a whisky, listened to the last call of the birds in the setting sun and feeling like a pasha on a rickety throne, contemplated the comings and goings of the campsite. We had picked up a cook in

Karo man of Omo Valley

Jinka and when my team of three were not laughing, they prattled away like a cageful of parakeets. The cook's name was Gezacho; naturally I named him Gazpacho. With scarred cheeks he looked like a savage but was gentle, sweet natured, soft spoken and never without a knitted scarf in the national colours of red, yellow and green tied around his head and knotted under his chin. When he smiled, which was often, white teeth split his shiny black face in half. It was as though the lid had been lifted off the keys of a Steinway. He was trying to educate himself, studying by night and cooking (learnt from his mother) by day. At 28, he was in fifth grade (usually reached at 15), but he was a poor country boy with no father and only two sisters to run the farm. While here he lodged in a shack in the town and the day before had walked the two miles to the tents at three in the morning. He had no watch and was anxious to ensure that he was in time to cook breakfast and make up the lunchtime picnic; I adequately rewarded such conscientiousness. His chicken dish the previous night started off live in the market and I had just seen that night's kid stew trot by on the end of a string. There the cooks have to be butchers too.

The Omo Plain stretches widely on each side of the river, its western side reaching into Sudan and across its surface the gravel road to Omorate was straight and level – a welcome change from the bone-jarring, chassis-twisting, rutted, boul-

Galdo woman
of Omo Valley

dered, corrugated tracks of the past few days. Along the way were black backed jackal, dik-dik, gerenook, vulturine guinea fowl, quail dusting themselves in the dirt, and storks, vultures and other assorted raptors perched with menace and anticipation in dead trees. The town was a dump; a couple of dozen shacks and a few breeze block dwellings bordering a dirt street full of the litter of uncaring inhabitants who exhibited even greater listlessness and sedentariness than other southern towns. A branch thrown across the road marked the town boundary and details of my passport and the car were noted in a torn exercise book. 30 miles (50kms) from the Kenyan border, smuggling was the local business.

As I stepped into the hollowed log with a hole in its side, I regretted my request to cross the Omo River. I squatted in two inches of mud as a boy who cannot have been more than eight years old, poled the log up the river's bank and then out in to the main flow where water dark as treacle, swift and eddying, miraculously took us across to the far bank. It was Nationalities Day and villages sent in troupes of dancers, male and female, to perform. They were patient of a dreary speech through a malfunctioning megaphone and then, with much crowd support, each team sang, whooped and stamped its way around the police compound, all giggling with the fun of it.

It is amazing what can be done with hair as short and thick as a door mat but no two heads are alike in The Omo. Beaded, woven, shorn into intricate patterns, rubbed with clay, saturated with fat, tied up on top, knitted, knotted, knobbled, knurled and even plaited; each man and woman sported something distinctive. Further down there was scope for greater imagination and artistry. Bright pieces of plastic were a particularly popular addition and were twisted and shaped, dangled from ears, threaded through noses and stuck into hair. Married women got to wear necklaces sized for an ox – three necklaces if you were number one wife, and they were solid metal. Beads were big in these parts – in size, in number and in fashion. Strung long, short, light or heavy they were multicoloured, plain or patterned and they hung them from their necks and wrapped them around their waists, arms or ankles. A metal watch strap dangled from one ear, a bunch of aluminium pull tabs formed a necklace and a picture of Osama bin Laden was threaded through a length of wire and hung around a neck. Through Melkanu I asked if the owner knew whom he had jiggling against his chest. The dialect was difficult but it seemed he had no idea and when I told him it was a picture of the most wicked man in the world he beamed with pleasure; I had probably doubled its value. When it came to the main canvas of the body, inventiveness was the name of the game; a pot of white clay and ten fingers were all these artists asked for. There was no pattern too weird, too elaborate, too eccentric or too bizarre. I was not the first to see them and they knew their worth in front of a lens: 5p a shot and they counted the shutter clicks. The women of the Mursi came more expensive but if you have got a saucer jammed in your upper lip and earlobes down to your shoulders, a premium can be expected. Most of the men had a Kalashnikov slung over a shoulder and bullets in the magazine. I checked one – an extra 10p; in the circumstances I thought the price very reasonable. There are about 25 different tribes and, like the Dogon of Mali, they are all an anthropologist's dream.

At Konso it was dusk and lorries laden with labourers leaving for outlying villages were throwing clouds of ochre coloured dust into the setting sun whose rays, equatorially horizontal, were split by the roadside eucalyptus. St Mary's Hotel in the jargon of the travel agent was 'the best available'. It may well have been but it was rough even by local standards. It also occupied a prime site at the junction of four roads where a loudspeaker blared a cacophony of music in between pep talks on Aids; no one stood and listened. Outside my room there was an enamel bowl in which appeared to be the entrails of some animal. Peering closer they turned out to be the entrails of a lavatory cistern, mine. After a dampening from the drip of a shower, I found that the tiled floor was higher than that of the bedroom and there was now a small lake around my bed. A group of Japanese arrived a little later – I wondered when they would turn up. Their 4x4s were numbered 1, 2, 3, 4 and 5 and ten identikit women and two men tumbled out – several wearing masks over their mouths. They had brought their own food and two cooks were setting up their stoves in a corner of the courtyard. In another corner there was a bar crowded with locals and at the back a workshop for maintaining road construction machinery; a low loader was inching its way past Landcruisers 2 and 3. The bar turned on its music and the restaurant opposite was keen not to be audibly left out. My iPod reluctantly conceded defeat and the whisky bottle lowered a notch or two.

Yergalem is at the heart of the coffee growing area, and Aragash Lodge provided a sanctuary; on a Sunday, I was the only guest. Huge roundels of split bamboo formed the individual lodges and had bathroom appliances that actually worked. The cool of the altitude and the cooing of mourning doves did much to relieve the splitting headache and queasy stomach I had brought from the hell hole of Konso. Alone in the dining room, the Greek/Ethiopian owner came to chat. We discussed the difficulties of attracting upmarket customers in downmarket countries but he was confident that quality will win out eventually and smiled inscrutably as only a Greek can. He had 11 brothers and sisters all of whom live abroad – a sister in Bradford sent him lettuce seed for the hotel garden.

Longing for more cool and clean air, I headed for the Bale Mountains. It was two days' drive to the north through coffee, wheat and barley plantations and passed people wrapped in woollen cloaks astride small, bony horses and villages each with a square mosque of corrugated sheets and sporting a minaret economically painted with windows, balconies and cornices. Whining in first gear, Teckle nursed the car up to the Sanetti Plateau – the highest road in Africa. The Afro-alpine moorland, well above the tree line of the juniper forests, was dotted with giant lobelia and patched with spreading groups of *kniphobia*, sage and helichrysum. The air on the summit of Tullo Deemtu was thin and crisp and cloud covered all the land around. At 14,100 ft (4,300m) it is the continent's third highest mountain. 600 miles (375kms) to the northeast is the Danakil Depression, the lowest point on earth – what a country!

But I tired of contrasts, the struggles to survive, the inefficiency that poverty is careless of, the stares, the drab and dreary, 30 year olds going on 60, the squalor and the half-finished. I longed for things fat and fleshy, ironed sheets and a smooth road. I lack any missionary zeal and such conscience as I have was not moved to change the lives that I saw here. Churches of all kinds, NGOs by the score, aid agencies, governments, The World Bank and United Nations have all tried or are trying; I could not see a detectable dot of success.

Melkanu planned to open a tour agency. I told him to import bicycles – he would make a fortune. He smiled wistfully and waved a fluttering hand in sad farewell. "Abyssinia," I cried. Well – maybe.

Postcard Home

Here near the Omo, I'm in the deep south,
The men are all scarred as mark of respect,
The women are slim which is what you'd expect
If you got a large dinner plate stuck in your mouth.
They told me the Omo was dusty and hot,
Now I've been here a week, I can tell you it's not,
I've been drenched every day and in mud to my crutch,
I doubt whether Noah saw such rain or so much.
But the mountains are green and the tribes strange and queer,
It's untamed and untraveled and I'm thrilled to be here.

Burma II

January 2007

'To get to know a country you must have direct contact with the earth. It's futile to gaze at the world through a car window' – Albert Einstein

On New Year's Eve the champagne exploded like a firecracker turning heads in the Golden Banyan, a small restaurant open to the street in Kentung in the Eastern Shan State. Moving the ashtray with its 'No Smoking' notice attached and contemplating the menu of Half Fried Egg, Wet Fried Pig's Colon and Pig Ear Salad, I poured out the contents of the bottle into three unmatched tumblers for my two travelling friends and myself where it frothed and sparkled in pink anticipation of further celebration but none came. Here, with the Chinese border only two hours' drive away (as is that of Thailand and Laos), the party for Chinese New Year is in February. But tomorrow is my birthday and I have more fizz in the hotel fridge.

I had met up with my friends in the chaos of Rangoon's airport's internal departure lounge (I use the word colloquially – you do not lounge at a Burmese airport) and our plane had then hopped via Heho, Mandalay and Tashleik to this town in the hills. Each airport was a clone of the other, sporting a terminal building externally decorated with multi-pitched roofs and the intricate carving of a Buddhist temple. Earlier on in the evening, we had looked in on the cathedral that sat solid and plain in a prime spot overlooking the lake and adjacent to a huge gilded figure of a standing Buddha whose outstretched right hand and raised finger was a look-a-like of Uncle Sam in that ubiquitous poster 'Your Country Needs YOU'. Above the cathedral doors the words 'The Gates to Heaven' had been chiselled into the brickwork. Clearly this celestial frontier appealed as the church was packed for Sunday vespers. Headscarfed or veiled women were in

BURMA

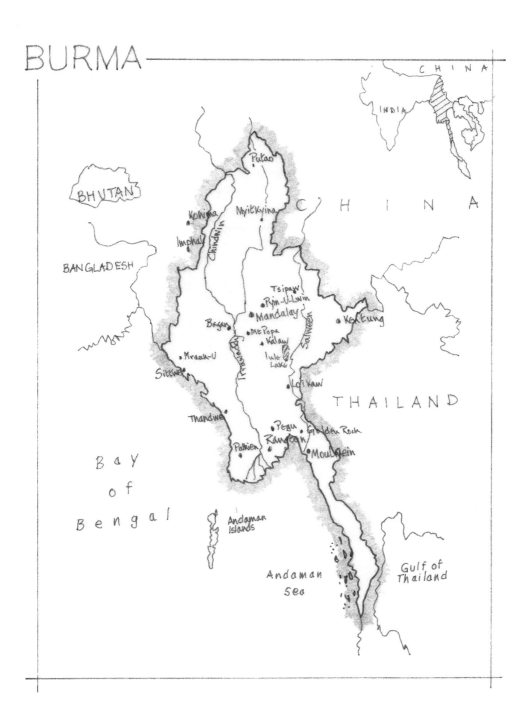

Akha head dress

the nave while the men occupied in the side aisles; an interesting antithesis to Muslim etiquette. Strings of coloured lights for Epiphany flashed on and off around the altar as we lustily sang out *Adeste Fidelis* guided by a hymn book in phonetic Burmese. I bet they did not have so much fun at the frowning Buddha next door.

At dawn I watched the town wake up; the noodle makers, the dumpling steamers and the tea boilers all doing their best to disperse the early morning mist. Commuters on mopeds, looming out of the watery gloom, wore helmets based on the German WWII model. It was as though a panzer division was advancing into town. It was a sleepy town, whose empty shops seemed content to remain so, whose dogs yawned as they lay in the dust and whose inhabitants had no need to hurry. But not wishing to disappoint my friends and family, I wrote on the back of the little watercolours I sent them:

'Here in Kentung it's a smuggler's lair,
There is blood on the floor and intrigue in the air.
The women are pretty but the men look mendacious,
It's a place to be cautious and not too audacious.
The cops and the army are all on the make
And opium warlords have set out their stake.
In the smoke of the braziers a furtive shadow
Slips down an alleyway dark and narrow.
Is he searching for women, for drugs or for rubies?
You need to be sure who the friend that you choose is.
If I get into trouble through some trifling mistake
I shall offer some crumbs from my birthday cake.'

Later, squeezed into a tiny, tinny Honda van, we set off on the road to China occasionally dwarfed by lumbering, overloaded trucks stirring the dust and belching the black diesel smoke of an engine pushed far beyond the limits set by its manufacturer. Dormant paddy fields, newly flooded, were being prepared for the spring harvest by rows of women wrapped against the morning chill and wearing coolie hats against the later sun. Rice nursery beds of the brightest viridian dotted the flat landscape like scattered emeralds.

After two hours of rattling, climbing and twisting along the road cut out of the red soil of the hills by Chinese engineers, we stopped amongst lush vegetation and Paul, our guide, led us up a narrow, steep and slippery path. Music, filtered by the jungle, gradually became louder and curiously familiar; it was those same hymns from the cathedral. Arriving in the village square, a stage had been set up decorated with tinsel and palm fronds and crackling loudspeakers, powered by a car battery, carried the tune to rows of villagers. Women in the elaborate headdresses, tunics and leggings of the Akha people were singing their hearts out (the men were gambling round the back). A missionary would have sunk to his knees in gratitude for work fulfilled. It was the same priest from the cathedral and his parish included scattered mountain villages and competed with the Baptists, Buddhists and those who still clung to animist traditions. In his mid-forties, he was urbane, charming and fluent in English and several tribal dialects. After he had doled out communion wafers and given a short sermon, he revved up his trail bike with its panniers stuffed with vestments and sacraments and skidded off to another jungle service. Around and about, potbellied pigs rootled in muddy corners, chickens roamed, dogs panted and families crowded the verandas of their stilted wooden houses.

The most northern Burmese province of Kachin stretches 215 miles (350 kms) beyond Myitkyina where the railway ends and from where the mule caravans used to start, travelling to China, the jade mines and the outposts of the Empire. Distance here is reckoned by days not miles; there are only tracks and the Irrawaddy, still 1,000 miles (1600kms) from the sea, is un-navigable even in the wet season; now, it drowsed 40 ft (12m) below its top banks. On three sides, the blue mountains hemmed in the plain, curving down southwards like horns; high on the China frontier, lower towards Tibet and Assam. Kingdon Ward came this way in 1928 collecting plants. He clearly wanted it known that he was not on holiday:

'These are the wild regions which the tourist who does Burma in three days only dimly hears of. For six months the mountains are swathed in impenetrable mists and drenched with rain, the paths are washed away and the rivers inflamed. The dense and evergreen jungle is alive with blood sucking creatures – leeches, horse-flies, sand-flies, blister-flies, mosquitoes, ticks and other horrors. There is an orgy of blood-thirst for salt.'

And just as you have got your breath back and are wondering whether in the circumstances the plants were really that important on the next page he carries on:

'Here whole mountain ranges have been in conflict; there is dense jungle and all the discomfort

that this entails with impassable rivers, snowbound passes, incredible rain and a total lack of roads and shelter. Add to this that the tribes who inhabit the North-East frontier are some of them hostile and most of them unfriendly, and it will be realised what the traveller has to expect.'

I had not expected temple bells, languorous maidens smoking cheroots, pagan gods with ruby eyes or strong silent men struggling with dacoits but I had not come to be punctured by flying insects or confront hostility. Even Lonely Planet talks of *'One of the least visited regions on earth'*. It was, therefore, both a pleasure and a little disappointing to fly into the little airport of Putao to find waiting to greet us the tall, charming Ma Lay with a smile sweet enough to spread, a pashmina over her shoulders and 'gloves' on her feet. The town dozed, children skipped home from school and cyclists slalomed through the potholes. (A bike with a crossbar is rare in this country where longyis are everyday wear.) A vehicle of great age and with several bolts less than its manufacturer intended, an exhaust that sounded its arrival a mile in advance and blowing smoke and steam so dense that it seemed to float, carried us and our smiling team of porters to the government rest house. This was dismal and soulless and had a plastic bucket for a bath, but no blister-flies, no raging rivers and no conflict. You were having us on, K. Ward.

In the venerable, belching jeep we made our way via a track of round river stones to the Mekila River where two elephants were hauling great teak logs up the bank. Such was the great weight of their load that they took only two steps at a time, wheezing and grunting with the effort. Compared with the elephants I had seen at Taungoo on a previous trip, they were making heavy weather of their tasks; perhaps they were overdue for retirement. Boarding a long boat, whose engine spurted oil in prodigious quantities onto the static water and whose helmsman's young son screamed in terror at the alien passengers, we chugged downstream. Bamboo hung over the river like giant fishing rods and women, washing metre-long hair on the riverbank, quickly adjusted their longyis in modesty. At a sandy bank by the village of Nam Kahn, we came ashore and settled into the teak-floored, stilted, thatched house of our host and his delightful young family. Word had spread of the arrival of foreigners, something of a rarity, and neighbours aged between six and 70 crammed themselves into the house to stare. Having been amazed at our eating habits, wondered at our complexions and examined our clothes, they launched into a long and impressive repertoire of generally tuneful songs. Our response was several rounds of *Frere Jacques, Old MacDonald had a Farm* and *Jerusalem*. Our performance was pathetically lame at first but whisky and audience participation soon raised the tempo, volume and enthusiasm. Later, as we struggled into sleeping bags, the household gathered for a final moment of voyeurism.

Heading south again, the chilly mists of Putao lifted at the prescribed time of 10.30 am allowing the Air Bagan flight to take off. Snow on the mountains to the east dribbled down countless little valleys from the knife edge of the ridge before vanishing into the jungle tree line. Mykitina was hot, dusty and noisy and with avenues shaded by cinnamon trees of great size and age. We had caught up again with the Irrawaddy and had lunch beside its pale brown, languid water in an establishment imaginatively named The Riverside Restaurant. When we left, we had renamed it The Bonking Cats on account of the energetic and continuous performance under the adjoining table. Outside, huge piles of oranges, glowing like embers, were being sorted and graded in readiness for tomorrow's festival.

At the stadium had gathered all the tribes of Kachin state – Jingpaw, Lisu, Law Waw, Lawang Waw, Rawaung and many subtribes. Old men had dusted off their ceremonial swords and donned a jaunty headband and younger men had the chance to show off their best kit. After the tedium of speeches from generals keen to impress and assured of an audience, a military band, uniformed entirely in white and playing all-white instruments, struck up including in their repertoire *Auld Lang Syne* and *Colonel Bogey*; how the Empire lives on! They marched in their plim- solls with a curious skipping motion so that the most enter- taining part of their programme was the euphonium players

Fisherman. Lake Inle

Anauk Gawt Gaw Pin
Monastery c1700

dancing and puffing their way around struggling to keep their balance and retain their formation. There were many military contingents on parade including the Kachin Independence Army. This band of guerrillas had been brought into the national fold for the first time in 100 years and in a tented exhibition of Kachin history, there were photographs of leaders from the '40s whom my father would have shot on sight. The four senior Kachin chiefs in satin robes of scarlet and emerald and headdresses of a freshly painted hornbill and three foot (1m) high peacock feathers, led the procession each holding a huge *parang* held vertically before them. Ko Ko, the *Mikado's* Lord High Executioner, would have cringed to see himself so comprehensively upstaged. 1,000 or more, decked out in their traditional best, swayed and sung their way around the stadium for two hours. Then, for tradition's sake or maybe just for the hell of it, they formed into a sinuous and multicoloured conga line. The drummer at the stadium centre beat out the rhythm on an immense drum and then they all did it twice more – and that was only the morning session.

The previous evening we had hoped to see a dancing competition between various tribes and villages but we caught the performance only at a half time interlude when we were 'entertained' by several of the local talent. It was unfortunate that the best of these, a slim hipped, long haired heartthrob in jeans and a leather jacket, was so enveloped by his smoke machine with its green and yellow lights that it looked as though he was struggling to find his way out of an old-fashioned pea souper. The firework finale was enlivened by the exploding rockets which only reached 40 ft (12m) and set off the alarms of the parked cars.

One evening we searched out the weaving district for which Mykitina is well known. We heard the racket a couple of streets away. The slap, crack, snap of the hand looms and the whirr, crash, slam and rattle of the mechanical looms – 100 or more of each. The handlooms were all worked by young girls nicely dressed and sporting lipstick and eyeliner: they seemed to enjoy the camaraderie. They wove fabric of great complexity with astonishing skill and slowly, very slowly, a party longyi appeared. The machines wove the everyday stuff of green and purple and where grease had not congealed with dust and cobwebs, they spurted oil into glistening and slippery puddles. They looked as though they were the cast offs of a Liverpool industrialist in the '30s. At any rate, in dim light with their flapping belt drives and little space between them, they were horribly hazardous to the dogs and small children that played amongst them.

Burmese rubies are prized worldwide and in Rangoon I searched for one, with a picture in my mind of a stone the size of a pigeon's egg, the colour of its blood and all for the price of a squab. I was much mistaken but U Win, whose day job was Professor of Geology at Rangoon University, was clearly the man to set me on the path to reality. So late one evening we went to 'an associate's' house in Rangoon. This was how the trade operated, I thought: a furtive guard at the gate, a whispered password in the shadows and precious stones unwrapped from a clandestine hiding place. I was wrong. A middle-aged couple welcomed us with charm and English fluency to their large, brightly lit new house and spread out a great array of stones, precious and not so precious, on a sheet of black velvet. The largest ruby weighed in at about a carat and a half and about the size of two grains of rice. So much for romanticising. I eventually settled for something blood red, flawless and fingernail sized that seemed to me (and I hoped to M) good enough for a princess. Before we left, our dealer host brought out a pair of sensational diamond earrings. "At $44,000, who can afford those?" I asked. "Oh, a general or two," he replied. In Bangkok or Singapore they would be half as much again and in London or New York, double.

In the great cities of Rangoon and Mandalay, a pot of dissent may well be bubbling but in the backwoods areas of our travels the controlling hand of government was apparent but not oppressive. In Kentung the public right to fish the lake had been arbitrarily removed in favour of a military owned company. In Mykitina, the cost of taxi permits had doubled and doubled again and all tourist guides were licensed and had to file a report as to their proposed programme and later, whether it had been carried out. I was sure that the same man was on every plane we travelled in. All our guides spoke of stricter controls in all parts of daily life. The national exchequer spent extravagantly on prestige projects of high visibility so that the international arrival halls at Rangoon and Mandalay were clean, sanitised, huge and empty; domestic departures was dirty, cramped, overflowing and chaotic. 'Technical colleges' sat unused in the countryside, too far from town for a reasonable bicycle ride and lacking any supporting community. A 750 mile (1,200kms) dual carriageway was almost completed between Rangoon and Mandalay. "It will be empty of cars but clear for the military," said our guide.

The Buddhist temple on the east bank of the Irrawaddy trumpeted its presence at 4.30 am and then, like an alarm clock, continued intermittently for another half hour. This irritation was no doubt tolerated by the Hindus, Baptists, Catholics, the Bethesda Church, Our Lady Queen of Heaven and the other evangelist churches sprinkled around since this is a land of equanimity and toleration. I never once saw a hand raised in anger, a dog kicked, neither a shouting match nor an angry gesture. In the crowded buses and in the paddy fields, the jokes seemed to start at first light and end with the last flickering candle. Whether this is the antidote to oppression, the healing salve of Buddhism or the stoicism of a people who for centuries have been the pawns of power struggles, invasion and persecution, is hard to tell. All are probably linked but against all odds, on the surface (albeit a thin and polished surface), this is a land of laughter.

Postcard Home

The skin of the Chin is a web of tattoo,
To the ways of the Wa this is par to taboo.
Among the Hmong, striped sarongs strike a pose
But a Naga's content with a bone through his nose.
I've travelled by jeep, cart, train, plane and boat
To hills, shores and cities and places remote.
It's sad for the people of beautiful Burma
That unrest is suppressed and now only a murmur.

Gabon

August 2007

'One always begins to forgive a place as soon as it is left behind' – Charles Dickens

No, I was not sure where it was either but it came with good credentials. A stable ex-French colony, the third highest income per person in Africa (oil and timber), 35,000 lowland gorillas (*Gorilla gorilla gorilla*), a sub species of elephant that live in the forests, troupes of mandrills 1,000 strong, hippos that surf in the sea and humpback whales in the Gulf of Guinea. The country has the largest intact forest area in all Africa (covering 80 percent of the country) and has the greatest diversity of birds and plants on the continent. Its forest is part of the Central African rainforest which, aged 60 million years, is probably the oldest in the world and the River Ogooue delta is the second largest in Africa. On the practical side, the country was due South (*so* due south that the Greenwich meridian almost touched its western coast), so no jet lag. Its capital, Libreville, sat on the equator and is the nearest town to that topographically mystic spot where zero degrees longitude meets zero degrees latitude. All in all, worth a look.

The new French president, Nicholas Sarkozy, had left the morning I arrived and huge posters showing him shoulder to shoulder with President Omar Bongo were at every crossroads. The reflected glory was obvious but it seemed strange that Sarkozy should have chosen Gabon (population 1.2 m) for a second foreign state visit (Germany had been the first); no doubt the oil pumped offshore by Elf had something to do with it. O. Bongo's presidential palace was in the worst possible taste and its two shades of brown were overdue for repainting. Considering that the national exchequer had been badly dented by its construction, its interior must be top heavy with glitz to compensate for its bland but crenellated exterior. The Hotel Meridian ran the palace a close second in size and brashness and in

216

Forest buffalo
Gabon

the huge entrance lobby the Libreville Gospel Choir, all in grey suits and flashy ties, was belting out *Mine Eyes Have Seen the Glory* – it sounded strange in French. The restaurant was empty but here the evangelical harmonies were replaced by a trio of elderly, spectacled and greying locals who ran through a repertoire of Charles Trenet and Dusty Springfield on an unlikely combo of guitar, panpipes and tom-toms.

My homework on the country was limited to the flight out and the only published guide book by Bradt but it was enough and there were some entertaining snippets of history. It was only in 1839 that a French naval lieutenant named Bouet-Willaumez obtained a large tract of coastal land from a native chief in return for two sacks of tobacco and ten white hats. Fifteen years later Paul Belloni du Chaillu mounted a three year expedition into the interior, survived 50 separate attacks of malaria and wrote a book describing 2,000 different birds and 200 different mammals (if you want to sell, think big and lie). Forty years after this, the formidable Mary Kingsley (she of *Travels in Africa*) made her own explorations. The natives addressed her as 'Sir'- entirely apt considering her fortitude. A passage from her book runs:

'Falling into a wild game pit I found myself sitting on nine ebony spikes. It is on occasions such as this that you realise the blessing of a good thick skirt.'

Spending the night in a Fang chief's house she recalls opening a putrid bag that disturbed her sleep.

'...there was a human hand, three big toes and two ears. The hand was fresh.'

217

She explained to her readers that human flesh was nutritious and a good food source. As a colony, the French did nothing except sell concessions for rubber plantations. Death, disease and hatred for whites were rife. They eventually gave up in 1960. El Hadj Omar Albert Bernard Bongo (names that seem to cover most of the useful nations and religions) was elected with a 99.9% majority a few years later and he and his majority have been there ever since.

There was alarming confusion for the flight to Port Gentil. The queue was long and largely comprised huge women in extravagantly patterned robes with matching turbans pushing forward great parcels of cardboard and string. The policeman did not like my visa, the clerk did not like my ticket (I did not like it either – a single, flimsy piece of paper with details of the flight scribbled on it) and worse, this was the last flight for three days. It was overbooked and certainly overloaded. But suddenly I had a more convincing ticket – No.1 and a boarding pass for Air Gabon flight 202 and found that there were only five others on it. These included a young European couple so amorously engaged in thoroughly getting to know each other that I was sweating too.

And then it was by open boat. Powered by three Evinrude 200 HP outboards, we twisted and turned down countless watery paths beset with mangrove, palms and papyrus, sometimes doubling back to find a shorter route, sometimes zooming across an inland lagoon. Every mile looked the same but every inch was different. The helmsman handled his 600 horses with nonchalance and skill and how he found his way amongst the myriad streams seemed a miracle but perhaps that is said of a London cabbie too. My fellow passenger carried an impressive metal-bound suitcase, strengthened at all corners and secured by a small bolt and a huge padlock. It turned out that he was delivering the monthly wages, in cash, for 70 employees at the lodge where I was going. He did the same trip at the same time on the first of each month. Slight of frame with a thin moustache and mock croc shoes he was the double of the accountant in *The Untouchables*. Had we been ambushed, and it was a miracle that we were not, I would have been left to fight the bandits while he handed over the cash. After the lagoons came the open sea and with it, spray, rain and skies as grey as a Welsh slate quarry. I had come prepared for malaria, dengue, yellow fever and encephalitis but not pneumonia; we were on the equator and this was the dry season for heavens' sake! Berthing at Omboue, cold and shivering, I sought refuge in the waterfront hotel where the patron, a greying French *roué* who was finishing a fishy lunch in the company of a local lass talented in all the right places, offered me a mouldy bathroom, a tepid shower and a threadbare towel.

Loango Lodge sat on the edge of an inland lagoon which was open to the sea.

Conceived by a million-
aire Dutchman, Rambout
Swanborn, as a place for
scientific research and conservation, he was the sole
source of finance. Rec-
ognising that the Gabon
infrastructure was not up
to the requirements of
the well-heeled traveller,
he set up his own internal
airline and fleet of Landcruisers. Back unexpect-
edly for lunch one day and
as the only diner, the cook
appeared looking mourn-
ful.

*"Je regrette mais j'ai seul-
ment un filet mignon, des har-
icots verts et de la salade. Pref-
erez-vous de la sauce béarnaise
ou des champignons?"*

Hurrah for French colonialism and rich Dutchmen. The lodge was kept in tip top working order by a human dynamo named Phillipe du Plessis de Grenedan. On the last day of my stay he twice reorganised a complicated rescheduling of jeeps, boats and planes as though that was what contemporary French aristocracy was best at.

The River Mkita, as black as the mud beneath it, snaked through banks of papyrus, rubbed up against patches of forest where sometimes a tree of great age and presence dominated its local kingdom and meandered over flooded grasslands. It seemed as if we were slowly sliding over glass, so still and placid was the water in the quiet of the evening and in that suspension of time that comes just before dusk and the anticipation of the drawn curtain of darkness. All that broke the surface of the water and the surrounding silence was an occasional fish rising to a mosquito. Under a benign moon and an indigo sky, it was if earth was drawing up its duvet. Dawn seemed almost indistinguishable from dusk except that breakfast was clearly on the menu. A profusion of fish eating birds from fish eagles to pygmy kingfishers were busy, hadeda ibis and wood storks foraged for frogs and herons took off in languid resignation as we passed by. Only hammerkops remained imperturbable. Solitary forest elephants, smaller and darker than their east African cousins, slowly munched their way through reed and papyrus without so much as raising a trunk in recognition of our pontoon.

Later, back beside the sea, I went in search of humpback whales. The helmsman of the rigid inflatable was securely strapped as if in an acrobatic aircraft but the passengers were left to their muscles and the realisation that a relaxed grip meant a catapulted push overboard. Two marine biologists came along for the ride and what a ride it was. We bumped and slammed our way through the waves, turning 90 degrees in as many milliseconds and careering from crest to trough. My stomach tightened to snapping point, my arms ached and my fingers were white from immersion and strain. I found myself screaming from pain and exhilaration as the laughing steersman tried to anticipate the next breaching. We were saturated with warm tropical salt water and exhausted by the need to survive. All the while, I was gripping a camera for the shot of the year but the whales seemed to be resting under the restless sea. But suddenly, one breached magnificently off the port side. It was enough; 40 tons of barnacled blubber leapt out of the sea streaming spray from fins and flukes, crashed back in to the salty turmoil and vanished.

On the Isle de Petit Evengue there was a gorilla sanctuary built and financed by the ever benevolent M. Swanborn. As usual in this area of lagoons and waterways, our journey was by boat and I was handed a life jacket.

"Nagez-vous?" the boatman enquired. Answering, *"Qui,"* the jacket was abruptly taken back; perhaps it was felt wise not to test it too far. Gabon's gorillas are slowly being reduced by disease (ebola), loss of habitat (oil and logging) and hunting (bush meat) but disappointingly, this sanctuary of three acres held only two orphaned boys and an old man of 27. The old man and I looked at each other through the electrified fence but his expression showed no sign of interest in life. He was magnificent with vast shoulders and arms of formidable power and his body was solid muscle under its silver hair. Too old to be habituated to the forest he would spend his remaining years, 20 at least, as a lonely lord in a pint sized kingdom.

The German Pilatus pilot, with a baseball cap that said 'Butch Cassidy' and aviator dark glasses of the type favoured by James Dean in the '50s, flew so low up the sinuous River Lope that we scared the birds roosting in the forest canopy and banked left and right in almost equal turns in the two hour flight from Ombroue to Lope. "Shall we have a little fun?" he had asked. I was not sure that I wanted any fun in a small plane flying into the interior of a country with wall to wall primary rain forest. He had come from Cameroon and was off to a logging concession in Congo after dropping me, so I smiled weakly hoping that these journeys indicated a long established skill rather than a wish to show off and the twisting flight did in fact turn out to be fun. We landed on a grass strip the length of a cricket pitch and as I recovered on the veranda of my chalet with a double malt whisky, a six strong squad of grass-cropping black and white goats (or they may have been sheep) came by. Their chums were six black and white cats that hung about the dining room and putting their heads through the timber fence, they went muzzle to muzzle in friendly conversation.

The lie of the land was different here with rolling savannah, small sharp hills and paltry patches of forest. In two safaris, each of half a day, I saw little except for two groups of forest elephants. My companion, a Dutchman with hands like hams and a face to match, kept up a commentary of all the animal encounters he had had since arriving three days ago. It seemed that he had been within a few feet of buffalo, red river hogs, hippos, fishing owls and elephants. I wished him dead. I moaned to my guide that luck was not on my side. He replied, "On safari, you may see nothing the first day and again, nothing on the second day. On the third day all the animals come out in large numbers but by then you have left!"

At dinner I ordered a bottle of Baron de Listrac 2002 in compensation and fed the black and white cats my gristly lamb chop. The garish paper flowers on the table and the raffia bread basket were made in China, the tinned pineapple came from Cameroon and so did the morning's cornflakes and yoghurt. Here were the consequences of a country resting on its oil wealth and a people too lazy, or perhaps simply too African, to make any effort themselves. When the oil dries up and Bongo is dead, both likely in the next ten years, where will the entrepreneurs be? Sadly, they may be back to swinging in their hammocks on their front porch.

The instructions for the mandrill tracking expedition were clear:

Be ready at 0730 – please be prompt.

Wear dark clothing.

Wear boots or wellingtons.

My team of Vincent and Salvador appeared around 0900 dressed for a Caribbean carnival and wearing flip-flops. I signed a form absolving the National Park authorities from any responsibility as to my safety and in particular, expressly waived my rights under Sec 1542 of the Civil Code of California and we set off for the forest. After a number of triangulation hits of a radio collar fitted to a matriarch mandrill, a spot by a stream was chosen as being on the likely path of the troop. Camouflage netting was thrown over the base of a tree and two of us squatted for over an hour in a space the size of a tea chest, encumbered by roots and accompanied by large ants, small spiders and a host of tiny black, biting flies. Suddenly, there was a roar from a male mandrill and a troop of some 200 rushed past in the deep shadow of the far side of the stream. They were gone in 20 seconds and I caught a glimpse of a disappearing blue bottom. I had paid extra for this.

I cannot blame the galloping mandrills on my guides; wild animals do not perform to order but I tired of Lope and longed for the food and efficiency of Operation Loango. Devoid of energy and enterprise, any organisation eventually collapses and action does not form part of the average African day; it is simply a way of passing time. In every village, non-committal women with folded arms leant against doorposts and listless children tumbled with their dogs and chickens in the dust. I ceased to take note of them and joined the local ways: smile, resign yourself, things will work out. In any case it's too hot, too wet and whatever you might think of doing, it's too hard. African scenery is spectacular, its wildlife sensational but its people drive me mad.

The twice weekly Train l'Equateur from Libreville trundled in an hour late but for those waiting it was an opportunity to chat to friends. The station, clean, tidy and well maintained, adjoined a huge marshalling yard for the logging industry and a train half a mile (400m) long was being loaded for its trip to the coast. Trees five feet (1.5m) across were stacked six high; 600 year old giants sought out for their sovereignty were now felled, scarred and chained and awaiting banishment to a foreign land. There was a trainload every two weeks and in addition, a constant flow of timber lorries and large rafts on the rivers. From time to time the station master appeared from his office, donned a waistcoat emblazoned on its back with SETAG – *Societe Transportation de Gabon* – and wrote the expected arrival time on a blackboard; taking off his waistcoat he then disappeared again into his den. Alterations were made several times each hour but I never saw anyone read them. The porter never did as he was fast asleep on a pile of mattresses; his legs twitched now and again and his shoes did not match. Instead of a trolley he had a wheelbarrow which was now filled with bananas and a microwave oven. The barrow was new – perhaps it was part of the luggage.

The deep interior of an equatorial rain forest is a quiet, benign and shadowy environment. Life lurks in these shadows and stares from the canopy but it seldom threatens and is seldom seen. In the rainy season, it would be unpleasantly abuzz with insects but it was now dry and I accepted an invitation to visit Mikongo, a small camp run as a scientific station and staffed by five women researchers all of different nationalities (but none Gabonese or even African). We rattled for a few hours due east down the main road to the Congo over the ruts and corrugations caused by 40-ton, 18-wheeled logging lorries driven fast and carelessly to the railhead at Lope by drivers paid by the trip and high on marijuana. Passing one meant driving blind in an impenetrable cloud of fine and choking dust; a dozen times my life was in the hands of chance or the Angel Gabriel. After a further two hours along a narrow track cut through the forest and which snaked around great trees and plunged down steep banks to cross over streams, we reached a little clearing with six wooden huts spread around the perimeter in a circle. My Gabonese guides had the unlikely names of Janvier and Jeremy and we set off along barely discernable paths a foot wide, slithering down slimy slopes and crossing streams on fallen tree trunks. I simultaneously tried to find life in the canopy 200 ft (60m) above and avoid the hazards of the track two feet below. After 30 minutes, I was already dripping with sweat and every muscle ached and there was another five hours to go. The wildlife had clearly heard I was coming and scurried away but what remained was spotted by Janvier with the fine-tuned ear and far-seeing eye of a forest hunter; Jeremy sat down at every opportunity. Along a wide stream bed of damp sand there were the tracks of leopard, mandrill, bush pig and antelope, the paths we followed were cut or brashed by forest elephants and I heard, but seldom saw, hornbills, turacos, parrots, manabe and vervet monkeys. Perhaps I was unlucky, perhaps the time of year was wrong, the weather too damp and dull or perhaps I did not offer up the right incantations to the right gods but the wildlife had conspired to stay hidden.

Leaving Lope, Vincent (the ham-handed animal spotter) looked at me as he mangled my fingers in a goodbye crunch.

"Vat have you done viz your hair?" he asked.

I had no idea and the mirror in the gloomy gents showed nothing amiss. But later, back in the tasteless pile of the Meridian Hotel and a brightly lit bathroom, I discovered my hair was satsuma orange. I looked like a Belisha beacon. The culprit was clearly a new and novel anti-sunburn liquid that I had been liberally applying to my thinning pate. At a supermarket I miraculously obtained a pack of Garnier 'ColorGo' whose contents (two powders and a liquid) came with instructions in French. The only part of these I could understand was 'It is important to apply the contents in the correct order'. Having no idea of the correct order and with a plane to catch I risked powder, powder, liquid, avoided the stares of curious passengers and sank low into my aircraft seat. It took a month for orange to turn to grey.

Gabon will be spared a return visit.

Postcard Home

Deep in the forest the shadows are parted
By a leathery hand the size of a plate.
It's a female gorilla as big as a shed
But she's still just a tiddler compared to her mate.
Here in Gabon on the plains and the foothills
Are hundred-strong gatherings of blue nosed mandrills.
As I swing in my hammock the drums from the Congo
Are beating a greeting to President Bongo.

Tibet

September 2007

'I should like to spend the whole of my life travelling abroad, if I could borrow another life to spend afterwards at home' – William Hazlitt

The Shankar Hotel in Kathmandu was once a palace but surplus to royal requirements in the '50s it had been converted from its ground plus two floors, into ground plus three. Our bedroom on the new mezzanine third was the top slice of the previous ballroom and had a three foot (1m) deep cornice and the top pane of the ballroom window so that to look out required lying on the floor. Two weeks before we arrived, there had been a more radical distribution of royal residences and all 16 of the countrywide palaces had been confiscated, the king stripped of all executive powers and the kingdom declared a republican state. These dramatic political changes seemed to have no visible effect on the street jams of worn out lorries, Suzuki taxis or Honda motor bikes, nor had three hour queues for just two litres of petrol dampened the Nepali enthusiasm for motorised wheels. However, three bombs (two killed and 19 injured) allegedly planted by Maoist terrorists on the evening we arrived closed off Durbar Square, adding to the press of traffic elsewhere.

The *Kathmandu Post* naturally described these atrocities the next morning but the more disturbing front page news was a report that the chief engineer of Nepali Airlines, baffled by a persistent mechanical problem, had sacrificed a goat to encourage a divine solution. Since we were about to fly with Nepali over the highest and most inhospitable mountains on earth, I wished that at least he could have run to a buffalo.

In Lhasa, the Chinese had rolled out a great carpet of commercial concrete over the fertile valley so that there was a grid of dual carriageways and rows

225

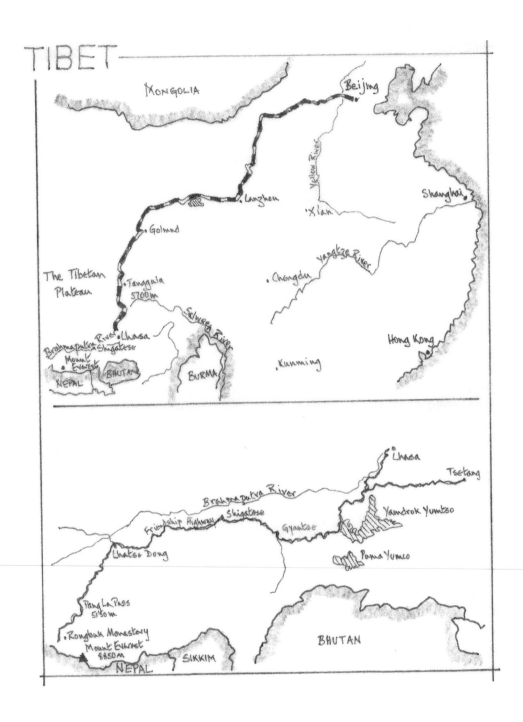

of identikit tenement blocks together with four army barracks and several open spaces for mass rallies. To those nurtured on the sentiments of a mystical city inhabited by a living god, a tough and resolute people under the protection of high mountains, this garish, insensitive and overbearing example of Chinese dominance was initially shocking. However, the Han Chinese have outnumbered the Tibetans in Lhasa for almost 40 years and Tibet with a quarter of China's land mass (equal to France, Germany and Belgium combined) has only six per-cent of its population. The dreadful destruction of the Cultural Revolution had been halted for some of the buildings most precious to the Tibetan heritage, and the inner sanctum around the Jokhang temple was respectful of traditional styles and materials. The Potala Palace too had been left largely unscathed as an important draw for tourists. Part fortress, part prison, part shrine and part home, its dominating vertical plane and its monolithic structure of immense grandeur glowed white, pale pink, red and gold. The hill on which it rests and its own slant-ing walls (a structural necessity in the absence of mortar) combined to give it a powerful sense of stability.

Elsewhere, architectural devices from Ming to modern were deployed with hid-eous abandon. In Tsedang was embodied what is present in all Chinese cities: a stupefying architectural sameness based on an inanimate set of models. Streets of standard cuboid shops are followed by streets of standard cuboid shops. There is no basic variation in the design of flats, government offices, barracks, parks or bookstores. Only the street lamps differed although there, the model was art nou-veau meets Venetian. The Chinese ideal of harmonising with nature is absent in the stodgy, conformist architecture of its cities. At our hotel, a personal message from the manager welcomed us:

'Enjoy the enchanting sunshine and extensive field of view' ending, *'We are always your sincere friends; here is your sweet home from home.'*

I looked for a bucket to be sick into. The smarmy tone of the letter was some-what alleviated by a warning against *'...depositing hotchpotch in the garden.'*

Escaping the bling of the town and the supercilious manager, we set off for the Samye monastery following the course of the fledgling Brahmaputra River, whose flood waters had wrapped the stands of willow and poplar in a swirl of Brown Windsor soup. Along the way *ceratostigma*, pink and white *cosmos*, and a pungent low growing shrub – an *artemesia* perhaps – were all flowering and the mountainsides were covered by a thorny bush cautiously grazed by herds of sullen sheep and arrogant but perky goats. Rape was being harvested to be crushed for cooking oil and *quinke*, the hardy highland barley, harvested for bread and beer. The farm houses were solid, stone built and square, each with an elaborate door-way and prayer flags at the four corners of their flat roofs. We crossed axle deep an eager and intemperate river of clear water as it rushed to join the soup of the Brahmaputra and climbed to a pass where the whole of the valley could be seen through a tangle of prayer flags, torn and tattered by the bitter wind. The monastery stood alone in a desolate landscape and was the object of pilgrimage by many thousands of Tibetans, the majority of whom made the difficult journey in the winter when the land no longer required their attention. Many had travelled over these mountains for days, some for weeks enduring the harshest weather and the most rigorous conditions. At their goal, they prostrated themselves many times before their chosen Buddha or lama, caressed the door frame of a shrine's entrance already engrained with the sweat and dirt of 10,000 imploring hands, and kissed the pedestal of their god. Behind the temples were ruins of wood and clay, reminders of the fury of an extreme cultural intolerance. They are left to the nettles, an occasional hoopoe, mangy dogs and diseased peach trees. In the monastery's ill-kempt grounds were hollyhocks and delphiniums in profusion and a bed of pink roses which we set about dead-heading.

In contrast to the Potala Palace where backpacks were scanned and photographs forbidden, the monks here were welcoming and unconcerned as we poked about their temple and their home. Taking advantage of a sign crudely painted with the universal letters WC on a piece of cardboard torn from a box of tinned milk, I found a row of four unpartitioned squatters and a windowless opening to the outside. On a wall was a poster of David Beckham.

A quilt had been laid over the wide plain of the Yalumba River, its patches of unripened barley showing green, and those ready for harvesting glowing like crème caramel and matching the early autumnal hues of poplars along the river banks. Other patches, where barley had already been cut and stooked, showed like polka dots in the wide landscape and in between there was an occasional square of potatoes and a smear of rape or a flash of mustard. Harvesters took a break for yak butter tea, sitting with legs outstretched as though the bend at their waist was locked in place whether reaping or resting. My three Tibetan phrases drew more quizzical expressions than smiling acknowledgements but I stopped short of the local custom of sticking out one's tongue in greeting.

Each day there was another monastery – or so it seemed, each with its scattering of young monks sprouting the first hairs of manhood and with shy but sincere smiles. They looked implausibly healthy and cheerful on an unchanging diet of steamed vegetables and suffocating veneration. I could never have become accustomed to the stygian gloom of monastic shrines, the cramped interiors, the impossibly complex characters of Tibetan Buddhism, the pungency of rancid yak butter and the almost insufferable compression of spiritualism that they contained. On the other hand, the buildings' construction and decoration was admirable with

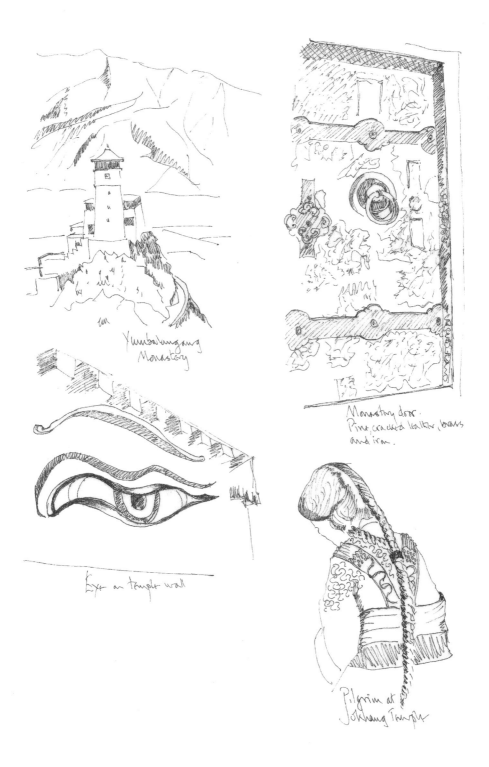

Yumbulangang
Monastery

Monastery door.
Pine, cracked leather, brass
and iron.

Eye on temple wall

Pilgrim at
Jokhang Temple

their massive structural timbers, lacquered and bound with studded bands of steel and copper. Their exquisite wall decorations, minutely illustrated religious texts whether painted on leather or fabric and their effigies were beautifully fashioned from clay and gold; Buddha's past, present and future, Guanyins and Sakamunis all with a different posture or gesture. At each of these monasteries, pilgrims, the devout or the simply curious were chanting, praying, shoving and spinning prayer wheels which engendered a pitch of religious enthusiasm I found both exhilarating and disturbing. Everywhere there were silk brocades, banners and smoke; lamas in maroon or saffron robes sat in alcoves intoning scriptures; a novice scrubbed the floor and in a corner there were brooms and thermoses. A thousand small Buddhas looked down from niches and there were macabre *tankas* of Kali. Through all this solemnity, cut the deep jangle of the bell whose frayed rope was pulled as pilgrims pressed past, the endless chant of *'Om mani padme hum'* and the brilliant clang and muffled thud of a great cymbal-drum echoed through the resonating halls.

The pilgrims and Chinese tourists with their squawking leaders pushed slowly through the corridors, halls and shrines of these labyrinths. Implanting coins in wax around the doorways, they dragged rosaries along the vermilion doors of closed rooms. Monks attended to lamps with strainers, tongs and trimmers. Dogs barked at rival dogs. Children carried younger children on their backs, adult sons carried their mothers. A woman prostrated herself full length before an image of a Buddha top-knotted, long-lobed and with an indescribable sense of peace on his unlined features. Before him there were offerings: a china cup, peacock feathers, teapots, incense sticks, plastic gladioli, toffees, hair slides, oranges, four yellow roses, coins brimming over in a copper bowl, a portrait of the Dalai Lama and barley grain. The golden statue itself was swathed in sashes of white, saffron and yellow, fastened to its robes with safety pins. A fire extinguisher and a huge aluminium kettle stood by the door. The smell of incense permeated the dark rooms. I longed to escape, to breathe the crisp, clear high altitude air, search the great sweep of the valleys and gaze on the mountains.

On the way to Shigatse we wound up a gorge along whose base flowed a river so awash with white water that it resembled cappuccino froth. The northern wall had twisted contortions of rock while on the southern side, the strata was turned vertically into slivers of grey stone. This was worked by groups of cheerless men who levered it out, chiselled it into long thin strips and heaved it down to the valley to be stacked beside the road and to await prospective purchasers. Small patches of ripe barley stood in tiny terraced plots and caught the sun like scattered gold coins. The rock ridges were tinged pink and slate and cinnamon with dark cloud shadows marching over them. On the tops of north facing peaks there was fresh snow and then came a feast of geological transformations. Isolated nude dunes of seductive contours; black hills, oily and stony and, like a tricolour of an imagined republic, a distant blue lake, a strip of flowering pink mustard and in front, a line of emerald grass. A sole mountain glowed gold in the late light. The grass was thin but goats and sheep nibbled a meagre meal. Plants, stunted and well-spaced, strived to maintain a foothold in the loose textured surface and rock falls were a constant hazard. Later, the slopes were riven with deep runnels as though scarred with the tears of the weeping mountains. At the Gyatso-La pass (17,100 ft, 5,220m) the scenery opened out on to a high plateau and yak herds were frequent. If grazing by the roadside, they looked up with a benevolent and bewildered expression as if we were the first vehi-

laughing monk

cle through in a month and then bolted in alarm. A nomadic herder plodded wearily along, the poles of his tent dragged by one of his beasts and some way behind a calf struggled to keep up. A glacier had slid this way many millennia ago and the ground was strewn with boulders. Astonishingly, at 9,800 ft (3,000m) above the tree line, wild clematis and *buddleja* were growing and the inhabitants of isolated villages were harvesting barley and beans. The sky was immense and the mountain ranges, set one beyond the other in infinitely fading shades, were barren but magnificent. Tingri, the last settlement before Everest, was like a small town in a Western movie: brown, broad and dusty with a few stores strung out along its single street. A horse with richly patterned woven saddle cloths stood patiently beside the modern cowboy's steed: a motorbike of extravagant chrome and its own decorated saddle cloth. Packs of savage looking dogs roamed around.

We took the back road to Everest beside the chalky white Ra Chu River, along a track rutted, bouldered, swampy, mountain-sliced, gravelly, jarring and jolting. Later this joined a wide, graded road where barriers were being installed on the open side. In five years there will be tarmac and neon. At the end of the track, the world's highest monastery had a lucrative sideline in providing accommodation – at least that is what they called it. No doubt they believed that an upgrade

Potala Palace, Lhasa.

on a monk's quarters would be sufficient and so were happy with a nicely painted restaurant which only served boiled rice or noodles. Patrick Leigh Fermor's comment on a bad meal came to mind. *'The cooking was so appalling that a stretcher may profitably be ordered at the same time as dinner.'* There were four beds to a room (torn curtains to match torn wallpaper), running water (a glacially cold dribbling tap 60 ft (20m) down the hill) and lavatories (a long drop, 130 ft (40m) down the hill and no clothes peg supplied). We pretended it was all a bit of an adventure – pioneers exploring up the sharp end; no room here for wimps and sissies. Had we needed a second night there would have been a mutiny.

And so to our journey's goal. We passed a collection of small tented 'hotels' that sported such names as Heavenly Peace or California Dreaming, providing accommodation for those prepared to accept even less than the spartan amenities of the monastery and the usual stalls of imported amphitrites, amber and beads and bangles. The transport for the last three miles (5kms) was by obsolete traps and we rode in a little patched and rattling cart pulled by a weary and bony pony whose driver was as old and weary as his beast. The way was hard and slippery and our driver whacked the rump of our struggling beast until I snatched away his whip of a length of fan belt and yelled *"Mind!"* – No! And then, rounding the last bend there was Jomolangma, Sagarmartha, Goddess of the Mountains, Everest. Not as dominating as I had expected but nevertheless imperious, authoritative and head high over its acolytes of Lhotse, Makalmond and Cho Oyu. For the hour that we were at the deserted Base Camp the wisps of cloud around the summit lifted, parted and vanished and then, as we turned away a storm came in from the North and drew a dark curtain across this empyrean stage.

At 8 am, the architecture of Lhasa's new railway station seemed imposing and intimidating. No doubt this was intended but to those who scurried through its concrete caverns, the concerns were about form filling, the fear of losing the flimsy paper train ticket and the bewilderment of where and when to board. After filing through ever narrowing barriers like sheep to be dipped, the Sky Train suddenly appeared like a mile long tethered dragon that was eager, snorting and impatient for the journey. On board there was chaos with boxes, bags, suitcases and provisions, pushed into spaces too small and too few to accommodate them.

The permafrost high plains spread to all horizons as we slowly climbed East up to the Tangulla Pass (16,900 ft, 5,150m) that marked the boundary between The Autonomous Region of Tibet and the Qinghai plateau of China. White tents of nomadic yak herders sparsely dotted the plain like little mushrooms as we continued through gorges and wide open spaces at a leisurely and confident pace. On board, cards came out onto impromptu surfaces of a sack or unsteady knees, babies were breast-fed, grannies were spoon-fed, pot noodles reconstituted and melon seeds cracked. Dozing, sleeping, laughing, chatting and texting, this pot pourri of the Chinese nation was trapped and transported in the world's highest train. One of our compartment's occupants was a young military officer as inscrutable as a brick wall and addicted to films of the Fu Manchu/Genghis Khan type which he watched continuously on his laptop. Not a muscle moved nor a lip twitched whether the barbarians were routed or a princess rescued. When he left at Tianshui, two elderly passengers arrived who both occupied the lower bunk; they coughed, spluttered and drank tea all night. Amid this fervid travelling community, the train's staff, smart in their dark green uniform emblazoned with stars, badges and chevrons (how the Chinese love their uniforms), moved aloof and efficiently, guarding each carriage as their personal fiefdom. At Lanzhou, the three diesel engines were replaced by a single electric engine and the pace quickened as we followed Hon Wey, the Yellow River; first east, next south and then, leaving behind this lifeblood of central China's agricultural valleys, headed north to Beijing. Towns became larger, monoliths of bland apartment buildings blander, the skyline a fretwork of tower cranes and the pollution denser.

An unwanted, unscheduled but unfortunately necessary visit to the 20-storey granite block of the Bureau of Public Security in Beijing was an irritating transit stop before we moved on to Hong Kong. There, the burnished steel and polished crystal of the skyscraping towers were as astonishing as ever. In the smog that sullied the air for our three days, they glowed ghostly grey but at ground level, in every small space that remained unbuilt, exquisite little gardens and landscaped areas were squeezed in or, when the ground was sloping as it so often was, torrents of water gushed and bubbled. On the pavements, people worried and scurried, twisting little human trails between the monster stalagmites '...*through caverns measureless to man down to the sunless sea.*'

I looked down from our hotel window to a swimmer in the turquoise pool 48 stories below. He seemed trapped, arms and legs slowly moving like a gnat caught in a jam jar: a modern Xanadu's sapphire lake – regulated, enclosed and sanitised. Two thousand miles to the northwest, the shoreline of the sapphire lake, Yamdrok Tsa in the Shannan mountains, wandered free, fed by snow melt and nurtured the valleys below, where the wind was chilled by the Himalayas, the water reflected the sky and the horizons slowly vanished in ever diminishing tones.

Postcard Home

The roof of the world is majestic but barren
In contrast to temples and smiling Tibetans.
It seems it's just monks who inhabit Tibet
But for the yaks (there's no yeti yet).
We're both in good spirits (in spite of the drains)
Tomorrow it's Ev'rest, the king of all mountains,
Then two days by train, two days in Hong Kong.
How we long for some wine and a comfy chaise longue.

Burma III
January 2008

'You cannot see the whole sky through a bamboo tube' – Burmese saying

Air travel in January brings extra hazards. If in this season of *'good will to all men'*, you are fortunate enough to escape a baggage handlers' strike, an air traffic controllers' go slow or a caterer's walk out, the wheezing, coughing and sputum spraying on board ensures that you add another 300 colds to the one you already have. The need for a panacea to winter's blues was not the primary reason to visit Burma again; there were corners not yet discovered, a tribal festival and in that troubled land, the appealing tranquillity in its people.

Form filling goes hand in hand with dictatorship: an obsession with control, the gathering of statistics and the busybody state, so it was no surprise to find that the immigration formalities at Rangoon's flashy new international airport were a lengthy affair. The form, printed on a large piece of pink card, was longer than on my last visit; perhaps the authorities were getting nervous. I have never understood the need to 'State your occupation'; I usually put 'enjoyment'. 'State your profession' is a little trickier; this time I entered 'trapeze artist'. Once, when entering Sabah I was asked for my interests. Where, I wondered, would the filing clerk have put my entry of 'foghorns'? I had considered 'pantaraxia' (a word that I had come across by chance when researching *Who's Who* for the credentials of a keen but insipid boyfriend of one of my daughters; it was the entry of that splendid millionaire and eccentric Nubar Gulbenkian) but then I thought I might be considered some sort of deviant.

The River Kaladin discharges into the Bay of Bengal on the northwest coast of Burma at the town of Sittwe. Built by the British to control the troublesome people of Arakan, it is home to a largely Muslim population, the product of

236

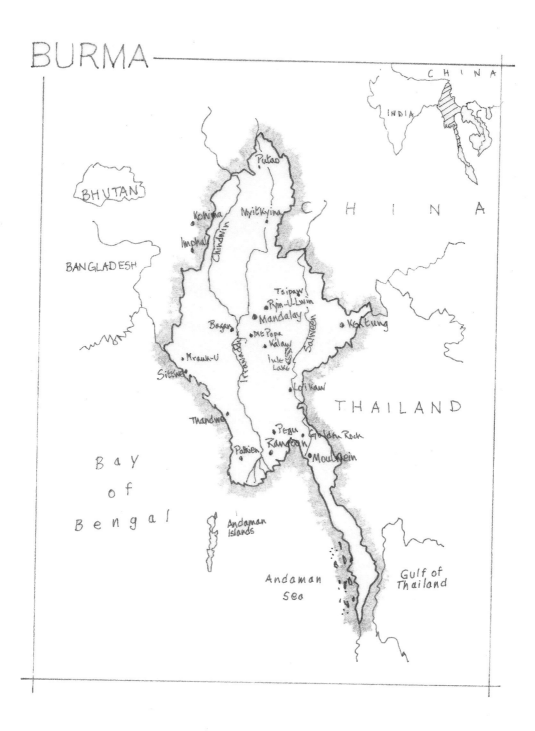

Naga bark basket

Bangladeshi labourers brought in to work the paddy fields and build the railways. In a tributary near the river's mouth a great assortment of craft were each secured by frayed rope knotted around one of a number of angular and dismembered trees scattered along a bank that was muddy and malodorous at low tide. Newcomers jostled for a gap and many had to tie up two or three abreast. Chanting stevedores, glistening with sweat, were working on cargoes of wood, coal and bricks, passing them up hand to hand. Irrespective of the tides, the air was tainted with the stench of fish – both fresh and rotten, detritus and diesel fuel. There was clamour, clutter, rust, ropes and the cries of helmsmen squinting into the low sun as they judged their run in to a vacant slot with a precision born of 1,000 such previous manoeuvres. Out on the river, the horizons of the broad plain were scalloped by distant hills whose silhouettes were blurred in the evening haze like watercolour smears. The banks were covered by a rich velvety turf and clumps of waterpalm had been kindled by the setting sun into a glowing, green fire. Large flocks of egrets on their way to roost, the largest I had ever seen, splashed the sky like an unseasonal blizzard. Pagodas had been placed like little follies on hillocks that thrust up like nipples from the unwrinkled meadows and pale mountains were reflected in the dark waters.

To celebrate my birthday, my delightful companions had laid out on the deck a feast of foie gras, cheeses, Pfeffernusse and Amaretti, arduously carried here from the best London emporia and these joined the noodles and spiced shrimp bought from harbourside vendors. Approaching Mrauk-U at dusk, a tropical sunset stained a sky as sanguineous as an unstaunched wound, which then gave way to a raven night where the Pleiades, Orion and the Milky Way were mirrored on the dark plains by the scattered, flickering fires of 100 braziers fanned for the evening meal.

The Kingdom of Arakan in northwest Burma traded rice and slaves with India's Coromandel Coast and Indonesia and spices and timber with the Portuguese. It amassed great wealth but having no expansionist ideals, instead built temples, stupas and pagodas of substantial size and in enduring stone. These are dotted over the countryside like molehills in a rich meadow and at the centre of Mrauk-U, the kings established a huge palace. But the Burmese, jealous of their peaceful and wealthy neighbour, invaded, conquered and destroyed the kingdom and by 1758 it had been absorbed into the great central plains of the Irrawaddy. One hundred years later the British, irritated by the resolve of the Arakan people to cling on to their inheritance and re-establish an independent state, completed the destruction of historic buildings but the spirit of the people and their distinct and fierce Arakanese pride, was still very much alive in Zan, our guide. We looked at four temples (a fraction of what was on offer but two too many to my unrefined views) and all had dark, dank and dim warrens of internal passages. The Temple of 80,000 Buddhas was only marginally preferable to The Temple of 90,000 Buddhas by the fact that halos of sparkling, blinking lights around the principal 16th century statues were inscribed with the name and telephone number of the sponsoring local restaurant.

The town was delightful; a little grubby and decayed but car free and seemingly carefree. Well-fed ponies pulled traps with delicate wheels and hooped coverings against the sun, while bullocks lumbered along with the carts whose oversized wooden wheels are of a design that reaches into every corner of Burma. The universal bullock cart, hand crafted with the inherited skills of many generations, its wheels turning on greaseless axles, will outlast any mechanical machine. Norman Lewis found tonality in the wheels' ponderous turning: '*.....four notes of a pentatonic scale that repeated endlessly until distance and dust faded out their irritating and melancholy plainsong.*' Two-storied houses with fretted balconies, brightened by flowers lined the streets; an occasional vulgar arriviste with a tiled façade and neon lighting had carbuncled the scene but no doubt these contemporary touches established the credentials of its owner. Several Willys jeeps, abandoned by the Americans pushing down the Burma Road in 1943, were still in use but judged on their condition, it would not be long before there was only a single survivor from its cannibalised companions.

The Lee Maw River runs into the Chin Hills and on another river trip in another boat, we sat one behind the other in pink plastic chairs of the kind usually seen on the patios of Weymouth bungalows. The seasonal floods bring with them rich alluvial soil and the paludal land on either side provided perfect conditions for sweetcorn, peanuts, flat beans (dried and exported to China), cauliflowers, great gourds as long as a cricket bat that hung from bamboo frames and pasture which was grazed by fat, grey water buffalo wallowing in fat, grey mud. Many people here originated from Chittagong and Dacca and are dark skinned. Some women were almost incendiary, so bright were their saris but these costumed flames were dampened by sombre men with black beards and white, crocheted skull caps. Although there was much activity, the flow of the river and the heavy hardwood structure of the craft made for slow travel. Great lumbering lighters of wide beam and high prow and loaded with stones or timber were laboriously poled along close to shore, sometimes with a tattered handkerchief of a sail. Long rafts of bamboos were even slower and took great effort to control around the river bends, sometimes having a man on the land heaving on a rope while the raft was edged around the boulders and the vegetation of the shoreline. There were patient fishermen, laughing, waving children, market-day housewives and the twice daily ferry packed as tight as any commuter train and overloaded to an inch of the water line with market cargo stacked on the roof. Boys bathed, women washed, girls fetched water and dogs, pigs and chickens scurried and scavenged among the river's detritus. The celebrated Chin women, whom we had gone to see, looked sad and burdened with the grotesque web tattooed over their ancient faces. These grandmothers are the last to carry this deforming ritual and were now trotted out as an anthropological oddity for the few who journeyed this far.

At the uncomfortably early hour of 3 am we sailed again under starlight for the return trip. The waning moon threw no light as we negotiated slippery, steep planks laid from one boat to another, our only saviours being a dim torch and willing hands. Trying to rescue the robbed hours of sleep on the damp teak deck of a boat which shuddered from the capricious camshaft of its ancient diesel engine proved hopeless. Additionally, there were the cries of the boy at the prow as he spotted for obstacles and there was spray from choppy water.

From Maymyo, an hour's drive from Mandalay into the cool hills, we journeyed by train. I do not know the age of its carriages (the engine was a diesel electric upstart), but to judge from their condition and design, they may well have carried my parents when they were resident here in the late '30s. We travelled first class, the only perceivable difference from the second class being thin, brown seat cushions and an attendant. His principle job was to prevent the ticketless from riding the train while hanging from the exterior or from finding a toehold in a doorway. For the most part he slept. An exception was a sudden realisation of a duty to be performed near the Gokteik Viaduct. Built in 1903 by the Pennsylvania Steel Co on behalf of the British, this was the second-highest railway bridge in the world. Unaccountably, it is considered a strategic structure by the authorities which should not be photographed. The attendant made a half-hearted attempt to inform the passengers of this fact and ignoring the tourists who then crammed the windows for the best shot, went back to sleep. At each station stop there was an unchanging routine. At a moment that seemed solely at the whim of the platform superintendent, he took a bell from under his arm and on ringing it the train lurched forward. Those passengers already asleep awoke and others, crowding the space in between, fell on top of them and then picking themselves up, smiled with dazed pleasure and settled in any space available while those still on the platform made a sudden dash for the doors and hawkers attended to their last customers running alongside the train.

At the northern edge of Thibaw (or Hpisaw depending upon which map you are reading) and at an idyllic elevated spot above the Dot Htawaddy River, is a building simply known as The Shan Palace. But there is no gilded carving, no crouching lions nor suppliant servants. Here is a substantial and elegant house of the '30s with a porticoed veranda, double height bay windows of pleasing proportions and a *porte-cochere* shading the panelled entrance doors; it would sit happily in Hampshire parkland. But at this mansion, the paint peels, the gutters sprout weeds, the garden is made over to corn and most windows are shuttered. Barking dogs announced our arrival to Fern, the elderly niece of Soe Ohn Kya, one of the last Shan princes. Her husband Donald was imprisoned two years ago on spurious charges and she now lived alone in the faded glory of influence and privilege, surrounded by photographs of relatives lounging on cushions of tasselled silk. The heavy and nervous hand of government is also intent upon crushing the spoilt but revered hereditary tribal leaders.

Our guide on this eastern part of our travels was Hubert, a beaming and charming man with a penchant for hats – a Breton beret, a pink

Maymo taxi

woolly confection or a cotton slouch. His trousers were a little short, his flat feet were shod in red canvas plimsolls and he managed to combine the idiocy of Monsieur Hulot with the beatitude of the Dalai Lama. As a former missionary boy, he paused for grace before even the humblest meal, suggested vainly that we visit each Catholic church we passed and sang a repertoire of World War II patriotic songs. Along a forest path *'Roll Out the Barrel'* would echo through the bamboo or *'Bluebirds Over the White Cliffs of Dover'* ripple over the river. Each song ended with a giggle of delight. Breakfasting on doorstep-sized slices of toast and fig jam in Mr. Charles's Guesthouse, where the gloom of the teak boarded walls was lifted by candles in elaborate table candelabra, I chatted to an elderly white-haired woman from New Zealand; her broad smile so creased her face that it seemed a delicate exercise in origami. After Thibaw she was going west to travel on a local cargo boat down the Chindwin for four days sleeping on deck and eating with the crew. Here was the epitome of New Zealand's pioneering spirit. Mr Charles and his wife Liz (both Chinese/Burmese) ran their establishment with their five daughters and had cornered a niche in the limited tourist market. In my bathroom the towel was embroidered with two blue bears and *'If you go down to the woods today...'* The flip-flops had 'Manchester United' on their soles.

Besides Mr Charles, there was Miss Maureen (an Australian whose little riverside establishment served coffee at a price only slightly less than the Palm Court of The Ritz), Mr. Book and Mr. Food. The latter, a Chinaman, had a double row of largely gold teeth and displayed this investment often and willingly to potential customers. In his restaurant, a cook naked to the waist displayed tattooed dragons that writhed up his arms before they ended open-jawed across his chest. A cling-ing snippet of intestine was flicked off a finger to be caught mid-air by an expectant cat. A discouraging collection of cellular, membranous or sinewy objects lay in a chipped enamel bowl, some black from lengthy displays, others startlingly red or blue. Over the double wok hung a lantern that spread an unsympathetic light over this tapestry of viscera.

river steamer barge

In spite of a large contingent of military in celebratory mood, our food arrived within minutes of ordering; a dish heaped with scrawny chicken limbs, jaundiced with curry and blanched with rice and ton yam soup brimming with river prawns, watercress, baby turnips, lemongrass and carrying a raft of coriander.

Back in the west at Homalin, the foreign contingent of 40 who disembarked from the military plane were as diverse a bunch of travellers as ever ventured into the mountainous jungles of North West Burma. It was the variety of their hair that initially surprised. Pigtailed, shaven, permed or lank; as black and glossy as a guardsman's boot or so blonde and flowing it caught the sun and the eye of local lads. There were those slim in body and light on luggage, those corpulent and overburdened, those gone native in local homespun and those in tailored jackets. Enthused by adventure, they huddled in great discomfort on metal seats narrow even for a slight Burmese, first on a Chindwin river boat (four seats wide and 20 long) and then bounced on dusty tracks perched on racks welded onto the backs of requisitioned pickups, shrieking in agony or excitement. Four hours in each unforgiving vehicle separated the hardened adventurer from the soft and curious. One of the traveller's worst enemies is the pernicious optimism of informants. "Will we arrive before dark?" "Oh, for sure." "Does the hotel have bathrooms?" "But of course." And so it was for the journey. The information was that it would be short, the seats comfortable and the scenery spectacular. But we were off to see the Naga and apart from an extortionate premium of £600, a sore bum, rattled bones and a late night arrival, a package of misinformation was an acceptable part of the price.

On the switchback track which cut like a whiplash through primary forest, the truck in front ground its way uphill, grossly overloaded in the usual manner with cargo both human and vegetable. Suddenly, it gave off a startling crack and simultaneously, like a beast shot through the heart, collapsed to the ground. In the dark, the panicked human cargo leapt off, the panniered vegetable cargo rolled off and there was much yelling and confusion. Our pickup seemed vulnerable to the truck sliding backwards and we too scrambled to safety but it was soon clear that with the shackles of its rear springs snapped and its axle broken, it would be there for a long while. It was so immobile, in fact, that a large section of the high bank to one side had to be excavated by mattocks under the pale light of faltering torches before the convoy of eight vehicles lurched past, pushed, pulled, wheels spinning, engines screaming and all of us cheering. Another drama on this darkened jungle track was played out on the return trip but this time it was more tragic. The lead truck travelling too fast, too loaded, or too near a ditch turned on its side, pitching its passengers off. There were urgent calls for blankets, a doctor and torches. Several bodies lay groaning in the undergrowth and the truck's front

Ox Cart

wheels were splayed out with twisted and torn tyres. But assistance arrived by way of the dawn and a visiting general and his entourage of nine vehicles including a doctor. There was nothing we could do and we went on our way like unfulfilled Samaritans, alert at every perilous corner.

The *Insight Guide* describes the Naga Hills *'as isolated and remote as anywhere, completely off limits and inaccessible'*. Well, not quite. Two helicopter pads and an excavated hillside for our bamboo sleeping accommodation scarred the forested hills that surrounded the little town of Leshio perched at 10,000 ft (3,000m) on the border with Assam. The people here are the stuff of legend and fulfil every preconception of tribal ferocity. Glorious in hornbill plumage and parangs thrust upwards to the sky, they are beset with boars' tusks, bears' claws and tigers' teeth. Tarzan might have cried, "Run while you can!" Their language and customs are so diverse they have difficulty in conversing from one village to another (they certainly don't speak Burmese). And they like to kill each other. At least they did, until the Burmese government introduced a sophisticated policy of engagement which included a New Year Festival. The headmen are seduced by TV sets, sheets of corrugated iron and bags of rice and the young by tee-shirts, ballpoint pens and fizzy drinks. The Nagas are a proud people, tough and even brutal but they also have charm and humour and abound in the courtesies effected by remote peoples to passing strangers. But for me the festival was a monstrous sham, hijacked by the army and sponsored by a Rangoon travel agency, with the local people dragooned into providing huts and entertainment for foreigners. The £600 per person was apparently a loss leader but to a government intent on providing an acceptable face of peace and harmony, the publicity was vital.

The antidote to the jungle clad hills lay 800 miles (425kms) south on the Bay of Bengal. Here at Ngwe San, where a perfect cyan sky met the azure water on a line drawn spirit level true, a small blemish appeared as though a speck of dust had landed on this page of paradise. Moving slowly, a silhouette of a fishing boat could be made out. A lobster lunch was coming ashore and the previous day's 19-hour journey was already forgotten. Each hotel strung along the coast had progressively pretentious names so that in order of construction, there was Sunny Beach, Palm Beach, Treasure Cove, Aurium, Paradise, Emerald Paradise and Glorious Paradise. We were settled in Hotel Bay of Bengal which seemed to trump the lot by encompassing the whole 200 miles (320kms) of Burma's western coastline. On the beach fronting one of the more extravagant of these establishments, men were digging out building sand and filling sacks that required two of them to lift. These were then placed on the head of a young woman to carry to a waiting truck: the slim, fragile body of a female Burmese disguises a physique of steel hawsers. At first light, long low fishing boats with a dozen or so men aboard rowed out to sea a little way and then spread a net perhaps 300 ft (100m) long. Returning to shore, the net was pulled in from each end with great effort and after an hour or so a modest basket of little silver fish was gathered in, each adorned with an emerald stripe. They sparkled in the sun like misplaced *cloisonné*. In the afternoon, four squawking Japanese arrived and splashed around in the pool and then two more foreigners, gasping at the view. The 200-bed hotel in which the four of us had been the only guests was becoming crowded, the gates of paradise were opening too wide and it was time to move on.

On a previous trip, I had taken the public ferry from Mandalay to Bagan enjoying the village shore life from a deckchair on the upper deck. I was looking forward to a repeat voyage, some hours of enforced meditation, a lassitude in the cool evening air and a period of reflection aboard a battered old relic of a boat of susceptible safety but reliable machinery, making its way mid-stream at a pace commensurate with that of Burmese life. The sight of the hordes of waiting passengers on the dockside at Pathien immediately destroyed such an indulgence in dreams.

The ferry terminal had some resemblance to Waterloo Station on the last working day before Christmas: unwittingly, I had hit upon the end of term at Pathien University. Booking clerks were shouting, porters were yelling, vendors were clamouring and the ferry was hooting. To add further confusion, the down ferry was late in and disembarking passengers clashed with the forces intent on home and holiday – 400 students carrying 400 bicycles and as many sacks, chests, trunks and cases. Once on board, this paraphernalia was stacked six feet (2m) high around the perimeter of each deck. In the event of an accident, a total loss of life would have been assured. There were four cabins and I had paid double (£18) to secure one all to myself. The guidebook had spoken of *'spacious cabins each with private facilities and air conditioning'*. These facilities were confined to two wooden beds, each with a grubby mattress and a sheet that may once have been washed and a hole in the window's fly screen; neither the light nor the fan was in working order. As far as I could tell there were only two WCs on board but by drinking my remaining whisky, as an anaesthetic rather than a pleasure, I then had a useful empty bottle. Burmese students are little different from any others; however, since few could afford alcohol, they were for the most part good natured, laughing and playing guitars most of the night, while those who had scaled to the roof (and the ceiling of my cabin) seemed to prefer dancing. Having opted for a policy of self-imprisonment as soon as the sun had set, a group of girls then made a little more space for themselves by leaning against the outside of my door and like a sophomore choir, crooned into the early hours. At 1 am we berthed near Hinthada and the pandemonium of boarding was reversed. In the morning there was not a student left and litter was the only evidence of their passage. The lower decks, which I had come to photograph and on which I had hoped to mingle with its passengers, were locked off and I contented myself with the flat agricultural plains of both banks, fishermen attending their nocturnal nets and stupas gilded by the early morning sun.

The Shwedagon Pagoda, *'where the prodigious glamour of the ancient orient endures'*, remains the heart and soul of Rangoon, a great and glorious monument of the Buddhist faith. The 320 steps of the southern entrance were lined with flower stalls, religious souvenirs in the most garish and vulgar taste and votive offerings. Apart from a handful of Tibetans whose tenacious piety is never daunted and groups of tourists awestruck by the gilded splendour, it is now only the Burmese who kneel penitent or beseeching before their chosen shrine. The remaining Buddhist world which regards a once in a lifetime pilgrimage to the Schwedagon as an obligation to be undertaken in the same manner as those that make the journey to Mecca, Santiago de Compestela or the Khum Mela, has been discouraged by the recent unrest. The heavy dictatorial yoke that so tragically burdens the Burmese people is becoming weightier, but the nation stands on foundations of extraordinary solidarity. Wonderfully fertile, materially abundant in coal, gas, oil and timber, its people have a resilience that has pulled them safely through a millennia of historic crises of the gravest kind. The current isolation and retrenchment could be the gravest yet. May the gentle, industrious and hospitable people of this beautiful country have faith enough to again pull them through to safety.

On the evening of my return I found myself in a packed Oxfordshire village hall where a judge conducted an auction for a ton of manure and a basket of chutneys, a professor of genetics was in a flap about the readiness of her sausages and a plump and merry hairdresser was on her feet, just, swaying to entertainment from the local postman's Elvis impersonations. Here were tribal rituals of a different kind and of such is life richly spiced.

Italy

July 2008

'As a member of an escorted group you don't even have to know that the Matterhorn isn't a tuba' – Fielding's Guide to Europe, 1963

The presence of the Florence football team, ACF Florentina, at our Kastelruth hotel was unexpected and unwanted. To a man – and there were 50 of them including managers, physiotherapists, trainers, publicists, security bouncers and a team and a half of reserves – they were handsome, tanned, with black or blackened gelled hair and universally clad in purple tracksuits (courtesy of Toyota). These were worn from breakfast onwards – they may well have been worn in bed. Several passionate young women were overcome, small boys clamoured for autographs and a crowd gathered outside the hotel door chanting in adoration. For us, six friends who had banded together to tackle the higher slopes of the Dolomites, the team and their admirers were an irritation that distracted staff from our alcohol order.

Our alpinist, Charles, authentically clad in breeches, checked shirt and a hat that bore the sweat of a thousand ascents, was intent upon the most direct route to the high plateau. Our walking notes for this option were headed boldly: **'Do not undertake this route unless you are exceptionally fit and experienced'.** We were all well past 60, had seldom ventured off a well-worn Cotswold path and carried between us the handicaps of a broken toe, a damaged knee, acute cystitis, attacks of vertigo and legs whose ligaments needed stretching at regular intervals and this was our first day. The option was universally accepted. The warning on the notes was wholly accurate; the route was alternately slippery with mud, strewn with boulders, laced with roots and so vertical that ropes had been secured into the rock to assist survival. A waterfall opened its net of whis-

pers, rinsing the air and mingling with our sweat. Boosted by mutual encouragement, an instinctive will to live and fearful of the stigma of failure, miraculously
we achieved our goal. Along the way, nature's dazzlers in the form of aconites,
orchids, arnica and martagon lilies nodded their heads in admiration.

The little hamlet of Compatsch wallowed comfortably in a fold of the plateau.
The storm that had threatened the day finally opened its dark clouds in the late
evening, encrusting the ground with marble-sized hail that rolled into gutters and
hollows glinting there in glassy piles under the street lights. But the storm left
behind skies bright and clear so that at dawn the jagged teeth of El Massiccio del
Catinaccio could be seen in all their ferocity: it was clearly a day to climb Mount
Pez. The farmers were cutting their wild flower meadows and the hay would
have been of such sweetness that the cows must have anticipated the pleasure
of winter. But if ever the absurdities of the Common Agricultural Policy needed
visual proof, here it was. Each field, some barely a couple of acres, was being cut
by a machine that was either new or so little utilised as to look new. At one point,
five of these were operating within a few hundred feet of each other. And not
just a machine for cutting, there was another for turning and drying and a third
for picking up and transporting. All these, when a single machine for each task,
co-operatively owned or contracted, could have done all the work in a week. No

doubt there was a second crop to take later but each machine was employed for two days of the year: extravagance beyond reason.

At a scenic point there was a choice; to the east the Salterhutte with a cappuccino and maybe a cognac while to the west was a two hour vertical hike to the summit of Mount Pez – 8,408ft (2,563m). I had nothing better to do and as I was to receive a new knee on the operating table of Mr Dodd in a couple of weeks' time it seemed sensible to get the full mileage from the current one and so I steered to the west where the solid red line on the map and accompanying text confirmed a mule track. It was not a mule track, although a mule that was severely thrashed and had the certain knowledge of an unlimited supply of the sweetest carrots might have once ventured up it. On the path there were few who matched my age but a number who could have been my grandchildren. Two of these had frolicked past me and I found them later sitting on a wayside rock. The girl was in a skirt and wore plimsolls and her brother, if that was who he was, had on a tee-shirt emblazoned with the motif of The Waking Dead. I first thought it said The Walking Dead in which case I might have asked to be buried in it there and then. As I passed, the girl held out a dozen sugar lumps wrapped in newspaper and on gratefully accepting one, her brother squeezed on fresh lemon juice. Whether they thought I was a grandfather in need or whether this was the natural generosity of alpine trails, I do not know but I skipped the next few steps with gratitude in my heart and the way distorted by tears.

M (who had needed to visit the clinic earlier) had spent the day reclining with an entertaining book and a team of good looking waiters who from time to time brought her herbal tisanes and slices of fresh fruit. Returning in the late afternoon I recounted my adventures; the vertiginous ascent, the crumbling track, the torrents of cascading storm water shredded white by boulders and the hazardous bridges. I described in detail the pinched path chiselled from the granite rock face, the sections that were accessible only by the iron ladders of a *via ferrata* and the bus sized boulders. The only thing that impressed her was the sense in staying where she was.

The wildflowers often drew me down to my knees to marvel at their ability to survive let alone bloom from a crack in a rock or the dark shadows of a pine forest. They did not group themselves by hazard but in colonies of common need. A limestone scree was the home of toadflax (*linaria alpina*), Snow in Summer (*cerastium latifolium*), viola and alpine buttercup (*ranunculus glacialis*). Around heavily dunged farm buildings, large areas were covered with lady's mantle (*alchemilla alpina*), docks (*rumex alpinus*), the spires of monkshood (*aconitum napellus*) and red campion (*silene dioica*) while a shaded wood hosted martagon lilies, alpine sea holly,

Chiesa di San Zeno Maggiore
Verona. (14ᵗ

soldanellas and violets. On the pastureland, machines and scythes cut in a single sweep a dozen or more different varieties.

The Sudtirol carried its burden of tourism kindly and with custodianship. Some hotels had succumbed to external modernity but for the most part little seemed to have changed since the pictures in my parents' photograph books. There were well-ordered arrangements of flower meadows in prodigious variety, fretted balconies supporting cascades of geraniums, well-fed horses harnessed to open carriages piled with warm rugs and a coachman in a silly hat and puffing an oversized briar. Here were hearty, healthy hikers, hearty healthy helpings, huge woolly dogs, sweet gentle cows enduring the clang of their bell, black predatory ravens and all around fearsome, grey, saw-toothed crags.

Heading back down to the plains we called in on Ötzi, the Iceman who had fallen foul of a rival or maybe fatally slipped 5,000 years ago. Peered at through the porthole of his public tomb where he now rests in temperature- and moisture-controlled peace, his mahogany skin, tautened over bones and ligaments, shone as if polished like a favourite pair of shoes. One long arm was thrown defensively across his face as though in anticipation of a blow but now he looked helpless, cold and distraught with his arm shielding the gaze of the curious.

On reaching the plains, the massive marble slabs of Verona's pavements so reflected the heat of the northern Italian sun that it seemed that each of 10,000 tourists skipped lightly along their flagged route for fear of sizzling like a suckling pig. No wonder that *gelati* in 14 flavours and a corresponding palette were cooled at every other street corner. Awnings were stretched out on mechanical arms of astonishing length and width to shade those weary of Juliet, the cream and terracotta striped façades of the 12th century, renaissance palaces of conspiring princes, aggressive yet attractive market stalls and fashion shops with absurd prices. San Zeno Maggiore, a 14th century Romanesque church of sublime simplicity, frescoed walls and refreshing coolness was an antidote for these tourist lures. Its cloisters provided rest for feet and eyes and the opportunity for contemplation. The River Adige, clouded with alpine silt, washed the city's northern boundary, the fortifications against Napoleonic invasion massively formed the western edge and to the south, the land widened to the gentle contours of the Po. But at the centre, like a kernel of vitality within its succulent but soporific shield, lay the roman Arena. Forty one tiers of precision joined marble blocks formed an elliptical masterpiece and seated 25,000. During the Verona Opera Season, the stage is so vast and the theatrical settings so monumental that only half this number can be entertained but so perfect are the acoustics that under open skies, the softest *pianissimo* brings tears to those in the highest and furthest tier. In the first century, the arched perimeter would have been crowded with those anxious to witness the blood of wild beasts or the death of a gladiator. For us in the 21st century, the blood was Carmen's and the tragedy Tosca's.

Leaving the Arena at 1 am, pushing through curtains of crimson velvet a storey high and joining the throng of post-opera diners, I spotted a group of handsome, tanned men, with black or blackened gelled hair, wearing purple track suits and surrounded by adoring young women; ACF Florentina were on their way home.

Canada

September 2008

It was only clouds that were stampeding in Calgary at 4 pm on September 11th but they were also competing to see which could dump the most rain. The immigration officials were in flak jackets, the car hire procedure had been unnecessarily long and the official grumpy, it was rush hour, the traffic on the TransCanada Highway crawled through the town and we were on 2 am UK time

But Banff banished the Calgary blues. Its homely architecture in pine and stone and its streets named Elk, Wolf, Beaver and ten more seemed charming, like some child's game, and early snow had dusted the mountains that surrounded the town. All this cheered the spirit and astonished the eye. But at this southern tip of the Canadian Rockies this girdle of grandeur was just a teaser for what was to come.

Towering sternly over the town in turreted magnificence was the Banff Springs Hotel. Completed in 1888 by the Canadian Pacific Railway, it was in its day (and its day lasted many years) the most magnificent hotel in Canada. Chateau Louise up the road would attract more publicity later. We approached the hotel from behind, climbing up steeply from Bow River and skirmished around its cavernous interior, universally decorated with mock stone walls and wall lights in the form of braziers; only the paisley carpet constrained the resemblance to a medieval dungeon. Enquiring of foreign maids as to the whereabouts of the lobby, alarmingly they did not know. Like moles, we eventually surfaced for an eight dollar hot chocolate and an astonishing view. In the lobby there was a display of old photographs, menus and the bills of previous guests who came for three months and trundled off in

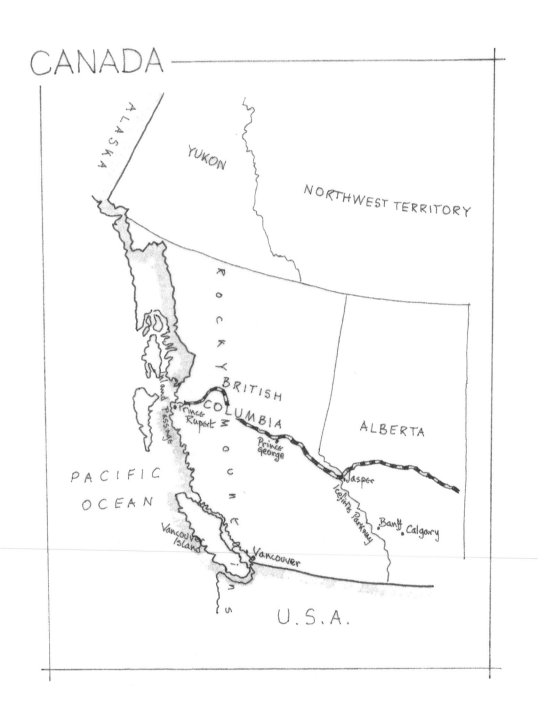

CANADA

ALASKA

YUKON

NORTHWEST TERRITORY

ROCKY

BRITISH

COLUMBIA

Inland Passage

Prince Rupert

Prince George

ALBERTA

PACIFIC

OCEAN

M O U N T A I N S

Jasper

Icefields Parkway

Banff · Calgary

Vancouver Island

Vancouver

U.S.A.

Brewsters' charabancs to gasp in wonder at nature's magnificence and return for jellied consommé, boiled gammon, peach melba and a foxtrot or two.

We knew Moraine Lake was near when we came upon the cars parked four miles (6.5kms) from its shores. It was after all a glorious sunny Sunday and the lake, with its water of aquamarine surrounded by fearsome mountains and a couple of glaciers, was displayed in astonishing beauty. From above, the water looked clouded as if in solidified solution, as though all the artisans of Murano had conspired to pour in molten glass and tint it with Titian blue. But nearer to the surface a strange and magic mutation occurred; the milkiness dissolved, the solidity vanished and in its place was water of such exceptional clarity that stones and sodden tree trunks were clearly visible 13 ft (4m) down. Our hotel (the only one there) had the only canoes and we paddled one of these across this magical surface to escape the visitors from the tour buses and the four mile queue. Our course mirrored the saw-toothed silhouette of the mountains and no doubt caused amusement to the shore-based.

By 6.30 pm, the last visitor had gone, the magic lake turned from Titian to gentian, its 3,200 ft (1,000m) granite walls took on a wet on wet wash of pink, indigo, straw and violet and the forest with its lynx, elk and bears became exclusively ours. We listened to its noises in the night where, in the honeymoon suite, we searched for each other in a bed ten feet (3m) wide.

The weather was so close to perfection that it seemed that every jagged peak was etched with the precision of Durer. Each glacial lake was dyed with a turbid tincture of cobalt, azure, sapphire or emerald and their shores scumbled with chrome yellow larches and poplars gilded with the richest butter. When all this delight is augmented by a backdrop of glaciers that overhang or burnish the highest summits, the scene is almost too intense. And such scenes come readily along the Promenade de Glaciers – The Icefields Parkway and left us gasping as we tried to absorb one view before the next usurped it. Here were formidable ramparts of sheer granite with serrated ridges as if they had sawn their way through the earth's crust. I have travelled some of the world's great mountain highways – the Karakoram, the Ollague in the Chilean Andes, Sapa to Dien Bien Phu, Kathmandu to Lhasa and the Valeta in the Pyrenees but this beat them all.

Jasper, at the northern end of this wondrous road, had a backwoods feel and attitude. Jaunty but purposeful, tidy and colourful, its low rise, clapboard houses were painted in placid shades that soothed our restless eyes. Front gardens were still bright with autumn flowers but in two months they would be insulated under six feet (2m) of snow. Our hotel, Jasper Park Lodge, which had looked so attractive on its polished website, was a mini town with its main building fashioned like an overgrown railway station in which vacationing parties wandered, helpless

Mount Robson 3954m
Highest mountain in Rockies

and lost in its internal maze. Our 'deluxe with sitting area' was in a distant siding and came with an invitation to call Bites on a Bike for 'snacks and beverage'. So awful and alien was all this that we drove into town each morning for a cosy and cheerful Breakfast Special at the Grizzly Inn along with maintenance men, long distance bikers and bleary-eyed motorhomers.

The genuine railway terminus would have fitted snugly into the front hall of the mock one and was adorned with geraniums and a totem pole and here we clambered up from the pavement level to board The Skeena and a two day train trip west to the Pacific. In the Caribou Mountains we stopped at McBride, one of many quintessential railway communities with its cluster of wooden houses, a general store, a farm shop advertising 'Feed and Hay' and swarthy men who strolled around in dungarees. The little Victorian station building was jolly with nasturtiums and petunias. The track doubled up here to allow trains to pass – and what trains! It needed half an hour for them to rumble through, one with flat cars loaded with cut, planed, kiln-dried and shrink-wrapped timber – 102 cars and just under a mile long. The other, with containers stacked two high and with four engines, was even longer. Both were en route to or from Prince Rupert and its deep water port.

Now virtually nationalised, the Canadian railway system amalgamated Canadian Pacific Railways (*Can't Pay the Rent*), Canadian National Rail (*Certainly No*

Rush) and Grand Trunk Pacific (*Get There Perhaps*). The Skeena was independent of these but was a nostalgic reminder of the 1950s and a designer's dream with its stainless steel VistaDome internally fitted out with Perspex, vinyl and glass mosaics. Here were the ghosts of Gregory Peck and Maureen Swanson, the clink of cocktail glasses and laughter. These ghosts were banished by a party from the American equivalent of SAGA who busied themselves with fat books of Su Doku puzzles and when halted by the 'Malicious' section,

Grizzly at Knight Inlet

turned to discussing their medical problems real and imagined. In our mid-60s, we had felt the youngest on board by 20 years but were now depressingly well prepared for a variety of problems we had not yet considered. As we trundled along, thistledown and fireweed growing on the track side was scattered like an early snowstorm and were reflected on the surface of the numerous lakes as we passed. On the second day, the names of Scottish and Irish pioneers give way to native Indian glottalstoppers such as Gitwinksihlkw, Ginglox and Gitwangak and then we rolled downhill through mists beside the Fraser River, surprisingly the home of sturgeon – North America's oldest and largest freshwater fish.

The Inland Passage is not part of a digestive system but the route of British Columbia Ferries that twists through the many hundreds of islands of the West Coast. Every island, creek and community has a name from the pioneering settlers of the 18th century interspersed with a few of those from of the native Indians – oops, First Nation, but give a patronising nod towards the royal family of the time: Prince Rupert on the Alaskan border is followed southerly by Queen Char-

lotte, Princess Royal and then Victoria on the Washington State border.

On a day that a storm blew in from the Pacific raising the waves of Johnstone Strait to a height that led to our grizzly bear expedition being cancelled, we killed time by a trip to Alert Bay. Confusingly, this is an island and it was about as alert as the crowd of crows that languidly pecked at the rubbish that rotted in every corner. The island was home to Namgis Indians and was a miserable, unkempt and sad place. When tired of a sofa, washing machine or child's toy, it was thrown out on to the front lawn. Slim was size 18 and shoppers heaved themselves out of large, rusty pickups to stock up on a fresh supply of the carbohydrates that made up an unhealthy proportion of the single supermarket's shelves. In the Memorial Park – a roomsized paved area beside the jetty – we lunched off a sandwich that would have fed a family. In a corner was a tablet whose carved inscription recognized the achievements of Gilbert Popovich, an ex-mayor. Ending *'He lived with grace'*, some wag had added *'but died with Gretel'*.

But we got to see our grizzlies another day. On Vancouver Island there are only vegetarian black bears (*ursus ursus*) and on the mainland, only omnivore grizzlies (*ursus horribilis*) and consequently they seldom meet and would never wish to socialise. At this time of year, pacific, pink and sockeye salmon were spawning in succession and provide an irresistible meal for grizzlies so, after a bumpy ride on the open water of the strait, we found ourselves dressed in bright orange survival suits stumbling though undergrowth to a fenced platform overlooking the junction of two gravel streams. A presumption that any sensible bear would have spotted us and scampered off in fright fortuitously turned out to be mistaken. Over a couple of hours, five females wandered through, one teetering with her cub on a rock mid-stream as she taught it the tricks of salmon fishing while others took a casual attitude to the fish that could be clearly seen in the water. A huge male, with a malicious look in his eye and claws long enough to flay an ox, came along and we held our breath and focussed our cameras in case he took a fancy to a female or tragically attacked the cub, but in the event he went on his way as he had arrived, irritable and ill-tempered. Bald eagles, with scowling expressions and ferocious beaks, perched patiently in pine trees dripping with Spanish moss, waiting to clash over the prize of a fishy scrap.

The Pacific Rim National Park is a slender strip of white sand, backed by some of the last primary rainforest in Canada and runs for 81 miles (130kms) along the west coast of Vancouver Island. This ancient forest that has been spared devastating fire and nurtured by the buckets of rain that are tipped up by the clouds hitting their first landfall in 3,000 miles, contains trees of astonishing grandeur and maturity. The four major species – western hemlock, douglas fir, sitka spruce and western red cedar, can all reach well over 260 ft (80m) at which height they would be at least 500 years old and the grandfathers amongst them would have been mature at the time of Christ. At the northern end of this unspoilt wild and windswept park lay Tofino – a fishing village out of season and an overcrowded tourist trap in season. Its clapboard façades reflected the sultry colours of the landscape and weather with a meld of olive drab, murky green, rusty red, cedar brown and sky grey. Smart, waterside summer houses are mixed in with the shabby homes of the first nations Indians whose wastrel teenagers roamed the streets mid-morning chewing on crisps and wedges of pizza so large that they might have been sliced from a millstone.

On 30th September we were on the seasonal cusp and the Visitor Centre had already closed but at the Wickanninish Inn where we lodged (a far grander establishment than its name might imply), they relished the coming winter, advertising a special rate for the storm watching season. Our room on a top floor corner with vast windows looking west was clearly a favourite with honeymooners, since the folksy guest book recounted the names of at least a dozen couples who had got married on the beach and no doubt started their married life sighing at the beauty of a Pacific sunset. There was a bald eagle perched in a nearby ancient hemlock and a couple of blue jays squabbled in a stunted sitka spruce that overhung the balcony. Our chambermaid left a personal note to say she had seen us on the beach and hoped we had had a lovely day, and the fresh flower arrangement in the lobby Gents would have been the envy of Moyses Stevens. It was that sort of place.

At the moment that the morning sun lights up the mountain tops to the east of the city of Vancouver, the harbour area of Canada Place wakes up. Float planes and helicopters zoom in, ferries crisscross the bay, trains local and transnational hoot their arrival and giant cranes dip and swing as they attend to container ships. We observed all this activity with wonder and interest from our waterfront hotel. A few miles to the west on Vancouver Island, an eagle would have viewed a less active scene but from the branches of an ancient douglas fir that would have reached four storeys higher than our room on the 22nd floor.

Postcard Home

The Rockies are stunning, the weather is gorgeous,
The leaves butter yellow, the mountains stupendous.
We've done Yoho, Banff, Jasper, Sunwapta and Wanka,
Tomorrow two days in a train, then up anchor
For islands, moose, eagles, elks, whales, wolves and bears
Three days full of thrills but sore derrieres!

Burma IV

March 2009

'A man of ordinary talent will always be ordinary, whether he travels or not; but a man of superior talents (which I cannot deny myself to be without being impious) will go to pieces if he remains forever in the same place' – *Wolfgang Amadeus Mozart*

The scent of jasmine and frangipani lay so heavily in the room that it seemed reluctant to be disturbed but a lazy fan gently stirred the sweet, exquisite fragrance while the barbets chatted in the *callistemon* outside the shuttered windows. By the street entrance stood a soldier of unquestioning alertness, an AK-47 cradled in his left arm and under his helmet were eyes that scanned the movements along this road of embassies. Cocooned in the teak-built Governor's Residence in Rangoon, I was back to my roots again.

Pa-an straggles along the muddy banks on the Salween River, 150 miles (240kms) to the east of Rangoon, as the crow flies across the Gulf of Martaban. It is an old and bustling town that marks the last gasp of the river before it broadens to end its journey from the Himalayas at Moulmein, an hour's boat trip to the south. The Zwe Kaybin Pagoda Festival was in full swing and we visited this three day jamboree when it reached its loudest and jolliest on the night of the full moon. From every part, banks of Tannoys hurled out deafening music with a different tune for each stall; whistles and drums competed for attention and bingo callers were amplified to the point of pain. All manner of lighting was employed and in descending order of stall keeper affluence, strobes flashed, fluorescent tubes threw flat stark shadows, bulbs shone with naked effulgence, coloured lights winked, paraffin lamps glowed and candles flickered. Gambling and food were the predominant attractions. The former mostly comprised a square of canvas painted with numbered squares onto which the punter piled his money. A dice

261

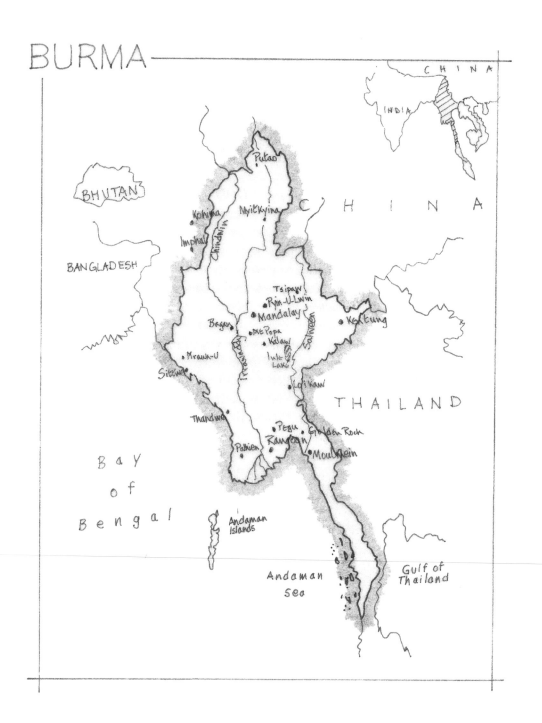

was then rolled, a disk twirled or a drum revolved to determine the winner. There must have been 100 or more of these in many variants but I never discovered how the owner controlled the odds. Charlatans abounded with exponents of the Three Card Trick, Guess the Dice and the usual devices to fleece the gullible and all were doing good business. There is nothing a Burmese enjoys more (or is worse at) than gambling. Food came bright or brown; the bright was lurid with clashing colours of incandescent intensity. Ice cream, dyed desiccated coconut and drinks all played their part in this edible kaleidoscope. Near the entrance, a lady stall owner had spooned jelly of hideous hues on to slices of white bread which in turn were balanced on upturned glasses. Each ghastly arrangement trembled like some exotic sea slug sending out danger signals to potential exterminators. The brown food was curries, roasted meats, kebabs and a miscellany of offal and entrails in tones of umber and maroon. At the centre of these festivities was a Ferris wheel on which were suspended four seater bamboo cages. At first sight, it seemed that agile but foolhardy young men were daringly hanging beneath these cages while others clambered through the rotating spokes. However, these men were the engine of this machine. After coming to rest to change passengers, the foreman blew a whistle and with great speed and energy, half a dozen of these longyi skirted gymnasts climbed to their positions around the wheel so that their combined weight started the revolutions. As speed increased so did their actions – swinging from seats, jumping from one to another, pushing with their feet or riding the outer circumference. Here was manpower at its most literal. As a spectator sport it was fascinating for surely one of the human components of this fly wheel would fall.

Later, at the Grand Hill Hotel (a few small bungalows so recently constructed that my bath and basin still had their manufacturer's paper labels), sleep was disturbed by the remembrance of this vibrant festival and was further denied by the skirmishes of rival gangs of dogs, the television next door, the faulty bearing of the bathroom fan (there was no visible switch), a soulful tomcat, the plaintive call of a nightjar, a nearby factory that seemed to work a night shift taking deliveries of corrugated iron sheets and, at 3 am, blaring speakers along the road that intoned Buddhist chants. Frustrated by these disturbances, I opened the jewel case of Ann Fadiman's latest collection of sparkling essays. Along with Dickens, Jan Morris, H. H. Munro and Perelman, she would be on my desert island bookshelf – well, that was that night's choice.

We set off down the Salween in a boat of clinkered construction and seemingly great age, the three of us sitting one behind each other, on fully upholstered chairs borrowed from a local restaurant. Approaching Moulmein, the first glimpse was of stupas that formed a seductive girdle of gilded breasts above the coconut palms.

Caught in the slanted beams of first light they shone with polished allure. Kipling's town, *'lazy by the sea'*, still had an air of languid indulgence. Lives were unhurried, the market busy but unaggressive and rickshaws were pedalled by lean men whose insouciance reflected a wish for a regular bowl of rice rather than a desire to trade up to a better model. The back streets were a model of tolerance where the Buddhist majority were neighbours to Christians (Catholic, Baptist, Methodist, SPG and probably more), Hindus (their temples awash with crocodiles, elephants and devils) and bearded Muslims. Scattered through the town with apparent abandonment of the principles of prime location, were the old, grand, rotting wooden mansions of previous merchants and colonial grandees.

Like Miss Haversham, they rested in sad and decaying splendour under a web of lianas that twisted their way over fretted balconies and decorated dormers. A sunbeam sometimes caught the coloured glass of a door so that a brief splash of green, red and blue appeared as a jewelled brooch on a withered façade. Possibly loved, universally uncared for but occasionally occupied, they were the remnants of the commercial success of this teak trading town. Along the seafront, Chinese investors had erected the contemporary symbols of success: hideous buildings draped with ceramic tiles, stainless steel balconies and neon signage.

With the lassitude of previous untroubled times, Kalaw spreads itself over hills sprinkled with stone pines and alder. These also clothe three valleys that meet in a glittering collision at the silver mirrored stupa that marks the town centre. A favoured hill station in colonial times, half-timbered clones of Surrey gentility occupy the spots with the best views. Most would sadden or even break the hearts of their original inhabitants with their slipped slates and wayward gutters and the tropical exuberance that has overtaken the gardens but some carry the evidence of suburban home county gardens with sweet peas, roses, marigolds and dahlias. My parent's old house is one of these. Perched on a prominent mound to catch cooling breezes and the pleasure of the setting sun, Arakan Lodge hints at Arts and Crafts with its quoins of stacked tiles, oversized chimneys, bow windows and leaded panes. Now it was part of a primary school occupied by the head-master and two other families and with a single storey block of eight class-rooms built where lawn and trimmed beds would once have been carefully tended. My mother was pragmatic, generous and concerned for children's welfare and she would be happy that they were benefitting from her old home. I took photographs to record the current slip from better times and also of the school as a model for ones that I might be able to build myself. Else-

where around the town, these relics of Guildford's environs were having some-thing of a renaissance with rich men or military commanders returning them to their previous domestic origins, recognising the value of their superior views, solid construction and practical arrangement.

The in-flight magazine of Yangon Airways carried four pages of cosmetic advertisements that presumably appealed to the ambitions of the hip and cool. They included Super Whitening Foam, White Pore Radiance, Crystal Brightening Essence, Noni Fruit Detangler, Cherry White Cream, Dumb Blond Highlights and Chocolate Head Massive Hair Treatment. The tourist may be fooled and amused by these signs of modernity, perhaps unaware that they are for the priv-ileged minority. The reality is sombre and bordering on the tragic, for the great majority live in poor conditions and carry the burden of an oppressive regime. The challenge for the international community is how to engage effectively with this secretive and opaque regime and, at the same time, act in the best interests of the country and its neglected people. The election promised for 2010 (ten years after the last election when 86% of the electorate voted for Daw Aung San Suu Kyi's Democratic Party) did not give rise to any optimism for any slackening of control or an increase in transparency, domination and secrecy since these were

Fisherman off beach at
Ngwe Saun. Bay of
Bengal

fundamental to the ruling authorities. As to control, laws and regulations are made without reasons given. In October 2004, 2,000 intelligence officers were arrested or dismissed; a year later diesel prices rose by 900%; in April 2006, civil servant salaries were increased tenfold and in August 2007, petrol and diesel prices were hiked up another 500% overnight and motorcycles were prohibited in Rangoon. As to transparency, the composition of the cabinet (which has ruled since 1962) was unknown, although it could be assumed to be overwhelmingly military or ex-military and of these, reputedly only two were from the 135 ethnic groups of the country. Fifty percent of the GDP is spent on the military. Driving east out of Rangoon through the suburb of Mingaladon you pass the new Gynaecological Hospital for Women of the Army and there is a storage area for hundreds, perhaps thousands, of military vehicles obviously visible from the highway. 80 percent of health treatment is borne by the patient, 86 percent of children do not continue education post primary school (Burma may be the only country in the world whose current generation is less educated than their parents) and this from a country whose education system used to be the envy of the Orient. Inflation is the highest of the ASEAN group of countries in spite of its natural resources of oil, coal, gas, teak (80% of the world's supply), hydro power, copper, precious stones (90% of the world's rubies and the finest jade in the world) and vast rice-producing areas. All these made it once the richest country in south East Asia.

Most bizarre of all is the world's newest purpose-built capital: the remote, mad, gleaming city of Nay Pyi Daw. At 6.37 am on 6th November 2005 (the exact time designated by the astrologer to General Than Shwe, the mysterious and all powerful head of the ruling junta), a convoy of government trucks started to move thousands of civil servants from Rangoon. The new capital was not marked on any map; neither was the six lane, deserted, unsignposted highway that leads to it. In this country of gentle people, all are afraid of their rulers but their rulers are so afraid of their people that they hide themselves away in a crazy capital 100 miles (160kms) from anywhere. The abandoned government buildings, many forming part of Rangoon's architectural heritage, had lain empty so long that weeds and even trees had already grown out of their upper stories. This great seaport's heart had become a sort of tropical East Berlin. Whether there was hope in the rumour that some of these ex-government buildings had been sold to Malaysian and Chinese investors remained to be seen. The 100 year old, 100 acre (40 hectare) campus of Rangoon University in the city centre had been empty since the student protests of 1996.

But this is not a piece on geo-politics or socio-economics and certainly not on doom and gloom, for the overwhelming and frankly baffling fact is that the people bore these yokes with fortitude, resilience and even cheerfulness. No doubt Lord Buddha has a hand in this tolerance (and Christ too, for there is a significant and earnest Christian community). With this in mind, the current regilding of the Schwedagon with a ton of gold leaf (at £600 an ounce, about £7.5 million), or the mega project of the world's largest reclining Buddha at double that, may seem like money well spent. In desperate and troubled times who can blame such a poor people contributing what little they have to ensure that life in the next world is better than this. Perhaps future salvation can be bought; it certainly will not be provided in the present.

Like a ribbon the colour of moonlight on cream velvet, the beach at Ngwe Sang follows a gentle curve of palm fringed land for nine miles. A few thatched fishing villages are shaded by the palms and a group of sturdy wooden boats ride the surf of the Bay of Bengal while a multitude of little red crabs scuttle to the safety of their sandy dugouts at the approach of a footfall. Here is the epitome of a travel agent's brochure, the fashion photographer's dream location and the setting of those romantic paperbacks that seem only to be available at airports. The morning rush hour was between 8 and 8.30 am when four mopeds and four women skirted the surf on their way to one of the three hotels at the Northern end of the bay. For the hour before this commuter activity, this idyll had been mine. Not a soul, a dog, a wandering Crusoe nor a servant Friday. For myself it was perfection but for the country and this seaside community, tragic. Here were three hotels of great comfort, the match of any on eastern sands, which together with a few more modest establishments and a scattering of bungalows stood forlornly empty. Cooled by air conditioning, with cooks at the ready, tables laid, staff alert, crystal clean pools and trimmed grass there was not another guest in sight. Marching monks and a devastating cyclone had scared off the tourists while the more worldly and experienced travellers avoid the heat of March. As the sun sizzled into the ocean and the idling evening breeze gathered a little strength, I made my way to the expectant barmen, the attentive waiters and the table beside the impossibly perfect sand. I turned my thoughts to daffodils, to hyacinths and to tulips, the soil to be tilled, the myrtle to be trimmed, welcoming dogs and loving arms. It was time to go home.

Uganda

October 2009

'No one realizes how beautiful it is to travel until he comes home to rest his head on his old, familiar pillow' – Lin Yutang

Thunder rolled around the Mountains of the Moon, the sky was black with menace and lightning cracked an apparent hand's breadth above our roof. The tumult increased until it reached a crescendo that Wotan himself might have orchestrated and then subsided as the storm sulked its way over to the Congo in sullen abatement and the sun restored peace. Pairs of scarlet-chested sunbirds were nesting in the thatch of our bandana and the crater lakes shimmered pink in the pale dusk competing with the flowering erythrina that glowed with red hot embers; it is not called the Flame of the Forest for nothing. The mountains mark the boundary between Uganda and the Democratic Republic of Congo and the lakes that border Rwanda. Ndali Lodge, shaded by a giant fig tree that drips with the homes of hundreds of black headed and Viellot's weaver birds, perches on a promontory at the end of a long and sinuous dirt road and looks out on all these wonders.

Kenya Airways – The Pride of Africa – had taken us to Uganda, The Pearl of Africa (there is much jostling for superlatives in these parts) and the drive from Entebbe had taken us through the depressing suburbs of Kampala. Evangelism has found fertile ground here, spilling over from gospel halls to The Hosanna Restaurant, The Blessed Clinic, The Glory of God Primary School, The Light of Christ Correspondence College and The Back to God Salon. We sped by too quickly to discover whether this last one was for hairdressing or downing a pint. St Adolf and St Theresa were uncomfortable neighbours a block down from Paradise Shopping and Desire Hall. For another six hours we passed clusters of

269

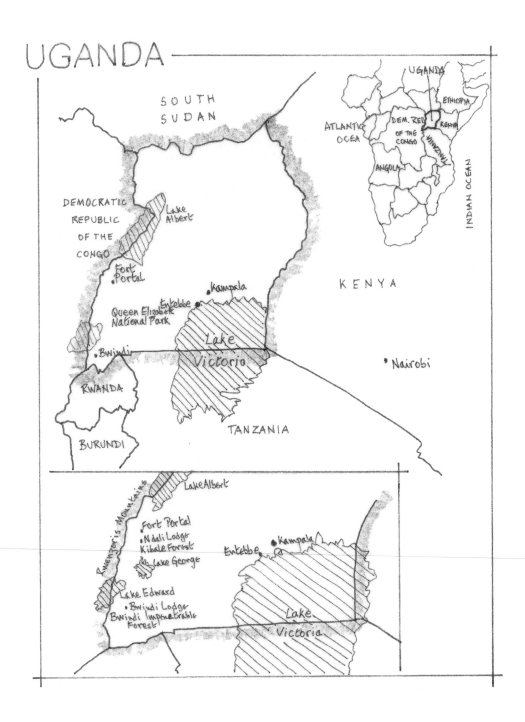

pathetic single roomed shacks, built by their owners, judging from the uneven courses of rough bricks. Many of these had succumbed to the offers of cell phone companies and received an external paint job that as part of the bargain, had the company logo stretched across the façade. Drab villages were much brightened by splashes of bright puce (Zain –'We Care'), sunflower yellow (MTN –'It's all about U') and red and white check (Warid –'Making Life Better'). Others had caught on to this marketing wheeze so that soap, beer and washing powder manufacturers offered their own bright palettes.

We passed through rolling acres of tea plantations whose leaves were so continually harvested that they seemed close cropped by sheep. They were divided by neat and orderly rows of pine and eucalyptus. Many had English names as did Fort Portal (named after Sir Gerald Portal, a former Special Commissioner). 'Fort Portal – The Trumpet of Life', whatever that may mean – announced the sign on its outskirts.

Ndali Lodge had the usual flow of guests that sustain these establishments and dinner at a long table was convivial and lively as views and adventures were exchanged. There was a lean and bearded doctor attached to Medecins sans Frontieres and his girlfriend from Manhattan, a previous rock DJ turned pastry chef who looked a little out of place in her pencil skirt and sparkly blouse. There was a husband and wife team of ex-teachers who had come to find old pupils who had fled their Kampala school during the terrible massacres of the Amin regime, a loud mother in plaits from Idaho with her 45 year old son and a Scotsman from Thurso with his mincing fiancée – a strip of a thing from Basingstoke. M and I seemed to be the conventional social glue around the table. There were also five resident dogs, all related to each other and, some while ago, a Rhodesian ridgeback. The two youngest, Sybil and Polly (of Fawlty Towers), engagingly adopted us and when not sleeping on our veranda, encouraged us to take them for a walk.

The lodge and the adjoining land had originally been the property of a Yorkshireman, Major Trevor Price. His son, Mark, was driven out by the tyrant Idi Amin but coming back following the 1993 Act of Reconciliation to reclaim his property was astonished to find that it had not been trashed by its military occupants. Getting on in years, he left the house to his son Aubrey and the land to a young cousin, Lulu Sturdy. Aubrey, realising the potential of the incomparable views, persuaded 20 friends to invest in building a tourist lodge. Lulu, then aged 30, showing similar grit and entrepreneurial talent, was also determined to make a profitable enterprise from her inheritance. After building a house for herself, she experimented with coffee, avocados, bananas and cocoa before hitting on vanilla. This last experiment, involving extraordinarily time-consuming, labour-intensive and complex manufacturing procedures, proved highly successful and Ndali

Vanilla Extract is now sold in major UK supermarkets. We paid a visit to the vanilla farm with Ronald, a local naturalist, together of course with the five dogs. Along the way he pointed out the medicinal qualities of plants. One, he assured us, was used to promote big breasts. "But I prefer small breasts and big bums," he candidly admitted. Judging from the number of nursing mothers we saw (the population has trebled in 40 years), his preferences seemed thin on the ground.

The chimpanzees of Kigali Forest were an unpredictable bunch (maybe all chimps are). Displaying all the conventions of an unruly and dysfunctional family, they crashed around the forest sometimes stopping to rest, to sleep, to eat or, in a sudden explosion of shrieks and cries that sounded as though half were being dragged away for slaughter and much thumping on tree buttresses, they all careered around the treetops, hurled sticks and raced around the ground before settling again in peaceful harmony. Females in season and the establishment of pecking orders were usually to blame.

Moving to the south-west corner of the country where it collides with Rwanda and the Democratic Republic of Congo (known locally as DRC) in a string of volcanoes that had spent their fury (although a few fume on), we came to the Bwindi Impenetrable Forest. The dirt road of our route passed first through the grasslands of the Princess Elizabeth National Park and miles from any obvious habitation, small groups of men and women wielded mattocks in a listless and futile occupation of weeding the verges. The park was littered with termite mounds scattered over the land; some were like the untidy turds of a wandering dinosaur, others were pinnacled like the fantasy castles of Ludwig, King of Bavaria. In between roamed small groups of Ugandan kob (the national animal), baboon troops, elephant and buffalo.

Bwindi Lodge occupied an enviable patch of hillside above a small river that engorged by recent rain, rushed over granite boulders and was bordered by arbours of daturas whose flowers dangled in a profusion of white trumpets above the frothy water. From the veranda of each thatched bandana and the sweeping terrace of the main lodge, the forest created an unbroken backdrop – dark, verdant and forbidding and full of the promise of intimidating and mysterious giant beasts. We first explored its mysteries at Ruhija, an hour and a half's drive along a road cut through deep forest, which coiled and squirmed its way through small hills scattered with steep cultivated plots of maize, cassava, beans, bananas and yams. After climbing to 7,500 ft (2,300m), we stopped at a remote outpost of The Ugandan Wildlife Service before setting off with our guide Joanne (whose rotund figure we found later belied her formidable fitness), two trackers, two armed guards to scare off any marauding elephants and two porters to carry our bags of wet weather clothes. More usefully, they pushed or pulled our struggling bodies up or

Gorilla's hand

Chimpanzee in Kibali

down vertiginous slopes carpeted with every kind of vine, creeper and thorn that might catch, snare, tear or entwine. We cursed these obstacles, the altitude, the oppressive conditions, the relentless pace, the flies, the oily mud, the hidden pits of rotten trees and the impossible steepness and then we forgot them all in an instant of wonder as we came upon gorillas.

The mastery of his position as neither predator nor meal sets the male gorilla apart from the petty squabbles of monkeys. His notoriety in countless films and books affords him a cult status but only when you are face to face and his eyes meet yours do you succumb to his presence. His huge sumo bulk and arms that could crush one to pulp are tempered with gentleness, languid movements, the human gestures of scratching an ear or inspecting toes. There was a casual dis-regard for visitors and a single grunt that seemed to come from an unfathomable depth of gut. Staring straight into my eyes I saw no interest and certainly no fear but there was a perceptible intelligence. Neither was there any disdain, only an imperial recognition that unchallenged superiority did not need to be paraded.

On another day in another lower but equally difficult environment, we came across a family group. An infant was captivating with its exploration of a young tree but the silverback leader of the group, a giant named Ruhondeza, displayed such contemptuousness that awaking from a snooze to find five visitors with their fingers on their photographic buttons, he let out a fart that rocked the under-growth and fell back into contented sleep.

Driving back towards Kampala, we were struck by the proliferation of schools and Moses our driver told us that you paid no income tax on any part of your earnings if you built a school. 'Built' was the crucial thing, and many schools had been built and were devoid of pupils. But there were clearly establishments that were properly up and running: Uphill College suggested a rigorous routine, St Theresa's Convent of the Sacred Jesus Child was a branch from Calcutta, The Divine Mercy Renewal Center seemed worth considering for enrolment and, if only for its knockout name, there was The Isaac Newton College School Total Learning Academy.

We spent a happy hour in the 48 acre (19 hectare) National Botanic Gardens at Entebbe, laid out in 1898 by A. Whyte and the setting for the Tarzan films of the '40s. As we walked around with a young botanist who displayed an impressive knowledge and a winning smile, the grassy park with its magnificent trees seemed far too benign for swashbuckling deeds of jungly valour. Then the thunder rolled farewell and the rain washed away our footprints.

Postcard Home

The natural world has nothing thriller
Than face to face with a gorilla.
500lbs of flesh and fur
Whose stare reflects a king's hauteur.
We've followed chimps through trees and swamp
(For us exhaustion, them a romp)
Then, in this land of mists and rain
We found the mountain's suzerain.

Kalimantan

November 2009

'The real voyage is not in seeing new landscapes but in having new eyes' – Marcel Proust

The introduction to Bertram Smythies' great two volume classic *The Birds of Borneo* is succinct.

'Borneo is the third largest island in the world after Greenland and Guinea. It is five times the size of England and Wales. It is one enormous forest.'

Redmond O'Hanlon in Into the Heart of Borneo gives the island a more alarming spin.

'As a former academic and natural history book reviewer, I was astonished to discover, on being threatened with a two month exile to the primary jungles of Borneo,... the strength of that irrational desire to find a means of keeping your head upon your shoulders; of barring 1,700 different species of parasitic worm from your blood stream and Wagler's Pit Viper from just about anywhere; of removing small, black, wild-boar ticks from your crutch with minimum discomfort (you do it with Sellotape); of declining to wear a globulous necklace of leeches all day long; of sidestepping amoebic and bacillary dysentery, yellow and blackwater and dengue fevers, malaria, cholera, typhoid, rabies, tuberculosis and the crocodile (thumbs in its eyes, if you have time).'

Elsewhere I read that encounters may be had with the Mangrove Cat Snake, the Mock Viper, the Grass Green Whip Snake, the Common Malayan Racer and the Banded Coral Snake. Kalimantan (part of Indonesia) is the southern two thirds of Borneo. And Lonely Planet says:

'Kalimantan is one of the world's last, vast wilderness areas. Few tourists make it and travel is difficult.'

It seemed just the place to visit.

Indonesia is the world's largest Muslim nation and of its 124 million people, 90% are Muslim. Of the country's 17,500 islands, Bali has the only Hindu pop-

KALIMANTAN

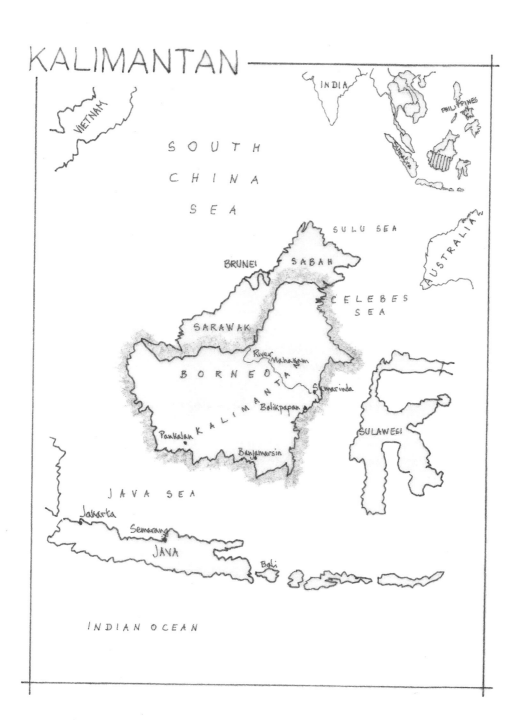

ulation, East Tenjgara the only Roman Catholic population and Papua the only Protestant population. On the day of my arrival, the Jakarta Post reported that the Corruption Eradication Committee was to be disbanded and that the Commission for Disappearances and Victims of Violence was to be terminated for lack of witnesses. But first I flew to Yogyakarta to see the Borobudur temples. It turned out there was only one that seemed worth seeing: a square, multilevel lump elaborately decorated with Buddhist images. School children in a uniform of Hawaiian shirts lit up dark enclaves of the volcanic stone and a troop of crew-cut soldiers were racing up its stepped sides singing out a chant of mutual encouragement. Spoilt by the wonders of Angkor Wat, the Pyramids and Mayan temples, I was uninspired.

Of the three passengers on the plane from Semarang on the northern coast of Java to Pankalan Bun on the southern coast of Kalimantan, I was the only Westerner. I was not sure whether to be grateful or alarmed at the lack of interest in *'the wild, untouched, wildlife paradise'*; O'Hanlon again. I was met by Aidis Usanto – "Call me Eddy". He was only a touch over a metre and a half and had the teeth of a giant. For once 'tombstones' were appropriate; they could probably crack rocks. He was cheerful and resourceful, particularly in obtaining beer. I had read that alcohol was banned in Kalimantan but with his graveyard grin, Eddy explained that the source of beer was a secret that was universally known and stopping off at a karaoke bar – well that's what he called it in spite of the six leggy and listless young women playing cards in the porch – he later appeared with six bottles in a bin bag.

My boat, *Mama One*, was painted in Cambridge blue from the top deck canopy to the waterline. Built to accommodate six, the top deck (open on every side) was all mine. Hassein steered, Samy cooked, squatting on the rear deck beside the loo that overhung the stern and Alam did the chores. We chugged peacefully along the slack and muddy windings of the Seikonyer River, 350 ft (100m) wide from one dense *nipah* palm covered bank to the other where local fishermen in slim and sleek skiffs fished for crayfish with rods that a fly fisherman would be proud of. As the water lost its salinity, *pandanus* palm crowded the banks and would have closed up the river if constant traffic had not kept it controlled. At dusk, proboscis monkeys squabbled for the best spots in the trees overhanging the river and long tailed macaques made Olympic-length jumps. The proboscis is one of the eccentrics of the primate world. Endemic to Borneo, their body is reddish-brown down to their waist but with white arms and legs, they seem to be in pyjamas. The males have a grotesquely droopy nose and on an elderly male, the nose can drop so far that he has to lift it up with one hand while eating with the other. Younger males can straighten out their nose like Pinocchio through which they then let out a shriek like a party whoopee whistle. They also glory in an almost permanent erection and, if this was not enough to attract a bride, they make almost suicidal leaps into water. No wonder they are shunned by zoos.

The beer the previous evening was a mistake. Four journeys to the stern were needed during the night, each hazardous even by the dim light of a quarter moon. There was the mosquito net to be opened with its yards of enveloping muslin, then the garrotting cord that held it up to be avoided and next, the trapdoor to five unprotected steep steps. Continuing through the dining area I hoped not to step on any of the cockroaches that flew in earlier (each as huge as a mouse and considerably faster), and then there was the bargeboard to be stepped over before the final sanctuary. The stillness of the night brings an audible focus to each individual sound. Whoops, whistles and wails; cackling, croaking and clucking; hooting and honking; and sounds mechanical such as clanking, tinkling and whirring. And laying layers of aural continuo, the cicadas and frogs keep up a desperate search for a mate. In the river things splash, plop and squelch. Fish are leaping at moths, a crocodile lurches after prey or fruit falls. In the forest, unknown beasts scavenge for a meal so that there are shrieks, crashes and an occasional roar. At dawn I awoke to the twe, twe, twe of the drongo, the babblings of babblers, the flutings of pittas and the chattering of bulbuls. All these slink mysteriously away as a female gibbon hoots the coming of day, a woodpecker drums into a tree for breakfast, hornbills cackle, the silver macaques search for the tenderest leaves and others take up the aural challenge calling across the river or announcing a territorial claim. And it is only 5 am.

Turning off the main stream down a creek so narrow that it seemed to squeeze the timber planks of *Mama One*, the banks were hung about with pandanas, lianas, great green spiky water plants and overhanging trees and then the water clarified from cappuccino to espresso. It also started to rain. Great plump drops hurtled down, bubbling the brown water, bending branches and obscuring the way. An hour before, the sun had shown from a clear blue sky and I had lathered on the Reiman P20. But then, like the valve of a fountain being turned off, the waterfall stopped, the clouds vanished and the water became as polished as jet and pacific swallows took to the air once more.

An orang-utan is so endearing, a twenty stone (280lbs, 127kgs) male excepted, that there is an impulse to rush to it for a hug. I had spotted a pair from the boat intent upon gathering the fruit from *nipah* palm, but at Camp Leakey (a research station now in its tenth year), they are habituated so that a hug seems possible and tempting. Add to this a baby (there were five when I was there) and the impulse is almost overwhelming. With huge, brown, innocent and naïve eyes, clinging instinctively to its mother's back with 20 gripping fingers and toes, an infant orang-utan is a universal favourite. Strung out like furry laundry as they limber up on a liana, they melt all hearts. Two hours and 100 photographs later, it was hard to leave.

My plane from Pankalan Bun to Banjamarsin had been cancelled. With admirable efficiency, the message was sent upriver as we were about to moor. As an alternative, cars had been arranged to drive through the night and so we chugged on in the dark with fireflies dotting the banks in a profusion of flashing bulblets. At the dock, a youth was waiting with a car; he appeared to have just passed his 14th birthday. Once, in Costa Rica, the pilot of my ten seater Cessna looked similarly immature and was so small that he had to sit on a cushion. At the end of the trip (through a scary thunderstorm) I enquired as to the age of the pilot and was told that he was 26 and had been piloting cargo planes for six years. I hoped my driver was as experienced but in any case we shot away before prayers and protests could be mustered. After three hours, at midnight, I was transferred like a DHL parcel to the care of Ali. I took him aside and carefully explained that should I detect so much as a twitch of a yawn, he was to stop and sleep. I also made it clear that if we reached our destination, eight hours away, there would be a substantial tip and the possibility of a glowing letter to his employer. The first of these instructions appeared to be understood since we covered the next few miles so sedately that the next day's programme seemed in jeopardy. We made stops on the way for a pee and a prayer; the former at a police station and the latter at a mosque that appeared to be open 24 hours. Providence prevailed and as I sank into the arms of the Swisshotel at Banjamarsin, Ali turned around for the eight hour return journey. As I wrote this in the 'cocktail lounge' (the only non-Indonesian word there), a chanteuse was belting out *My Way*. Taking a call on her mobile phone during the second verse, she stopped to read the text for a minute or so before carrying on to the end of the song.

The diamond mines at Chempana were surreal and close to hell. Here was the *'basso loco'* of Dante's *Inferno*, the sunless place of restlessness and now the ultimate despair of any health and safety officer. Several great craters had been excavated and huge tree trunks, buried for a millennium, had been preserved in the gravel at haphazard angles and at different depths so that as the pits grew deeper, these trees were left, sometimes bridging across a cavity while men laboured underneath and struggled to lever out boulders and direct high-powered water jets. Eight inch (20cms) diameter hoses were manipulated to suck up the sludge to filtering trays mounted in four layers of bamboo scaffolding 80 ft (24m) above. From these Heath Robinson contraptions, the silt was washed into other smaller pits where men and women stood up to their chests in muddy water panning the residue for specks of diamonds. Each retrieved a teaspoonful of these in a day. As

Proboscis monkeys on
Kinabatangan River

Waterside village at
Sandakan

I photographed this place of the damned and those who earned little more than three bowls of rice a day, I encountered smiles, thumbs up and that magic name that keeps the oppressed cheerful – Beckham.

Banjamasin, the capital of East Kalimantan, is a watery city reputedly below sea level. Given that the city is only a few miles from the sea, this seems to have a medieval disregard for geographical facts. Half of the town's inhabitants live, or at least exist, either beside the Jorong River which cuts through the centre or along the canals that spread out like pulsating arteries. Outside its impassive and dreary modern centre, it is a city of shacks, wooden planked, corrugated-iron-roofed and stilted to rise above the eight feet (2.5m) tide. Each has its own floating privy and the water is the universal depository for these and other rubbish of all kinds. In this oily, salty, filthy, fetid and scummy environment, hair is washed, clothes scrubbed, pot and pans cleaned, bodies soaped, teeth cleaned and dreadfully, children swim and play. Oven baked in summer, pounded by monsoon rains, odorous and of doubtful stability, these are homes to people who seem remarkably healthy and certainly cheerful. Travelling down these watery lanes, children cried 'bale', meaning white man. I was assured that this was only out of curiosity and without exception all gave a friendly wave. They also called out 'Kodak' whenever I raised my camera. Upriver the scene is less intense, with the houses still stilted but neater and the water here littered with bunches of water hyacinth storm torn from the banks. Groups of hyacinths stud the river in a profusion of little green islands. A number of taller buildings played recordings over a loudspeaker of the songs of swifts to encourage their nesting, bird's nest soup being a highly prized and expensive delicacy.

Syahdian, "Call me Shady," was 29, tall, bony and with a mass of black hair as untidy as a mop. He could have been a Bedouin but was more like a dervish. He whirled, jerked and fidgeted; his windmill arms waved around and his hands and pianist fingers gestured as though helpless with palsy. As he explained the history of Dutch colonisation, this spring-loaded marionette clutched at some imaginary fly and emphasized some point of importance with a desperate semaphore of twirling limbs. He was an English language graduate and his brain seemed always three words in front of his speech so that as they tumbled out, his mouth made a futile effort to catch up. A single word, 'whatd'youknow', ended every sentence and I ducked to escape the manic gyrations that accompanied it. He was well informed on history and politics, hopeless on birds and plants and inquisitive of the facts and customs of other lands. He also laughed a lot, was reliable and willing and I felt he would make a good companion for the ten days ahead.

The reed-covered marshes of Nagara oozed over a huge area that was ingeniously sliced through with a web of canals and streams that drain parts for the cultivation of rice and vegetables and other parts for the breeding of ducks and water buffalo. Small towns have grown up accessible only by water and I went to explore them. A white foreigner was clearly rare around there and a crowd gathered, probably intent on seeing me tumble into the soupy stream as I stepped off the slimy steps into a small and slim plank of a boat with an outsized outboard motor. To hoots of laughter, we shot off at astonishing speed down ditches barely wider than the plank. Often the ditch was clogged with plants but opening up the throttle to achieve maximum speed (and maximum fright from its occupant), we cut through or simply leapt over the obstacles. Pacific swallows zoomed around and stork-billed and common kingfishers perched on every pole. Black crowned herons and lily trotters meticulously lifted their wire-drawn legs as they hunted frogs, a greater coucal with its plumage of *feuillemort* tawny tones looked out from a withered tree and a brahminy hawk drifted lazily over the eutrophic wetlands. And there were eagles too; they preceded us with leisured wing beats, alighting on a branch until we neared and then taking off again like an avian vanguard. These pathfinders were yellow eyed lesser fish eagles and the more sluggish grey headed fish eagles.

Making a two day detour to Loksado, an attractive little town spread out along a bank of the River Amandit in the Meratus Mountains, Shady suggested a forest walk and I eagerly agreed. There were two options on offer: short and steep or longer but gentler. I chose the latter thinking that if rain came, the steeper route would be tricky. A thick coverlet of mist hung over the forest as we started and a strange pharmaceutical smell leaked out from the trees with the odour of medicinal roots or benzoin. The air was as flabby as the captured moist warmth of one's last exhalation and at 8 am the heat and humidity squeezed around one like the rank coils of a hungry python. After ten paces I dripped with sweat, after 20 paces I was soaked and at 50 I was awash. The walk became a trek and the way three degrees off vertical – heavens knows what the steeper option would have been. There were streams to cross on a single length of bamboo, streams that required leaps from boulder to boulder and streams that we walked up, sometimes struggling against the flow coming down. The trail grew to be as narrow as my foot. I cursed the humidity, my misplaced enthusiasm and the pace that Shady insisted on. "We must go as we cannot walk in the dark," he yelled over his shoulder. I hoped the dark would come in the next few minutes. "If I die," I cried, "you will have to carry my body."

"Please die at the lodge," came the reply, "the ground is softer for a grave." My blood boiled, my camera (weighing in at 6lbs (3kgs)), came close to abandonment and after four hours we were still climbing. "I am fat and old," I whimpered. "You are like a deer," came back down the mountain side. I skipped for two paces. At least I was unaffected by mosquitoes which are clearly unequipped for wet land-ings on sweaty skin. Labouring on through little plantations of maize, peanuts and dry rice and through villages crowded with small brown children and smaller black pigs, we eventually made our goal of the Harati Waterfalls. As I lay down on a boulder that seemed as soft as a pillow, two Indonesian sightseers appeared – one was wearing a fleece anorak for goodness sake! They insisted on taking my photograph; no doubt in some kampong a group are gathered round a mobile phone, giggling at the picture of a fat old Englishman, puce in the face, dripping with sweat and eating a pot noodle. We rafted back – blissfully cool, with my feet awash in the frothy, tepid water. The locals are on to a good thing here. They need to sell their bamboo downriver so they bind 20 or more together and then charge a panting tourist for sitting on top of them, legs astride a stool.

I have never encountered so many mosques as there were in Banjamasin. A network covers the town in astonishing profusion so that a larger mosque, topped with four or more tiled domes and perhaps a slender, balconied minaret, spawns a group of smaller ones. Some are painted, others are plainly planked but all have a distinguishing polished metal dome. Their loudspeakers squawk raucously, five times a day, and woken by the first of these squawks, we set off in the tranquillity of first light for a floating market that operated on the edge of the Barito River, the widest in all Kalimantan. It is in an area that receives timber floated down the river from logging operations, legal and illegal. Towering over the huddle of little boats full of fruit, vegetables, coconuts, chickens and rice, was a massive barge laden to the water line with huge tree trunks – 200 year old veterans, slain in the forest, trussed as a raft and then piled end to end in a sawmill morgue of sacrificial and profitable anonymity.

After a plane journey north, I rode the River Mahakam in lordly but lonely splendour. The top deck of the *Budi Serati* was mine and below were the captain, two deckhands, two cooks (they were sisters) and Shyadhian, still as my guide. Set-ting off from Loa Janan at dusk, the banks sparkled in a ribbon of light from river-side settlements and timber factories processing plywood, spewed acrid smoke. We chugged along all night, the whole boat throbbing from the diesel engine. I moved my mattress out on to my veranda to distance myself from the exhaust and lay there restless and sleepless, watching the weak searchlight on the bows sweep the river as the helmsman sought a safe route and warned other craft of our presence. We tied up at dawn beside a rotting jetty and behind a sleek river taxi taking an elderly couple on a *hadj*, the Islamic pilgrimage to Mecca. They were both dressed in the obligatory white, symbolising purity and equality and a party of friends, a group of schoolgirls and a few of the simply curious were gathered to see them off. It was a solemn farewell, since the pilgrims would be away for six weeks or

Riverside settlement at Banjumarsin

Coal Barge, on Mahakam River

more and many do not return, having succumbed to the difficulties of the journey followed by the rigours of the inescapable impositions of the *hadj* precepts.

Transferring to a smaller craft, I zoomed down a tributary of a darker tone of brown water, first calling at a fishing village that had been created by people from the north of the province, escaping the Japanese in 1940. Shyahdian disdainfully referred to them as immigrants. The village was a ramshackle conglomeration of planked houses perched above the water on a spillikin confusion of feeble supports, its roofs as patched as the clothes of the inhabitants. All manner of fish traps lined the river edges. There were huge affairs on booms that needed winching up, lines of bamboos that led the fish into an internal prison and woven tubular wicker traps with a bulging end. Another type of netted enclosure had somehow been infiltrated by a stork billed kingfisher and it flapped about in a vain attempt at escape. I hoped the fisherman would be merciful to such a spectacular bird. Lines of whiskered terns sat on the trap structures in long lines like targets at a funfair shooting booth and there were grey and little herons, egrets in variety and mournful looking adjutant storks which slowly paced the banks as though intent upon solving a philosophical puzzle. Later on at Waja, a plump youth with a Suzuki motorbike (both unusual in these parts) was employed as a taxi and we skidded along a dusty road to a famous dayak longhouse. It lived up to its name being a good 260 ft (80m) long and richly ornamented with lattice openwork and fronted by a long line of grotesquely carved totem poles. Two days before there had been a 'second burial' of a dayak chief at which two buffalo were sacrificed. An old man with a sagging body and lacklustre eyes offered to take me to the killing ground. Despair hung about him like a squalid and stained garment and he brushed off the accompanying band of bright and cheerful children as though irritated by troublesome flies. At the sad sacrificial spot, blood stained the earth in front of a huge pile of dung.

Night falls fast on the equator and by 6 pm the lights on board attracted a host of flying bugs. My guide book had advised, '*What you need on the Mahakam River is a good long book*' and I read *Blood River*, Tim Butcher's account of his heroic but insane journey following Winston Stanley's route down the Congo. As I sat expectant of dinner from the sisterly duo, it did not seem too fanciful to think of Stanley as he made his way, as I was, on a river of viscous brown soup, bordered by jungle and bombarded by bugs. Tropical rivers are all much the same but what was different and a surprise about this one were the coal barges that lumbered ponderously down to the sea pulled by tugs. We passed several conveyor belts that leant over the river to fill these floating giants with 2,000 tons (2million kgs) of coal apiece that had been ripped from beneath the jungle carpet. In a single morning I counted 11 of these behemoths.

At Balikpapan airport on a Saturday morning there was chaos and confusion as passengers and their cardboard boxes spilled out into the car park and groups of schoolchildren shouted at each other and their mobiles. Shyadian spun in a whirlwind of fluttering handshakes and contortionist hugs, grinned and was gone. I swept on to the ordered and manipulated calm of Singapore. The city was locked down for an APEC summit attended by the presidents or prime ministers of America, China, Japan and 24 others and was aglow with Christmas decorations. I escaped by the first plane out.

Postcard Home

Here in an outpost of Asian jungle
There's rain, lushness and a wild ensemble
Of bears, birds, monkeys, Dyaks and Iban
And that 'man of the forest', the orang-utan.
Up a Borneo creek in a dugout canoe
I've thrown up on yam and snake ragout.
My boat smells of diesel, fish and carbolic,
Banished at night by draughts alcoholic.

Colombia

February 2010

*'The traveller is active; he goes strenuously in search of people, of adventure, of experience.
The tourist is passive; he expects interesting things to happen to him. He goes 'sight-seeing'.'*
– Daniel J Boorstin

Manaus scattered itself peripatetically along the Rio Negro. Only the Teatro
Amazonica seemed in good order and very fine it was. Elsewhere the crumbling
façades of 19th century elegance stood, or were more often propped, to await
salvation. This may come with the 2014 World Cup which has matches to play
in the city stadium. This woeful disregard of architectural heritage is all the more
unfortunate considering that Manaus in its boom days of rubber and gold from
1864 to 1928 was one of the wealthiest cities in the world with a population of
100,000 ; now it is one million. Other cities on a traveller's schedule and in a par-
lous financial state have done things better. Kathmandu, Havana and La Paz have
adapted; Rangoon has sold off the best to hotel chains and Lijiang has turned
itself into a historical pastiche. Here nothing has been done. Once, after jour-
neying to Alexandria to find the world of Justine et al, I was disappointed to find
nothing remained. It was the same here: where had the past gone? Where was the
legacy of the French and Spanish architects, the extravagance on an epic scale –
marble and craftsmen from Italy, laundry sent to Paris, horses rubbed down with
champagne, Les Halles reproduced by Eiffel? Here the fault lines of age have had
no cosmetic assistance, the gentle charm of the elderly has been simply ignored
or covered in a shroud of hoardings, weeds and opportunist market stalls. In the
evening I went with Carlo my guide (at six, the Brazilian junior bridge champion)
to look at the celebrated opera house. It was a strange affair with its rectilinear
form, mock classical façade and topped by a dome which mixed Moorish geomet-

COLOMBIA

ric mosaic with Picasso's invention. Inside was opulence to match any European equivalent with painted ceilings, intricate parquet, gilt on every protuberance and chandeliers of Versailles proportions. Strolling around its piazza, a covey of fireworks sprang into the sky and little plops left balls of smoke hanging in the air. Rockets are as numerous in Brazil as exclamation marks in a debutante's correspondence. The birth of a saint, the death of a patriot, the birthday of a relative and the outbreak or conclusion of a revolution will all be sparkled with fireworks.

I have been impressed and a little confused by the courtesies afforded me. In an airport bus, a young man of sickly appearance and a weight of silver in his right ear, gave me his seat; in Manaus, a featherweight chambermaid insisted on carrying my luggage and for the flight to Tabatinga, I was singled out (along with nursing mothers and cripples) for prior boarding. Was I really that old or that foreign? It seems that balding, greying and white skinned is not on the Brazilian indigenous menu in spite of the genetic stew with its original ingredients of Spanish soldiers, African slaves and Aztecs and a later seasoning of immigrants from just about everywhere.

Down by the river bank, my boat seemed loaded for an expedition of several months. Moored by a pontoon to which were tethered another dozen longboats and on which sat an assortment of mothers, children, Indians of varying authenticity and piles of cardboard boxes, sacks and paraphernalia of all kinds, my boat was stowed gunwale to gunwale. Here there were drums of diesel, smaller drums of petrol for the outboard, boxes of fruit, sacks of flour, cold boxes, coils of rope, stacks of eggs and a block of ice the size of an armchair. There was also a lump of *carne seca* the size of a suitcase that lay unwrapped in a torn sack and so charred it could have been roasted in a volcano. Within minutes of leaving our mooring, I was soaked through with the warm spray of the river. But what the hell, we were off up the Amazon.

But first, out on the Rio Negro, grey river dolphins showed their dorsal fins and a pair of pink dolphins – as pink as calamine – surfaced for an exclusive but elusive moment. River traffic was plentiful but such was the scale of the river, running silently and slowly but with immense strength, that fishermen and water taxis seemed like gnats on a Scottish loch. Only ill-maintained and foul-looking river ferries (four days to Manaus from the delta – I had flown in three hours) streaked with the rigours of age and the ardours of Amazonia, were noticeable by their bulk. The day before, I had been rowed out to the Meeting of the Waters. Here, the Rio Negro, cold, acidic, and grey meets its watery master, the Amazon – warm, calcalareous and brown. Both embrace to finish their combined journey to the Atlantic.

Four hours later, wet through, deafened by the outboard but exhilarated just to be there, we turned off the main river, up a lesser one, then a smaller one, across a lake and after wriggling through the tops of a forest of shrubs in this flooded environment, we came upon Heliconia Lodge. In the gathering darkness, monkeys crashed around as they trooped off to their treetop dormitory, the whistles of the orependulas slowly subsided and silence crept in. The Javari River, our nearest waterway, marked the boundary between Brazil and Peru where clocks were set one hour later. For the time conscious, this was a confusing part of the world but time was seldom on the mind of those who lived here and in any case, Brazilians seemed immune to any notion of punctuality. Delay is indigenous and procrastination an element of every decision; in Brazil, a man in a hurry is a man of misery. The local Indians (a few of whom worked at the lodge) had little concept of numbers. "How many fish do you have?" Answer, "Enough." "What time is dinner?" "When it is ready." "How far is the village?" "Not far/very far/too far."

An armadillo had made its home under my cabana – under the loo in fact. It shuffled about after dark looking for termites and worms but in the silence of the night it might have been a pig. I had not seen it but Santiago, the Indian guide, had identified its burrow. The loo, whose raised floor so conveniently protected the armadillo's home from the rain, was spacious and occupied a three sided corner of the cabana. The fourth side did not exist and so one sat, enthroned, looking out into the forest. It was oddly liberating and disturbing at the same time. There were ants the size of battleships that scurried about the planked floor; it was not a place to linger. As there was no electricity, little jam jars of paraffin with a cotton wick were placed around including one outside the shower, similarly open to the forest. If you were engaged in ablutions at 6.30 pm when the lamplighter came round, he simply wished you a courteous *boa neite*. Outside my room, a branch heavy with blossom was bent towards and into a window as if to eavesdrop on any conversation within.

One afternoon, a group of the indigenous Indians came to visit the lodge. There were five men wearing an assortment of western cast-offs and two women in grubby skirts and blouses with four small children. They all had fingers as stubby as their toes and none had shoes. The women had long, black, tousled and shiny hair while the men's were as neat as if they had just stepped out from a barber. They were all short and sturdy with muscular legs and wide feet with splayed toes. They arrived in a boat about 30 ft (nine metres) long, its whole length covered by a hooped roof of woven palm and this was their temporary home in which they all slept, cooked and travelled. They had started their journey eight days before. Apparently they made this journey twice a year, visiting lodges and selling finely woven baskets and hunting weapons. These weapons were magnificent; a long bow, taller than any of them and made of black polished

Stew maker at Bogota market

Doorway in Old Bogota

wood and arrows, six feet (two metres) long which were beautifully feathered and with their sharp ends protected by a woven sheath. All these were decorated with intricate braiding of coloured twine. They were a cheerful lot, no doubt happy that they had sold all their goods to the lodge for its collection. We waved them goodbye but they did not wave back as they started on their long return journey to their home in the deep forest. Unknown birds sent out stealthy, isolated calls across the still water, a dog barked in a far off settlement and fish broke the surface with a surreptitious splash. Against a lambent western sky and the embers of sunset, the jungle was sharply defined. To the east it was indeterminate in the little mist that writhed along the smooth dark water. A morpho butterfly, loitering and aimless, flopped by in resplendent slivers of electric blue. Unable to rest, it spread its gorgeous cloak over the water as though its vanity required that there be a mirror image. It was all a little improbable but in accordance with the best traditions of exploration.

At Tabatinga, the town straddles the border with Brazil and this is marked by a plastic barrier of the kind commonly seen protecting an excavated hole in the road. On the other side of this and the other side of the street is Leticia in Colombia. There are no formalities. This town of adjoining nations is spruce and soulless on the Brazilian side and unkempt and lively on the Colombian side. Each half boasts its own international airport although 'international' must be taken with a degree of circumspection around here: Peru is round the corner, Venezuela is over the hill and Bolivia is down the road. Leticia's cracked pavements, its muddy riverbanks and its lively cafés were sprinkled with all those characters that move through the movies of South America from *Saludos Amigos* to *Romancing the Stone*. At a street corner a Jordanite was haranguing a few apathetic loafers and a suspicious policeman. He wore a long white robe and a white turban; a drowsy small boy sat in the dust beside him was holding a large and scuffed bible. Their name is derived not from the river but from a Mr Jordan from Jamaica. Seeing myself as the only white man, he became a little flustered and cracking the boy on the head, demanded the bible from which he then chose a text to preach on. Here were local girls, generous with their lipstick and mean with their skirts, Indian families bewildered in urban surroundings, old men with faces furrowed by time and climate, nodding in conversation or sleep and tall, lean and bony backpacking men, trousers threadbare, hair awry and eyes too bright. A nun or two added solemnity and an elegant *senor* with a pencil moustache, polished shoes – crocodile he would like you to think – and dark darting eyes that searched for a break in the queue and the short cuts of life; the kind that had a ready smile for authority and a sneer for the humble. Elsewhere, you might have imagined this cast but here they were real.

Victoria, the receptionist at El Marques, one of a new breed of boutique hotels in restored old merchants' houses in the old town of Cartagena, had only a smattering of English. So we had a computerised conversation. "May I delay my check out?" "How do you get to the church of St Pedro?" "Did you know you are the prettiest receptionist in Cartagena?" All instantly translated into Spanish or blushes. The old town had much the same characteristics – pretty façades that hid modern technology; the new town housed a million in urban high rise and a few chic villas.

The historic centre was so picturesque it was almost a caricature of postcard kitsch. It was saved from this fate by the contemporary reality of the real people that lived here and, every now and again, crumbling masonry – the town is built of limestone and coral. Bright colours in painterly profusion, but nothing as crude as the primaries, were washed on to the street façades from an attractive palette and many balconies overflowed with flowering climbers. Wooden doors patterned with little pointed studs like a tableau of metal nipples, guarded the older and grander houses. There was genuine beauty, no outstanding elegance (pitted and pockmarked coral does not lend itself to ashlar and fine detailing) and it was attractively approachable and homely. In some ways it had echoes of Dubrovnik. A massive fortified perimeter wall protecting a huddle of streets, stone buildings under tiled roofs and all surrounded by a great spread of modernity.

The tourist office's historical handout had much to say about the position of Cartagena as the treasure house of Spanish South America and the impregnable fort of St Filipe, the bastions and stupendous walls of the city that were built to protect the gold, silver and the emeralds. Many were prepared to risk men and ships to obtain this fabulous fortune and the guide drew particular attention to 'the notorious pirate' Francis Drake. I watched the sun dip into the Caribbean from Café del Mar, a fashionable spot set around rusting cannons, still aimed seawards towards the approach of pirates and a place for the locals to flirt and loosen their inhibitions with a caipirinha or three. The sea was grey, the sky leaked a drizzle and the wind blew my umbrella inside out.

There were many heroes of those times but none more heroic than Don Blas de Lezo. A Spaniard of noble birth, he had lost a leg in combat, a left eye in Toulon and his right arm in the Battle of Gibraltar. His legendary fighting spirit (that's about all he had left) led him to being commissioned by Cartagena's citizens to defend the city against a massive assault by the British under Admiral Vernon. In the subsequent attack, de Lezo lost his other leg but now, with only one limb and one eye left, he demanded to be carried to the thickest of the fighting to urge his men on. Vernon, realising that he was up against a man who rose above any normal human disabilities, wisely withdrew.

Plaza Santa Dominico was the place to be, post 6 pm. The ochre façade of Inglesia Santa Dominico dominated one side, Paco's and another four restaurants the second and third sides and Immobiliaria Bustamante, true to its estate agency business, was in a handsome house that completed the fourth side. In its window was a poster advertising the Hay Literary Festival. I rubbed my eyes to read it carefully. It was true; in a couple of weeks, Simon Schama, Michael Ondaatje, Ian McEwan and others were all lined up for a bookish weekend. The Spectator later reported,

'At the Hay Festival in Cartagena, the popular conception of Caribbean literary festivals that freeloading writers enjoy sunshine, mojitos and rumbas till dawn, conformed to every detail of the stereotype.'

In the centre of the square were acrobats, dancers, guitarists, cigarette sellers, swindlers and tricksters and the restaurants' prettiest waitresses to drum up trade. The square was no bigger than an Oxfordshire market place but here, music throbbed and the cabaret of after dark life pulsated in amiable abandon and all for a plate of *ceviche* and a Club Columbia beer. A gust of warm wind sneaked round a corner scattering papers and crumbs, lifting skirts to squeals of laughter, blowing hair and adding to the fun. And then it was gone, dashing down Calle Domingo to make mischief elsewhere. Lovers returned to interrupted intimacy, an itinerant guitarist spotted his romantic moment and a carriage pulled by a grey horse munching its supper on the move, rattled over the cobbles. The dancers, hawkers, buskers, slinky waitresses, nimble accordionists, sellers of beads and bags, excited matrons, bored children, photographers, caricaturists, sellers of CDs of unknown performers and posters of well-known footballers and Africans with unsellable leather things, all returned to business. Bright yellow taxis – all Fiat 500s that could squeeze through the streets – buzzed around seeking custom from the passengers of a cruise ship. These elderly and flabby vacationers, each tagged like sheep, were herded around in numbered flocks. Some needed support, all needed guidance. I was ready to move to another carnival but this time it was to be on a blockbusting scale.

The El Prado Hotel was in chaos. It had not only been fully booked for months but there was a wedding to cope with too. The biggest and best of Barranquilla's hotels was noted in my ten year old guide book as in need of modernisation. The management had clearly not read the book but it was in carnival spirit with elaborate and jolly decorations and, by reputation, had the biggest and best party. It may have been the biggest but in my book it was far from the best. The 1,000-watt amplification system seemed to be in my room – probably under my bed. The furniture bounced and glass was close to cracking. The hotel's only real asset of a magnificent swimming pool was wisely roped while the wedding guests mingled around it. They also had music, different music and 500-watt amplifiers. This cacophony met below my balcony in competitive disharmony until the wedding gave in at 1 am allowing the megawatts to triumph until 6 am. Then the rush hour traffic started. My package at the hotel included a bed for three nights, tickets for the carnival and a bottle of whisky; forlorn and alone in this festive city, the bottle was empty well before the wedding ended.

They are big on decibels here, at least at carnival time. You could hear the beats from 100 sources five blocks from the carnival route – a dual carriage way that ran through the city centre. My seat was beside a 20 ton low-loader, stacked a storey high with loudspeakers. I shall be deaf for a week, I thought. At ten in the morning and three hours before kickoff, the stands were almost full with an audience decked out in neon hair, sombreros of every colour and size and glitz, glitter, dazzle and bling. Any effulgent colour would do provided it was fluorescent and sparkled and there were confetti, balloons and flags too. This was not the opulent extravagance of Rio. Here it was homemade, earthy and folksy enjoyment for the people and by the people and they loved it, calling to their friends in the parades and waving to their families. They were dancing on the way here, laughing when they arrived and never stopped either all day.

Legend, folklore and fun seemed to be the order of the days (there were four of them) and scattered through them, Caribbean met the jungle, Aztec and Inca danced with Spaniards, *penos* and witchdoctors mingled with a dozen Minnie Mouses and there were pirates, prisoners and gorillas by the score. All the Colombian states were represented as well as individual towns and wealthy estancias. Here were Congo Grande, Toro Grande and Cipote Marimanda. Two hundred and sixty six groups in all and each came with 100 or more dancers and their own marching bands. They swirled in a frothy sea of gingham or tailored suits of short jackets and tight trousers in elegant and carefully choreographed displays of *congas, cumbiambas, gavabatos* and *toritos*. In between them came every kook in the land in costume and paint, the brighter, the more brazen and the more bizarre the better. Robin Hood, Don Quixote and Gandhi were there along with Osama bin Laden, Che Guevara, Chavez and Castro. Rebellious renegades of all kinds were popular and this seemed a healthy indication of a democratic nation but Pablo Escobar, the notorious drug baron, was noticeably absent. Romans, Red Indians, Spidermans, Supermans and Batmans by the dozen ran about. They came on roller skates and stilts and waved banners, flags and pennants. A group of spastics earned particular applause and a bunch of outrageously camp guys, a crescendo of wolf whistles. A Michael Jackson lookalike, stick thin and mad as a hatter, split his shiny, scarlet, vinyl trousers from his crutch to his waist in a ground level limbo. His shoes split too. I thought my neighbour might be sick with laughter. There were holes in the fencing and exasperated police spent much time in the futile effort of trying to catch infiltrators who then reappeared through another hole further down the course. It all added to the fun.

How the crowd loved it all. It had started an hour late and many stood in the hot sun for six hours or more but who was caring. We laughed, slapped each other on the back, pointed, cheered, yelled at friends in the parade and swayed to the music – and what music! Toe tapping, rhythmic and joyful, it was belted out by trucks loaded with great banks of speakers (they towed an industrial generator to power these) and overflowing with gyrating performers. The crowd knew every number and sang along as these musical monoliths lumbered through. If there was a celebrity singer on board, the crowd developed near hysteria. But if there was one national icon that seemed to be worshipped above even their music, it was pulchritude. Not for nothing have long-legged, sublimely shaped, sparkling toothed Colombian maidens regularly held the Miss World title. Here they dazzled us all once again. There was *Reina del Carnival, Exit Reina* – last year's winner, *Reina del Reina* and of course, *Reina del Mundo*. All carried sashes that spelt out their name and their attendants and all the runners

Teatro Amazonas, Manaus.

up added extra glamour. In between, adorning floats with gorgeous cheesiness, were other *Reinas* whose lesser status was only apparent by the lack of their name.

I was at the starting line, so there was the additional entertainment of frustrated marshals, the jockeying for position in front of TV cameras, late arrivals and general chaos. But this was Colombia and a four day national carnival with 15,000 participants cannot be expected to work with precision. One of the hazards that disrupted any attempted precision was an overhead cable that spanned the dual carriage way of the route. These are a regular problem in an urban environment but the height of the leading float – an extravagant giant cockatoo of painted polystyrene against whose breast nestled one of the *Reinas* – had not been properly measured. It was two feet too tall. Long poles failed to lift the slack of the cable and as the monstrous bird inched forward, the crowd fell silent with alarm. Would the cable snap, was it carrying electricity, would it bring down the poles supporting it? There were thousands of performers behind and as many spectators in front. The strain on all concerned but critically on the cable was too much. It snapped with a whiplash that missed the six foot beauty queen by as many inches and simultaneously demolished the bird's crest. The crowd roared in relief or entertainment, I missed the photographic scoop of a dozen bystanders being either electrocuted or crushed by a falling pylon, the carnival procession moved on and part of Barranquilla was deprived of telephones.

Four-phone Filipe took me to Tayrona National Park on the Caribbean coast – a two hour drive on the empty roads of a holiday Monday. One phone was at home but the other three were in the car and in use, often two at once. Had the third rung, I was ready with, *"Momento, por favor."* Filipe had gone to New York, speaking no English, 20 years ago to find a better life, before moving to Miami with his wife. Now divorced and his children American citizens (one in the marines and another training as an accountant), he drove a taxi in Barranquilla and said he was happy. He certainly had a lot of mobile-owning friends.

The jungle of the national park spread itself over the foothills of Pico Cristobal Colon (Colombia's highest mountain at 18,700 ft (5,700m), with a snow covered peak all year long), and tumbled into the Caribbean Sea. Since some cataclysmic explosion had sent them helter skelter down the mountain side, great boulders littered the slopes and piled up on the beaches. This was primary rainforest territory and there were many ancient trees although nothing huge. The steep slopes washed off the nutrients that are necessary for giants. Lianas crossed the track like cables over an urban carnival road. Pack horses provided the transport here. Nothing else could have manoeuvred through the gulches, roots and boulders. Suitcases, beer crates, groceries, chairs and all the paraphernalia to maintain a comfortable lodge, were strapped on, with smaller items being stuffed into jute bags.

Several of the 176 steps to my hilltop cabana were crossed by lines of leaf cutter ants. They worked tirelessly day and night but were clearly programmed as there was a great store of leaf bits at the entrance to their nest; management had over ordered. Some ants were too ambitious and carried a section of leaf like a great sail. If this got caught by a breeze, they got blown over. Someone should have warned against the wind hazard of oversized leaves, like those notices to pantechnicons at the approaches to the Severn Bridge. Once, a scared agouti scuttled from underneath the cabana and a blue crowned motmot was a regular early morning visitor. No doubt, both were scavenging for bits of fruit tossed away by guests.

The capital is officially Sante Fe del Bogota. Known locally as *'A despelote'* – chaos – its streets are a battlefield for wild traffic, whether mules or Maseratis. *'An impression of visual and mental disarray.'* I stayed in the old quarter that was protected from the battle by pedestrianised streets and a policeman on each corner but in a tour around the more modern areas, it seemed no more restless or disorganised than any other South American city. At 8,500 ft (2,600 m) it is the third highest capital on the continent (after La Paz and Quito) and the mornings were chilly and the mountain tops obscured in mist. There were splendid colonial churches, impressive modern buildings, wonderful museums – including the Gold Museum of astonishing Columbian craftsmanship, shanty towns, a city centre park of pine trees in which cows were grazing, bootblacks, thieves, drug dealers, traffic jams and interest and fascination around every corner.

Throughout my brief visit to the country, I had questioned my guides and drivers on their perception of modern Colombia and its neighbours and they were universally in accord on two points. Firstly, Chavez in Venezuela next door was an idiot and a menace. Secondly, the country had been at the mercy of drug barons but this was now a matter of the past and all the towns were safe. If you were foolish enough to adventure into the great rainforests of the East, you might never return but elsewhere things were good. They did not look that good to me with the prominence of police and military but, in comparison with the past, perhaps things were safe and stable. For myself, whether on an Amazon long boat, strolling colonial streets, enjoying a multicoloured crowded carnival, accompanying a line of pack horses or admiring the Spanish architectural legacy, I found only a happy and friendly people anticipating security and prosperity.

Postcard Home

I've left the flooded Amazon
The dolphins, otters, hoatzin.
(I failed to find an anaconda
But had I done, I'd quick absconder).
Banditos hide round every tree,
I hope they're not observing me.
Oh! There's a bandit over there.
No, just a one armed guerrilla.
The carnival at Barranquilla
Runs on rum and neat tequila.
I may, with luck, lose my demeanour.
How sad my dancing days are over,
I'm quite a dab at bossa nova.
Tomorrow, Bogota. Hurrah!
The next day, the UK. Hurray!

Malta for the Weekend

March 2010

'Leave the home, O youth and seek out alien shores' – Petronius

I had come to the island with other choristers to sing *The Messiah* at St Paul's Cathedral, built on the site of a previous Norman church in the walled city of Mdina. From the air, I counted 20 ships steaming past the island. No wonder this rock, placed in the middle of the Sicilian Channel, has such strategic relevance. It guards the central Mediterranean and Phoenicians, Greeks, Romans, Normans, Turks, French and British (roughly in that order), all had their eye on it and most fought their way ashore and left their mark.

Geologically, it is a lump of limestone. Every house, road, wall, cathedral (there are three), church (there are 363) and, above all, bastion, is built from it. If you threaten one of the principal naval routes of an expansionist world, bastions are what you need and here they do not come thicker, higher or better designed. The immense fortifications owe their construction to the military monks of the Order of the Knights of St John of Jerusalem who had the money, the religious zeal and the contacts to employ the best, to pay the highest wages and capture the strongest slaves. 5,000 were paid and 5,000 enslaved to construct the bastions following The Great Siege – the four month attack of Suleiman the Magnificent in 1565.

In only a weekend, there is no time for academic research, foot slogging exploration of nooks and crannies or local conversations. Minimalism is the watchword and my miniature world was the capital city of Valletta. Here were crystallised history, religion, homes, markets and contemporary living. There were also little pockets of greenery, struggling to support casuarina pines, stunted holm oaks and huge oleanders. Elsewhere, handkerchief sized patches grew barley and irregular lines of vines.

Street in
Valetta

The promontory of Valletta protects the harbour of Marsomxett to its north and Grand Harbour to its south, the latter being one of the world's great natural deep water ports. The promontory itself has sides so steep that streets career down to the sea, sometimes so steeply that they are all steps. At the shoreline, the perimeter walls tell the story of a turbulent past; here are the English Bastion, Abercrombie's Bastion, the French Bastion and the German Bastion along with a dozen others named after salvationist saints. The Knights reconstructed the town on a grid system and, on the principals of good town planning, provided a central backbone of a wide street that cleaves the town in two like the slash of a cutlass. At the centre lies the great Grand Masters' Palace, a fine National Library and the Co-Cathedral of St Johns with its astonishing chiaroscuro interior, *pietra dura* memorial tablets that cover the nave floor, two Caravaggios and a number of great tapestries woven from cartoons of Rubens and Poussin. Here also in Republic Square, is the plaque that reads:

'To honour the brave people, I award the George Cross
to the island fortress of Malta to bear witness to a
heroism and devotion that will be famous in history.'
April 15th, 1942   George R I

Malta well deserves its nickname – *Superbissima*, 'Most Proud'.

The architectural styles ranged from severe classical to runaway baroque with a smattering of mannerist and *belle époque*. The majority of the public buildings date from renaissance and very fine some of them were. "A city built by gentlemen for gentlemen," as Disraeli declared. The standard and extent of decoration diminished in proportion to their distance from the backbone, Republic Street, but everywhere the residential façades were hung about with balconies. All no more than three feet wide, enough for a chair perhaps but in an astounding variety of lengths, colours and materials and all enclosed with glass from waist level, like little slimline conservatories clinging to a cliff face. Avert the eyes from street level and it could have been Aleppo or Damascus. I never saw anyone in these balconies; with streets so narrow they must have compromised privacy – perhaps they were just for pot plants.

On a Sunday morning, I hurried to catch the sung Eucharist at the cathedral of St Paul, the HQ of the Anglican Church of Malta and Gozo. Its neo-classical exterior with a robust portico of ionic columns, was matched by an interior plainness that made a restful contrast to the overwhelming elaboration of its Catholic cousins. Opposite was a modest and severe building for the accommodation of Carmelite nuns whose adjoining domed church towered hypocritically over St Pauls and St Johns. Beside the convent cowered a tiny shop whose hand-painted notice read 'Joe Agius – Coffin Maker'. On the cathedral doors a notice read 'Go to church now and beat the Christmas rush!' I had tried to beat the rush but there was no 9.30 am service. I told the verger of the disparity between the Times of Services pinned outside and reality but he only opened his arms, shrugged his shoulders and smiled, as though in acknowledgement of human frailty. Wandering away, I came across a small band of banner waving, musket toting, helmeted men clad in doublet and hose and marching to the solemn beat of a muffled drum. Expecting an enactment of the changing of 18th century guard duties, I followed them to Freedom Square, where they disappeared into a bakery, placed their helmets on a table, leant their pikes against the door and ordered coffee and cake.

On the other side of the square, was the bus terminal from which 98 routes were served by a fleet of assorted buses. They seemed to be the last survivors of manufacturers long gone. They were all here: Daff, BMC, AEC, Reliance and Cummins. MAN was well represented, there were a dozen Leyland and as many Reliance. One had 'Premble Beach, NSW' across its rear. They were not as old as those of Rangoon or as flamboyant as Karachi's but each had clearly seen 40 years or more of service and each was a 'transport of delight'. Universally painted bright yellow, they looked like a box of bruised bananas.

The Maltese language is a strange blend of several others having a base of Semitic, a layer of Sicilian and topped up with Arabic. Oddly, those from the Levant of the eastern Mediterranean are alleged to understand the language. Discussing its origins with the captain of the little ferry boat that runs between Valletta and Sliema, he sadly but accurately explained, "We have been the football of so many jealous countries that we have a little of them all." 'Good morning' is *bonju*, 'thank you' is *gratsi*, while 'how are you?' is *keef intee?* So there is French, Italian and Arabic for a start. But to throw you off course, the road out of the banana bus depot was Vral Dwardu VII. How fortunate that the friendly, helpful and charming Maltese all speak English.

Under the Mosta dome of the cathedral, one of the largest in the world, the

Malta Philharmonic Orchestra did their best. Every note ricocheted around the marble walls, every square foot of the floor had not less than two feet on it, side chapels were crammed and the tombs were swamped. The free performance (churches are not allowed to charge) may have boosted the numbers – apart, of course, from the reputation of the choir. Brian Kay, our brave conductor, triumphed against the odds and alleluiahs and applause reached to the top of the dome and rattled the chandeliers. In 1942, a bomb was accidently dropped on the cathedral when 300 worshipers were gathered there. By a miracle, no one suffered even a scratch.

On our last day, a storm swept in from the west and we holed up for a farewell meal in the British Hotel, a modest establishment that smelt of Dettol and stale cooking oil. A local resident had described it as having the best view and the worst food in Malta. He was right on both counts and the grey meat and warm beer were forgiven for the panorama of Grand Harbour from the dress circle of St Barbara's Bastion.

Postcard Home

It's springtime here in gay Valletta,
Put on the shades, discard the sweater.
I'm here with members of my choir
In this cathedral – for Messiah.
Let's hope our notes succeed to please the
Congregation of Maltesers.
We're safe with Brian Kay as boss,
Mishandling Handel can make a Maltese cross.

Kamchatka

August 2010

'I would rather wake up in the middle of nowhere than in any city on earth'
– Steve McQueen

The goodies bag on Aeroflot's Boeing, the Anton Chekhov, contained only a pair of slippers whose soles were substantial enough for a country walk; there was no room for anything else. My neighbour had a florid complexion, a snub nose, a hideous shirt of lime green horizontal stripes and a plate sized watch. He was flicking through *'Elite'* – The Private Jet Life Style Magazine – and regularly summoned a stewardess by waving a chubby hand; courtesy was not a word he had yet encountered. He seemed an unlikely visitor to Kamchatka.

At the north western corner of 'The Ring of Fire' – the girdle of volcanoes that is spread around the rim of the Pacific Ocean and nine time zones east of Moscow, lies a peninsular that dangles off the end of Siberia. By a freak of geophysics its capital, Petropavlovsk-Kamchatskiy, and Chipping Norton are on the same latitude of 51 degrees 56 minutes. To those familiar with P-K and Chippy, that is all they have in common. Residents of Chipping Norton are used to wind and cold but here, arctic winds from the Siberian Anticyclone combine with the cold Oya-Shio Sea current to produce a bitter winter that extends from October to June. *'Summer is short with only a few snow showers.'* The peninsular is 620 miles (1,000kms) long (about the size of the United Kingdom) and 245 miles (400kms) wide at the broadest part of its spear head that plunges into the convulsion of the Bering Sea and the Seas of Okhotsk. At its tip, like dripping drops of blood, are the string of volcanic Kuril Islands that reach to Japan. There is a single dirt road that reaches half way up the spine; 300,000 inhabitants – most of whom live in

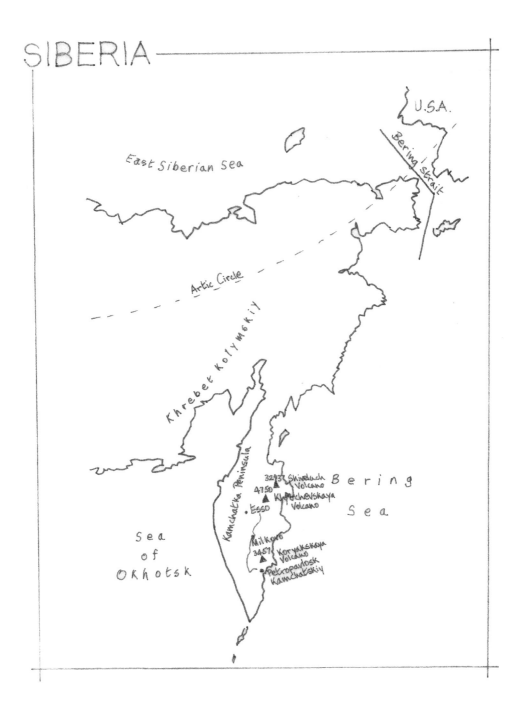

P-K; the population density is .02 per square kilometre (the equivalent in Hong-kong is 28,000) and there are 300 hundred volcanoes, of which 29 are active and include Kluchevskoy, the most active in Eurasia. The cones rupture the surface like boils on a careworn face, some suppurating in steam, others waiting their time, but nevertheless it is also a land of spectacular beauty. The International Dendrology Society, to which I belong, thought it was an interesting place to visit and so did I.

It was high summer but snow lay in all the crevices of the rumpled landscape and crowned the higher volcanoes. Flying in from the west, the sun reflected off lakes that sat in the numerous calderas so that the land was dressed in a scattering of sequins from mineral waters of green, blue, red and yellow. We flew over the dusty line of the province's only road as it snaked through the central valley following the path of the Kamchatka River before this spread its limbs into a delta of 1,000 curled fingers, exhausted by its journey. Our hotel, the best in town, had peeling paint outside and dazzled with the glitter of mirror and chrome inside. *'Your cosy home when far from home'* was its slogan. *'Seventy rooms with all the necessary stuff'*. Its restaurant diners were breakfasting on dumplings, several varieties of pickled vegetables and tiny cups of instant coffee. Several were drinking beer. In my bedroom, the instructions ran to 18 pages in Russian and four lines in English; these set out the procedure in case of fire: 'Inform the administration and wear out the fire on the balcony'. There was no balcony. The whole town was without water for two days while the annual maintenance was carried out so buckets proliferated. It was as though the roof was leaking in 100 places. Perhaps it was.

On the first evening (actually the morning to those who had flown from London and were on a 12 hour time difference), I and a fellow traveller (an elderly, eccentric and distinguished aristocratic Scottish lady with an impressive knowledge of trees and an inexhaustible stamina), stumbled upon a 30th birthday party where tables had been spread around the bar area with an extravagant array of champagne, wine, brandy and vodka and great platters of soused herring, salmon caviar and blinis. Spontaneously and generously we were invited in and we joined the birthday boy (a helicopter pilot), his glamorous wife (a banker) and their friends, only leaving when the music changed from '60s Western to '90s Slavic. The floor shook with stamping, the tables rattled with the clapping and the glasses clinked as the toasts moved from shots to tumblers and occasionally over a shoulder. The previous week, President Medvedev, shocked by the average weekly consumption of almost a litre of vodka, had declared War on Alcohol; in Siberia, the war would be lost in a week.

On a glorious day whose cerulean sky showed off the cloud-capped Kronotskay volcano (11,574 ft, 3,528m), we took a boat to Starichkov Island, a celebrated bird sanctuary passing by immense floating docks of the ship repair industry. Outside the protection of the headlands, the swell deepened and we pitched and rolled our way accompanied by tufted puffins, guillemots and redfaced and pelagic cormorants. Vertical slabs of rock supported large colonies of slaty backed gulls and black legged kittiwakes. We had a diver with us incongruously clad for the boat trip in a suit of cream linen who, when introduced as a scuba diver, was quick to correct this. "I am a free diver, is that clear?" The message and his English were perfectly clear. Later he brought up a net full of sea urchins, some inedible starfish and a couple of sea slugs – horrible slimy, spongy creatures which he kept to sell to the Japanese. The urchins were split open and scarlet mucous was scattered over the deck while those who like sucking out the entrails of strange sea creatures indulged themselves.

The town was drab, ill-kempt and unloved. Weeds flourished in every crack and waste ground accumulated the worn out and the thrown out – the discards of a careless society. Cheerless men in felt trilbies and grey anoraks were camouflaged against this urban desolation but a few young women sported high heels, long legs and bright colours in defiance of soviet conformity. Like townspeople throughout Russia, their dachas provide an escape from the tedium of life; nothing grand or substantial but simply a wooden shack with a stove pipe through the roof and a plot large enough to grow potatoes, some beans and a bower of flowers. The rural roots of the Russian people run deep and the soil of Mother Russia nurtures their soul. Communities of these dachas were scattered around the town's perimeter.

The lone road ends its journey north at the whimsically named Esso (meaning 'larch tree' in the language of the indigenous Even people). After ten hours on this desolate dirt track, unfurnished with any habitation, we tumbled out to an enthusiastic welcome from Tatiania, as substantial a fairy as ever could be imagined. We squeezed into her ramshackle guesthouse that spread itself over a weedy patch of land in three buildings of dubious stability and eccentric plumbing (cold only on the ground floor, hot only on the top). Tatiana's jolly demeanour and carefree attitude were infectious and her establishment was clearly her own idiosyncratic design. The swimming pool was unrefreshingly warm, heated by the town wide geothermal hot water system that blasted out central heating even in August. It was a shame that it did not run to ground floor showers. The kitchen she presided over produced delicious, though unusual breakfast fare including *tvorog* – a patty of fried cottage cheese and semolina served with sour cream and wild honey, rice pudding with a substantial lump of butter and best of all, crepes smothered in sweetened condensed milk. There was a sofa of palace proportions on the veranda and in the morning, before others stirred, I sat on a tenth of it writing in the early sunshine. The resident tom cat snuggled the back of my neck and scratched my shoulders with sharp claws to demand attention. From this vantage point he was able to control his territory and he frequently leapt off to chase away any furry intruder, knocking my *tvorog* in his haste.

As might be expected from members of the International Dendrology Society, the accumulation of expertise was formidable. Trees, of course, but also woody plants and herbaceous perennials were studied, photographed and discussed, hand lenses brought out for minute examination and adaptability and taxonomy vigorously debated. Victor Kuzevanov, the Director of the Irkutsk Botanical Garden, botanical boffin and polymath, fielded questions on everything from habitat to politics and his delightful wife Elena, herself an experienced ecologist, soothed the temperamental and provided a constant ear for worries. Amongst us we had representatives from Scotland, Wales, France, Italy, Belgium, Luxembourg, Holland, Russia, America, South Africa and Australia. English was the common conversational denominator, although the European aristocrats (of which there were six) could never make up their mind as to whether French, English or Italian suited their mood best. These aristos behaved true to their lifestyle, interrupted conversations, expected attention, were unprepared with maps or money (one had brought seven copies of *Country Life* just to read the bridge column) but nevertheless were impressively knowledgeable on flora of all kinds.

We flew into the Valley of the Geyers in a rattling army M20 helicopter. On the way, there had been spectacular views of the snow covered summits of volcanoes whose icy slopes were patched with bare shale areas that released steam from their centrally heated interior. At 13,000 ft (4,000m), the helicopter must have been flying at its maximum altitude but to those inside, crouched on the metal deck and jockeying for a view from the open portholes, this was of no concern. The rear double doors were done up with string and there were cracked panes in the forward cabin but, as if to compensate, there were three pilots. Unaccountably, all the military helicopters was painted bright orange so there was some measure of comfort that hostilities were not expected. The valley – a UNESCO World Heritage Site – is apparently frequented by 155 species of bird, several hundred brown bears, wolves, marmots and red foxes. I saw only a few insignificant birds and a single squirrel.

But all around us and very visible were the elements of volcanic activity. Blue ice slid into fumarole fields, asphyxiating gases seeped out of the earth, streaks of aluminium sulphate, iron, calcium and magnesium stained the valley. Billowing clouds of sulphur poisoned the air as though yellow dragons had vented their wrath with open jaws and decaying fangs. Tiny vents in the crust of soil whistled like boiling kettles, larger fumaroles roared like the Flying Scotsman tackling a gradient and mud pots slurped their ooze like grey suppurating sores. Pyroclastic

House in Esso, Kamchatka

Woman at Esso

Moscow.
Demonstration
by supporters
of old USSR

blasts from 18 miles (30kms) below the surface brought up iron hydroxides that flowed in hot streams of orange, red, maroon and violet and tainted the air. Black foam covered boiling pots and on a greater scale, all this hydrothermal activity produced acidic lakes of startlingly coloured azure, carmine or yolk yellow. It was as though these mountainous hillsides, so verdant and in August still shaking off winter's deep blanket, had caught some dreadful disease which, ebola-like, threatened to gnaw at its flesh. It was all malodorous, rather disgusting, strangely fascinating and oddly attractive.

In this land of natural plenty on which the indigenous people have lived for a few hundred years, it seemed odd that there was little evidence of any introduced animal. Travelling up the 310 mile (500kms) road, I saw six cows (two of which freely grazed the verges of Esso's dirt streets) and two sheep. But there were no goats or pigs or herds or anything on four legs. Perhaps the climate defeated them or the inhabitants were content with fish and potatoes; the diet was certainly plain but the people were undoubtedly healthy.

For three hours we climbed up from Paratunka in first gear. Our intended six wheeled, cross-country, altitude-defiant, insulated, go-anywhere vehicle had broken down so instead, a school bus was requisitioned. This gallant little 20-seater, piled with luggage underneath, on the top and inside down the aisle, took us from sea level to 3,350 ft (1,000m) without a hint of trouble. It wheezed and groaned, its gears grated, its springs sprang and it complained every step of the rutted way but it did its job and its duty and earned our applause when we finally reached our destination of the geothermal station whose turbines supplied Petropavrosk with its electricity. Here were other leaking hillsides and great pipes snaked around carrying steam gathered from deep, subterranean sources. Steam escaped from every pore, sulphur stenched the air and there was a vaguely sinister, experimental feel to the place enhanced by military men on the gates and on patrol around the perimeter wire.

The chatelaine of the hotel attached to this explosive complex (possibly the only female on the establishment), had close-cropped banana yellow hair and wore a tunic (to call it a dress would give it a fashionable sophistication it did not deserve) patterned like a large chequer board; already broad, this emphasized her stoutness in all directions. She was emphatic in her instructions to remove our boots and glowered in the way that is reserved for Russian hotel managers who adopt the attitude that guests are privileged to be in their establishment. Dinner was precision cut wedges of pressed grey mincemeat – a variation from the minced theme of rissoles, meatballs, hamburgers or spoonfuls of grey grit. But the pancakes, smothered in sweetened condensed milk and honey, were so deliciously decadent that they obliterated all the previous horrors. Banana Hair gave a talk one evening on the geothermal station and the facts were impressive: the supply of all of the electricity for Petrovpavlosk, the steam brought up from 980 ft (3,000m) below ground, 300 tons (31,300kgs) of super-heated water per hour through turbines manufactured to a tolerance of one micron and the whole plant buried under 40 ft (12m) of snow in winter. For all this, the whole place resembled the HQ of a scrap metal merchant and traction engine enthusiast.

A better meal came later in the form of smoked sockeye salmon – blood red and served as a chunky steak – fresh rye bread and a jar of gherkins all laid out on windcheaters spread over the fine volcanic sands of the Gorelaya Volcano. Here was honesty, health and hunger. The volcano puffed intermittently as though enjoying a pipe of Capstan Ready Rubbed and patches of snow covered its slopes like the flanks of a gypsy piebald. On the highest edge of the tree line, some trees were still bandaged in snow. Intent on filling my cup from the stream that flowed through our encampment, I was quickly prevented by Victor who then explained the toxic cocktail of volcanic run offs. In the distance, the Avachinskaya volcano sent out its own smoke signals. Any plant here that is not herbaceous and has wisely disappeared into the ground for the long winter tends to be prostrate. To be flattened by snow up to 40 ft (12m) deep from October to May and then battered by wind would keep anyone prone on the ground. The carmine flowered *Rhododendron kamcatchiensis*, which covered hillsides in splashes of blood, was no more than a foot high; even lower was a willow (*Salix acturus*) that crept sideways for perhaps 100 years and there was an azalea that barely achieved three inches. Elsewhere, larches had been so buffeted that they leant over at an angle of 45 degrees.

'On Wenlock Edge the wind's in trouble,

The gale, it plies the saplings double.'

Heaven knows what Houseman would have made of the saplings here.

One evening at Patunka we were invited to a local knees-up. Alexander Yastrebov, "Call me Sacha," also called himself a farmer running to two sheep and half an acre of cabbages and whose ramshackle establishment was indistinguishable from any other of the litter covered, half built, half broken 'farms'. He was a bear of a man and had a sideline in entertaining tourists who wandered to this remote place. "I am the best musician farmer and the best farmer musician," he growled as he introduced us to the meal that he was to serve. It was growing wild beside the track – *artemesia*, hogweed, thistle, garlic and a couple of other unlikely candidates and we looked at each other in much the same way that those gathered at Tyburn may have considered their imminent fate. However, seated in his giant tepi shaped *chooma*, warmed externally by a log fire and internally by vodka from a mountain of bottles, we tucked into all of these local weeds; cooked, sweetened and seasoned, they were excellent eating. All the while, we clapped to the beat of the bear's Russian folksongs and marvelled at the ability of his piano to withstand the thrashing it got from his massive paws. We joined in toasts to friendship, marriage, health, happiness, universal tolerance and at least another seven and wobbled home singing *Kalinka* and *Moscow Nights*. Sobered and sore headed in the morning, the majority opinion was that Sacha was an incompetent farmer, a good musician and a genius at milking susceptible tourists. But who cared, we had all had fun.

Flying back westward and homeward, I stopped off in Moscow. The city was sweating a temperature of 100°F (37.5C) and enveloped in smoke from 800 disastrous forest fires to the east. Hotel Kempinski offered salvation with a huge bed, a choice of five different pillows (including cherry stones and horsehair), a music system with seven pages of instruction and breakfast at £40. The contrast with Kamchatka could not have been greater and for two nights it offered outstanding comfort.

At 9.30 am on a Sunday morning I shared the Kremlin only with a group of Japanese women, masked for a plague and waving menopausal fans. Large, bored women with dyed hair sat grumpily at the entrance to each of the eight cathedrals. The sublime interior of the Archangel Cathedral was almost as obscured with billowing incense as the absurd exterior of St Basil's Cathedral which loomed up eerily in the noon gloaming. I felt sorry for the wedding couples who clearly did not expect their wedding day photograph in front of the cathedral to have the clarity of a November fog. At 3 pm five couples queued up for their murky reminders and five stretch limos each with a roof smothered with a confusion of organza and plastic roses waited patiently. I wondered if they had seen the advertisement in the Moscow Times, English edition (Editor, Scott Machesney) – '*We will perform the wedding of your dreams with beautiful music, lovely photographs, a huge cake and a hundred metre wedding trail. (Yes, really!) Together we will build the Cathedral of All Being in Love. Also kid's program*'. Later at Dom Kingie, Russia's largest bookshop, I wandered the un-airconditioned literary acres asking, "*Vi gavarri pa angliski?*" The po-faced staff had one reply, "*Nyet,*" but a friendly customer helped secure the Bears of Kamcatchka that I was searching for.

In the huge amusement area of Gorki Park, the grass was brown, the trees withered, the booths shut, the rides unridden and the pools algae green, and it was August holiday time! Only the fountains displayed any pleasure. Scarcely any birds fluttered in the reeky haze.

'*….few sparrows twitter in the smoky trees as though they called to one another "Let's play at country".*'

The city was domineering and graceless with streets motorway wide and buildings of great size and solidity. There were no cyclists or mopeds and no taxis. The

Russian soul, so deep and so full of passion, was absent. Paris has beauty, London is cosmopolitan, Rome has history and Vienna elegance. Moscow has only brutality but this is leavened by the world's most lavish and gilded underground stations, exquisite 13th and 16th century churches and art museums of world class. I admired the Metro, delighted in several churches but being a Monday all the galleries were shut. Instead, I took a long and dreary walk along grand but grey streets to the Novodevichy Cemetery, the resting place of the country's great and good. The giants of literature, music, the military and politics were scattered among other lesser notables. I had marked my map for the tombs of Chekhov, Eisenstein, Gogol, Khrushchev, Oistrakh, Prokofiev, Rubinstein, Scriabin, Shostakovich, Stanislavsky and Yeltsin. Such was the tangle of headstones (some large and beautiful) and the difficulty of interpreting their Cyrillic inscriptions that I found none of them. There were many fine and distinguished faces – aviators, commanders of all kinds and heroes of the Soviet Union; they were cast or chiselled as they no doubt lived, proud and distinguished. It seemed a sad end to a visit full of expectation.

'Thus step for step with lonely sounding feet
We travelled many a long, dim, silent street.'

I headed for the indulgent arms of the Kempinski and then the green, green grass of home.

Postcard Home

The wild and lonely landscapes of Kamchatka
Have barren beauty but here the gnats are
Spitfire sized and meals are fish with vodka.
(The dateline could provide a stimulant –
Another mile, it's up my fundament!)
By helicopter or by truck our days are spent
Discovering the flora – stunted, rare,
With eagles, reindeer, salmon everywhere.
Volcanoes steam, bears roam without a care.
Tomorrow Moscow and nothing clean to wear.

Ladakh

March 2011

'Mountains are not chivalrous. Indifferently, they lash those who venture among them with snow, rock, wind and cold.' – *George Schaller*

To camp at 15,000 ft (4,500m) in a Himalayan winter needs help, at least it does for me, and I sought this at Atkinson's homeopathic pharmacy in New Cavendish Street. With 1,000 little boxes arranged round the walls, it is like a Chinese herbalist but without the romance and intrigue. Strangely the assistant was Chinese; an attractive young woman with a green butterfly slide in her shiny hair and nail polish to match.

"Some coca pills please."

"What strength you like?"

"The strongest."

"To suck or chew?"

I was thrown off balance as I looked at the exquisite young lady and hesitated.

"Melt in mouth or crush with teeth?"

Crushing sounded more fun.

"How many?"

"About 50 I think."

"Ah, big expedition. Please wait."

She was back soon with a small glass tube of saccharin sized pills – not much to chew on.

"One, three times a day. Not too many at once. Might make you little bit happy."

Really? Perhaps another 50, just in case. But reason got the better of romance and I left Miss Green Nails to her next customer.

The crumple zone of the Himalayas reaches five miles into the sky, its snowfall is

Ladakhi woman

the largest outside the poles and its glaciers feed the great rivers of Asia; the Indus, Brahmaputra, Ganges, Salween, Mekong, Yellow River and Yangtse. Here, the power of raw nature cradles the fragility of life. Bar-headed geese fly higher than Everest (their blood is high in haemoglobin to increase oxygen takeup at -50°). Snub nose monkeys live on lichens at 14,000 ft (4,200m) and a four eyed spider lives at 22,000 ft (6,700m), the highest living animal in the world. At around 15,000 ft (4,570 m) live about 4,000 snow leopards in an area that stretches from Afghanistan to Mongolia and I had come to find one.

The rain in Delhi had helped to clear the gutters but not the smog. I took a nostalgic ride in an Ambassador car to look at the 12th century tower of Qutub, drove down the Rajpath and left for the dry, clean air of Ladakh in the Himalayan foothills and the most northern state of India. The capital Leh has a winter temperature of -20° and a height of 11,200 ft (3,400m) and is a town of dogs, tourists and poplar trees. The dogs were large, woolly beasts and when they were not scavenging in ditches they lay around in the sunshine like somnolent bears. They left their faeces everywhere and fought noisily for territory and mates during the night. Donkeys and cows also populated the streets and care was needed as to where you trod. In winter, the town hibernated but spring would bring trekkers, river rafters, botanists and those intent on yoga, Zen and meditation.

Over two days we took a car and driver and Sonam Gyapso to visit the hilltop villages of the surrounding valleys. Sonam was a marvel; soft spoken with excellent English, he was a man of culture and humour whose severe military moustache was at odds with his broad smile and impossibly white teeth. He was the leading expert on the region's historical buildings but was also keen to ensure that his guests understood the Buddhist way of life and its deities. My western mind cannot grasp the concept of a family of gods or the fact (and they truly believe it to be a fact) that a person can be transfigured to return to earth as the embodiment of a previous being. In Tibetan Buddhism a *tulku* (a high ranking lama) can choose the manner of his (or her) rebirth; it could be the same again or even an animal or insect. Not only that, they can make known the place of their next birth and details of the house etc; this greatly assists the monks who are assigned to locate the reincarnated being. But engagement in metempsychosis, metamorphosis, materiality or any other such wordy mores would have spoilt the day. The poplars with their uncannily slim posture reached up to an azure sky and marked the roadsides like sentries along a ceremonial route. Dzos, dzomos (the females), donkeys, cattle as small as their owners (some of the cattle apparently crossed with Jerseys!) and shaggy ponies wandered the tracks and withered apricots still clung to bare twigs. Great wide plains of uninhabited gravel stretched to the snow clad mountains and down the centre of this dry, uncompromising landscape flowed the River Indus, benign in broad reaches but savage in ravines. The previous August, engorged by exceptional rain, the river had carried away property and lives.

At the village of Basgo, we happened upon their annual *puja* under the direction of a wizened lama whose embroidered tunic and various elaborate garments had never experienced the cleansing properties of soap and neither, it seemed, had he.

'A lama of the sect of Yuru
Got more dirt as the holier he grew.
He was once heard to say
"It's twelve years to the day
Since I washed." And to smell him it's true!'

In bright sunshine, 100 or so villagers ate a lunch of rice, lentils and beans served from great cauldrons with a side order of coleslaw. In an orchard of almond and apricot trees, families sat around gossiping while black cows with unkempt and hairy coats (no Jersey genes here) wandered amiably around hoping for an unfinished plate. These were polished off with a cinereous tongue as though they might be a hungry dog. Lunch over, the village assembled in the temple courtyard for an hour or so of chanting. In the orchard the cows scavenged the last of the rice and beans.

With China to the east and Pakistan to the west, the Indian army has large cantonments spread throughout the valley. I was told that they numbered at least two divisions, along with the air force and the Ladakhi Scouts, *'The Mountain Tamers'*, who specialized in alpine warfare. Each regiment declared their motto of military bombasticism. *'Faith and Valour'*, *'Fire, Fury and Fidelity'* and *'We Serve the Nation'* were signposted in bright colours. Along the road, equally colourful signs warned *'Stay*

Alert, Accidents Avert', 'After Whisky, Driving Risky' and *'Safety Brings Cheers, Accidents Bring Tears'.*

The gods of the mountains had blessed us on our first day of trekking with glorious skies; iridescent and cloudless, passionless and bitter, they were the deep, dark, saturated blue that is only found in the purest, highest and coldest areas of earth. The going was generally easy with a steady ascent up the winding valley of a frozen river. Granite walls 1,000 ft (304m) high sloped back on each side, occasionally overlaid with shale so small it was like pulverised bark. Sparse willow and poplar occurred in little naked copses and a sprinkling of withered sage provided seeds for coveys of mountain partridge. Jigmet Dadul, our snow leopard expert, dashed about setting up scopes to scan the mountains for signs that a leopard had passed though. Paw prints in the snow, scat, the discarded feathers of a meal of snow pigeon or the oily stain on an overhanging rock from its rubbed neck glands; all marked its passing. As the narrow path followed the valley that twisted as a vine searches for light, the sun and shade alternated. All around, the sun fired the summits yet this steep valley was so shut away that it remained dim and foreboding two hours after daybreak. A lammergeyer circled above on its great nine feet wide wingspan, trailing its shadow on the snow as it searched for carrion. In atmosphere this cold it seemed impossible that there could be sufficient thermals to ride but no beat was needed to keep it aloft. It vanished into the leaden light of the ravine and its place was taken momentarily by a golden eagle that alighted on a rocky ridge and sat haunched and glowing, its nape feathers lifting in the wind before it disappeared over the tops of the cliffs. Further on, a pair of blue sheep scurried up a slope to become silhouetted against the sky. Like tightrope walkers, they made their way along the ridge; perilous to an onlooker but an easy game for them. One, as though intent upon a demonstration of its skill, leapt to a pinnacle and while standing there with its feet clamped together on the rocky needle point, it turned its head to accept the applause. Later, in the violet light of dusk and the approaching bitter cold of the night, Eliot came to mind:

'...*the evening is spread out against the sky*

Like a patient etherized upon a table.'

We pitched camp beside a track that linked the village of Zingchen on the banks of the Indus below us, with the hamlet of Rumbak that lay close to glaciers above us. Six shiny orange domes sprang up on stony ground in a grove of coppiced willow, through which small herds of sheep and goats came to nibble on the young shoots. Groups of pack ponies and donkeys regularly made their way down this local highway. Sometimes they were loaded with the equipment of an expedition, at other times with wood brought up from the valley or unladen, they wandered through the orange mushrooms risking entrapment from guy ropes and leaving piles of dung as they went. So mixed were the genes of the goats that their ragged and shaggy coats ranged from dark cinnamon to pale cream and their horns were straight, curved or corkscrew and swept backwards or sidewards. As they passed they tangled with the willow twigs or the briars of *Rosa sericia* and the coils of *Clematis montana*.

Beneath the frozen surface of the Rumbak River, water rumbled like the grumblings of some mountain deity who resented our intrusion. Rusty, sludgy green, black and beige daubs were splattered over rocks where an assortment of lichens cohabited. A waterfall, frozen with the stalactites that marked the sudden start of winter, was adorned with lengths of prayer flags which danced on its glassy surface and were so worn by the wind as to be diaphanous. In the river, stands of willow were up to their knees in ice; miraculously they were starting to bud. There were walnuts too entombed in the ice and on the river margins, 15 ft (4.5m) tall roses, protected by savage thorns from scavenging donkeys, still had scarlet hips clinging on from the previous autumn. *Caragana* thorns, their bare black snaky stems armed with clusters of pink but vicious spines were adorned with the wool of passing animals. Occasionally there was a scattering of hare droppings. The hares would make a good meal for the red fox I had heard barking in the night. In the shadow darkened creases of the ravine, the temperature dropped ten degrees from the sunny parts. I had on six layers of arctic clothing but in these darkened areas I was shivering. Two nights ago, under clear skies and a full moon, the temperature was -32°. We crossed and recrossed the frozen river, fearful that the groaning river god might have laid the ice thinly to catch a disbeliever. I trod warily, testing each step, glad of the earth that was sometimes scattered to provide a grip.

Camping is no fun; it may be the only option in places such as these but it is uncomfortable, exhausting and in cold and wet conditions particularly unpleasant. On waking (something of a misnomer considering that one has no recollection of being asleep), there is a struggle against recalcitrant zips to rid oneself of the sleeping bag in which the night has been spent plugging draughty gaps. The inner surface of the cramped nylon igloo is covered in ice. Then, with courage akin to sea bathing at Christmas, the five layers that have masqueraded as warmth during the night are peeled off and gasping at the cold, the long johns are discarded and the daytime substitute, crisp with frost, is pulled on in feverish haste. A small bowl of hot water was placed outside the tent during these handicapped, hunchbacked, knock-kneed and misshapen movements. I was astonished to find that it was even colder outside the tent than inside. The flannel for the minimal of ablutions was as rigid as cardboard and the frozen toothpaste needed a good warm soak before it could be squeezed. The ironic wonder of all this unpleasantness is that I had paid for it.

Ladakh mules on way
to campsite

Meals were cooked on a kerosene fuelled pressure burner and from a collection of battered aluminium pots, delicious vegetarian dishes of eccentric variety were served up in huge portions. Spicy soup, tofu stew, chow mein, tuna momo (boiled dumplings) and cheese pizza were typically and collectively on the plate; hot fruit salad was the cook's favourite. In the sanctuary of the warm dining tent, the talk is of our objective, *Panthera unica*, the snow leopard. It is rare, elusive, mysterious and so well camouflaged that from a few yards away it can be almost invisible. Its coat of pale, misty grey is patched with black rosettes whose edges are blurred by the rich depth of its fur. It is a solitary beast and an adult weighs in at around a 100 lbs (45 kilos) and is six feet long including a tail that is as long as its body; as soft as pashmina and as heavy as a marine rope, this tail is both a scarf and a counterweight. It is a crepuscular hunter capable of killing creatures three times its size, has enormous paws and is able to leap 15 ft (4.5m) in a single bound. There are thought to be between 3,500 and 5,000 living in the horseshoe of high peaks that encircle central Asia and nominally belonging to a dozen countries including Pakistan, India, Nepal, Mongolia and China. This is a realm that has more affinity with clouds than nation states. In the state of Ladakh there are thought to be about 200. Put simply, we were searching an area the size of Switzerland for an almost invisible animal the size of a large dog, in inhospitable mountain terrain during a Himalayan winter.

We searched diligently for five days but then came The Great Leopard Day.

Breakfast was late: where was the porridge? At that moment the guide of our two neighbouring Indian photographers burst in.

"There's a cat up the Husing Valley."

Breakfast was abandoned and I set off at a run, shoelaces akimbo, tent flaps ajar and camera frozen. Namgyal the cook left the eggs, forgot that his apron was still around him and ran with me. The trail was hard; it crossed the ice river, slithered across loose dust and shale, wound around rock falls and then steadily and exhaustingly crept uphill through deep snow over scattered stones. My lungs hurt, the thumping of my heart could have been heard back at the camp and for an hour I trudged and panted and climbed and slipped and climbed and gasped and listened to the wind of my breath. Would I be there in time? Was the message clear? Would I die before I got there? But there she was, in the lens of the scope 500 yards (450 m) away across a valley, lying on a warm rock ledge, sunbathing and asleep. Posed and positioned like a Himalayan Olympia, she enraptured a dozen voyeurs, occasionally lifting her head to stretch a cramped muscle or move her tail which lay alongside her as thick and furry as a bell ringer's rope. She claimed suzerainty not only on this great rocky cliff face where she lay but the whole valley, and we claimed our prize.

With our steps lightened by the achievement of our goal, we wound our way further up the valley to the mountain village of Rumbak which lay at 13,500 ft (4,100m) looking out to a glacier and a multitude of interlocking valleys. All of these were mantled in snow. The nearest vehicle access point was a four and a half hour trek away from this isolated community of nine houses. A monastery of low, drab buildings was barnacled to the mountain side and manned by three ageing monks. All lived here harmoniously, if precariously. Alongside them, and sometimes with them, lived their animals: four pack ponies, a dozen donkeys, a few cows, several dzos and a male yak named Tashi who was entrusted with keeping the dzo population flourishing and at regular intervals performed his duties enthusiastically.

'The profile of the gentle dzo
Always seems so full of woe.
I'm afraid he worries so
Upon the fact that he's a dzo.
His mother was a buffalo,
His pa a yak – and that's a dzo.'

In our homestay house there was a framed certificate to show that Tsewang Dolma had attended a five day course in the Basic Skills of a Homestay Provider. This did not seem to include providing fuel for the primitive stove in the centre of our room, and a 200 rupee bribe to Dolma's father who did the root splitting (any other wood being scarce above the tree line) did not provide much either in spite of gestures that such largesse was intended to finance a woodpile the size of a bus. When the father came in to replenish the stove, he squatted for a while warming himself. Similarly, Dolma, on bringing spicy marsala tea and chapattis (their toughness eased with a generous spread of wild apricot jam), stayed to observe the strange ways of her guests. Electricity came from a village generator and a satellite dish allowed the India v England World Cup cricket match to be broadcast to enthusiastic applause by the whole village and its guests.

Down from the mountains and back in Delhi (a heavy fall of snow had brought travel to a halt for two days), I sought warmth and set out for Bharatpur in another creaking but sturdy Ambassador with Mr Subass at the wheel. On the way there were pedestrian crossings, roadside markets and whenever there was a blade of grass to crop there were goats. Anything mechanised was overloaded with goods and overburdened with people. There were tractors, pedalled rickshaws, two person tuk-tuks holding nine persons and buses with the roof as loaded as the interior; trucks of doubtful mechanical integrity were beaten, battered, bent, bashed, broken and bereft; insouciant, plodding camels pulled enormous carts of dried dung and there were individual wandering cows and a herd of sheep. All this is the familiar traffic of an Indian road but this was the dualled National Highway N2 from Delhi to Calcutta.

The Barg at Bharatpur had been the shooting lodge of a Rajasthani prince and a huge marble slab was engraved with the bag for the years to 1964. The King of Malaya was a guest in 1961 with a bag of 350 birds (an astonishing slaughter by 50 guns in half a day); the King of Afghanistan had topped this with a bag of 600 birds and 77 guns and more moderately in 1960, the party of General Sir Richard Hull KCB, DSO had a bag of 200 with 57 guns. The Barg's cool and spacious marble guest houses were the antithesis of everything I had left behind a few hours ago in the alpine conditions of Ladakh. It adjoined Keoladeo National Park, the premier bird sanctuary of India. Avian migrators rest together in this staging ground either going south for warmth or going north to escape the heat but in whatever direction, they were going to breed. At dawn, I joined my naturalist guide Balraj Singh in a rickshaw whose wheels were uncomfortably misaligned and pedalled by a giant and amiable Sikh, to discover the huge flocks of birds that make this temporary stopover. Sarus cranes, black necked cranes and the endangered Siberian cranes were fattening up on the frogs of the wetland, bar-headed geese (the ones that fly over Everest) grubbed around in the mudflats, herons in many varieties lunged into the water to catch their breakfast and 100 different resident species went their separate ways in the light of the rising sun. In the grass and the dry forest, golden jackals, spotted deer and porcupine lived in natural harmony.

temple trumpeter

Ladakhi princess

after Mollie Moltsworth

Connections for the homeward flight required a final night in Delhi and my agent's choice of the Ramada was an unhappy one. All the bedrooms were identical – a hermit would have been cramped in them. So bizarre was the décor that it mixed Italian renaissance, Russian glitz and contemporary furniture; there was a Watteau in the coffee shop and Vishnu in the gents. Byzantine columns supported chubby cherubs. I escaped to The Imperial, as classy as its neighbour was vulgar, but even so it was a little too extravagant in its use of scented candles that hinted of Laura Ashley. The inhabitants of the bar provided a pastiche of a decaying expat community. Two elderly but elegant European ladies, a couple of bellied and brash Englishmen disputing every decision of the World Cup cricket match being displayed and a tall forty-something in dinner jacket and pink scarf ensuring that his invitation would not be as dry as he anticipated. A selection of the lonely tinkered with a beer and rather disturbingly, a handsome fellow in a black tee-shirt and Piaget watch took the adjoining bar stool with a smile and an enquiry as to the rules of cricket. Having dined on the bar's nuts and poppadoms, I left before his friendly hand found mine.

Om shantih, shantih, shantih.

Postcard Home

Why am I here in this old town of Leh
(The highest, most time worn in all of Ladakh)
Embraced by fleece layers and a 30lbs pack?
I'm seduced by snow leopards, the rarest of cats.
If it snows they will vanish; smells me I'm lost.
It's above 12,000 feet and 30 below,
My heart's beating fast and my footsteps are slow.
Can this really be worth the sums that it cost?
But to find the Grey Ghost, the monarch of mountains
Will turn out to be the best of all bargains.

Australia

October 2011

'Modern travel is not about travelling at all; it is merely being taken to a place and is very little different from being a parcel' – *John Ruskin*

The greatest benefit of flying first class is the loo to passenger ratio; in the case of Thai Airways this is one to five. (This knowledge comes about from an accumulation of air miles rather than a generous bequest or an obscene salary.) This benefit was not available to the manacled convicts transported to Australia in rotten ships. *'An excrementitious mass', 'a swinish multitude'* – Burke; *'dreadful banditti'* – Nepean. Take your pick. The first of these arrived on 26th January 1788.

Our accommodation in The Rocks area of Sydney was built for a convict overseer and Geoff, the present proprietor, now wielded the whip. "In after two, out by twelve. Two or three rashers at breakfast?" The breakfast table was animated by a collection of foreigners who displayed their nationality by their preference for muffins and syrup, scrambled eggs and bacon or fried eggs and definitely no bacon. A small, fat, tailless terrier patrolled around the sandaled, booted, trainered or espadrilled feet begging scraps that would soon cause him to explode. The gathering included an American couple who, finding accommodation impossible in Auckland, New Zealand, on account of the Rugby World Cup semi-finals, had flown to Sydney. They were to fly back the next day to join their cruise ship whose first port of call was Sydney. Of such are the wheels of the travel trade indulgently oiled.

The convict association continued, at least in mind, when we tackled the Harbour Bridge Climb. Dressed head to toe in grey overalls; we were drilled on safety and set off shuffling in single file shackled to a wire. Snaking along a route that twisted through girders, along steel beams (one foot carefully in front of the other) crossing over transoms above eight lanes of traffic we arrived at the base of one

of the great arches. Like mountaineers nervous of slipping off the sides of a vertiginous col, we slowly shuffled our way up the outside stanchions marvelling at the view and our courage. At the top, resting under a huge flag, Sydney was set out beneath us with the sails of the Opera House set in miniature and boats buzzing about like toys in a bath. Nearby, workmen engaged in repainting, sauntered around unroped and as nonchalant as a pavement artist.

With our feet back on safe and solid ground, Asians seemed to make up a large proportion of the population and the city's taxi business had been commandeered by Indians but this vigorous city was full of the young and active that worked hard, played harder and were universally cheerful. It was all rather exhausting. Ferries constantly crossed the azure waters of the harbour, perhaps the greatest natural harbour in the world, and we boarded MS Lady Northcott to take a scenic trip to Manly on the Pacific coast. By a broad stretch of white sand bordered by neat Norfolk Island pines, families spread themselves on jolly beach towels while the bronzed and athletic played in the surf. The less active sauntered along the shops and played the gaming machines, clouds puff balled the blue sky, ice cream parlours had queues and dogs chased balls and bicycles. It was the first week of November and arriving from England the previous day, it seemed we had stumbled into a film set.

The Blue Mountains were blue, studded with vertical escarpments some of which carried waterfalls from their head that streaked the granite walls in wispy threads and isolated houses sent up smoke like strands of unspun silk. Surreally, we passed through Chipping Norton as we skirted Liverpool and then we headed north for the playgrounds of Queensland's coast and the Great Barrier Reef. This top right hand corner of the continent is only a few hundred miles below Papua New Guinea so it was surprising to find acres of sugarcane plantations, with their own railway system. Desolation Point, the landfall of Captain Cooke on 26th June 1770, belied its name with idyllic white sand sandwiched between a blue sea and a bluer sky but the reef had turned to the colour of putty, apparently a victim of pollution. This bleaching had not affected the fish and diving in the gin clear water; they stood out in technicoloured brilliance as they flitted through their concrete surroundings. The completion of our four hour flight to Adelaide in South Australia was something of a miracle since the Qantas boss, weary of union intransigence, without warning and evidently without regard to public relations, precipitately grounded every Qantas flight worldwide. The god of travellers can be vengeful but this swipe across all the flights of Australia's national airline missed ours by a whisker and we touched down in Adelaide, the last of the 802 planes of the Flying Kangaroo to land. All this was unknown to us until the audacity of the deed covered every front page the next day. Insulated from these commercial troubles by vacational tranquillity, we wandered the streets charmed by the Victorian ornamentation of the city's little villas with their frothy front gardens and wrought iron decoration. Leaving these pleasures behind, we headed down the Fleurieu Peninsular to the mainland's southernmost point at Cape Jervis. On the way, rolling hills were interspersed with ordered olive groves and vineyards, contented herds of Hereford cattle and sleek horses.

We continued even further south, taking the ferry to Kangaroo Island. Here, Snelling Beach is on the south coast and its azure water is all that there is between its eucalyptus fringed shoreline and Antarctica. The water felt that way too, but New Zealand fur seals like it cool and they flopped around the rocky foreshore. The island is home to 4,000 humans, several more thousand sheep, kangaroos, wallabies and sleepy, adorable koalas. A ban on non-native animals has ensured an untainted island fauna and flora. The koalas are everyone's favourite of course but when they are not chewing eucalyptus (a more unpleasant and indigestible diet would be hard to find), they pee and poo scattering the crowd of onlookers whose upturned faces are in the vertical line of fire. The straight dirt roads were regularly and tragically the mortuary of kangaroos, wallabies, wombats and monitor lizards but the koalas never seemed to wake up long enough to unwedge themselves from their tree and venture on to dangerous arterial territory. Eucalyptus trees of many species were spread over the island and none had a disciplined habit. In attractive disarray and with their mottled bark highlighted by the sun, they lined the roads like a queue of pretty girls whose hair is flying in the wind.

On a grey and windswept day we took a look at Vivonne Bay; the pleasant name, its position adjacent to a colony of fur seals and especially its accolade of 'Voted the best beach in all Australia' had tempted a visit. There was only one other person on this five-mile long, prize-winning beach: an old man who moved slowly with a stick that dug into the sand causing him to limp. As we passed he said "There's a chill today." We agreed. "Did you know this is the best beach in all Australia?" His face was veined and scarred with the rigours of the Southern Ocean's climate and time had dragged its harrow across his brow. In a *beau laid* face, a nose akin to that of Ernest Borgnine was set amongst the furrows of Wilfred Thesiger but his eyes, sunk deep into the chasms, were bright. His olive, quilted coat was sunbleached over its shoulders and a small black dog romped cheerfully beside him, jingling several metal discs on its collar. The old man had lived on the island where he had had a small farm, then his wife died and he had moved to Adelaide. His accountant daughter had no time to look after the dog so he had adopted it and was back for a while. Each day he exercised himself and the dog on Australia's best but deserted beach. Each time we gestured to move on, another chapter of his ordinary life trickled out. We indulged him, of course; one day we too might be alone and grateful for a stranger's attention. Then he held out a gnarled and cracked hand and limped away. We had not even asked the name of his dog.

We shared the ferry back to the mainland with a monster truck hauling Aberdeen Angus cattle. The cows headed north to Adelaide and we turned east for the Great Ocean Road – ten centimetres away on the map, 1,000kms (620 miles) on the ground. We learnt of the birth of our fourth grandson at Port Fairy (not an omen, we hoped) where avenues of huge and ancient Norfolk Pines overpowered more little Victorian cottages. In one of these, we ate spaghetti in a French restaurant run by a Turk. Out on a promontory, 10,000 pelagic sooty shearwaters arrive each year within a day or two of the tenth of September. Many corpses were spread around where birds had landed only to die of exhaustion from their non-stop flight over the Pacific from Alaska. On the nearby marshland were Australian white ibis, yellow billed spoonbills and black winged stilts. In the ponds there were black swans and on the rocky shore pied cormorants hung out their wings. The hinterland was sprinkled with mimosa, elderflower and angelica of giant size, at least to a European, and casuarina pines spread their spiciness all around.

The claim of the Great Ocean Road to be one of the great drives of the world was somewhat dampened by grey skies, a drenching mist and a southerly gale but even in these conditions the startling clarity of the blue sea was apparent. The more scenic parts of the eroded coastline had been christened with fanciful names such as The Arch, The Grotto and Loch Ard Gorge. We stopped at most of them since it seemed wasteful not to indulge in these wonders; we would not be passing again. Were we to do so, it seemed doubtful that many would still remain. Previously great bays were reduced to a modest bite, London Bridge had lost one of its two arches and only five of the Twelve Apostles remained standing.

By a quirk of climate and geology, The Great Otway Forest covered the high hills that bordered the coast for many miles and we stopped off at Mates Rest (named from a British forester who regularly watered his horse there on his monthly patrol). We took a trail cut through rain forest dense with massive tree ferns, Australian red cedar (*Tone ciliate*) 100 ft (30m) high, lush undergrowth in every shade of green and noisy streams of clear water. A Japanese women's tour group in strange dresses and high heels tripped along in front negotiating the muddy paths and dripping vegetation and taking giggling photographs with tiny cameras that could have shown only a fraction of the great size of these magnificent trees. Then, as the road descended again, the lushness vanished when altitude-specific plants demanded more space and light. The resort town of Apollo Bay was busy with weekenders who patronised boarding houses and hotels with colonial names such as The Victoria, The Blenheim and The Royal. The high street was awash with tourist tat and fish and chips outlets. On the town's edge

Sidney Opera House

Sidney Harbour Bridge

Koalas

neat little clapboarded houses in pastel shades had clumps of pampas grass in the front gardens, the signature of seaside suburbia. Further on this gave way to natural stands of six feet (2m) high *artemisia* and beech myrtle. The Queen was in Australia at the time (an astonishing seventeenth visit) and the heartfelt welcome she received was surprising and stirring. The more so since the Welsh-born Prime Minister had been elected partly on her Republican sentiments. These were emphasized by a welcoming handshake rather than a deferential curtsey.

Melbourne on a hot, summer Saturday was in marriage mood. Women in chiffon and silk, topped with fascinators and tottering on six-inch heels, decorated the city centre, twittering and twirling in mutual admiration outside several pseudo gothic churches. With their scrubbed and suited beaux they rode the trams, jammed the pavements in jolly groups and added bonhomie to a city of pleasant parks, towering glass and solid stone institutions. Here was the epitome of Australia; cosmopolitan, one foot clad in the solid brogue of colonial history and the other squeezed into contemporary and comfortable footwear – immigrants justly proud, prosperous and cheerful. The convicts, their overseers and the impoverished settlers that followed them would have been astonished.

Postcard Home

We've walked through Wooloomooloo
Done Wagga-Wagga, Way-Way too.
We've tramped the Krungle-Bungles,
Climbed Harbour Bridge and cut through jungles.
(Even been to Chipping Norton, it's north of Liverpool!)
Dodged dingos, dingbats, wombats, 'roos,
Seen lorikeets and cockatoos.
Found platypus and possum
And trees weighed down by blossom.
Chewed billatong and bully beef
And Moreton Bugs on Barrier Reef.
And then, of course, there's billy tea
Brewed beneath a cool'bah tree.
Now we stretch out the chaise longue
By a shady billabong
And glass in hand unravel
Reminiscences of travel.

India II

January 2012

'The normal stigmata of a travel book are the fake intensities, discovering the 'soul' of a town after spending two hours in it and the boring descriptions of conversations with taxi drivers' – George Orwell

Mrs Varughese sat huddled but dignified in a corner of the sleeping compartment – 'First Class with AC'. I knew her name from the number of packages strewn around, each annotated in pretentiously large letters. Also strewn around were three of her 20-something-year-old daughters. They were considerably larger than Mrs V and the fact that they were two too many for the four berth compartment did not seem to worry them a jot. They readily acknowledged that a pair were 'on the waiting list' but it was quite apparent that waiting list or not they were here to stay and had probably slipped a sufficiently fat brown envelope to the conductor to ensure this was the case. In contrast to the depressing and depressed condition of the train, there was taped to the outside door a typed list of the authorised occupants of cabin B, carriage 26 of the Gondwana Express, train number 1268 departing Delhi at 1515 on Friday December 30th 2011. There were Varughese S, Varughese M, Chilton J, and Waters M (my 15 year old grandson, Max) – four persons in four berths. The Varugheses had a great deal of luggage since, as they explained, six of the brown boxes tied up in brown paper or sacking were for a friend in Jabalpur, the station after Katni where we were to disembark. None of this was of the slightest interest to me nor was the small talk which covered the weather, a cousin in Manchester and the London Olympics. My only concern was the matter of a maximum of four persons in four berths in a small, largely airless cabin for the 14 hour journey through Madya Pradesh in central India.

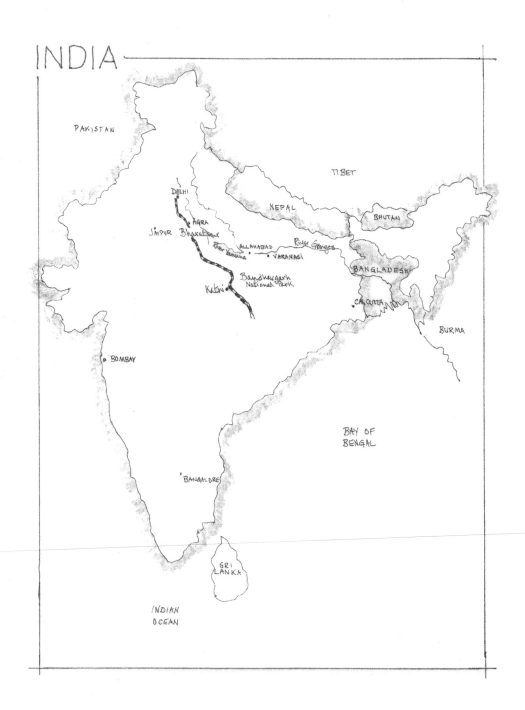

As it turned out, the adjoining cabin was not only a two-berther but at the time of departure it had not been claimed by those on the typed manifest. There was no sign of two sprinting, yelling late passengers nor were there any packages to indicate earlier possession. Experience had told me that there are those who, if accommodated less comfortably, will roam the carriages hoping for a chance encounter with empty berths; so, gathering up our modest luggage we said goodbye to the undeserving Varugheses, swiftly moved next door, locked the door and drew the curtain. At each subsequent station, we waited nervously the appearance of Singh M and Singh T but providence favoured our opportunism.

Bandhavgargh National Park has the reputation of being India's best tiger sanctuary. On New Year's Eve it seemed that most of India knew this as jeeps, packed up to eight occupants strong, each woollen-wrapped up to eye level against the chilly dawn mist, waited in eager anticipation for one of the entrance gates to open. There was a gate for each of the four sections of the huge forest and there were strict regulations. Each jeep had to conform to a standard specification (4WD, mechanically sound, no noisy exhaust etc) and have an accredited driver. Additionally, the park authorities placed a guide in each jeep as a naturalist and to report on misdemeanours. No food was allowed, no use of mobiles, no getting out of vehicles (those with weak bladders had no alternative but to suffer), no music and no smoking. Each of the jeeps (a maximum of 36 were allowed at any one time) was given predetermined routes. All this kept out sightseers, deterred the riff-raff and apparently gave the tigers a relaxed environment to wander about. But disappointingly they were not wandering about during any of the five visits we made; at least not visibly. With our driver Chitty and guide Allin we bounced around the rutted sandy tracks and saw few other jeeps but not a tiger either. There were fresh pug marks as big as my palm and on hearing roars from behind a rocky outcrop, there was a deep urge to sneak over the stones but self-preservation held this in check. Then we had to race for the gates, since to arrive late would have meant a month's suspension for our guide and driver.

Our room at the Tree House Hideaway was so hidden away that we were given a sketch map with distinguishing natural markers along the route. Right by the termite mound, left by the bamboo clump and mind the pit dug by the boars. But we carried no flag to raise above the shoulder-high grass should we have strayed, no whistle was provided and our cries would have gone unnoticed. Speke and Livingstone must have felt this way as they cut their way through the Congo but without their train of 200 bearers, driven cattle and a straggle of camp followers, our two man expedition moved faster.

The rain was expected. Saubar the manager said, "In three days."; Chitty the guide sniffed the air and declared, "Maybe a drizzle tomorrow." They should have known it was imminent with the air smelling crisp and metallic, as though it had been seared by the lightning buried in the clouds. It came during dinner, overwhelming, drenching and powerful. Like a cannonade, a sudden and thunderous roar rocked the glasses, lifted our teak table and sent a dog whimpering into a corner. Simultaneously lightning shafts stabbed the ground, the rain sheeted down as dense as the Niagara and instantly flooded the earth which in turn enveloped the open dining area. Staff rushed to lower heavy canvas awnings but the rain summoned its ally, the wind. The awnings blew in, snapping the fastenings, more glass shattered, a second salvo loosed off and then a third. The sound was immense, the curtain of rain impenetrable and the lightning spectacular. Sensing a slight easing of the tumult, we made for our treehouse, running on paths treacherous with mud and as heavy with water as a flash flood down a Saharan wadi. Reaching the salvation of our room, the barbarous elements were kept at bay although they hammered in frustration at the windows. We thought this was the climax but we were fooled. In a finale, hail sugared the ground and blasted the metal roof in a din that seemed to gather all the snare drums on earth, lightning was like photo flashes in the face of a celebrity and rolling crescendos and rockslides of thunder bombarded us for another hour. Then exhausted, the players retired, returning from time to time to crash a cymbal or two lest it be thought that their stamina was weak. We too were exhausted, in awe of the elements, exhilarated by its power and thrilled to be at its core. By noon the next day the paths were dry, the prairie rinsed and green, tendrils of steam rose from the grass, the damage was repaired and Thor's spectacular performance only a memory.

Leaving the tigerless forest, the road to the west was snarled with trucks for all of the four hour drive to Jaipur. Snaking along the edge of the highway was an almost continuous line of establishments to cater for the needs of their gaudy,

Delhi railway station

Taj Mahal

Street food, Agra

overloaded vehicles and their drivers. Tyre changers, oil changers, money changers, mechanics, places to eat and ladies to sleep with. You can feel the vibrancy of the city while still on the approach to its boundaries. The number of trucks increases even beyond the congestion of the highway, camel carts plod the main road to hobble the traffic, the colours of saris notches up from bright to dazzling and metal beaters, stone carvers, bus repairers, bed makers, car breakers and all the noisiest, dirtiest workers that crowd around a city's periphery make their presence known on the kerbside. Plunging into the city's heart, you are assaulted by the odours, the colours and the frenzy that occupies an orderly configuration of streets. The great Rajput, Mahahraja Sawai Jai Singh built Jaipur as a planned new town in 1727 and so it remains today with buildings of a single style, balanced on either side and at each end of a grid system of streets with no building more than two stories high. Five generations later when Ram Singh II was to receive a visit from the Prince of Wales, he was concerned that the intense glare might be too much for his royal visitor. This anxiety was solved with the declaration, "Paint the town pink!"; he owned the town after all. Now a city of over two million, its original central concept and buildings remain and are still pink – well, pinky/orange/apricot. Turning down a small side street that would usually take courage or naivety to enter, you come across Samode Haveli. This former merchant's house sprawls in so many lateral and vertical directions, up so many little stairs, across so many hidden balconies and down so many narrow passages that it is suggested that a guest calls for a guide to return him from his bedroom to reception. But this maze is also an infantile pleasure of hide and seek with the knowledge that you will always be found. The place is an oasis of hospitality, peace and comfort and we were gratefully seduced by its charms.

We were seduced too by the dogs we befriended at the next stop. Indians have no affection for dogs. They are tolerated as all life is and they roam around every town and village, related in appearance if not in genes. They are left to themselves to scavenge and breed and if one is killed by a truck, no tears are shed. It was a surprise therefore, on arriving at the tented camp of Chhatra Sagar, to be greeted by a Harlequin Great Dane that stood as high as my waist and around whose legs darted a trio of Jack Russells. Here was Sarko and his three small friends Castor, Pollux and Pluto. We took them all for a walk one evening and they relished chasing monitor lizards, wild boar, antelope and anything else that moved.

The camp was the inspiration of two brothers, Raj and Nandi Singh. Urbane, educated and charming they had erected a dozen spacious, elegantly decorated and well equipped tents stretched along the top of a dam. The dam had been built by their great grandfather at great expense to provide a reliable source of water to irrigate the land of his tenant farmers and their villages. Following Inde-

340

pendence, the land had been taken away from the family and distributed to their tenant farmers on whose behalf the great grandfather had almost bankrupted himself a few years earlier. The political expediency of providing social justice can slap the good with the injustices of the grasping. But now there was harmony and the evident prosperity of the local farmers was evident from the machinery and solid houses that were scattered over the former Singh estate. And efficient farming too; cumin, aniseed, chilli, aubergine, millet, barley, henna and fenugreek were all grown rotationally (with exception of henna that remains as a shrub annually cut to the ground) according to their water requirements and the marketplace. The irrigated fields needed constant attention to the ditches, the little mud walls and the diversion of water. In the community there was a hereditary division of farming skills: either you grew crops or you shepherded sheep and goats. The latter grazed the stubble and in return provided manure; additionally, the fields had a scattering of Neema trees that are pollarded annually (the grotesquely hacked stumps looked as if they had been chewed by some monstrous passing beast) and this was the shepherd's job at the end of the summer, when the shade the trees have given is no longer required but light is needed for the winter crops. The prunings are given to the sheep and goats.

The divisions of the fields were marked by vertical stone slabs, the most abundant local material. Since the stone is naturally layered like slate, it is easy to split into pieces two feet (50cm) wide and six feet (2m) long. These are dug into the ground at random heights since wild antelopes are confused by this uneven line. The stone is expensive but is justified as it is not only long lasting but it is an investment that can be realized in times of hardship. The nationwide law that prohibits the killing of any wild animal or bird results in large numbers of ducks on the reservoir and great flocks of pigeons and laughing doves who are an irritating scourge to the hardworking farmers.

Back in Delhi, the salute from the turbaned Sikh doorman at The Imperial Hotel presaged the elegant interior. The historical paintings and lithographs that crowd its public spaces in profusion form a gallery of imperial pomp and maharajas' extravagance. At the street entrance, framed by marble columns that support gates of extravagant curlicues, we hailed a dented tuk-tuk and plunged into the squalor and exuberance of Old Delhi. In a few minutes the suffering and insufferable divisions of India were manifest; the mutilated beggar appealing to the suited; the makeshift hovels that border the world's most opulent hotels; Hindus, Muslims and Sikhs coexisting in wary harmony; the odour of diesel smoke, the perfumes of the flower market, the retching nausea of blocked drains, the sweet pungency of spice; the calm order and wide avenues of New Delhi and the frenzied, crushing alleys of Old Delhi. Lives being led leisurely or distraught, indolent or desolate.

Elephants at Agra Fort

Postcard Home

Tiger, tiger burning bright
In the forests of the night
What spark caused you to ignite?
Thrilling us with savagery
Elephants to trace your route,
Tusk high grass in slow pursuit.
Took careful aim, prepared to shoot,
Captured you in imagery.
A detour then to Bharatpur,
Taj Mahal and pink Jaipur.
Always spice in plats de jour
Flavours near incendiary.
India washed in shades of sepia,
Frenzied, unfamiliar.
Sights to stimulate and stir.
Always extraordinary.

American Train Trip

March 2012

'I have seldom heard a train go by and not wished that I was on it'
– Paul Theroux, The Great Railway Bazaar

The Windy City lived up to its name. Gusts swept across Lake Michigan and played hide and seek amongst the canyons of downtown Chicago. Turning a corner meant leaning forward at an angle that would have found one scrabbling on the pavement had the wind suddenly dropped. The James R Jardine Water Processing and Purification Plant (America's largest) had white horses and salt from the pavements, scattered two days before in preparation for snow, whipped up like sharp gravel. Writing in the early '50s, Jan Morris was disillusioned by what she found. *'This festering place... in a desolate expanse of depression. There is a persistent rottenness of the place.'* She talks of The Syndicate, that central office of vice but nevertheless is heartened by *'the endearing braggadocio'* of the city's traditions. Now, these traditions have transformed the place. Better still, the snow had gone, the wind had vanquished the clouds and blue sky was now the backdrop to the architectural wonders of the city.

And what wonders they were. Here was the world's classiest vertical city. Confident and elegant, its buildings spiked the sky in shards of steel and glass in unexpected nobility. Stone structures came first following the great fire of 1871 when on 7th October and the subsequent three days, 17,000 buildings were destroyed and 100,000 inhabitants were made homeless. Myth has famously attributed the cause to Mrs O'Leary's cow that kicked over a kerosene lantern but history has recognised the anti-Irish sentiment of the time and the principal concern of newspapers to sensationalise. The facts were mundane and dreadful. The whole city including pavements and roofs was constructed of wood; in the better parts

AMERICAN TRAIN RIDE

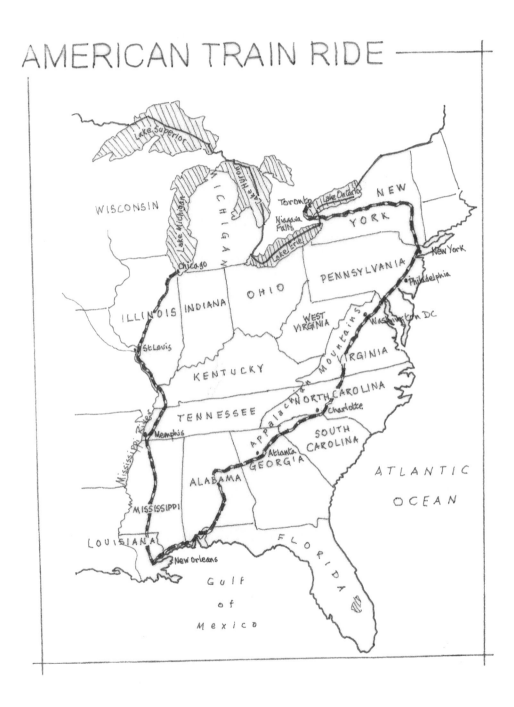

of the city even the streets were of wooden blocks and insulation was generally of horsehair. The previous month was the driest on record and on the previous day, a fire in a suburb had left the fire crews exhausted. After the fire started, the wind got up and blew the embers towards the gasworks which exploded and rendered any effort at containment useless. In circumstances that reflected London's Great Fire of 1666, a charred but clean scar presented itself and before the embers had cooled, rebuilding began but only, by ordinance, in stone. A few of these early buildings remain and are largely churches and institutions, but now there stands a textbook for architectural historians and students. The brightest and the best are there; Frank Lloyd Wright, Corbusier, Renzo Piano, Alan Johnson, Frank Gehry, Mies van der Rohe, Ralph Johnson and a whole galaxy of architects employed by their corporate clients to build higher than the last, assisted by technology that saw iron replaced by steel and air conditioning that chilled the consequences of vertical acres of glass. All these trophy structures culminated with Sears Tower, where Adrian Smith of Skidmore, Owings and Merrill in 1973 built the tallest building in America; at 1,450 ft (442m), it held this title for 25 years. (Smith famously went on to design the world's tallest building, the 2,716 ft (828m) Burj Khalifa in Dubai.)

At the concierge desk of the Sofitel Hotel, I teamed up with a diminutive grandmother to share a taxi to The Museum of Science and Industry. On her head was a knitted beret (she had bought the wool from a hospice bring-and-buy) and around her shoulders she had what appeared to be a colony of weasels with long flapping tails and several pointed noses. Her head was so sunk into this furry miscellany of a trapper's livelihood that only the beret showed. On the twenty minute ride she crammed in a generous slice of her life which included a law professorship, eight grandchildren, a passion for Wagner and a love of Bob Dylan. She was on her third visit from Texas to explore the museum and in particular, the captured German submarine U-505, which was preserved intact in a subterranean tomb and above which flew a Spitfire and a Heinkel. On the way we passed Soldiers' Field, whose classical pastiche would have been more at home on the set of Spartacus than as the stadium of the Chicago Bears. This anomaly was compounded by additional seating that floated above the façade of ionic columns and was known locally as 'The Toilet Seat'. The museum was also fashioned in a classical idiom. The eclectic mix of all these images may be the cultural meat of Chicagoans but it gave me a headache.

An Amtrak Superliner does not ride on the ocean but sometimes the irregular condition of the railway tracks so sways the coaches that nervous passengers might well reach for a lifebelt. Nevertheless, my bedroom on the upper deck was a model of compact design and comfort. Instead of a stubble-chinned, black, elderly

346

car attendant, Kiesha was thirtyish, pretty and efficient. The City of New Orleans pulled out of Union Station at eight in the evening from a bare and bleak platform that contrasted with the magnificence of the porticoed station entrance and the Grand Hall with its classical motifs of *torcheres*, dentil cornicing and vaulted roof. At the time of its completion in 1909, Chicago was pre-eminent in east/west rail traffic and it ensured it retained this position. I had dinner with an articulate architect, a jolly nun and a silent pharmacist with a red chiselled beard. Breakfast was in the company of three college graduates on their first train trip who were going to New Orleans, "To get away,

get hammered and get laid."; presumably in that order.

Memphis, the home of The Blues, The King, Muddy Waters, Casey Jones, Johnny Cash and other folk legends, was passed at dawn and beyond the Tennessee/Mississippi state line swamp cypress, greening willow and dispirited, dreary stubbled fields combined to an indifferent landscape. Crumbling shacks, the detritus of abandoned machinery and deprived humanity lay in sad and squalid communities. Here was the begetter of the tales of Twain, Steinbeck, Faulkner and Williams but then Yazoo went by and cherry trees were in bloom along with azaleas, camellias and magnolias. The Louisiana bayou followed, sinister with rotting logs, alligators and stagnant water occasionally enlivened with Cajun or Creole clapboarded settlements. And then, New Orleans itself, the prize of Generals Jackson and Sherman; the backdrops of *Mississippi Burning, Easy Rider, A Streetcar Named Desire, Steel Magnolias* and *Dead Man Walking*. My stomach called for jambalaya and gumbo but the streets of the French Quarter were clogged with fans of The Southern Basketball Championships universally clad in blue. They choked Bourbon Street where traditional jazz had been elbowed out by blaring pop. The Hustler Club and its ilk, with long-legged and slim-hipped temptresses, dazzled the street with neon signs but tradition survived at classy Galatoire's which kept the blue shirts at bay with a jacket-only policy, although Arnaud's had succumbed to allowing its sneering, black tied waiters to serve a jacketless visitor such as me. *Breakfast at Antoine's* was one of my mother's favourite books and in a loving and nostalgic spirit I knocked at its doors at 8 am but no one came. But at Brennan's, another local foodie institution, the queue was into the street waiting for their breakfast of five courses, each with a different wine and kick started with an absinthe cocktail. Seventy three million visitors swamp the French Quarter each year; it seemed that half of them had come early. I escaped on a tram whose final stop was in the Garden District and wandered the neat and tidy streets and admired the white, porticoed mansions of the city's old established families. Here, on high ground in August 2005, their owners could have looked down on the devastation of Hurricane Katrina that broke the levies and swept inland for 40 miles (64 kms) in the worst natural disaster in American recorded history. The single-storey timber homes in the Ninth Ward were under 20 ft (6m) of sea water and today the area remains derelict and abandoned.

The swamps of the bayou are only a short ride from the city centre and on one of them, I stepped aboard a perilously frail craft with a huge and deafening aft propeller which shot across the water, the reeds and hyacinths with exhilarating speed. I shared this flat bottomed craft with a raucous but good-natured group of eight young men on a stag weekend. They brought with them a crate of beer which was so soon finished that a detour was made to purchase another. This too went as quickly as the first so whenever an alligator was spotted, it was greeted with boozy yells of salutation. This did not deter the beasts in any way since bizarrely, they were more concerned with snapping up the white marshmallows that were scattered on the water to attract them. Back on Bourbon Street in the early evening I was heartened to find a group of hobos, either penniless or artfully distressed, plucking at guitars and banjos, scratching a washboard, scraping a violin and blowing a battered clarinet. They were first class. On another corner, four young black people made good music from dented cornets and a squeaky trombone.

The long haul north on The Crescent first passed by 100-year-old Cypress Grove Cemetery where 14,000 bodies are encased in tombs of granite, marble and cast iron. Since these are all intentionally above ground, they have escaped all the floods; the living may have drowned but the dead have endured. In the dining car, a southern breakfast of crab cakes, grits and cinnamon bread was shared with Sallie and Vincent who were on the last lap of a 19-day train journey of which only six nights had been spent in a hotel; they were planning to do it again. The swamps of Mississippi gave way to the gentle slopes of the Blue Ridge Mountains of Virginia and the Appalachians. Aberdeen Angus cattle were scattered through undulating pasture and stands of shagbark hickories and pecans. Sometimes the sun caught a group of dogwoods whose upturned flowers covered long drooping branches, like an extravagant serving of fried bantam eggs. Up through Maryland and West Virginia the fields became neatly fenced, the grass greener and peeling paint was a source of neighbourly disapproval. By the time The Potomac was crossed, affluence flourished to the edge of the tracks.

On a morning that sparkled much like that dreadful day in 2001, the 9/11 Memorial was crowded and long lines snacked around the hoardings of the surrounding building sites. The police presence was overwhelming with command cars, chase cars, patrol cars, cameras, X-ray checks and a burly, surly cop at every corner. No chances were being taken although it seemed unclear what assault could be mounted on the two immense, square pits that mark the sites of the World Trade Center's twin towers. The four walls of each pit (collectively named Reflecting Absence) cascaded with a perpetual torrent of water that vanished into a central void. Lost friends and lost hopes? It was simple, dignified and monumental. As the sun dipped behind the crenellated sky high roofscape, I walked The High Line. Here a railway, raised above the street and constructed to serve the wholesale warehouses of meat and vegetables, fell into disuse and disrepair following its commercial submergence to truck deliveries. Nature claimed the tracks for a while but then spawned an imaginative idea of a second-storey parkway that would twist along the unproductive rails in a three kilometre walk. Piet Oudolf was commissioned to spread his prairie planting in linear appeal and birch, willow, *daphne, aralia* and hazel supplied structure. Benches, chairs and picnic tables completed an urban felicitation that was being appreciated by many strollers on a barmy evening.

With an appetite honed by a day of walking, I tried to reserve a table at the legendary steakhouse of Peter Luger in Brooklyn and was offered the last remaining place of the day at 4.45 pm. Unwilling to indulge in a teatime slab of meat, I went later to The Strip House, having been assured by my hotel that the flesh on offer was for the peckish rather than the prurient. In spite of the heads of the waiters being covered in black skull caps that suggested that a pigtail should hang down their back, a prime, corn-fed, thirty-day aged, USDA-certified, 14-ounce filet mignon, seared at an industrial 1,800 degrees was brought to the table with the reverence it deserved. Taste and texture merged in juicy heaven.

While New Orleans was packed with basket ballers, New York suffered an onslaught from the school Spring Break. Most of these holidaying students disappeared into the Apple Store and I went to MoMA – the Metropolitan Museum of Modern Art. Here are gathered a representative collection of the world's greatest confidence tricks, also known as contemporary art. White on White, Scribbles on White, Heavier Scribbles on White, A Wall Pitted by a Single Rifle Shot. Since they are all worth countless millions my judgement seems to be awry.

The last leg of this rail journey started at New York's Pennsylvania Station

Amtrak, City of New Orleans

Street musicians, New Orleans

where even at 6.30 am commuter trains were rattling in from the suburbs. The Maple Leaf was not a sleeper train but there were comfortable seats. The track ran beside the Hudson River and on its high, steep banks, houses were perched on tall concrete columns. Across the aisle, a middle-aged far eastern couple gabbled away incessantly. The man was smart in a grey silk suit and new white trainers while his wife had amber rings threaded through her long hair. I asked them where they came from but was met by wide smiles and wider arm waving. Curious I asked, "Passport?" and was shown a pair of brand new Canadian passports. They had not even enough English to say, "No speak English." Two rows up were a couple of Tibetans in national costume. The formalities at the border required all the passengers to disembark and on re-joining the train, Mr and Mrs Silk Suit were absent.

The scenery became wild and open with great wet areas bordered by reeds and populated by ducks, geese and an occasional swan. Further north near the towns of Amsterdam, Utica, Rome and Syracuse there were areas of deserted and disorderly industrial land and abandoned factories. In contrast, having crossed the border into Canada at Niagara, for many miles the landscape was precision planted with orchards and occasional vineyards. There were greenhouses too, very tall and covering many acres. In Toronto at the formidable Fairmont Royal York, there were reassuring portraits of the Queen and Prince Philip in the cavernous lobby. This huge, stone-built establishment is the grandmother of the city's hotels and her arms enfold a thousand bedrooms, measureless corridors of flock wallpaper, chandeliers to rival Versailles, 20 lifts of elaborate brass work and several acres of Axminster in colours of mud and gold. Anxious to escape this stygian labyrinth, I enquired of the concierge about a trip to Niagara Falls and he regarded me for a while before suggesting I would be best served by a private car and driver; the round trip would be $480. The next morning I took a Megabus for $22. One fifth of the world's fresh water pours over the Falls and it seemed that half of that fell in spray over the land beside the gorge. In spite of a bright, cloudless sky, the air was as saturated as a Braemar mist. The rush of water was undoubtedly impressive and emphasized the stupidity of falling over it in a barrel.

The next day I was to fly home and as always the anticipation was heart-warming. I reflected on the trip: Chicago, the epitome of a skyscraper city – stylish but with panache, grand, dignified and even noble. New Orleans' French quarter with the vulgarity of Bourbon Street but fringed by back streets of charm and personality. New York, brash, demanding, part overpowering, part empathetic. Toronto, cosmopolitan, polished, thrusting, with high-rise glass and high living. Amtrak, utilitarian, slow and scenic. I do not expect to return to any of these but they will linger long in my thoughts.

Postcard Home

I'm riding the rails of the US of A
From Windy City and all the way
Past Nashville, Yazoo and Memphis music,
The blues, The King and all that's rhythmic.
Through the land of Faulkner, Steinbeck, Twain
To voodoo, Big Easy and bayou's wet plain.
Jambalaya and jazz feed body and soul
Then Amtrak speeds North to its final goal
Through eleven states and The Appalachians
To bite the Big Apple. But the journey still runs
To Canadian Niagara and its frozen fall.
Then, odyssey over, I reach Montreal.

Guyana, Tobago and Panama

November 2013

'For day wear, drill or palm beach shirts or light suits are general. Revolvers are not usually necessary' – South American Handbook, 1947

On Halloween there was only a single sandpiper on the mile long beach of silver sand. As it tried to scale the sandbar we both dodged the froth of the incoming tide; she scurried, I plodded. Barbados seemed to be half built bungalows with paint in short supply but an airport's edge is never prime and I had to leave early the next morning.

Guyana yields only to its neighbour Surinam in claiming to be South America's smallest country but it punches far above its weight. Area aside, everything is big or biggest: giant otters, giant anteaters, the giant armadillo and the giant river turtle; here lives the world's largest rodent, the capybara; the largest snake, the anaconda; the largest bat, the false vampire; the Americas' largest eagle, the harpie; its largest cat, the jaguar, and the world's largest water lily, victoria amazonica (three feet across). Some countries have some of these but no other country has all of these. Added to these are 1000 species of trees, 815 different birds, 420 different fish, 300 reptiles and amphibians and 225 species of mammals. I have always been seduced by the colourful splendour of tropical birds and their evocative names. How could anyone resist these local residents:

Bronzy Jacamar, Zig-Zag Heron,
Golden Sided Euphonia
Guinian Puffbird, Crimson Fruitcow,
Rufus Crowned Elaenia.
Violaceous Trogon, Dusky Purple Tuft,
Spangled Cotina, Painted Parakeet.

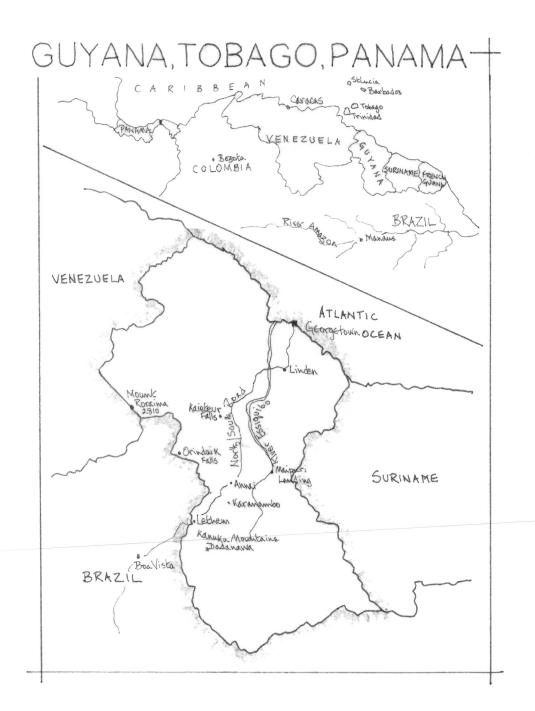

They may defy scansion, but they did not defy a glimpse of all these and there are 800 others.

There are also 1,400 rivers, including the Essequibo, South America's third largest and the Kaieteur Falls, the world's highest single drop waterfall at 817 feet (250m). This staggering biodiversity is spread over a country the size of the UK but it has only one road; with a gravel surface it runs 400 miles from the Atlantic Ocean to the Brazilian border in the south. The three historical Guyanas (British, Dutch and French) are the only part of South America that are neither Spanish nor Portuguese. Of its three million English speaking inhabitants, 95 percent live in the capital, Georgetown. There is no natural harbour on its 900 mile muddy coast and 80 percent of the country is covered by forest. All this makes for an explosion of life, lushness and fecundity. With this agglomeration, it would seem that there was no room for a traveller but this country is big on space too. The population density is 3.4 persons per sq kms – the UK's is 388. Guyana attracts 2,500 tourists a year; Machu Picchu matches that every day. All these superlatives and numbers can be exhausting before one has even landed.

In 1595 Sir Walter Raleigh came this way believing it to be the fabled El Dorado, city of gold and wrote it up as *The Discoverie of the Large, Rich and Bewtiful Empire of Guiana*. Robert Schomburgk in *Riesen in British Guiana* wrote, '*We stood on the borders of an enchanted land*' but by 1882 a visiting English yachtsman described it as '*... a hopeless land of slime and fever*' and James Rodway in his book Guiana says, '*Formerly a land of mud and money, it is now a wilderness of mud and mosquitoes*'. In between, the country changed hands nine times and its borders, particularly those with Venezuela to the north, are still in dispute. V.S. Naipaul and Evelyn Waugh came and went dispirited and fractious. Waugh in particular had nothing good to say about any part of the country but then he had journeyed 100 miles on a horse and no doubt was a mess of saddle sores, ticks, bites and boils. In 1970, the country was granted independence and became The Co-operative Republic of Guyana.

The population today reflects its troubled past. Only three percent are native Amerindians; the genes of the remaining human stew have come from pirates, pioneers, and pathans; seekers of gold and salvation, Scottish herders, Irish adventurers, Indian and Chinese labourers and displaced slaves. The Abolition of Slavery Act and the refusal of the native Amerindians to work the sugarcane plantations (too hot, too arduous and too demeaning), brought in indentured labourers from Ireland and Scotland; the famine in Portugal of 1848 brought in 30,000 Portuguese which was followed by 11,000 Indians and, in the early decades of the twentieth century, some 15,000 Chinese. Sugar production was gradually reduced, cotton could not compete with the US and rice took its place.

Storehouse at Karanambu Ranch

Whites now make up less than one percent of the present population and Indians more than 50 percent.

I took a look around the capital Georgetown first. Perhaps it was a midday, midweek lull but the city seemed empty and unloved. For the most part the buildings are low rise, wooden, and have charm and personality. The exceptions are the city hall designed by a Father Scholes, with a turreted, concave spire and multi-balconied façades that would sit within Disneyland without further embellishment and St Georges Cathedral – the largest timber building in South America. It seemed to be inside out with an interior lavishly furnished in black and white timber and a plain painted exterior. With its plaques to previous British notables, it was as if an overgrown Shropshire parish church had sprung up in the tropics. Apparently, the roof timbers are of English oak but, if true, this would have been a bizarre extravagance when a forest of hardwoods the size of Britain was on its doorstep. So full is the town of fretwork, spindles, clapboard, porches and turrets that it gives an impression of fluttering but another church, St Andrews Kirk, provides an anchor of ecclesiastical and architectural severity. Built in 1818, it nevertheless displayed the original sign- 'No negroes or animals allowed'. Andrew Gimlette in his entertaining book on the Guianas, *Wild Coast*, says of Georgetown '…*there was something about the city – its breezy architecture, its see-through homes, its open arms and its open drains,… here was a place with nothing to hide.*'

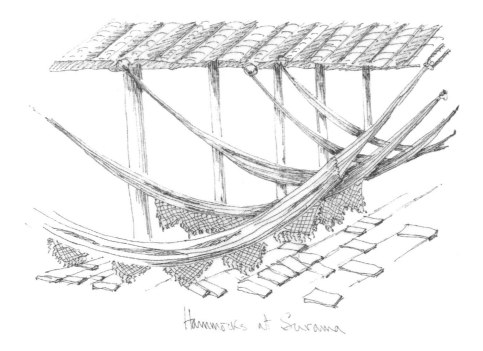

Hammocks at Surama

My taxi driver was called Vicky (inspite of being male) and had a voice of such rasping tone it could probably penetrate walls; it certainly drilled straight through my brain. I hesitated to ask questions in case my hearing was left damaged. Not that many questions were necessary since information came in a sustained stream like firecrackers at a Chinese festival. However his opinion of Georgetown tallied with my own. It was like an iced fruitcake; the icing was chipped and although the cake was largely intact the fruit had all gone bad. Now it was only edible for the dogs of corruption and the scavenging poor. As we drove through the town, Christmas trees were springing up at every cross roads and piles of rubbish malodorously littered every corner. Christmas is taken seriously as the Hindus and Chinese join in as well; there is mutual religious tolerance and the country takes a day off to celebrate each religion's main feast days. We picked up Vicky's three year old daughter from her nursery school. At the end of her day she was still neat and clean in a blue gingham uniform, polished shoes and hair tied in bunches with matching ribbons. She stood on the torn moquette of the car's back seat, leaning into the corners like a slalom racer.

In 1977, the Rev Jim Jones founded The People's Temple of the Full Gospel. He bought 27,000 acres (11,000 hectares) in the north of the country, called it The Promised Land and himself The Prophet and persuaded 900 kooks and the dispossessed of all kinds to follow him from California to build a utopian nation.

But a utopia with a watchtower and a barbed wire boundary. A year later, in 1978, following an investigative visit by a US senator, Jones gunned down the senator and his team and declared that all his followers must die too. In a mass suicide, mothers cut the throats of their children, men squirted cyanide labelled Flavor Aid into the mouths of women and themselves and others blew out their brains. 909 died, including 276 children, dogs, cows and Mr Muggs, a chimpanzee. Since that day, no one has lived in Jonestown, that promised land; it has been erased from the land and the Guyanians pray, from memory.

I shared the two hour flight to Karanambu Ranch with a Guyanian cattle man and his 20 stone (128kgs) wife. Also on board were two dead chickens and two small children; these last being very much alive. The smallest of these children at maybe six months old, made it clear that it was lunch time and this was provided from an exposed milk bar so conspicuously full and all enveloping that the child almost disappeared from view. My fascination got the better of modesty, as I watched to see if the poor mite would surface from underneath this balloon of succour. As he did so, the other child was sick. In a six-seater Cessna some activities are a little too neighbourly for equanimity and indifference.

Diane McTurk is a Guyanese living legend. Now in her eighties, she came down to the river to greet me at the landing stage of Karanambu with a sprightly step. Her face, deeply furrowed by the ravages a lifetime in the tropics, broke into a wide smile.

"How lovely to see you. Did you have a pleasant river journey?"

She has similarly put a thousand guests at ease. Her ranch of 102 square miles (265 square kms) is largely coarse savannah grass and scrub but her legendary status and the reason that these guests come is rooted in her work with giant otters. Orphaned pups, damaged mothers and a one eyed male have now slipped away into the Rupununi River, directed by instinct for the wild ways. Micro-chipping proved useless and tagging collars slip off their oily fur and in any case do not work under water, so the intimate details of their lives remains largely unknown. Princes and presidents, Attenborough, Durrell, all the world's best zoos, have come to Karanambu to kick off their shoes and succumb to the gentle and persuasive charm of its willowy chatelaine. I was her only guest for two days and listened enthralled to her quiet voice recounting the ranch's history. Diane's father, Tiny McTurk (he was six feet six (2 m)) built the ranch in 1922. He had 'an appetite for hardship' and taught himself to hunt with bow and arrow. When Brazilian rustlers stole his cattle he followed them across the border, took their guns and burnt down their houses. You didn't mess with Tiny. One of his three children was Diane, born in 1932 and now the incumbent of Karanambu. Educated in Jamaica and Oxford, a one-time member of the Savoy Group PR

Department, Chelsea party girl and drama student, she devoted herself to the welfare and protection of giant river otters for many years. When she told her tales in the crisp consonants of an English education she smiled often and even more creases than seemed possible came across her fissured face. "I was born here, a wild child," she said.

A bookshelf that screened the kitchen from the dining room was full of old classics. Here was Waugh, Cooper, Walmisley-Dresser, Cecile Hulse Matschat et al but almost all had their bindings exposed to the bookbinder's string and cotton webbing. I had assumed this was from the corrosion of the tropics, bookworms and parasitic wasps. The reality was more prosaic; a pet goat had discovered that the glue was palatable and overnight had stripped the books of their titled spines.

Each single-roomed benab was of a size that would have been welcomed by a whole Amerindian family and was constructed on a timber frame. There were brick walls nine feet (three metres) high but they were only there for privacy and did not reach to the eaves, allowing for ventilation. A small colony of bats shared my accommodation hanging in a line under the ridge of the thatched roof. A large sheet of plywood was suspended over the bed to catch their "precipitation", as it was modestly described. During the night they flew around with much squeaking as they gorged on night-time insects and there was a little pitter-patter of their "precipitation". A tarantula, like a hairy hand, sat in a corner waiting for an unwary bat and frogs belched in some nearby ditch. Food was always cold in these lodges and here it was colder than most. It came from oven to table via chat and pleasantries and then lay panting on a side table until someone became aware of its existence and rang a bell or banged a log whereupon diners shambled towards the table, sorted out their preferred place, took a seat, were given a cold plate and then stood up again to help themselves from the once-warm dishes.

On a Sunday, I found myself in the nearby village of Yurupakari, a few miles upstream. A team of BBC wildlife film makers had arrived at the same time and while they shifted their mountain of gear, I looked in at the three churches in the village. With only 750 souls to provide for, there was an element of competition. The Christian Brethren offered a keyboard and familiar A&M hymns sung in Makushi, the Blessed Church of Christ had a couple of guitars but the Anglicans offered nothing except half-hearted a cappella singing, but two woolly dogs and a cat added an inclusiveness that was absent at their rivals'.

As dawn crept over the Karanambu mountains (at a lowly 3,000 ft (920 m)), I set out on a hunt for a giant anteater. We bumped over the tussock grass of the savannah disturbing hawks, pippets and other avian early risers until we arrived at the homestead of a *vachero*. In this single roomed, single windowed, shingle-roofed, breeze blocked, dirt floored, stained, grimy, dusty, home lived the *vachero* and his wife, two teenage boys, four small girls and a babe in arms. The mother was pregnant again. A tin roof covered the veranda under which a wood fire was heating a great metal griddle that glistened with oil and on which cassava bread was baking. These were flat, steering-wheel-sized rounds and several had been tossed onto the roof to dry into a long-lasting crispbread. A horse with open saddle sores waiting to heal stood patiently in the shade of a huge mango tree. The two small girls were in plaid frocks and played with a puppy and a pet toucan whose clipped wings condemned it to hopping. I photographed the children, looked at the penned herd of Brahmin cattle and waited for the crackle of the short wave radio. In an hour or so it came – an unintelligible mixture of Creole, Makushi and English, all distorted by radio squelch – but an anteater had been found. I could see the vachero and his sons on their horses two miles or so away and as we reached them, the poor creature was clearly exhausted from being harried for so long. As I crouched for a picture it ambled towards me, its bizarre snout leading the way and its rudder of a great hairy tail waving behind. With its poor eyesight it probably thought it had reached the sanctuary of a tree. As a nocturnal animal it had had a rough morning and I left it to find peace in the shade of the scrub.

I moved on to Surama, down the Rupununi River, whose high clay banks were perforated by the nesting holes of many varieties of kingfisher – Amazon, pied, ring-necked, little and pygmy. The village sat in a wide and lush valley bordered by the Burro-Burro River and the Pakaraima Mountains and in the morning, I set out to climb Mount Surama. The fact that its summit was shrouded in cloud should have warned me that this was not going to be a stroll and additionally, it was smothered in forest. A fellow guest, as dark as a southern Indian Tamil (it turned out he was a southern Indian Tamil but came from Coventry) had earlier knocked on my door to beg something for his stings – eight livid spots on his face that astonishingly had turned white. He had been walking through the same forest that shrouded the foothills of my mountainous destination.

My guide was to be with me at 5.30 am and I looked around for a gnarled and craggy forester with a *parang* stuck in his waist band but there was only a slip of a girl in tight jeans and a tighter top. As it turned out, the curvaceous Melissa was my guide and she carried a handbag decorated with raffia roses and a plastic sack that contained our breakfast. She wore flip-flops, had painted nails (red on her feet, and blue on her fingers) and a mane of hair to rival an anteater's tail. She was impressively knowledgeable on birds and rainforest inhabitants and at a welcome pause on the vertical route, she told me that Brown University was funding her course in Avian Calling as part of her Master's Degree in Biodiversity. At one stage she made such strange guttural sounds; I thought she was vomiting, but this was the call of the black spider monkey. I stumbled along behind, along

Handsewn Saddlery at
Karanambu

Tapir at karanambu

Tcbngo
resident

Policeman at Georgetown shootout

a path tunnelled through the jungle caverns and with sunbeams trickling through the canopy. From time to time I was caught on razor grass, snared on 'catchme' – a sort of green and growing barbed wire with extra spikes, avoided the spiny palms, slipped on boulders that seemed smeared with engine oil, crossed streams on rotten logs and miraculously reached the summit sweating so profusely I was wetter than an otter. Melissa was laying out breakfast and repairing her nails.

Back at the lodge, replacing the lost perspiration with a gallon of fruit juice, a swarthy and disreputable looking fellow dressed all in black rode up on his trail bike to a skidding halt. He flashed a lascivious grin at Melissa and produced a revolver from a back pocket. Melissa did not seem too impressed until he proved its working order by firing off a couple of shots and then scattering the remaining bullets over the floor. This country is full of oddballs and dropouts but bullets were a different matter. Before I had judged that the dining table was the safest refuge if things got nasty, he had packed away the pistol and sped off to whatever banditry and seduction he had planned next. Melissa simply studied a broken nail and said he came by every week.

Melanie's aunt had invited me for lunch and on the way, a man with a face like a squashed strawberry crossed the road towards me. "Where you from?" he asked. When I told him he thought about it for a while as though mentally arranging a geographical puzzle and said, "That's nice," and shuffled away. He wore a black baseball hat that said 'Connect with Christ' in silver letters. On the back was a telephone number.

Aunty Paulette was round from every angle and spoke in a torrent of humour, information and wisdom. Her five children and nine grandchildren all lived in the village and came together for each evening meal. Cooking for this family platoon was as nothing compared to the meals she cooked for an army of committees and social gatherings of all kinds. She had two cookers, fuelled by bottled gas, and an open wood fire but no refrigerator. Fish, meat and vegetables were dried or salted. Her husband Drango was a hunter and used only a bow and arrow; three types of bow and four types of arrow all fashioned by himself with great skill and beauty. Different designs were required for game, animals and fish – pimpla hogs, dogs and sakiwinkis in Drango's language. Three words were a conversation. "You eat guan?" (the forest turkey that had been prepared for lunch). "You come far?" That was it, he had exhausted his repertoire and went off to fashion more weapons and construct a mini fortress to protect his chickens from foxes and vampire bats.

I moved on to Iwokrama where for many thousands of years the forest had been unmolested by man and was one of the few places on earth were his activities had barely left a mark. From a lodge that claimed sanctuary in a small clearing, I set out to find a jaguar but the expedition was not quite the adventure I had been anticipating. This was no jungle trek, following a track and listening to the alarm calls of possible prey, nerves taut and eyes scanning the position of each unfamiliar noise; it was a drive down the north/south gravel highway. My guide was Viktor, a young man the size of the King of Tonga, who overflowed his seat in the Landcruiser like a beached whale. "Why Viktor?" I asked. "It is from the Italian," he replied. This seemed unlikely but I was none the wiser and neither, it turned out, was he. Viktor steered his tank around the cratered road with a chubby finger from one hand while the other hand waved a spotlight into the wall of the forest to pick up the glow of eyes. I stood on the back seat with my body through the roof following the eccentric light as it moved from treetop to verge while Viktor, from his position on the front sofa seat, yelled upwards his life story. "My grandfather Theodolphus built Surama village," he boomed up into the night air. After a catalogue of relatives, it turned out that his cousin was Melissa – she of the painted nails. There was no jaguar, but only a red rumped agouti, a disappearing tapir and an embellishment of red eyes but the forest noises as dusk fell were as magical as ever. Unseen creatures hooted and howled, there were cries of pain and the roadside swamps gurgled and thrummed with their colonies of amorous frogs. In this crush of vegetation, new species have continually emerged, most recently a frog that glows fluorescent purple. In the evening, this belly worshipper guide fuelled up with pancakes, six at a time, loaded with cheese and slavered with chili sauce. Pitta bread stuffed with peanut butter and honey was taken away as a precaution against any hunger pangs later.

Flying from Lethem, Guyana's second city, a spread of arboreal shag pile was draped over the contours. In between, the crushed velvet of the savannah, still green from seasonal rains, clothed random patches. Threads of Bisto-brown streams dribbled across the carpet and sun-silvered rivers wriggled their way to embroider the flat landscape. On still black lakes, little blobs of green showed up the metre wide leaves of *victoria amazonica*. Nature has strengthened them with an upturned lip and protected them with thorns but this is no deterrent to the nocturnal beetle that pollinates them at night, attracted by their huge, scented white flowers. Following pollination the flowers turn pink and four days later, die. Pockets of rusty earth showed up goldmines, scratched from the earth by *garimperos*; "One Brazilian, two girls," as the locals named them. A single road jigged at eccentric geometric angles as though pursued by a fly. Then as Georgetown neared, there was the Essequibo River blotched by sandbanks and its edges serrated by forest as it squirmed its way in a great, grey gash across the land. This serpent opened its gigantic jaws in a twelve mile wide yawn at the shore of the Atlantic. Somewhere in the mysterious interior there were bands of maroons, the descendants of emancipated slaves and Kwintis, N'Djukas, Bonis and Saramac-caners – the tribal detritus of failed colonisers, indentured labour, buccaneers and mercenaries. Creoles were largely along the coast and the native Amerindians were scattered throughout the country. In the deep south, the Wai-Wai still used blowpipes and lived on bushmeat. Georgetown now had a majority of Indians and their temples were everywhere sporting king cobras, many headed serpents and the elephants of Ganesh. Once, while waiting for a plane, I heard a passenger turn to another to ask, "What mix are you?" To have a genetic potpourri is a standard ingredient here. Added to this racial salmagundi were colonies of Java-nese and Chinese who had the capital to build hotels, roads and dams but all with labour imported from China. Each coloniser had left their mark on the urban landscape so there were areas named Nassau, Zealandia, Ruimveldt, Vreed-en-Hoop and Stabroek; La Penitence, Le Repentir, Affiance, and Mon Repos (yes, really). More recently, Doobay, Anamayah, Ganges and Chandranagar had been added and there were Scottish, Welsh and English names in profusion.

English binds most of the spoken languages but there is tribal language too and Makushi was the unintelligible dialect of the Rupununi but in and around Georgetown, the lilt of the Caribbean is in the markets, the wayside shops and the bus tops. Elsewhere, in the wild countryside, the conversation was often in Talkie-Talkie. To hurry up is *mekie hesie*, a boat is *boto*, tomorrow *tamarra*, enough is *onofo* and when everything goes wrong it's *alasoni fuk-up*. I was not here long enough to discover more of its idioms and sounds but the nationalities that have passed through so far – English, Dutch, French and of course the African slaves – must all have contributed. Now, the Indians, the Chinese, and educated Amerindians may add their influence.

Reports of the shoot-out at Melinda's Beauty Spot were carried on national radio into my taxi from the airport. Four policemen and the parlour receptionist were dead and another four were on their way to hospital and all this next door to my hotel. I spurred the driver on. Roads were blocked, crowds were gathering and blue lights were flashing including those of an unwanted fire engine. Hold-ing up my Press Pass and my long lens, I surged through the crowd. "London press! London press!" I cried. "BBC, let him through. Go man!" the crowd yelled encouragingly. This was terrific. I climbed a barrier, jumped a storm drain and took multiple pictures of bullet holes, armed police and assorted senior officers in crisply creased beige uniforms and polished shoes. The police presence included a number of disreputable looking fellows who seemed to be a mixture of the Con-golese Lord's Resistance Army and the Tonton Macoutes of Papa Doc. Dressed in T-shirts and shorts they strode around with revolvers in their waistbands. Since it then turned out that the gunman was still in the building, my enthusiasm for

OCEAN COLOSSUS

Panama Canal

on-the-spot reportage took a more cautious turn. I crouched behind a battered pick-up that itself might have survived a previous shoot-out, with a nervous cameraman sporting several plastic identities round his neck. I suggested to him that his job was to be out in front photographing the blood and bullets. "Hey, man! Are you crazy?" he shouted. "I don't wanna get shot. I'll wait 'till they get the bastard." When one of the track-suited Macoutes dropped a revolver the crowd yelled enthusiastic abuse. Even in the pursuit of a deranged and dangerous gunman and with four of their colleagues dead, the corrupt police were still jeered.

On the trip to Kaieteur Falls obesity followed me again. My seat neighbour was another overflowing passenger but this time in three shades of pink and ringlets like a cascade of candyfloss. She reminded me of Victoria Woods' Winnie, *'Like barracks in a pinny'*. Additional shades from her raspberry palette were added in nails, lips and shoes. On the pre boarding scales, she checked in at 130 kgs (290 lbs) (I was 90 kgs (210 lbs), including a hefty camera). When I complimented Miss Piggy for brightening the day, her laugh showed that she had no teeth. In contrast, there was a pale and willowy English girl from Manchester amorously entwined around a Rastafarian as shiny black as she was chalky white and there was a German from Manheim who spoke only of the immigrants who were robbing his country of jobs. The willowy Mancunian told me that her father was a Methodist minister in Guyana and I asked if he ever felt the pressure of gathering into his own exclusive flock different souls that worshipped the same god. This is a country where evangelical diversity is rife and the telephone yellow pages in my hotel had listed 26 different Christian denominations. "Oh no," she replied loyally, "He is grateful for any that knock on his door." Her own part in this work seemed limited to procreation as the chinkies got down to some serious smooching. The falls themselves were impressive- twice the height of Victoria Falls and five times the height of the Niagara Falls. They were scary too; the vertical cliffs on either side of the approach to the falls had no protection and a too enthusiastic look over the edge would have been fatal. I stood at the lip of jasper stone as every second, an Olympic swimming pool was tipped over to cascade 30 stories before fluttering away into the abyss of the Potaro River where the water recovered its poise and benignly sauntered on its way.

Sir Walter Raleigh, Melville, a thousand hopeful colonisers, and those with whom I stayed loved this country with its undoubted wild beauty and extraordinary diversity but the past provided the prospects for the future. The failed sugarcane, rice and pineapple industries; the Dutch, French and English who came, never conquered and left. In the South Rupununi, the Dadanawa Ranch is one million acres (404,000 hectares) – twice the size of Suffolk – and has been another failure, at least on the grand scale originally envisaged. The plan to fly out frozen carcasses proved far too expensive; now the planes fly out the quick but not the dead. The ranch also used to lose 400 cattle a year to jaguars, which were shot as pests. The Guyanese diaspora have a distinguished record in many fields but they found nothing to stay at home for. In the end, the countless schemes and colonial ambitions foundered, defeated by the heat and humidity, the people's indolence and the onslaught of the rainforest.

□ □ □

I stole away to Tobago and the little village of Speyside on the island's eastern tip, where the water spread itself over the sand like liquid lapis lazuli. In the gloaming, I walked down a rainforest track whose leafy borders sparkled with fireflies to celebrate my arrival with a lobster at Betty's Tree House but was deflected on the way by a group of youths who sat on a log and were also in celebratory mood. The dress code for this band of ruffians was dreadlocks, plaits, great bundles of hair stuffed inside a woollen cap and T-shirts emblazoned with blood-dripping daggers under some unintelligible gothic text.

"Hey, man! Dat's a real spicy outfit you'd be wearing. Comes and say hello."

In my red check shirt, I put one foot forward.

"Is this a party?" My Oxford accent was poorly disguised.

"OK, man! Always is a party. You drink rum?"

He offered a bottle labelled El Dorado, the best rum of the Caribbean but I doubted its authenticity. "Actually, I would rather not," cautioned my brain, common sense and prim reserve. To my surprise I heard myself saying, "Of course, what else is there to drink?"

"Spot on man. Comes and loosen up, we're all God's chillun."

A draught of bitter but strangely sweet alcohol found itself warming my throat. Toothy, white grins split tangled beards. Back at my posh lodgings the bar would be crackling with, "Chin-chin. Such a lovely sunset don't you think?" When Rastas Number Two offered a third slug, I slunk away from this thieves' kitchen for another that would be more hygienic. Never has lobster tasted better.

Continuing north to Panama, I wandered the crowded canyons of the airport for an hour as I searched for a sign to Immigration or someone to ask. The Panamanian customs' declaration form was inquisitive about money. Under *Procedencia del Dinero*, translated as Procedence of Money, there was a requirement to declare its origins – *Negocios/Familiar/Personal/Juegos de Azar* (Business/Relations/Personal/Games of Chance). A tick in this last box needed *Especifique* – an Explanation. At the centre of Central America and midway between the north and south Americas, it is at the hub of a vigorous and restless commercial wheel but also the distribution point for the drugs going from south to north. My driver, Mario, had skin as dry and wrinkled as a date discarded from a previous Christmas and was intent on ensuring that not a single fact or feature escaped me. While we cruised around, I asked Mario if there were guns and drugs. He gave an indifferent shrug as if to indicate that vices were an inevitable by-product of progress. Another question that enquired if the police were corrupt produced a similar shrug; but there were plenty of them – police that is:

Presidential Police in blue and red
Traffic Police in grey
Special Police in camouflage
and just Police in black.

All wore bullet proof vests and carried revolvers in open holsters.

The heavily accented torrent of information was regularly interrupted by one of his two mobile phones. One of them had a ring tone of the Honduras National Anthem (he just liked the tune) and was at such a volume that it might have been played by a band on the back seat. There were new car showrooms at every junction and huge sixteen-wheeled trucks jammed the main roads. Tower cranes reached to the sky as did the office buildings they had constructed. Panama City had symbols in height and architectural exuberance to rival Miami. My depressing couple of days in Georgetown and another couple in Trinidad had prepared me for indolent inhabitants that lived in lackadaisical torpor, but here was the turmoil that came from a frenzy of activity where the people were building, making, selling and learning.

This small country of only three million people runs on money, lots of it and in spite of the requirement to provide *en Especifique*, it does not much care where the money comes from. It was not until I got to the Panama Canal that I saw the source of most of this money – an astonishing two billion dollars per year. Here was a treasure chest that was growing in size year by year, not just physically but practically guaranteed and Panama had the only key. The Canal itself is immense. It is impossible to see each end at the same time and, in any case, there is a huge manmade lake in the middle, but it seemed appropriate that when I was at the Miraflores locks, the enormous tanker that was inching its way through pulled by little electric engines either side was named Ocean Colossus. On each side within the lock, there was no more than 12 inches (30cms) between steel plate and stone walls but this monster left without a single scrape. Ships that are able to squeeze through the locks are known as Panamax vessels but this epithet of 'max' might well be more realistically changed to 'min'. Its owners would have paid $250,000 for the shortcut.

Panama City was occupied by one and a half million souls of all shades, unem-

368

ployment was a paltry 3 percent, car ownership was an amazing 90 percent, politics were largely democratic and unsurprisingly, President Domingo expected to be re-elected the following year. The Americans left a useful legacy when they abandoned the day-to-day running of the Canal. Apart from the currency of American dollars, they left behind a city-sized military establishment with all its attendant facilities of barracks, offices and workshops including a vast airfield and acres of tarmac and all in good working order. There was also, Mario whispered, a small mountain said to contain seven floors, excavated internally from solid rock. This is a green country of tropical rainforests and although in Panama City, glittering buildings punched the sky downtown, uptown and around town, the Parque Metropolitan was untouched forest. Its edges had been encroached a little by universities, the biggest of which was The University of Central America – The City of Knowledge.

The blue and red police were on every corner around a presidential palace that had clearly been expanded with every incumbent and now took in an adjacent block or two. My cursory ride through the adjoining streets of the old city showed up the charm of old Spanish buildings that were being extensively restored. The Plaza Mayor, like all Spanish colonial towns, had a church on one of its sides; in this case, it was the cathedral with a spectacularly elaborate *chiaroscuro* altar screen.

On the airplane to Havana, a party of Cubans was jubilant. They joked and laughed to the point of hysterics and one got up and danced in the aisle as others beat out a rhythm on their bags and parcels. They were celebrating a successful shopping trip in Panama; had they come from Guyana, they might have been celebrating a successful escape.

Postcard Home

They say the Guyanas will drive you bananas
But as humming birds hum, I'm near to nirvanas
As I watch them collect a selector of nectar.
Nature's full throttle on this Mosquito Coast
(But the day starts at boiling and continues to roast!)
There are jaguars, ocelots, otters and tapirs
And waterfalls higher than many skyscrapers.
Next on this ramble is calypsoed Tobago.
Hey, amigo! Let's tango and stomp the fandango!
Then up the canal that splits Panama
And Bacardi and rum in old Havana.

Acknowledgements

Heartfelt thanks are due to a number of rare and helpful individuals. Foremost, to my wife Maggie for her indulgence of an absent traveller, her forbearance as first in line for the tiresome task of reading a first draft and for her pithy advice. I am grateful to the Authoright team of James Wharton who gathered me into the self publishing fold, Chris Sansom who held my literary hand during this book's gestation and to Jordan Koluch for deciphering my scribbles and for her skills in the design and setting out of the text and sketches. I was also fortunate to have the corrections, suggestions and improvements of Mary Douglas-Bate, Margie Charnock and Rosie Morton Jack, and special thanks are owed to Vicky Jardine-Paterson for her professional proofreading, sentient comments and encouragement. In America, the constructive review of the manuscript by Allan Talbot and Judy Goldring has been most valuable as has been their support.